Courtwatchers

Courtwatchers

Eyewitness Accounts in Supreme Court History

Clare Cushman

PUBLISHED IN ASSOCIATION WITH
THE SUPREME COURT HISTORICAL SOCIETY

ROWMAN & LITTLEFIELD PUBLISHERS, INC.
Lanham • Boulder • New York • Toronto • Plymouth, UK

Published in association with the Supreme Court Historical Society

Published by Rowman & Littlefield Publishers, Inc.
A wholly owned subsidiary of The Rowman & Littlefield Publishing Group, Inc.
4501 Forbes Boulevard, Suite 200, Lanham, Maryland 20706
http://www.rowmanlittlefield.com

Estover Road, Plymouth PL6 7PY, United Kingdom

British Library Cataloguing in Publication Information Available

Library of Congress Cataloging-in-Publication Data
Cushman, Clare.
  Courtwatchers : eyewitness accounts in Supreme Court History/ Clare Cushman.
   p. cm.
  Includes index.
  ISBN 978-1-4422-1245-9 (hardback) — ISBN 978-1-4422-1247-3 (electronic)
  1. United States. Supreme Court—History. 2. United States. Supreme Court—Officials and employees—Selection and appointment—History. 3. Judges—United States—History. 4. Judicial process—United States—History. 5. Clerks of court—United States—History. I. Title.
  KF8742.C875 2011
  347.73'2609—dc23

2011019794

∞™ The paper used in this publication meets the minimum requirements of American National Standard for Information Sciences—Permanence of Paper for Printed Library Materials, ANSI/NISO Z39.48-1992.

Printed in the United States of America

To my husband and children, without whom
I would have finished this book much sooner.

Contents

Foreword

Each year, hundreds of thousands of Americans visit the Supreme Court of the United States. They are justly proud of this great institution, yet most are struck by the anonymity of the seventeen Chief Justices and one hundred Associate Justices who have served on the Court over the past two centuries. Some of the portraits that line the Court's halls are readily recognizable: Oliver Wendell Holmes is sternly majestic; Hugo Black is captured in radiant color; while Felix Frankfurter appears in a modernistic pastel sketch. But even history buffs steeped in the lore of the Court are likely to be stumped by the names beneath some of the other portraits. Just who are these people?

Clare Cushman's latest work, *Courtwatchers*, helps to answer this question. She has written an informative survey, drawn from firsthand accounts, that brings the Justices to life. Drawing on recollections and recorded observations from a wide sweep of sources, the book provides what a good anecdote conveys—the sense of personality. Ms. Cushman has organized her book around topics that capture the human element of the jurists. She places them in the context of their times by examining the Court's early history and forgotten hardships, like circuit riding. She explores both the process of becoming a judge—including appointment, confirmation, and "learning the ropes"—and the poignant process of stepping down from the Court. But she also sets aside the black robes and delves into the private side of life on the Court, capturing vignettes of relations among friends, family, and one another.

Art critics tell us that good portraiture engages the viewer in two dimensions by commingling the subject's objective appearance with the artist's subjective impressions. Ms. Cushman's collection of firsthand observations—many of which, by virtue of resting on recollection, are open to historical debate—add depth to the Court in both those dimensions. Her book will delight all those who want to look beyond the portraits and gain an intimate view of the individuals who have quietly contributed so much to the work of the Court and the advancement of justice.

Chief Justice John G. Roberts, Jr.

Introduction

In the early nineteenth century, the Supreme Court sessions were considered the best show in town. One now-forgotten case argued over the span of ten days by an all-star lineup of orators, including the thrilling Daniel Webster, drew overflow crowds in 1844. A spectator reported:

> Daniel Webster is speaking. . . . There is a tremendous squeeze, you can scarcely get a case knife in edgeways. . . . Hundreds and hundreds went away, unable to obtain admittance. There never were so many persons in the Court-room since it was built. Over 200 ladies were there; crowded, squeezed and almost jammed in that little room; in front of the Judges and behind the Judges; in front of Mr. Webster and behind him and on each side of him were rows and rows of beautiful women dressed "to the highest." Senators, Members of the House, Whigs and Locos, foreign Ministers, Cabinet officers, old and young—all kinds of people were there. Both the President's sons, with a cluster of handsome girls, were present. . . . The body of the room, the sides, the aisles, the entrances, all were blocked up with people. And it was curious to see on the bench a row of beautiful women, seated and filling up the spaces between the chairs of the Judges, so as to look like a second and a female Bench of beautiful Judges.

During a more routine day in the Supreme Court, the same reporter compared the scene to a "ballroom," musing that if old English judges were to witness the sight, "each particular whalebone in their wigs would stand on end at this mixture of men and women, law and politeness, ogling and flirtation, bowing and curtseying, going on in the highest tribunal in America."

Watching a Supreme Court session today is still awe-inspiring. The line of would-be Courtwatchers waiting to take their turns in the seats reserved for the general public can often stretch down the steep white steps of the Marble Palace. The Supreme Court does, however, operate in a less theatrical manner than it did in 1844. It is definitely not a place to flirt.

Indeed, if Webster were to visit today's majestic Courtroom in session, he would be startled to see that women are no longer decorative spectators. One-third of the Justices occupying the bench are female, and the attorney standing at the podium may well be too. Webster would also be surprised that instead of enjoying the leisurely pace of oral argument that characterized his era—with no time restrictions and orators declaiming flowery rhetoric for days on end—advocates are now permitted only half an hour to make their case. And instead of listening deferentially, the Justices barrage them with questions, trying to get to the crux of the legal issues as quickly as possible.

Webster would probably be equally dismayed to watch oral arguments end abruptly, with the Chief Justice unceremoniously stopping counsel from going beyond the allotted time, even to wrap up a point. A current member of the Supreme Court bar, with more than twenty oral arguments under her belt, Maureen Mahoney has described the contemporary experience of being cut off in mid-sentence—something Webster and his peers at the Supreme Court bar did not even begin to contemplate until 1849, when time limits for each side began to be imposed. A former clerk to Chief Justice William H. Rehnquist, Mahoney was granted no special consideration in the Courtroom by her mentor, a strict stickler for time limits:

> The way the light system works in the courtroom is that it will tell you, when a light goes on, that you have five minutes remaining, and when your time is expired a red light goes on. In the Supreme Court, when the red light goes on, you are supposed to stop. When Chief Justice Rehnquist was presiding, you were really supposed to stop. I remember one time where Justice [Antonin] Scalia had asked me a question, and the red light went on just as he was finishing his question. I hadn't had a chance to say a word. I looked up at the Chief Justice, and he said "Counsel, I think you can consider that a rhetorical question." And so I just sat down. In fact, the press didn't know that the red light was on, so they reported that I was speechless in response to Justice Scalia's question.

The firsthand accounts related above are snapshots taken from two very different eras in the Supreme Court's development. Together, they give a sense of how the experience of being inside the Courtroom has changed, and are a preview of the lively eyewitness accounts featured in this book. Who better to narrate the Court's history than those who were on the scene: journalists, oral advocates, Justices, their spouses and children, clerks, Supreme Court staff, friends, and Courtroom spectators? Collectively, these accounts illuminate how the Supreme Court and its players have functioned as an institution. They reveal the workaday experience of life behind the marble pillars.

A few of these eyewitness accounts have been plucked from obscure sources. Many are old chestnuts, well known to scholars. Although efforts have been made to track down and verify the original sources, a few legends with uncertain origins are included simply because they are such a beloved part of Supreme Court lore.

And, admittedly, counterexamples to Courtwatchers' one-sided observations are not always supplied. For example, the loose-limbed Chief Justice John Marshall is amusingly depicted in these pages as a sloppy dresser who gave off an unfavorable first impression, belying his greatness. But there do exist accounts that mention his neat attire and his insistence that circuit court judges dress properly. Similarly, a journalist reported in 1824 that oral advocates were listened to "in silence for hours, without being stopped or interrupted" by the Justices, when in fact Court records shows that there was some interchange between bench and bar during the Marshall Court era.

Anecdotes in this book were selected for their educational or entertainment value, but readers should enjoy them with this, quite obvious, caveat. Although firsthand accounts may seem to represent the historical truth because they were recorded by an observer on the spot, eyewitnesses almost always have self-serving motives, if unwittingly. In this regard, skepticism is advised, for example in reading a clerk's description of his or her Justice's character, role, and work habits, because clerks tend to be so ferociously loyal to, and admiring of, the Justice they serve. A few Justices have even been known to chronicle events as much with an eye on posterity as to record the facts.

Memory is tricky. Sometimes eyewitnesses just plain get their facts wrong. For example, Malvina Harlan talks about how her husband Justice John Marshall Harlan's historic dissent in *Plessy v. Ferguson* (1896) "cost him several months of absorbing labor," when in fact the case was argued in April and handed down in May. No doubt it did *feel* like a long time. When an eyewitness is obviously mistaken or shows flagrant bias, it is so noted. But for the most part readers are left to evaluate these accounts on their own.

Another warning to readers: each chapter examines aspects of one thematic topic at different time periods in the Court's history. This enables one to compare, for example, how the Justices viewed their salaries or their workload at different junctures. But the norms of the Supreme Court—the institutional values and ways of conducting business—have of course evolved enormously over time (and from chamber to chamber). While historical context is usually supplied, sometimes it necessarily takes a backseat to the narrative. In comparing eyewitness accounts from two different eras, bear in mind that experiences which might seem similar may in fact be very different given societal and cultural norms both inside and outside the Court at the time.

Courtwatchers

1

⚖

Sink or Swim
The First Decade

In February 1800, Justice Samuel Chase was on his way to attend a session of the Supreme Court in Philadelphia (then the nation's capital) from his home in Maryland, a journey that necessitated crossing the very broad Susquehanna River. Because the river was frozen, no ferry was operating, and the only alternative was to cross it on foot. Chase, a large man, fell through the ice and narrowly escaped drowning. As he reported to his wife, Hannah:

> on Sunday before Day light one of the Negroes came into my Room. and desired me to get up, that the passengers were going over, that the Ice had been tried and would bear a Waggon and horses . . . two Negroes went before Me with the Baggage on a sleigh. I followed directly on the Track. . . . Myself and Son carried a long Boat-Hook. about 150 Yards from the shore, (in about fifteen feet Water) one of my feet broke in, I stepped forward with the other foot, and both broke in. I sent the Boat-Hook, & across, which prevented my sinking. Sammy immediately ran up, and caught hold of my Cloaths, and fell in.— he got out and lay on the Side of the Hole, and held Me and broke in twice afterwards.— I was heavily cloathed. my Fur Coat was very heavy when it got wet. . . . I must inform You of our Circumstance. I had just offered up a prayer to god to protect Me from the Danger, when I instantly fell in.

Chase was an unpopular figure in some quarters, and the anti-Federalist press made the most of this incident, with one paper reporting that fish in the Susquehanna were leaping into fishermens' nets "in preference to existing in an [element] become putrid by cleansing such a mass of aristocracy!"

1

Serving as a Justice in the first decade of the Supreme Court was indeed a chancy proposition. Wintry conditions made traveling to February sessions hazardous. Outbreaks of yellow fever during August sessions sent the Justices fleeing home. And the business the Justices managed to conduct in these first few sessions hardly made the trip worthwhile.

When Congress created the Supreme Court with the Judiciary Act of 1789, it did not provide a permanent chamber for the Justices to hold session. The first meeting was convened on February 1, 1790—in an upstairs room at the Exchange Building in New York (briefly the nation's capital)—but only three Justices appeared. Lacking a quorum, they immediately adjourned. A fourth Justice did turn up the next day, but there were no cases to hear. After six days of focusing on such administrative matters as hiring a clerk and admitting attorneys to practice before it, the Court ended its first term. The Court's second session took place in August and was even less eventful, lasting only two days.

Legend has it that Justice William Cushing arrived in New York from Massachusetts for the Court's first session wearing the big, white-powdered English judicial wig in vogue in state courts. After being followed up Broadway by a mob of boys who gawked at his extraordinary attire, Cushing dodged into a shop to buy a short, pony-tailed wig that would relieve him of the unwanted scrutiny. But even the more modest wig was controversial. Thomas Jefferson, then Secretary of State, thought that judicial robes should be the only official apparel: "For Heaven's sake, discard the monstrous wig which makes the English judges look like rats peeping through bunches of oakum [wadding used for stuffing timbers of ships]!" The Justices decided to go bareheaded. Some continued the tradition of English courts of wearing robes with a red facing; others donned their own academic gowns of varying colors.

When the nation's capital moved to Philadelphia in 1791, the Court found suitable space in the new City Hall, but was obliged to share it with the mayor's court. Although cases were beginning to percolate up through the judicial system, the Court continued to maintain a relatively low profile. When Chief Justice John Jay gave the President advance notice that he would be absent in 1792 due to his wife's difficult pregnancy, his letter also glumly noted a lack of business:

> As I shall be absent from the next [Supreme] Court, obvious Considerations urge me to mention to You the Reasons of it: Early in the next month I expect an addition to my Family __ Mrs Jay's delicate Health (she having for more than three weeks past been confined to her Chamber) renders that Event so interesting, that although she is now much better, I cannot prevail on myself to be then at a Distance from her; especially as no Business of particular Importance either to the public, or to Individuals, makes it necessary.

Associate Justice William Cushing of Massachusetts wore a horsehair wig and a black robe trimmed with red facing, the style for early colonial and English judges, to the first meeting of the Supreme Court in 1789. The Justices would decide to go bareheaded and don simple black robes. (Collection of the Supreme Court of the United States, painting by C. Gregory Stapko)

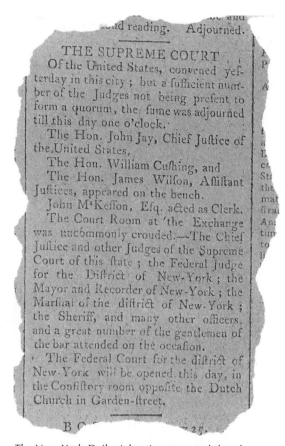

The New York Daily Advertiser *reported that the scene at the Supreme Court's opening day was "uncommonly crouded." Spectators had to return the following day to see the Court hold session, however, because not enough Justices had shown up to constitute a quorum. (Library of Congress, Rare Book Collection)*

One Justice, John Rutledge, resigned in 1791 to become Chief Justice of South Carolina—a job considered more prestigious. It took three tries before the President could fill his seat, as George Washington's first two nominees preferred to remain state legislators. The candidate who finally, if reluctantly, accepted the Associate Justiceship would resign months later. In 1792 the Chief Justice tried to quit the Court by campaigning to be governor of New York. He lost. In the first decade of the Court's existence, twelve different men served in six seats.

In selecting his nominees for the Court, President Washington based his decisions on potential candidates' character, experience, education, health, age, Revolutionary War record, and support for the Constitution. And, in an era when many people still owed their primary allegiance to their states rather than to the nation as a whole, he also strove for geographical diversity, attempting to ensure that as many states as possible were represented in his new administration. But it was not always easy to persuade good candidates to accept government commissions. He confided to Secretary of the Treasury Alexander Hamilton:

> What with the non-acceptance of some, the known dereliction of those who are most fit; the exceptionable drawbacks from others; and a wish (if it were practicable) to make a geographical distribution of the great offices of the Administration, I find the selection of proper characters an arduous duty.

In one instance, Washington's selection of a nominee was a little too hasty. In 1795, John Rutledge—the same man who had resigned from his position as an Associate Justice in order to become Chief Justice of South Carolina—heard that John Jay was soon to resign as Chief Justice. By now the Supreme Court had a somewhat higher profile—and in any event, Rutledge coveted the position of Chief Justice over that of Associate Justice. Rutledge immediately wrote to President Washington, informing him that he had "no Objection to take the place which [Jay] holds, if you think me as fit as any other person." Washington apparently did: the day after he received Rutledge's letter he wrote to him offering him the Chief Justiceship. Because the Senate was out of session, however, it was a recess appointment, subject to the Senate's later approval.

Rutledge did preside over the Supreme Court's August session that year, but around the same time reports began to circulate of an extremely intemperate speech Rutledge had made in South Carolina, denouncing the controversial Jay Treaty that his predecessor had just negotiated with the British. Beyond that, there were rumors that Rutledge was "daily sinking into debility of mind & body," and of his "attachment to his bottle, his puerility, and extravagances." When the Senate finally met in December, they rejected Rutledge's nomination by a vote of fourteen to ten. A few weeks later Rutledge made an unsuccessful attempt to drown himself in the waters off Charleston, rebuffing his rescuers (passing sailors) with the claim that "he had long been a Judge & he knew no Law that forbid a man to take away his own Life."

Perhaps, like Rutledge, one had to be a bit reckless to desire to serve on the Supreme Court. In addition to traveling from their hometowns to the capital twice a year to attend Court sessions, the Justices were saddled with an extra, often grueling, duty: circuit riding. The Judiciary Act had created circuit courts but Congress had not provided salaries for separate circuit court judges. The country was divided into three circuits—Eastern, Middle, and Southern—and each fall and spring two Supreme Court

Justices (later reduced to one) were required to preside over these circuit courts. They traveled by horse and buggy, stagecoach, or boat. Roads were muddy, rocky, snowy, or icy—if they existed at all. Hazards, including highway robbers, were abundant. Justice James Iredell once reported that his horse had bolted when the rein got under his tail:

> [T]he chair [a kind of carriage] struck against a tree, and overset, throwing me out, and one of the wheels went over my leg. I was able to proceed however (as the chair was not broken) about ten miles, but then was in so much pain, I was under the necessity of staying very inconveniently at a house on the road.

Inns and taverns were generally uncomfortable, noisy, and crowded. Sharing a room at an inn with strangers was not uncommon; a Justice might even find himself having to share a bed. Justice Iredell complained to his wife, Hannah, on one such occasion: "It has been this time very much crouded indeed. I suffered very much the first night, having to sleep in a room with five People and a bed fellow of the wrong sort, which I did not expect." But, Iredell added, the bed-fellow happened to be an acquaintance—"Col. Dudley"—"so that I suffered as little as I could do in such a situation."

Riding circuit did have its occasional compensations. It gave the Justices an opportunity to see the country and to represent the national government in remote places. Most inns lacked comfort, but a few proved a nice respite. Wherever possible, the Justices dined with social acquaintances, providing for some merry evenings in the company of local dignitaries. Despite his anxieties about leaving Hannah alone with the children at their home in North Carolina, Iredell reveled in the social opportunities that circuit riding often presented. In 1795 he wrote from Richmond:

> I receive great civilities and distinction here. I dined the other day with Mr. Hylton, and in the evening went with his wife and daughter to the play ("As you like it"), which was very indifferently performed, except by a Mrs. West, formally Mrs. Bignall, who is really a pleasing actress. . . . They have a neat little theatre.

Riding circuit paid off handsomely for Justice James Wilson, a widower. While presiding over a court in Boston, he met and wooed the young woman who would (very quickly) become his second wife. Hannah Gray was nineteen; Wilson was fifty-one and had six children ranging in age from eight to twenty-one. Although bespectacled and stodgy, Wilson did have the advantage of being wealthy and—as a leading legal scholar and one of only six men who had signed both the Declaration of Independence and the Constitution—exceedingly distinguished. By the time Wilson left town ten days after meeting young Miss Gray, he had already proposed marriage. "I long for an Answer," Wilson pleaded from Newport, Rhode Island, the next stop on his circuit. "Do let that Answer be speedy and favorable: Let it authorize me to think and call you mine."

The Justice's infatuation with a local beauty was remarked upon by several Bostonians, including future president John Quincy Adams. Like some other observers, Adams concluded that Hannah was marrying the Justice for mercenary rather than romantic reasons. He wrote to his brother in Philadelphia:

> The most extraordinary intelligence, which I have to convey is that the wise and learned Judge & Professor Wilson, has fallen most lamentably in love with a young Lady in this town, under twenty, by the name of Gray. He came, he saw, he was overcome. The gentle [Scotsman] was smitten at a meeting with a first sight love—unable to contain his amorous pain, he breathed his sighs about the Streets; and even when seated on the bench of Justice, he seemed as if teeming with some woeful ballad to his mistress eye brow. He obtained an introduction to the Lady, and at the second interview proposed his lovely person and his agreeable family to her acceptance; a circumstance very favorable to the success of his pretensions, is that he came in a very handsome chariot and four.
>
> In short his attractions were so powerful, that the Lady actually has the subject under consideration, and unless the Judge should prove as fickle as he is amorous and repent his precipitate impetuosity so far as to withdraw his proposal, you will no doubt soon behold in the persons of those well assorted lovers a new edition of January and May. . . .
>
> Cupid himself must laugh at his own absurdity, in producing such a Union; but he must sigh to reflect that without the soft persuasion of a deity who has supplanted him in the breast of modern beauty, he could not have succeeded to render the man ridiculous & the woman contemptible.

Unfortunately for Hannah Gray, her new husband was a real estate speculator on a massive scale. Justice Wilson's hunger for wealth had driven him to borrow heavily in order to buy into risky land schemes in undeveloped wilderness on the western frontier of Pennsylvania and elsewhere. For a while the profits enabled him to live in luxury, but in 1796 a general downturn in the economy prompted a number of his creditors to call in their loans, and Wilson was either unable or unwilling to repay them. As a result, he found himself thrown into debtor's prison—thus becoming the first and only sitting Supreme Court Justice to be jailed.

After his son Bird bailed him out, Wilson decided that Philadelphia— his hometown—was no longer safe and looked for some out-of-the-way place to hide from his creditors. Eventually he settled on Edenton, North Carolina, where his friend and colleague James Iredell lived. Wilson remained in Edenton for almost a year, living in a modest but expensive tavern, and was eventually joined there by his young wife. Hanna Wilson told Bird that the man she found in Edenton was quite changed from the grandee she had married. And, since Wilson had been flagrantly neglecting his judicial duties and missing Supreme Court sessions, Hannah knew that back in Philadelphia there was inevitably talk of impeachment:

> Mr Iredell has by this, told you what will surprise you, as much as it did me, that your Papa has requested the Southern Circuit, what he means to do with me, (as I cannot . . . go with him, as I have no cloaths, if it was otherwise convenient), I know not, a single Chair & horses will cost three hundred dollars. He certainly never could think of buying a Carriage, his cloaths are all going to pieces, he has not had any thing since he left home, which is fifteen months, it would take 60 dollars at least to furnish him with what would be necessary to go so long a Circuit. Besides the expences of the journey, your papa has never got a new hat, which was very shabby when you saw it, you may think what tis now. He intended to write you fully, and Mr. Iredell if he had been well enough. He will open his mind to you but not to me, but it is a subject that I have done speaking upon, as we think so differently. Write me what people say to our not coming home, you need not be afraid of distressing me, as I can hear nothing worse than I expect.

Despite the fact that Wilson had proved to be far from an ideal husband, Hannah appears to have remained devoted to him. When he contracted malaria in the summer of 1798, she selflessly nursed him through what proved to be his final illness. A few days after Wilson's death, she wrote to Bird from the Iredells' house, where she would spend several months recuperating from her ordeal:

> I never should have forgiven myself if I had left him, when he was sensible he took so much pleasure in seeing me by him, and requested me not to leave him, but that was not five minutes at a time, I had not my cloaths off for three days and nights, nor left him till the evening of his death, when I could not bear the scene any longer, I am astonished at myself when I think of what I have gone through.

Painful as Wilson's death was to his wife, it must have come as a relief to the fledgling federal government, ending as it did a scandalous situation and relieving the pressure to launch impeachment proceedings.

More detrimental to the development of the Supreme Court as an institution, however, were the prolonged absences of two of its Chief Justices during this period. In 1794 President Washington sent Jay, while still Chief Justice, on a diplomatic mission to Britain to ease lingering hostilities between the two nations. A good deal of opposition greeted this appointment—partly because of policy concerns about dual office-holding, and partly because anti-Federalists feared that Jay was too sympathetic to the British. These fears were confirmed when Jay returned the following year with a treaty that many felt had not extracted enough concessions from England. Protests were so violent that Jay himself is said to have remarked that he could find his way across the country by the light of his burning effigies. Meanwhile, Jay's year-long absence from the Court had increased the workload on the Associate Justices, who had to shoulder Jay's portion of the circuit-riding duties.

But Jay had been reluctant to undertake the mission, in part because, as he explained to his wife, Sarah, the work of the Court was now taxing enough:

> It was expected that the Senate would yesterday have decided on the nomination of an envoy to the court of London, but measures respecting the embargo occupied them through the day. To-day that business is to be resumed, and you shall have the earliest notice of the result. So far as I am personally concerned, my feelings are very, very far from exciting wishes for its taking place. No appointment ever operated more unpleasantly upon me; but the public considerations which were urged, and the manner in which it was pressed, strongly impressed me with a conviction that to refuse it would be to desert my duty for the sake of my ease and domestic concerns and comforts. I derive some consolation from the prospect that my absence will not be of long continuance, and that the same Providence which has hitherto preserved me will still be pleased to accompany and restore me to you and our dear little family.
>
> The court has unceasingly engrossed my time. We did not adjourn until nine last night. I feel fatigued in body and mind. But reflections of this kind are not to be indulged. I must endeavour to sustain with propriety the part assigned me, and meet with composure and fortitude whatever disagreeable events may occur to counteract my wishes or increase my task. I shall have rest in time, and for that rest I will not cease to prepare. I am very anxious to be with you; and the moment the preparatory measures here will permit, I shall set out.

Jay's absence from the Court was a strain. Congressman Jeremiah Smith of New Hampshire even worried about the potential lack of a quorum:

> The Supreme Court commenced their session on monday. ___ Much of the dignity of the Court is lost by the absence of the Chief Justice ___ Judge [William] Cushing has not attended every day ___ He is under the Care of a Physician for a Cancer on his Lip ___ He attends part of the Time & in those Causes where they cannot make a quorum without him.

Upon his return home, Jay found he had been elected governor of New York in absentia. He resigned his Court post immediately. Fortunately, his resignation prevented the negative repercussions of the treaty from undermining the Court's fragile authority. Despite the President's popularity both with the people and the Senate, George Washington had a hard time finding someone to succeed Jay as Chief Justice. Both Alexander Hamilton and Patrick Henry turned him down. He also tried to elevate Associate Justices John Rutledge and William Cushing. Rutledge was not confirmed by the Senate after the political blunder he made in denouncing the Jay Treaty, which angered the Federalists who dominated the Senate. Cushing simply declined because he was old and sick.

Finally, Washington turned to the well-qualified Senator from Connecticut, Oliver Ellsworth. Vice President John Adams described him as having "the Stiffness of Connecticut; though his Air and Gait are not elegant; yet his Understanding is as sound, his Information as good and his heart as Steady as any Man can boast." After serving for nearly four years, Ellsworth was tapped by Adams—since elected President—to be part of a three-man delegation to resolve differences with France and try to head off war. For political reasons, there was less opposition to Ellsworth's appointment as foreign envoy than there had been to Jay's, but the effect on the Court was similar: once again, the Chief Justice was absent for over a year. In addition to burdening the other Justices with more circuit courts to hold, these absences made it difficult for the Court to cohere as a group of colleagues led by a strong Chief Justice.

Chief Justice Ellsworth's health was so broken by his sojourn abroad that he felt he could no longer continue in office. His resignation in 1800 caused an important vacancy shortly before Adams's term as President expired. Adams's first impulse was to turn to former Chief Justice John Jay, despite Jay's recently announced intention to retire from public life. Jay, as many expected, declined the appointment, citing Congress's failure to eliminate the system of circuit-riding:

> [T]he Efforts repeatedly made to place the judicial Department on a proper Footing have proved fruitless—I left the bench perfectly convinced that under a System so defective, it would not obtain the Energy, Weight, and Dignity which are essential to its affording due support to the national Government; nor acquire the public Confidence and Respect which, as the last Resort of the Justice of the nation, it should possess. Hence I am induced to doubt both the Propriety and Expediency of my returning to the Bench under the present System.

Under severe time pressure—and preferring, for political reasons, to choose a Chief Justice from outside the Court rather than elevating one of the Associate Justices—Adams then turned to his Secretary of State, John Marshall. Many years later, Marshall would recall the circumstances:

> When I waited on the President with Mr. Jays letter declining the appointment he said thoughtfully "Who shall I nominate now?" I replied that I could not tell. . . . After a moment's hesitation he said "I believe I must nominate you." I had never before heard my self named for the office and had not even thought of it. I was pleased as well as surprized, and bowed in silence.

A new era for the Court was about to begin.

2

⚖

John Marshall Takes Charge
Establishing Power

When Joseph Story came to Washington in 1808 to represent his home state of Massachusetts in the U.S. Congress, he ventured down into the basement of the Capitol building to watch a session of the Supreme Court. The young lawyer was immediately struck both by the Chief Justice's lack of pretension, and by his genius:

> [John] Marshall is of a tall, slender figure, not graceful nor imposing, but erect and steady. His hair is black, his eyes small and twinkling, his forehead rather low but his features are, in general, harmonious. His manners are plain yet dignified; and an unaffected modesty diffuses itself through all his actions. His dress is very simple, yet neat; his language chaste but hardly elegant; it does not flow rapidly, but it seldom wants precision. His thoughts are always clear and ingenious, sometimes striking and not often inconclusive; he possesses great subtlety of mind, but it is only occasionally exhibited. I love his laugh—it is too hearty for an intriguer—and his good temper and unwearied patience are equally agreeable on the bench and in the study. His genius is, in my opinion, vigorous and powerful, less rapid than discriminating, and less vivid than uniform in its light. He examines the intricacies of a subject with calm and persevering circumspection, and unravels the mysteries with irresistible acuteness.

John Marshall had been appointed Chief Justice seven years earlier, when the Supreme Court was an institution that was still finding its way. Hampered by the resignations of several Justices who couldn't stomach the rigors of circuit riding, and by the lengthy absences of two Chief Justices who had been detailed as foreign envoys, the Court had not asserted itself strongly during the federal government's tentative first decade.

11

In the thirty-four years he served as Chief Justice, John Marshall embraced an expansive Federalist view of the Supreme Court as a coequal third branch of government. (Courtesy of the Library of Congress)

In his thirty-four years as Chief, Marshall would persuade the Court to embrace his expansive Federalist view and to speak with one, clear voice. This shift enabled the Court to claim its rightful position at the top of a federal judicial structure that was coequal with the executive and legislative branches.

A Virginia gentleman born on the frontier, Marshall made his mark in the capital city of Richmond, where he established a successful legal practice and served in the state legislature. While his formal legal education was unremarkable and his attire resembled that of a country bumpkin, his legal mind was sharp. Marshall was remarkably able to comprehend and distill the essence of cases with logic and rigor. From an early age he had developed the view that the country needed a strong national government. His fellow Virginians, Thomas Jefferson in particular, would continually and vigorously challenge this assumption.

Marshall was approached several times by the Federalist Party to accept posts in the new national government. He ultimately chose to serve in various capacities: as a diplomat to France, a member of the U.S. Congress, and President John Adams's Secretary of State. Although appointed to the Supreme Court by Adams, Marshall had been on the bench only a few months when Thomas Jefferson, his political and philosophical rival (as well as his cousin) became President.

The best eyewitness to life on the Marshall Court is undisputedly Joseph Story, who joined the Court as an Associate Justice in 1812 and shared the bench with Marshall for twenty-four years. The scholarly Story had practiced as a lawyer, served in the Massachusetts state legislature, and would in his later years teach at Harvard Law School. Although affiliated with Jefferson's Democrat-Republican Party, Story soon fell under Marshall's sway, sharing his nationalist vision and becoming his intellectual ally and friend. Through his writings and teaching, Story would also prove to be one of the most influential legal scholars in American history.

First impressions of Marshall were invariably unfavorable and misleading. His limbs were gangly and his manner of dress careless. A friend once described his attire as "gotten from some antiquated slop-shop of second-hand raiment . . . the coat and breeches cut for nobody in particular." But after half an hour in his company, according to one lawyer, his greatness became readily apparent:

> [T]he Chief Justice of the United States, the first lawyer—if not, indeed, the first man—in the country. You must then imagine before you a man who is tall to awkwardness, with a large head of hair, which looked as if it had not been lately tied or combed, and with dirty boots. You must imagine him, too, with a strangeness in his manners, which arises neither from awkwardness nor from formality, but seems to be a curious compound of both; and then, perhaps, you will have before you a figure something like that of the Chief Justice. His style and tones in conversation are uncommonly mild, gentle, and conciliating; and before I had been with him half an hour, I had forgotten his carelessness of his dress and person, and observed only the quick intelligence of his eye, and the open interest he discovered in the subjects on which he spoke, by the perpetual variations of his countenance.

Even after establishing his preeminence on the Supreme Court, Marshall retained his amiability and simplicity. Mused Story:

> Meet him on a stagecoach, as a stranger, and travel with him a whole day and you would only be struck by his readiness to administer to the accommodations of others and his anxiety to appropriate the least to himself. Be with him, the unknown guest at an inn, and he seemed adjusted to the very

Associate Justice Joseph Story, Marshall's close friend, provided the intellectual reasoning behind many of the Court's decisions. (Collection of the Supreme Court of the United States, photograph by Mathew Brady)

scene, partaking of the warm welcome of its comforts, whenever found; and if not found, resigning himself without complaint to the meanest arrangements. You would never suspect, in either case, that he was a great man; far less that he was the Chief Justice of the United States.

Marshall's ability to lead the other members of the Court was aided in no small measure by his likeable, down-to-earth personality and his jolly sense of humor. He had a quick wit and loved jokes, songs, and clever repartee. Even in old age Marshall retained his boyish, easygoing charm and sense of fun. Portrait painter Chester Harding described the celebrated Chief Justice, at the age of seventy-five, pitching quoits (a ring-toss game) at his sporting club:

> I watched for the coming of the old chief. He soon approached with his coat on his arm, and his hat in his hand, which he was using as a fan. He walked directly up to a large bowl of mint julep . . . and drank off a tumbler full of liquid, smacked his lips and then turned to the company with a cheerful "How are you, gentlemen?" He was looked upon as the best pitcher of the party, and could throw heavier quoits than any other member of the club. The game began with great animation. There were several ties; and, before long, I saw the great Chief Justice of the Supreme Court of the United States, down on his knees, measuring the contested distance with a straw, with as much earnestness as if it had been a point of law; and if he proved to be in the right, the woods would ring with his triumphant shout. What would the dignitaries of the highest court of England have thought, if they had been present?

Inside the Courtroom, though, Chief Justice Marshall apparently was all business:

> When, however, the time came for him to open court, a transformation came over him. Clad in the robes of his great office, with the Associate Justices on either side of him, no king on a throne ever appeared more majestic than did John Marshall. The kindly look was still in his eye, the mildness still in his tones, the benignity in his features. But a gravity of bearing, a firmness of manner, a concentration and intentness of mind, seemed literally to take possession of the man, although he was, and appeared to be, as unconscious of the change as he was that there was anything unusual in his conduct when off the bench.

Marshall broke with English tradition by wearing a plain black robe in the manner of the judges on the Virginia court of appeals. This was likely as much a political move as a fashion statement. He instinctively preferred simple dress, but he probably also wanted to show that he was distancing himself from the colors of the English court and from what he saw as the excessive hubris of the Federalists.

Chief Justice Marshall made another strategic decision by arranging for the Justices to live together in various inns and boardinghouses in the nation's capital while they attended the six- to eight-week sessions of the Supreme Court. Until 1827, they met from the first Monday in February until the second or third week in March. From 1827 to 1835, they commenced the second Monday in January. Wives and families were left at home, as life in the capital offered little to attract them. One nonplussed observer reported:

> There are few families that make Washington their permanent residence, and the city, therefore, has rather the aspect of a watering-place [for horses] than the metropolis of a great nation. The members of Congress generally live together in small boardinghouses, which, from all I saw of them, are shabby and uncomfortable.

It was in the spartan but hospitable context of boardinghouse life that Marshall was able to use his intellect and charm to influence his brethren in their decision making. The absence of family tightened the fraternal bond. It also allowed for rapid decision making: opinions were usually announced within five days of argument and seldom more than a few weeks later. Discussions of legal questions arising from cases the Justices heard in Court took place during dinner at a common table in the company of other boarders and continued after the meal in a private room. One year after his arrival on the Court, Story observed to a friend:

> I find myself considerably more at ease than I expected. My brethren are very interesting men, with whom I live in the most frank and unaffected intimacy. Indeed we are all united as one, with a mutual esteem which makes even the labors of Jurisprudence light. The mode of arguing causes in the Supreme Court is excessively prolix and tedious; but generally the subject is exhausted, and it is not very difficult to perceive at the close of the cause, in many cases, where the press of the argument and of the law lies. We moot every question as we proceed, and my familiar conferences at our lodgings often come to a very quick, and, I trust, a very accurate opinion, in a few hours. On the whole, therefore, I begin to feel the weight of depression with which I came here insensibly wearing away, and a calm but ambitious self-possession gradually succeeding in its place.

Story enjoyed the convivial atmosphere fostered by Marshall, with its mingling of business and pleasure, writing to his wife, Sarah:

> It is certainly true, that the Judges here live with perfect harmony, and as agreeably as absence from friends and from families could make our residence. Our intercourse is perfectly familiar and unconstrained, and our

social hours when undisturbed with the labors of law, are passed in gay and frank conversation, which at once enlivens and instructs.

Marshall had a taste for spirits and liked to frequent taverns when at home in Richmond. He arranged for cases of vintage wine to be shipped to Washington each term in bottles labeled "The Supreme Court." Story arrived at the Court a teetotaler because of a delicate stomach, but was pressured to join the other Justices in a glass of Madeira at dinner. He recounted to his friend Josiah Quincy, then President of Harvard University, that the Justices—mostly Federalist appointees—kept to themselves under the Jefferson administration, but nevertheless managed to achieve a degree of conviviality: "[W]e judges take no part in the society of the place. We dine once a year with the President, and that is all. On other days we take our dinner together, and discuss at table the questions which are argued before us. We are great ascetics, and even deny ourselves wine, except in wet weather." According to Quincy, Story paused and then issued a partial correction "as if thinking that the act of mortification he had mentioned placed too severe a tax on human credulity":

> What I say about wine, sir, gives you our rule; but it does sometimes happen that the Chief Justice will say to me, when the cloth is removed, "Brother Story, step to the window and see if it does not look like rain." And if I tell him that the sun is shining brightly, Judge Marshall will sometimes reply, "All the better for our jurisdiction extends over so large a territory that the doctrine of chances makes it certain that it must be raining somewhere." You know that the Chief was brought up upon Federalism and Madeira, and he is not the man to outgrow his early prejudices.

(There is a corollary to this much-repeated tale. It comes from Charles Henry Butler, who was the Court's Reporter of Decisions from 1902 to 1915, when the Supreme Court was hearing cases concerning the constitutional rights of territories in the aftermath of the Spanish-American War. At a gathering, the Justices were retelling the "Brother Story" anecdote when Butler questioned its authenticity. Justice David Brewer replied: "Why, Mr. Reporter, the story is not only true, but you ought to know that the Court sustained the constitutionality of the acquisition of the Philippines so as to be sure of having plenty of rainy seasons.")

The Marshall Court Justices did not limit their discussions to the law. They liked to dissect the day's political events and social gossip, and to analyze the manner and dress of the oral advocates who had argued before them that day. A visitor from Massachusetts was impressed by the convivial atmosphere he witnessed in 1834: "I dined with them yesterday. . . . No conversation is forbidden, and nothing which goes to cause cheerfulness, if not hilarity. The world and all its things are talked of as much as on any other day. Judge Marshall is a model of simplicity. He is naturally taciturn, and yet ready to laugh, to joke, be joked with." The Justices even debated the various attractions of eligible society ladies as suitable matches for the bachelors in their ranks. Again, Story:

> Two of the judges are widowers, and of course objects of considerable attraction among the ladies of the city. We have fine sport at their expense, and amuse our leisure with some touches at match-making. We have already ensnared one of the Judges [Thomas Todd], and he is now (at the age of forty-seven) violently affected with the tender passion.

While the Justices may have enjoyed the informality of their boarding-house deliberations, the fact is that they had been given little choice: the chamber where cases were argued in the Capitol building was simply too cramped to accommodate judicial conferences. Initially, only a single room was set aside for the Supreme Court in the basement of the Capitol, on the ground floor of the north wing. It was a committee room that the Court shared with the district and circuit courts of the District of Columbia. Because there was no shared bench, at least initially, the Justices sat at individual desks on a raised platform. No provision had been made for a law library or offices for the Justices. (They were not even permitted access to the stacks at the Library of Congress until 1812.) Nor were they assigned clerks or secretaries to help them. Architect Benjamin Latrobe, who designed the Capitol, lobbied President James Madison for better space, calling the chamber "meanly furnished and very inconvenient." Appraising the timbers propping up the low ceiling, a journalist said he experienced "a most uncomfortable feeling that there is danger of being crushed to atoms in this grim catacomb."

Visiting the Supreme Court with his father, a young boy named William Allen Butler was shocked to see that, for lack of a vestibule, Chief Justice Marshall and the Associate Justices put on their robes in the Courtroom in full public view:

> My boyish attention was fastened upon the seven judges as they entered the room—seven being the number then composing the Court. It was a procession of old men—for so they seemed to me—who halted on their way to the bench, each of them taking from a peg hanging on the side of the wall near the entrance a black robe and donning it in full view of the assembled lawyers and other spectators. This somewhat extra-judicial act impressed me more than any subsequent proceeding of the Court, and left a vivid picture in my memory.

The Supreme Court held session in this poorly ventilated chamber in the basement of the Capitol from 1810 to 1860. (Courtesy of the Architect of the Capitol)

So dismayed was Butler, that he later questioned his memory:

> Long afterward when I went to Washington to argue cases before the highest tribunal, contrasting the dignified formalities which attended the opening of the Court at every session with the robing method which I have described, I began to think I must have been mistaken and that I could not have seen Chief Justice Marshall, Judge Story and their associates doing so informal a thing as putting on their robes after entering the courtroom.

Butler even felt compelled to ask Chief Justice Roger Taney, Marshall's successor, to confirm that his recollection was indeed correct.

In 1810 the Court was given better accommodations when the Senate moved upstairs in the Capitol building and the Justices took over its cast-off chambers. These were redesigned as a vaulted, single-story Courtroom. But the new chamber was still inadequate and the Justices continued to don their robes in public. An English visitor thought the Supreme Court deserved better:

> It is by no means a large or handsome apartment; and the lowness of the ceiling, and the circumstance of its being under ground, give it a certain cellar-like aspect, which is not pleasant. This is perhaps unfortunate, because it tends to create in the spectator the impression of justice being done in a corner; and, that while the business of legislation is carried on with all the pride, pomp, and circumstance of glorious debate, in halls adorned with all the skill of the architect, the administration of men's rights is considered an affair of secondary importance.

Even more disparaging was this description by a New York reporter who came to cover the high-profile *Gibbons v. Ogden* steamship case in 1824:

> The apartment is not in a style which comports with the dignity of that body, or which wears a comparison with the other Halls of the Capitol. In the first place, it is like going down cellar to reach it. The room is on the basement story in an obscure part of the north wing. In arriving at it, you pass a labyrinth, and almost need the clue of Ariadne to guide you to the sanctuary of the blind goddess. A stranger might traverse the dark avenues of the Capitol for a week, without finding the remote corner in which Justice is administered to the American Republic . . . a room which is hardly capacious enough for a ward justice. . . . It is a triangular, semi-circular, odd-shaped apartment, with three windows, and a profusion of arches in the ceiling, diverging like the radii of a circle from a point over the bench to the circumference.

Space constraints were a problem as the Court was a fashionable haunt for society women who considered listening to gifted orators as entertaining as an evening at the theater. As oral arguments weren't subject to time limits in the early nineteenth century, it was possible for ladies to while away many hours in the Courtroom following a single case. They turned the proceedings into a social occasion, not always paying strict attention to the points of law being discussed. Dressed in their finery, including hats with tall plumes, these women arrived early to secure seats. Members of Congress and foreign ministers who attended high-profile cases often stood jammed in the back out of gallantry:

> The apartment is well finished; but the experience of this day has shown that in size it is wholly insufficient for the accommodation of the Bar, and the spectators who wish to attend. Many of the members [of Congress] were obliged to leave their seats to make room for the ladies, some of whom were sworn in, and with much difficulty found places within the Bar.

Advocates dutifully hammed it up, using grand rhetoric and lacing their speeches with allusions to Roman law and the Bible in an attempt to impress the audience with the breadth of their knowledge—even if the details were not always germane to the issue before the Court. To complement the oratory, Attorney General William Pinkney sported the latest fashions, including, on occasion, amber-colored doeskin gloves. He also staged his arguments theatrically, once even feigning unpreparedness so as to heighten the effect of his eloquence. A friend recounted Pinkney's subterfuge, having witnessed the intense rehearsals that preceded it:

> I did not fail to be at the courthouse the next morning. The court and bar were waiting impatiently for Mr. Pinkney. They were all out of humor; a messenger had been sent for him. He came at length, with a somewhat hurried step. He entered, bowing and apologizing: "I beg your honor's pardon, it really escaped my recollection that this was the day fixed for the trial. I am very sorry on my own account, as well as on account of others; I fear I am but poorly prepared, but as it cannot be avoided, I must do the best in my power."
>
> He was dressed and looked as if he had just set out on a morning walk of pleasure, like a mere Bond Street lounger. His hat, beautiful and glossy, in his hand, his small rattan tapping the crown. He drew off his gloves, and placed them on the table. He was dressed most carefully, neatly but plainly, and in the best fashion. His coat was of blue broadcloth, with gilt buttons; his vest of white Marseilles, with gold studs, elegantly fitting pants and shining halfboots; he was the polished gentleman of leisure accidentally dropped down in a motley group of inferior beings.

The stunt was evidently a success:

> The words and sentences seemed to flow into each other in perfect musical harmony, without sudden break or abruptness, but rising and falling, or changing with the subject, still retaining an irresistible hold on the attention of the listeners. No one stirred; all seemed motionless, as if enchained

or fascinated, and in a glow of rapture, like persons entranced—myself among the rest although some portions of the speech were already familiar to me, having heard them before, and this circumstance threatened to break the spell: but the effect was complete with the audience, and the actual delivery was so superior to the study, that the inclination to risibility was checked at once, and my feelings were again in unison with those around me. It was a most wonderful display, and its effect long continued to master my feelings and judgment.

But at least one observer, society writer Margaret Bayard Smith, disapproved of the way Pinkney pandered to the ladies:

The effect of the female admiration and attention has been very obvious, but it is a doubt to me whether it has been beneficial, indeed I believe otherwise. A member told me he doubted now, there had been much more speaking on this account, and another gentleman told me, that one day Mr. Pinckney [sic] had finished his argument and was just about seating himself when Mrs. Madison [the First Lady] and a train of ladies enter'd—he recommenced, went over the same ground, using fewer arguments, but scattering more flowers. And on the day I was there I am certain he thought more of the female part of his audience than of the court, and on concluding, he recognized their presence, when he said, "He would not weary the court, by going through a long list of cases to prove his argument, as it would only be fatiguing to them, but inimical to the laws of good taste, which on the present occasion, (bowing low) he wished to obey."

A single oral argument could go on for more than four hours at a stretch, and could consume more than a week of the Court's time. Although the Justices did sometimes ask questions of counsel, they mostly settled in and listened. Without law clerks or a law library, the Justices were grateful for the research and preparation that went into the speeches delivered by the advocates—some of whom even had firsthand experience in drafting the Constitution. Advocates chewed tobacco to keep themselves going; the Justices did too, placing their individual snuffboxes and spittoons on the bench. One of the greatest oral advocates of the era, Senator Henry Clay of Georgia, once brazenly helped himself to a Justice's stash in mid-argument. Recalled a Courtroom spectator:

[Associate Justice Bushrod Washington was] a small, insignificant looking man deprived of the sight of one eye by excessive study, negligent of dress and an immoderate snuff taker. . . . When Mr. Clay stopped, one day, in an argument and advancing to the bench, took a pinch of snuff from Judge Washington's box, saying,—"I perceive that your Honor sticks to the Scotch" and then proceeded with his case, it excited astonishment and admiration. "Sir" said Mr. Justice Story, in relating the circumstances to a friend, "I do not believe there is a man in the United States who could have done that, but Mr. Clay."

In 1812 the Court began reining in unrestricted oral arguments, adopting a rule limiting the number of counsel in each case to two per side. This revived the practice, common when the Supreme Court was based in Philadelphia during the 1790s, of hiring Supreme Court specialists, men who argued several cases a term. Among these talented advocates, oral argument became a competitive sport. On occasion it became cutthroat.

Most famously, the flamboyant William Pinkney once disparaged a young, up-and-coming opponent—Daniel Webster—before a packed Courtroom. According to Webster: "He pooh-poohed, as much as to say it was not worthwhile to argue a point that I did not know anything about; that I was no lawyer. . . . It was very hard for me to restrain my temper." Webster retaliated by luring Pinkney to an empty room in the Capitol, locking him in, and pocketing the key. According to Peter Harvey, a writer who interviewed Webster and put his reminiscences down on paper in 1877 (more than sixty years after the incident), an apology was extracted in a highly dramatic fashion:

Mr. Pinkney seemed to be waiting with some astonishment. I advanced towards him, and said: "Mr. Pinkney, you grossly insulted me this morning, in the court-room; and not for the first time either. In deference to your position and to the respect in which I hold the court, I did not answer you as I was tempted to do, on the spot." He began to parley. I continued: "You know you did: don't add another sin to that; don't deny it; you know you did it, and you know it was premeditated. It was deliberate; it was purposely done; and, if you deny it, you state an untruth. Now," I went on, "I am here to say to you, once and for all, that you must ask my pardon, and go into court to-morrow morning and repeat the apology, or else either you or I will go out of this room in a different condition from that in which we entered it." I was never more in earnest. He looked at me, and saw that my eyes were pretty dark and firm. He began to say something. I interrupted him. "No explanations," said I: "admit the fact, and take it back. I do not want another word from you except that. I will hear no explanations; nothing but that you admit it, and recall it." He trembled like an aspen leaf. He again attempted to explain. Said I: "There is no other course. I have the key in my pocket, and you must apologize, or take what I give you." At that he humbled down, and said to me: "You are right; I am sorry; I did intend to bluff you; I regret it, and ask your pardon." "Enough," I promptly replied. "Now, one promise before I open the door; and that is, that you will to-morrow morning state to the court that you have said things which wounded my feelings, and that you regret it." Pinkney replied: "I will do so." Then I unlocked the door, and passed out. The next morning, when the court met, Mr. Pinkney at once rose, and stated to the court that a very unpleasant affair had occurred the morning before, as might have been observed by their honors; that his friend, Mr. Webster, had felt grieved at some things which had dropped from his lips; that his zeal for his client might have led him to say some things which he should not have said; and that he was sorry for having thus spoken.

"From that day, while at the bar, there was no man," said Mr. Webster, "who treated me with so much respect and deference as Mr. William Pinkney."

Eloquent advocates with no shortage of stamina delivered such impressive performances that the Marshall era is considered the golden age of Supreme Court advocacy. Daniel Webster, who would argue close to two hundred cases and eventually eclipse Pinkney as dean of the Supreme Court bar, took particular pleasure in arguing before the great John Marshall:

> I can see the chief justice as he looked [at the opening of Webster's oral argument in the *Gibbons v. Ogden* steamship case, in which the Court broadened the scope of the Commerce Clause]. Chief Justice Marshall always wrote with a quill. He never adopted the barbarous invention of steel pens. That abomination had not been introduced. And always, before counsel began to argue, the chief justice would nib his pen; and then, when everything was ready, pulling up the sleeves of his gown, he would nod to the counsel who was to address him, as much as to say "I am ready; now you may go on." I think I never experienced more intellectual pleasure than in arguing that naval question to a great man who could appreciate it and take it in; and he did take it in, as a baby takes in its mother's milk.

Another distinguished advocate, Luther Martin, was bold enough to take a direct shot at Chief Justice Marshall when he argued *McCulloch v. Maryland* in 1819. Martin first raised the level of tension in the Courtroom by announcing that he would quote the words of John Marshall when, as a young man, he had been a delegate to the Virginia Ratifying Convention. Marshall reportedly "took a deep breath" when Martin began quoting him, but apparently was able to exhale with relief. Marshall later confided to his friend Story: "I was afraid I had said some foolish things in that debate; but it was not so bad as I expected." Marshall's nationalistic decision in *McCulloch*, which determined the distribution of power between the federal government and the states, would be one of his most important and eloquent.

But even the most skilled advocates sometimes taxed the Justices' patience with their lengthy speeches. In 1824 a newspaper reporter observed that the weary Justices did not hide their fatigue if oral arguments proved less than captivating:

The Court sits from eleven o'clock in the morning until four in the afternoon. It is not only one of the most dignified and enlightened tribunals in the world, but one of the most patient. Counsel are heard in silence for hours, without being stopped or interrupted. If a man talks nonsense, he is soon graduated and passes for what he is worth. If he talks to the point, he will be properly measured, and his talents, discrimination and industry reflected in the opinion of the Court. The Judges of the Court say nothing, but when they are fatigued and worried by a long and pointless argument, displaying a want of logic, a want of acuteness, and a destitution of authorities, their feelings and wishes are sufficiently manifested by their countenances and the manners which are displayed.

Another Courtwatcher found himself increasingly restless listening to a long-winded attorney's overly embroidered arguments:

Before this audience was the bench of reverend judges, listening with constrained patience to a ruby-faced spokesman; who, with his hair in full powder, but without any robe, which, like charity, might have covered a multitude of improprieties, was chopping law-logic, in a voice so loud as to be almost lost in its own reverberations. This was the third day of his speech; of which I heard nothing more than the peroration. But that was enough; for though, as well as I could catch the subject, there was a pervading strength of argument, and some coruscations of rhetoric, his gestures were so vehement, countenance so angry, and his continual digressions so entirely extra flammantia moenia mundi [outside the flaming ramparts of the world], that it was impossible to keep in view both the speaker and his cause; and indeed before he concluded, I suffered all the torments of restlessness, and a jaded attention, bewildered with vain efforts to sit still and understand.

The Court's docket was rapidly expanding during this time—from 98 cases in 1810 to 253 in 1850—forcing it to increase the amount of time allotted to oral arguments. The term stretched from forty-three days in 1825 to ninety-nine days in 1845. In response, the Court decided in 1833 that it would ask advocates to submit written briefs, a practice the Justices hoped would decrease the time needed for oral exposition. That rule was amended in 1849 to make printed briefs required.

After sitting on the bench all day hearing long-winded arguments, the Justices must have been relieved to return to the relaxed atmosphere of their boardinghouse to discuss the cases. And it was during these discussions that Marshall set about changing the way the Court issued opinions. Under previous Chief Justices, the Justices either delivered the Court's opinion as a single decision representing the will of the whole Court, or they each individually delivered "seriatim" opinions from the bench, beginning with the most junior Justice. Long the practice in English appellate courts, seriatim opinions tended to cause confusion. Observers would have to count up the votes to determine what result the Court majority had arrived at, and even then the Court's holding might not always be clear. On occasion Chief Justice John Jay had led the Court in speaking with one common voice, and later in the decade Chief Justice Oliver Ellsworth had tried to institutionalize the use of "Opinions of the Court." But Marshall solidified this trend, routinely issuing unified opinions that enhanced the Court's power. According to Story, Marshall's majestic delivery reinforced the Court's authority: "You heard him pronounce the opinion of the Court in a low, but modulated voice, unfolding in luminous order every topic of argument, trying its strength, and measuring its value, until you felt yourself in the presence of the very oracle of the law."

Initially it was the practice for the most senior Justice—Marshall—to write all the Opinions of the Court. But after Thomas Jefferson was elected President in 1801, he decided to shake up the Federalist-dominated Supreme Court by appointing a Democrat-Republican to rein in Marshall. He chose William Johnson of South Carolina, a ruddy, athletic man who took his seat in 1804 at the age of thirty-two. Johnson quickly concluded that the Associate Justices' weak intellects and advanced age made them willing to concur in Marshall's opinions because they craved a strong and astute thinker to lead them:

> When I was on our State bench I was accustomed to delivering seriatim opinions in our appellate Court, and was not a little surprised to find our Chief-Justice in the Supreme Court delivering all the opinions in cases in which he sat, even in some Instances when contrary to his own Judgment & vote. But I remonstrated in vain; the answer was, he is willing to take the Trouble, & it is a Mark of Respect to him. I soon, however, found the real cause. [William] Cushing is incompetent, [Samuel] Chase could not be got to think or write— [William] Patterson [*sic*] was a slow man and willingly declined the trouble, and the other two judges you know are commonly estimated as one judge.

The "two judges" to whom Johnson was referring were the Chief Justice and Bushrod Washington (1799–1829), the first President's nephew and Marshall's longtime friend and neighbor in Richmond.

Somewhat cantankerous, William Johnson liked his independence and fought to have his ideas taken seriously in Conference. In the face of Marshall's power and charm, and his brethren's desire for unity and harmony, this was not easy. Story would later reflect on Marshall's extraordinary ability to lead Conference discussions:

> [H]e excelled in the statement of a case; so much so, that it was almost of itself an argument. If it did not at once lead the hearer to the proper conclu-

sion, it prepared him to assent to it, as soon as it was announced. Nay, more; it persuaded him, that it must be right, however repugnant it might be to his preconceived notions. . . . He would by the most subtle analysis resolve every argument into its ultimate principles, and then with a marvellous facility apply them to the decision of the cause.

Nevertheless, Johnson did succeed in persuading Marshall to allow others to speak for the Court. This was quite a feat because the Justices were reluctant to air publicly the Court's differences about the law, fearing it would weaken the institution's prestige and stability. Johnson's first dissenting opinion appeared in 1805, only one year after he was appointed, and established a tradition of dissent in the Supreme Court.

By 1812 dissenting and concurring opinions were issued regularly, and Marshall no longer claimed to be the sole author of majority opinions. But by then Johnson had also changed. He gradually began to compromise, particularly when he saw that his new colleague Joseph Story, a fellow Republican, quickly adopted Marshall's belief in a unified bench and a strong federal government. By the 1819 Term the conservative nationalism of the Marshall Court was firmly in place, and the Court had increased its power and visibility. This was to be the apex of Marshall's authority.

In 1822 Thomas Jefferson, now retired but still the philosophical mentor of the Democrat-Republicans, complained bitterly to Johnson that many in the party had abandoned their Republican ideals and fallen under Marshall's influence. As Jefferson saw it, Marshall's undemocratic preference for unified opinions bred laziness and irresponsibility among the Associate Justices and masked their disagreements: "An opinion is huddled up in conclave, perhaps by a majority of one, delivered as if unanimous, and with the silent acquiescence of lazy or timid associates, by a crafty chief judge, who sophisticates the law to his mind, by the turn of his own reasoning." Jefferson wanted each Justice to go on record with his own opinion so the public would know exactly where he stood. He believed this would alleviate any suspicion that the majority had squelched dissent:

I must comfort myself with the hope that the judges will see the importance and the duty of giving their country the only evidence they can give of fidelity to its constitution and integrity in the administration of its laws; that is to say, by everyone's giving his opinion seriatim and publicly on the case he decides. Let him prove by his reasoning that he has read the papers, that he has considered the case, that in the application of the law to it, he uses his own judgment, independently and unbiased by party views and personal favor or disfavor. Throw himself on every case on God and his country; both will excuse him for error and value him for his honesty.

Johnson wearily explained to Jefferson that in practice compromise was sometimes the best tactic. It enabled him to avoid his colleagues' scorn and to remain effective:

> [After my appointment] some case soon occurred in which I differed from my brethren, and I thought it a thing of course to deliver my opinion. But, during the rest of the session I heard nothing but lectures on the indecency of judges cutting at each other. . . . At length I found that I must either submit to circumstances or become such a cipher in our consultations as to effect no good at all. I therefore bent to the current, and persevered until I got them to adopt the course they now pursue, which is to appoint someone to deliver the opinion of the majority, but leave it to the discretion of the rest of the judges to record their opinion or not ad libitum [as they please].

Spurred by Jefferson's rebukes, Johnson began reasserting his independence on the Court. In 1828 he was helped by the election of President Andrew Jackson, a Democrat who shared Jefferson's suspicion of a strong national government. Jackson would appoint four new Associate Justices who, like Johnson, would challenge the old Federalist order and threaten Marshall's dominance.

As Marshall lost his control of the Court, the collegial practice of sharing lodging began to fade as well. In 1828, Justice Story decided to bring his wife along for the Supreme Court Term. Although Marshall graciously offered to find Sarah Story living accommodations nearby and expressed his hope to her husband that she would join the Justices for meals, he was clearly displeased:

> [While Mrs. Story] may be tempted by gracing our table to shed the humanizing influence of the sex over a circle which has sometimes felt the want of it. She must however be forewarned that she is not to monopolize you, but must surrender you to us to bear that large portion of our [burdens] which belongs to you.

Sarah Story did not repeat the experiment.

Two terms later, Marshall was tied up at the Virginia state constitutional convention and was unable to arrive early to arrange his brethren's housing. Newly appointed Justices John McLean and Henry Baldwin thus made their own living arrangements: McLean stayed with his wife and children, who were already in Washington as he had been serving as Postmaster General; Baldwin, who complained about the high boardinghouse rents, lodged with his sister and brother-in-law in their home. (William Johnson had announced his intention to board separately, but he missed the entire term due to illness.) Marshall fretted that if the Justices lived independently they would revert to writing seriatim opinions:

I think this is a matter of some importance, for if the Judges scatter ad libitum [at liberty], the docket I fear will remain quite compact, [resolving] very few of its causes; and the few it may lose, will probably be carried off by seriatim opinions. Old men however are timid, and I hope my fears may be unfounded.

All seven Justices did board together one last term in 1834. But for the next twenty terms only a few of the brethren would lodge together; the others stayed independently in hotels or private homes.

With the solidarity of boardinghouse life eroded, his dear friend Bushrod Washington dead, and several new Jackson appointees sitting on the Court, Marshall in his later years found that the old days of camaraderie and easy domination of the Court were gone. But by then the Court had issued so many landmark opinions asserting the power of the federal judiciary—including the authority of the Supreme Court to overturn acts of Congress (in *Marbury v. Madison*, 1803)—that the Justices could afford to be less unified.

Age seventy-nine and with only a few months left to live, Marshall apparently still exuded a quiet power. English travel writer Harriet Martineau painted this scene of the waning days of the Marshall era:

> At some moments this court presents a singular spectacle. I have watched the assemblage while the chief-justice was delivering a judgment, the three [Justices] on either hand gazing at him more like learners than associates. . . . [The oral advocates] absorbed in what they are listening to, thinking neither of themselves nor of each other, while they are watched by the group of idlers and listeners around them,—the newspaper corps, the dark Cherokee chiefs, the stragglers from the Far West, the gay ladies in their waving plumes, and the members of either house that have stepped in to listen,—all these I have seen at one moment constitute one silent assemblage, while the mild voice of the aged chief-justice sounded through the Court.

When Marshall died in 1835, he left behind a Supreme Court that had fulfilled its constitutional promise. His old ally Story hung on for ten more years, conducting a rear-guard defense of Marshall Court jurisprudence. He was the last witness to an extraordinary era:

> I miss the Chief Justice at every turn. I have been several times into the room which he was accustomed to occupy. It yet remains without an inhabitant, and wears an aspect of desolation, and has a noiseless gloom. The table at which he sat, the chair which he occupied, the bed on which he slept,—they are all there, and bring back a train of the most melancholy reflections. Consider for a moment that I am the last of the Judges who were on the Bench when I first took my seat there. I seem a moment of the past age, and a mere record of the dead.

3

⚖

Justice by Shay, Stagecoach, Steamboat, Train

Riding Circuit

I have been elbowed by old women—jammed by young ones—suffo-cated by cigar smoke—sickened by the vapors of bitters and whiskey—my head knocked through the carriage top by careless drivers and my toes trodden to a jelly by unheeding passengers," complained Justice Levi Woodbury to his wife in the 1840s. The cause of his discomfort? A ride in a stagecoach, the main mode of transport used by the Justices to journey from their hometowns to attend Supreme Court sessions. But they didn't just log miles to travel to and from Washington. They also were obliged to sit as trial and appellate judges on regional circuit courts in the fall and spring. Distinguished elderly Justices thus found themselves facing the same hardships as traveling post boys for a couple of months out of the year. They dutifully performed this extra task—with some modifica-tions—during the Court's first century, but the burden of riding circuit weighed heavily on the Justices and they tried desperately to relinquish it. Although they repeatedly begged Congress to abolish the system, their entreaties were either ignored or rebuffed until 1891.

Requiring Supreme Court Justices to preside over circuit courts (with a local district judge) did have its merits. The system saved the government money by limiting the number of judges on the federal payroll because it didn't have to hire circuit court judges. Litigants were less likely to ap-peal their cases to the Supreme Court if a Justice had presided at trial on a circuit court. (For much of this period, circuit courts were primarily trial courts rather than appellate courts as they are today.)

Equally important, circuit riding kept the Justices in touch with local communities and helped foster respect for the national government by

Traveling by stagecoach, boat, and horseback to preside over regional circuit courts, the Justices found this added duty onerous and begged Congress to abolish it. Their entreaties were mainly rebuffed until 1891, when Congress finally provided for a separate system of circuit court judges. (Courtesy of the Library of Congress)

establishing a sense of federal judicial power. In the Court's first several decades, the Justices delivered charges to grand juries that explained the Constitution, the role of the national government, and the responsibilities of citizens. These grand jury charges were often published in the local press and helped people understand what the relatively new federal government was trying to accomplish.

When the Justices first set out on circuit in 1790, President George Washington asked them to report back to him their impressions of the new system:

> As you are about to commence your first Circuit, and many things may occur in such an unexplored field, which it would be useful should be known; I think it proper to acquaint you, that it will be agreeable to me to receive such Information and Remarks on this Subject, as you shall from time to time Judge expedient to communicate.

The Justices soon, however, became intimately familiar with the defects of the circuit-riding scheme as they found themselves journeying thousands of miles at a time when roads were rudimentary and travel conditions hazardous. Attending circuit court sessions meant spending lonely months away from their families, lodging in primitive roadside inns. As Congress required them to stay in public accommodations, they could not even accept the hospitality of friends or local dignitaries. To add further insult, the Justices had to pay their own expenses.

The Justices relied heavily on each other for travel tips and directions. Initially, the country was divided into three circuits: Eastern, Middle, and Southern. When Samuel Chase was about to embark on the 1,800-mile Southern Circuit for the first time, in 1797, he appealed to Justice Iredell for information about roads and horses:

> I have been advised to come from Savannah to Charles Town [Charleston, South Carolina], by Water. What is your Opinion? I take a Carriage with Me to Savannah, and, as at present advised, I propose to bring it with Me, by Water, to Charles Town; if I come by land I must purchase Horses at Savannah. Which would [you] advise?—if by Water ought I not (if in my Power) to ship my Carriage from there to Charles Town, to wait Me there? Can good Horses be purchased as reasonably at Charles Town as in Savannah; & what will probably be the Price of a proper Pair? As I am to go from Charles Town to Raleigh I wish to know if there is a line of Stages between those Places, and also from Raleigh to Petersburgh, or any other Place in Virginia, where a line is established to Maryland. I wish, if possible, to avoid the taking a Carriage, and the Purchasing of Horses. The trouble and Expence will be great . . . I imagine the Road from Savannah to Charles Town is good, and no Way difficult to find __ [I]s there no line of Stages between those places? __ If You could procure Me Directions of the Road from Charles Town to Raleigh I should be compleatly furnished, as Brother Paterson [Justice Paterson] has been so obliging as to send Me the Road from Raleigh to Petersburgh. I believe there is a line of Stages from this City to Charles Town, but I beg You will enquire, & inform Me, for fear I should be disappointed in a Vessel from home. You can also learn how many Days it will take to go from this Place to Charles Town in the Stage. I give You a great Deal of trouble, but hope You will excuse Me. I fear the Journey, and am [anxious] for Information.

The physical hardships of travel, compounded by their advancing years, meant the Justices were often in poor health. They wrote to each other outlining their numerous ailments and pleaded for help in covering their circuits. Typical is this letter from Chase, who suffered from gout, asking Justice William Paterson to hold circuit court for him in 1799:

> I have been unwell, for the last Eight Week, five of which I have been confined to my Bed-Chamber, and three to my Bed. this Day fortnight I left my Bed-Chamber, but am so very weak and low, that I have no Hope of being able to travel so as to reach New York by the first day of next Month. my Lungs are so very weak that I could bear the Motion of any Carriage for a few Miles, and a Relapse would be fatal. under these Circumstances I am to solicit the favor of You to hold the Court for Me in New York. __ This will afford Me ten Days longer, and if possible I will be at New Haven on the 13th

of April. If I find it impracticable I must submit to the unmerited abuse which fall on Me I wish that Congress had given the Judges of the District Power to try all Cases originating in the Circuit Court.

The Justices generally did what they could to help one another. When Paterson graciously agreed to take over the New York circuit for Justice William Cushing in 1794, despite his own imperfect health, he explained: "I . . . am happy in having an opportunity of obliging you. We must endeavour to accommodate, and save each other as much travelling as possible."

Initially, there were some injustices built into the system, particularly in terms of circuit assignments. Justice James Iredell arrived at the Court's second session in August 1790 to discover that he had been permanently assigned the most arduous of the three circuits, the Southern, which was dreaded for its vast size and poor road conditions. The other Justices had distributed the circuit assignments at their first meeting the previous February, when Iredell had not yet been appointed to the Court. They may have thought the Southern Circuit would be convenient for Iredell because he lived in North Carolina. But shortly after his appointment Iredell moved with his family to the capital, so the assignment required him to make a special trip back to the South twice a year. The one other Justice assigned to the Southern Circuit, John Rutledge, was from South Carolina. Iredell complained that he and Rutledge, who had been unable to attend the initial meeting because of illness, had both drawn the short straw:

> three Judges out of five (without consulting the sixth, [Justice John] Rutledge, who was on the spot, & tho' confined with the gout perfectly capable of conversing about business) determined that there should be <u>no rotation of Circuits</u>—in consequence of which the C.J. [Chief Justice John Jay] & [Justice William] Cushing considered themselves Proprietors of the Eastern Circuit—[Justice James] Wilson kept possession of the middle Circuit, and [Justice John] Blair . . . became entitled on the same principle to the middle Circuit also—and, Mr. Rutledge & myself were doomed to the Southern Circuit only. The Circuits were fixed in this manner at first by the former <u>four Judges only</u> (when I knew nothing either of my appointment, which was about that time made out, nor even of my nomination . . .) for this reason, . . . that the Judges could best determine in the Circuits wherein they lived on the propriety of the admission of Lawyers—In consequence of this arbitrary decision (for I can call it nothing else) I have gone the Southern Circuit three times out of four, (the last time I admit in some measure voluntarily) & upon the last Circuit alone rode 1800 miles—at least 1000 miles more than the utmost . . . of the others.

Iredell was the prime mover behind several of the attempts, both successful and unsuccessful, to eliminate or alter the circuit-riding system. At the Court's third session, in February 1791, Iredell wrote to his fellow Justices pleading for a system of rotating circuits, so that the Justices would take turns riding the lengthy and difficult Southern one. Chief Justice John Jay replied that while he agreed the assignments were inequitable, "an adequate Remedy can in my opinion be afforded only by legislative Provisions." Fortunately for Iredell, he had a brother-in-law, Samuel Johnston, who was a Senator. At Iredell's behest, Johnston managed to secure passage of the Judiciary Act of 1792, which provided that "no judge, unless by his own consent, shall have assigned to him any circuit which he hath already attended, until the same hath been afterwards attended by every other of the said judges."

While Iredell was no longer permanently condemned to ride the Southern Circuit, the remedy he—and his brethren—would have preferred was a complete abolition of the circuit-riding system. At the Supreme Court session that followed their first round of circuit riding, in 1790, the Justices—in response to President Washington's request for their thoughts on the subject—wrote a letter pointing out constitutional objections to the scheme. Washington himself was already aware of the problems inherent in circuit riding: only a couple of months after the Judiciary Act was passed he had observed that "a change in the system is contemplated." And even Congress seemed to have some reform in mind: in August 1790 it asked the Attorney General to report on whether the judicial system needed modification. A few months later he recommended that the Justices be relieved of their circuit-riding duties.

The prospects for reform looked promising—so promising that the following year President Washington assured a hesitant potential nominee, Thomas Johnson, that he probably wouldn't need to ride the Southern Circuit or any other: "it is expected some alterations in the Judicial system will be brought forward at the next session of Congress," including "relief from these disagreeable tours." But contrary to expectations, Congress did nothing. A disappointed Johnson resigned a little more than a year after his appointment, explaining to Washington:

> I have measured Things however and find the Office and the Man do not fit—I cannot resolve to spend six Months in the Year of the few I may have left from my Family, on Roads at Taverns chiefly and often in Situations where the most moderate Desires are disappointed: My Time of Life Temper and other Circumstances forbid it.

So desperate were the Justices to get out of riding circuit that in 1792, at the instigation of Justice Iredell, they even discussed proposing to Congress that each Justice forfeit $500 of his salary to help pay for a new class of circuit judges. Given that the Associate Justices earned $3,500 a year and the Chief Justice $4,000, this was not an insignificant amount. But Chief Justice Jay had reservations about the plan, and there is no evidence it was presented to Congress. The Justices did ask President Washington to convey their sentiments about circuit riding to Congress, explaining:

> We really, Sir, find the burdens laid upon us so excessive that we cannot forbear representing them in strong and explicit terms.
>
> On extraordinary occasions we shall always be ready as good Citizens to make extraordinary exertions; but while our Country enjoys prosperity, and nothing occurs to require or justify such severities, we cannot reconcile ourselves to the idea of existing in exile from our families, and of being subjected to a kind of life, on which we cannot reflect, without experiencing sensations and emotions, more easy to conceive than proper for us to express.

In the accompanying letter to Congress, which the President forwarded as requested, the Justices refrained from labeling the circuit-riding system unconstitutional—as they had done in an earlier representation to the President—but detailed its inconveniences and improprieties. Their strongest argument was that it was difficult for a Supreme Court Justice to be impartial in an appeal if he had previously decided the same case on circuit. The Justices made their case to Congress:

> That the task of holding twenty seven circuit Courts a year, in the different States, from New Hampshire to Georgia, besides two Sessions of the Supreme Court at Philadelphia, in the two most severe seasons of the year, is a task which considering the extent of the United States, and the small number of Judges, is too burthensome.
>
> That to require of the Judges to pass the greater part of their days on the road, and at Inns, and at a distance from their families, is a requisition which in their opinion should not be made unless in cases of necessity.
>
> That some of the present Judges do not enjoy health and strength of body sufficient to enable them to undergo the toilsome Journies through different climates and seasons, which they are called upon to undertake; nor is it probable that any set of Judges however robust, would be able to support and punctually execute such severe duties for any length of time.
>
> That the distinction made between the Supreme Court and its Judges, and appointing the same men finally to correct in one capacity, the errors which they themselves may have committed in another, is a distinction unfriendly to impartial justice, and to that confidence in the Supreme Court, which it is so essential to the public Interest should be reposed in it. . . .
>
> They most earnestly request that it may meet with early attention, and that the System may be so modified as that they may be relieved from their present painful and improper situation.

While the Justices did not get all the relief they hoped for, Congress did ease their burden somewhat: after 1793, only one Justice was required to hold a circuit court, meaning that each Justice had to ride circuit only once a year instead of twice. The Justices continued to hope that the sys-

Congress required the Justices to stay in public accommodations (such as this tavern) while riding circuit so they could rub shoulders with locals. They also had to pay their own expenses. (Courtesy of the Library of Congress)

tem might be abolished or further reformed, but in 1794 they resorted to self-help: they agreed among themselves that each would give $100 to the Justice assigned to the Southern Circuit.

The circuit-riding system made it difficult to attract and keep good Justices. Several candidates declined to serve on the Supreme Court because they feared the indignities of traveling and could not countenance being away from their families for weeks on end. In 1789 Robert Harrison turned down a seat on the Supreme Court after being confirmed by the Senate. He told President Washington:

> In the most favourable view of the Subject it appeared, that the duties required from a Judge of the Supreme Court would be extremely difficult & burthensome, even to a Man of the most active comprehensive mind; and vigorous frame. I conceived this would be the case, if he should reside at the Seat of Government; and, in any other view of my residence I apprehended, that as a Judge solicitous to discharge my trust, I must hazard, in an eminent degree, the loss of my health, and sacrifice a very large portion of my private and domestic happiness.

In 1801 Congress did pass a Judiciary Act that came as a reprieve—or so it seemed. It called for hiring a separate tier of circuit judges who would relieve the Justices of the most burdensome aspect of their duties. But all sixteen of these new circuit court appointments went to the outgoing Federalist President, John Adams. When the new Republican-dominated

Congress convened, it repealed the 1801 act, thus stripping the Federalist circuit court appointees of their commissions in apparent violation of the Constitution, which grants federal judges lifetime tenure. Congress then passed a new act that not only restored the circuit-riding system but actually increased the burden on Justices: the country was to be divided into six circuits, with each one assigned to a particular Justice, who would now have to ride it twice a year. And to guard against the possibility that the Supreme Court would declare the repeal of the 1801 act unconstitutional, Congress prevented the Court from meeting for fourteen months.

The Justices' subsequent entreaties to Congress did not, however, fall entirely on deaf ears. Some reform bills submitted to Congress over the years did make marginal changes in the circuit-riding system. But most were blocked by Senators who thought the practice was beneficial to the government. They believed the Justices should continue to educate the local citizenry about federal law and keep abreast of how the law was being interpreted at the regional level. In 1826 Representative Tristram Burges voiced his support for the Justices getting out and communing with the people:

> They must, however, have the benefit of travel; and if so, in the common method, in coaches, wagons, solos, gigs, carryalls; in steam-boats, packet-boats, and ferry-boats; receiving the full benefit, in eating houses, taverns, boarding-houses and bar rooms, of the conversations of learned tapsters, stewards, and stage coach drivers.

In 1848 Senator George Badger echoed this support for circuit riding, warning that the Justices would be perceived as aloof if they became only appellate—not trial—judges:

> We shall have these gentleman as judges of the Supreme Court of appeals, not mingling with the ordinary transactions of business . . . not enlightened upon the laws of the several States . . . by the discussion of able and learned counsel in the courts below—not seen by the people of the United States— not known and recognized by them—not touching them as it were in the administration of their high office . . . but sitting here alone—becoming philosophical and speculative in their inquiries as to law . . . unseen, final arbiters of justice, issuing their decrees as it were from a secret chamber— moving invisibly amongst us, as far as the whole community is concerned. . .

Another argument frequently offered in defense of circuit riding was that if the Justices sat only in Washington they would be unduly influenced by whichever administration was in office. In a debate in 1819 on the Senate floor, one Senator warned that the Justices would become "completely cloistered within the City of Washington, and their decisions, instead of emanating from enlarged and liberalized minds, would assume a severe and local character." Another Senator fretted that the Justices "might also fall victim to dazzling splendors of the palace and the drawing room [and the] flattery and soothing attention of a designing Executive." Senator John M. Berrien, who supported the abolition of circuit riding, felt compelled to challenge the conceit that the Justices could be corrupted by proximity to power. During an 1826 Senate debate, he reasoned:

> Sir, I have not myself been sensible of any peculiarly corrupting influence in the air of Washington. I do not believe that the integrity of a judge would be sacrificed by a residence here, and it does not seem to me that the confidence which that department of Government justly enjoys, is to be ascribed to the semi-annual visits of its members to the People of their respective circuits. On the contrary, I believe that it is derived from their personal integrity, from the intelligence and fidelity with which they have discharged their duties, and from the general correctness which has marked their decisions.

As the nation expanded westward, new circuits were added. In 1837 Congress divided the country into nine circuits and added two new Justices to the bench to oversee them. In 1844 Congress also scaled back the Justices' circuit duties to one sitting per year. New Justices were usually assigned to circuits where they had lived and practiced law because they would be familiar with local conditions and questions of state law.

The assignment of circuits could be highly political. For example, when Peter Vivian Daniel, a Virginia Democrat, was appointed to the Court in 1842, he was supposed to take over the Virginia–North Carolina circuit from the Justice whose seat he had inherited. But when the rival Whig Party, which had tried to block his appointment, came to power a few weeks later, it exacted its revenge. The Whigs abolished Daniel's circuit and created a new Southwest Circuit, forcing him to cover the remote Arkansas-Mississippi region. This meant a 5,000-mile trip from his home in Richmond, Virginia, which took him three months to complete.

While staying in a flea-infested inn in Jackson, Mississippi, Justice Daniel wrote to complain bitterly to President Martin Van Buren of his assignment:

> I am here two thousand miles from home (calculating by the travel record) on the pilgrimage by an exposure to which, it was the calculation of sad malignity, that I had been driven from the bench. Justice to my friends, and a determination to defeat the machinations of mine and their enemies have induced me to undergo the experiment, and I have done so at no small hazard, through the air of fever at Vicksburg and convulsive and autumnal fevers in this place and vicinity.

In 1851 Daniel traveled from Washington to Pittsburgh, spending two miserable nights on a canal boat:

> The discomfort of being about in immediate contact with all sorts of people, some of the most vulgar and filthy in the world, women more disgusting if possible by their want of cleanliness than the men; with squalling children and being required to use in common, two tin basins encrusted with filth, and one long towel for the whole male establishment, is a misery beyond which my imagination can scarcely picture any earthly evil. My washing therefore was limited to wiping my eyes and mouth with my linen handkerchief, but I neither took off my clothes nor slept during this purgatory.

On the way back he faced cholera—a foe more frightening than squalor. After witnessing five deaths, Daniel abandoned ship and took advantage of a new mode of transportation: the train. He nonetheless reported that the trip might have been worth it if the cases he heard argued on circuit had not been "most miserably routine."

As new states were admitted to the Union, it became impossible for the nine Justices to cover all the territory. They were stretched so thin in some areas that they could only nominally attend trials. When a tenth circuit was added in 1863, comprising California and Oregon, Stephen J. Field, a prominent California judge, was selected to be the tenth member of an expanded Supreme Court. (The Court would regain its nine-member composition in 1869.) Initially, he journeyed from Washington to the West Coast by steamship via Panama. The opening of the transcontinental railroad in 1869 would make the trip much shorter.

After the Civil War, the Supreme Court saw such an upsurge in cases that it could not keep up. An expanding population and rapid industrialization meant more cases on the docket, including ones interpreting the new regulatory laws passed by Congress. Lengthening the Court's term was out of the question as it would interfere with circuit duties. Again, Congress proposed bills to relieve the Justices. One, which passed in the Senate but failed in the House in 1866, was designed to create an intermediate appellate court manned by circuit and district judges. It would also limit the kinds of cases that made their way to the Supreme Court. Chief Justice Salmon P. Chase expressed his great hope in the bill to Associate Justice Samuel F. Miller, whose proposed modifications Chase feared might sink it:

> I have been painfully conscious of the delay of justice in the Sup. Court. I commenced agitating [on] the subject before you came on the bench, in a long communication to the chairmen of the judiciary com. of both houses. I thought when I left Washington there was a strong prospect of fair fruit for . . . these exertions, in the passage of the Senate bill. I am of course aware that

no bill can embody all that every person may desire. But as none of the court expressed dissatisfaction with that bill, except [Justice Nathan] Clifford, as it passed the Senate with near unanimity I had some ground to hope it would be accepted by the house, and pass.

In 1869 Congress did at last enact a significant reform in the circuit-riding system. After rejecting a proposal to expand the number of Justices to nineteen—some of whom would stay in Washington and some of whom would ride circuit, in a system of rotation—Congress created and funded a separate circuit court judiciary consisting of nine judges. Justices were still required to attend circuit courts, but only once every two years. Southern Senators, however, were worried about the lack of viable candidates for their circuit courts given that prominent Southern judges and lawyers at that time were tainted by their service to the Confederacy. Attorney General Ebenezer Hoar, who was advising President Ulysses S. Grant in his judicial selections, tried to make light of the difficulty of finding qualified Southern judges who were also Republicans: "My situation was somewhat like that of the parish committee who went to a divinity school in search of a minister, and were told by the president that the students fell readily into three classes, those who had talents without piety, those who had piety without talents, and those who had neither." Former Justice John A. Campbell of Alabama thought the solution was to import judges from other circuits:

The District Judges at all points are in bad odour for common honesty. My statement was to the effect that I hardly supposed that a man in any relation to the rebellion would be appointed to the Sup Court & that I know of no man in the Circuit who was qualified belonging to the republican party & not many of the other, who had the possibility of attaining the office. That under those conditions I preferred an honorable upright able man from another section to one that was thus selected.

In the 1870s the Senate debated a number of reforms designed to make the Justices' jobs less onerous. It considered requiring either that Justices be appointed from states within the circuits to which they expected to be assigned, or that a new Justice move with his family to the region he covered on circuit. Nothing came of these proposals.

By 1880, the Justices were beginning to slack off on their circuit duties. An aging Justice Miller said he dreaded the end of May because after the Supreme Court adjourned he would have to head out on circuit instead of recuperating over a leisurely summer:

I find myself more affected by the hot weather last summer and this than ever before and my experience of the benefit of sea bathing the two last summers has fixed my purpose of spending as much of each summer by the sea shore as I can. If I live out my six years, necessary to enable me to resign with my salary, I shall do but very little on the circuit during that time. I am feeling sensibly the need of more rest, and have earned the right to have it. In [Circuit] Judge McCrary I have a fresh hard working safe and acceptable Judge and can leave the business of the circuit to him and to the District Judges.

The relentless pace no doubt contributed to Miller's notorious irascibility on the circuit court bench. One lawyer who was slated to argue before Miller on circuit announced he was "going up to be stamped all over by that damned old Hippopotamus."

Circuit assignments were a perennial headache for the Chief Justice. Even his own draw could be problematic. When Morrison R. Waite became Chief in 1874 he hoped for an assignment in the Western Circuit, which at that time included his native Ohio. But he followed protocol for the Chief Justice, who was traditionally assigned the Fourth Circuit (then, as now, consisting of Maryland, Virginia, West Virginia, North Carolina, and South Carolina) because of its proximity to the capital. After John Marshall Harlan joined the bench in 1877, Waite told his friend Thomas Drummond, an Illinois circuit court judge, that he briefly considered switching circuits with Harlan so he could sit with Drummond on circuit:

> When I came to the Court, I desired a Western Circuit, but as the Chief Justices from Marshall down had always been located here, I made no serious objection to the allotment which was made to me. On the appointment of Judge Harlan, I hoped the way was open for me to go with you, but after an earnest effort on my part to make, some satisfactory arrangements to that end, it at last became apparent that a considerable number of my brothers were opposed to it, and I yielded to their wishes. I do not mean to be understood as saying that I could not have made the change if I had insisted upon it, but under all the circumstances I thought it better not to insist.

When Melville W. Fuller succeeded Waite as Chief Justice in 1888, he also coveted the Western Circuit (now called the Seventh)—in his case so he could look after his real estate and professional interests in Chicago, income from which helped bolster his modest government salary. Before accepting the job of Chief Justice, Fuller had broached the idea of swapping with Justice Harlan. But, like Waite, Fuller did not pull rank. Perhaps he held off because he had decided it was up to him to be the one to finally abolish the whole system.

In 1890 Fuller gave a dinner at his home in honor of David J. Brewer, a newly appointed Justice, and invited members of the Senate Judiciary Committee. The Chief Justice sounded the alarm about the menacing backlog of cases before the Court. It now took nearly four years for a case to go from docket to oral argument. Fuller's dinner speech evidently persuaded Senator William M. Evarts, who took up the cause and successfully sponsored a bill creating circuit courts of appeal. These intermediate courts would take appeals from district courts, relieving the Supreme Court of that burden. Perhaps more importantly, the bill provided that the Supreme Court had more discretion in choosing cases based on their importance; it no longer automatically had to review all appeals in federal cases. While the bill carefully sidestepped the question of eliminating the Justices' circuit-riding duties so as not to jeopardize its passage by Congress, the subject was left ambiguous enough that the Justices could effectively wiggle out of the responsibility. Chief Justice Fuller dutifully continued to ride circuit, but his brethren quietly dropped out. It was not until 1911 that Congress formally passed legislation abolishing circuit riding.

In the twentieth century the Justices did, however, continue to be assigned circuits and to preside over them as administrators. Currently, each Justice has jurisdiction over one or more of the thirteen circuits. Applications for such remedies as bail orders, injunctions, and extensions of time are addressed to the "Circuit Justice" assigned to the circuit from which the case arises. A single Circuit Justice can grant temporary relief unilaterally. Administrative responsibility for the circuits is most visible in death penalty cases, where a Justice can grant a stay of execution for a death row inmate in his or her circuit. A clerk to Justice Harry A. Blackmun in the 1980s described what it was like to be on the death watch:

> The Court tried to prepare as far in advance as possible for these execution-night ordeals. Each Chambers received copies of both sides' lower court filings as soon as they were made—often a day or two before the scheduled execution. This practice, born of necessity, permitted the Justices and their clerks to get a running start on the issues in the case. Next, the Circuit Justice for the state in question would circulate a memo summarizing the parties' claims and counterclaims as soon as they became reasonably certain, usually less than twenty-four hours in advance.
>
> Sometimes the Circuit Justice's memo made clear on the basis of past experience whether the Court (or a lower court before it) would grant a stay. . . . Quite a few cases, though, were not . . . predictable. Many stay applications required fine judgments about what had happened in the case and what legal precedents suggested or required. A single vote among the Justices often made the difference between a stay and an execution. These occasions were spent in tense assessments and reassessments of an inmate's final claims, frantic arguments with clerks in other Chambers over the merits of the case, and rounds of reluctant and stilted phone calls to a Justice's home, often continuing past midnight, about where matters stood as the last grains of sand passed through someone's hourglass. Such evenings were sheer, bleary-eyed agony, no matter what the outcome.

Being on call for emergency stays or other actions can intrude on a Justice's summer vacation. In August 1970 the American Civil Liberties Union (ACLU) sought an injunction against the Portland, Oregon, police, but had trouble locating William O. Douglas, the Justice presiding over that circuit. He was out doing what he loved best: hiking alone for ten days in the Cascade Mountains of his native Washington State. The ACLU attorneys had to trek six miles—dressed in business suits—to reach his camp, where they presented their arguments to the Justice. He told them to return the next day at noon; he would leave the decision on a designated tree stump. One hardy attorney dutifully hiked back to the now abandoned camp (covering twenty-four miles in two days), only to find a small note indicating that Douglas had decided to deny the petition!

Justices continue to have their preferences as to which circuit they are assigned, but it is often not possible to match them to geographic regions where they served as judges or lawyers before being appointed to the Supreme Court. In 1962 Justice Arthur Goldberg's wife, Dorothy, complained about the modest budget for the annual conference of the First Circuit (New England), to which the Justice was assigned, as compared to the more lavish spending on the Seventh Circuit, which encompassed their native Chicago:

> Unlike Chicago, however, where the judicial conference was open to about a thousand lawyers . . . the First Circuit Conference in Boston was a very exclusive affair confined to the presidents of the local bar associations (but not the women's bar association), the deans of the local law schools, and the local federal judges.
>
> Art was told by the Chief Judge of the First Circuit, Bailey Aldrich, that that evening there would be a dinner in his honor—a stag dinner—at the staid Parker House. The dinner itself was convivial enough, though limited to the same group as the conference. The food was good, the liquor good; in general, a most agreeable evening. Arthur was expected to make an after-dinner speech, and he did—a short talk in which he tried to portray how the Supreme Court was "doing." The dinner came to an end at a very early hour—also unlike the Chicago dinner, where the Seventh Circuit, in festive black tie, was able to dance to the music of a good orchestra later.
>
> As Arthur was preparing to leave the Boston dinner, after thanking his hosts for a pleasant evening, the clerk of the court discreetly told him, "Mr. Justice, the cost of the dinner for each participant is $7.50—either pay me now or in the morning, since our dinners are Dutch treat." I laughed. Art's only comment, as he shook his head in wonder, was, "My circuit is a Yankee circuit, that's all, and New England is New England."

When Justices retire, they sometimes fill in as needed as judges on lower courts, especially ones in their assigned circuit. When Byron R.

White retired in 1993, he slyly asked his colleagues to make their opinions as clear as possible:

> Since I remain a federal judge and will likely sit on Courts of Appeals from time to time, it will be necessary for me to follow the Court's work. No longer will I be able to agree or dissent from a Court's opinion. Hence, like any other Court of Appeals judge, I hope the Court's mandates will be clear, crisp, and leave those of us below with as little room as possible for disagreement about their meaning.

Ironically, a month after his retirement White found himself at a judicial conference in his native Colorado trying to defend to a group of appellate judges an unusually splintered double-jeopardy decision that the Supreme Court had just handed down. The decision had generated six opinions and dissents spread over eighty-six pages of text—including one by Justice White, who had concurred in the judgment and dissented in part.

4

Wives, Children ... Husbands

Supporting Roles

In 1965 Hugo L. Black asked his wife, Elizabeth, to host a dinner party. The purpose: to help him persuade Carolyn Agger, wife of Washington attorney Abe Fortas, to allow her husband to accept President Lyndon B. Johnson's offer of a seat on the Supreme Court. A tax lawyer at the same firm as Fortas, Agger was displeased that the move would mean a big cut in his salary; she thought he should spend a few more years in his lucrative private practice before becoming a judge. After all, he was only fifty-five. Elizabeth Black described the tense occasion in a diary entry:

> We had invited Carol and Abe Fortas for dinner in answer to an SOS by [Justice] Bill Douglas, saying they were having a serious crisis about Abe's going on the Court. Carol told me they had several big things going that now had to be given up [improvements to their house in Georgetown], that they can't live on the small Court salary and may have to give up their new home. Later Hugo talked to Carol in that dear straightforward way of his. I was almost in tears at the things he was saying and it did have a great softening effect on Carol, I could tell. He told how he had deliberately chosen public service; how invaluable his first wife's role was in his work; how unproductive he was in the years when he was alone; and, bless him, how much he was able to do after he married me. How a man needs a wife, in short. Carol asked indignantly if he was suggesting that she give up her law practice which was her life, and Hugo said "Certainly not." And as to whether Abe would have to sit out of some cases because of Carol's involvement, they were only a minute percent of cases. I do believe Hugo's advice helped. They stayed until after midnight.

Fortas relented to the pressure and let Johnson nominate him a few months later. Agger continued her legal career as a sought-after tax law specialist and became the family's principal breadwinner. She cut a colorful figure in Washington, driving around in her 1953 Rolls Royce and smoking cigars. But she refused to speak to President Johnson, a close friend, for months after her husband's appointment. Her "life had been ruined," she said.

Being the wife or, since 1981, husband of a Justice has always entailed some sacrifice. In the early decades of the Court, the Justices boarded together during the Supreme Court Term while their wives and children remained in their hometowns. These separations were exacerbated by the requirements of riding circuit, and the Justices often struggled to balance work duties with taking care of their families.

Hannah Iredell suffered more than most Supreme Court wives during her husband's absences because she was painfully shy. As long as the Iredells remained in their cozy hometown of Edenton, North Carolina, where Hannah was surrounded by family and old friends, her shyness was not a problem. Unlike most Justices, however, James Iredell moved his family to the capital after his appointment to the Court in 1790, probably for two reasons. First, the climate was thought to be healthier in New York and Philadelphia than in Edenton, where malaria was endemic. In addition, Iredell most likely believed the rumors that Congress would soon abolish the system of circuit riding, in which case he would never have to leave Hannah alone if they lived in the capital.

Circuit riding, of course, was not abolished, and Hannah was on her own in the capital for long months at a time, expected to participate in the elaborate social rituals of the new federal government—attending receptions and paying and receiving social calls or "visits." This would have been near torture for someone who described herself as "almost as helpless as a Child amongst Strangers," and sometimes it all became too much for her. Hannah wrote to her circuit-riding husband:

> I have made no visits. I could not prevail on myself to run about the town alone after people whom I had never seen & whom I did not care if I [ever] saw again. It is impossible for you to make a fashionable woman of me & therefore the best thing you can do with me I think will be to set me down in Edenton again where I should have nothing to do but attend to my Children & make perhaps three or four visits in the year, what a dreadful situation that would be for a fine lady, but to me there could be nothing more delightful.

Eventually, after three years in the capital, the Iredells returned to North Carolina. But Iredell still spent many months on the road, during which he fretted about how Hannah and the children were faring in Edenton's unhealthy climate. Two years after their move back home,

Iredell was still trying to persuade his wife (unsuccessfully) to consider a return to Philadelphia:

> I am perfectly well, but extremely mortified to find that the Senate have broken up without a Chief Justice being appointed, as I have too much reason to fear that owing to that circumstance it will be unavoidable for me to have some Circuit duty to perform this fall . . . I will at all events go home from the Supreme Court if I can stay but a fortnight—but how distressing is this situation? It almost distracts me. Were you & our dear Children anywhere in this part of the Country I should not regard it in the least—But as it is, it affects me beyond all expression.
>
> The state of our business is now such that I am persuaded it will be very seldom that any Judge can stay at home a whole Circuit, so that I must either resign or we must have in view some residence near Philadelphia, I don't care how retired, or how cheap it is. The account of your long continued ill health has given me great pain, and I am very apprehensive you will suffer relapses during the Summer My anxiety about you and the Children embitters every enjoyment of life. Tho' I receive the greatest possible distinction and kindness everywhere, and experience marks of approbation of my public conduct highly flattering, yet I constantly tremble at the danger you and our dear Children may be in without my knowing it in a climate I have so much reason to dread.

Justice William Cushing (1790–1810) routinely brought his wife, Hannah Cushing, along on his travels and even had his one-horse shay outfitted with special receptacles for the books she read to him during their trips. Although often in frail health, Julia Ann Washington also insisted on accompanying her husband, Justice Bushrod Washington (1799–1829). While the Cushings and Washingtons were thus spared the anxiety caused by long separations, the travel was nonetheless arduous and undignified. Writing to a relative, Hannah Cushing described herself and her husband as "traveling machines [with] no abiding place in every sense of the word." And in a chatty letter to her friend Abigail Adams, Mrs. Cushing recounted their difficulty in merely trying to get across the Hudson River at a time when New York City was the site of a yellow fever outbreak:

> We have been roving to & from, since we had the pleasure of meeting you. . . . To avoid N. York we crossed White plains to Dobb's ferry . . . & after staying there two nights without being able to cross, the wind continuing very high we went up 20 miles further to Kings ferry . . . where the river is not so wide & the boats better & after waiting there also two nights we safely passed the ferry, rejoicing as though we had been released from prison.

Not coincidentally, Hannah Cushing and Julia Ann Washington were the only Justices' wives in the Court's early decades who were childless;

the others generally had to stay home to look after their families and household affairs. Some of these women may have enjoyed the relative independence they had as a result of their husbands' absences. Chief Justice Jay's wife Sarah—who had six children to tend to—teased her husband when he was riding circuit in 1790: "We make out very well. Aint you a little fearful of the consequences of leaving me so long sole mistress?" But even Mrs. Jay had her moments of anxiety and distress about how her husband was faring on the road. In one letter, at the close of a litany of illnesses afflicting the family at home, she wrote to her husband: "Oh! my dear Mr. Jay should you too be unwell & be absent from me, & I deprived of the satisfaction & consolation of attending you how wretched should I be! . . . Oh my dear Mr. Jay how I long to see you."

Chief Justice John Marshall and his wife, Polly, also maintained a strong union despite their frequent physical separation. The commuter aspect of their marriage was compounded by the fact that Polly Marshall suffered nervous disorders and could not leave their Richmond, Virginia, home. At Polly's death in 1831 after forty-nine years of marriage, John nonetheless reflected on the critical support she had given him: "Her judgment was so sound and so safe that I have often relied upon it in situations of some perplexity. I do not remember ever to have regretted the adoption of her opinion. I have sometimes regretted its rejection." Marshall's friend Joseph Story sadly conveyed to his own supportive wife, Sarah, the depth of Marshall's grief and loneliness:

> On going into the Chief Justice's room this morning, I found him in tears. . . . I saw at once that he had been shedding tears over the memory of his own wife, and he has said to me several times during the term, that the moment he relaxes from business he feels exceedingly depressed, and rarely goes through a night without weeping over his departed wife. She must have been a very extraordinary woman so to have attached him, and I think he is the most extraordinary man I ever saw, for the depth and tenderness of his feelings.

In 1830, Justice John McLean, who had been serving as Postmaster General in Washington before his Court appointment, opted out of the group boardinghouse arrangement and chose to live with his wife, Rebecca, instead. As the city of Washington developed more pleasantly and the Supreme Court's term lengthened, other Justices began bringing their families to the nation's capital. Wives were tossed into the social whirl and expected to perform. This meant receiving and returning daytime social calls, and attending and hosting formal dinners in the evening—all while navigating the elaborate rules of protocol that governed polite society.

The arrival of the Court each year marked the beginning of Washington's social season. Each Justice paid a formal social call to all the Justices more senior to him and to all members of the Cabinet. These calls were then reciprocated. There was very little of the formal separation between the Justices and members of the political branches (or the Justices and members of the Supreme Court bar) as there is today. According to nineteenth-century protocol, Supreme Court Justices ranked above Cabinet officials in the social pyramid: they were on par with U.S. Senators (although the order of precedence between a Senator and a Justice was the subject of much controversy), just one rung below the President.

Arriving from Keokuk, Iowa, Eliza Miller, the wife of Justice Samuel F. Miller (1862–1890), threw herself into the role of Washington socialite. She immersed herself in the rules of protocol governing the Justices and fully leveraged the prestige of her husband's title. According to one society reporter:

> Mrs. Miller, a matronly lady, bearing a feminine resemblance to her husband, is held in high esteem among the ladies of the Court circle as the authority on the social etiquette which attaches to their position in fashionable life. The Justice being the senior member of the Court, in this respect even out-dating the Chief Justice, is recognized as the patriarch of the body, and Mrs. Miller is the acknowledged referee and umpire on all social questions.

Another reported:

> Mrs. Justice Miller . . . assisted by her grand-daughter . . . gives elegant dinners, not only to the Supreme Court, but other distinguished people at the Capital. She is a charming hostess. Her residence is in the best of taste, and in all her surroundings, there are many marks of luxurious refinement. . . . Justice Miller has abstracted hours, but is full of life and fun when wakened up in society. The nation owes them all a world of gratitude for their purity of character on the Supreme Bench. . . . [The Justices] all stand high in Washington, making no dinner or reception quite complete, without one or more of the Supreme Bench and their families.

But Eliza Miller may have been *too* socially ambitious. When Miller sought to be elevated to Chief Justice, his brother-in-law fretted: "I am afraid his wife will hurt him. . . . She is ambitious, imprudent & unscrupulous." Miller was indeed passed over, and Eliza's star faded as the city of Washington began attracting the newly rich and she was no longer able to entertain in style on a judicial paycheck.

Malvina Harlan, wife of Kentuckian John Marshall Harlan (1877–1911), was unquestionably an asset to him. She did her duty by receiving visitors at home on Mondays, the designated day for Supreme Court wives to host. This meant providing an elaborate spread for tea and music for dancing—often for as many as three hundred callers. But she also stepped beyond the hostess role to play a highly symbolic hand in inspiring John to write the Supreme Court's most famous dissent. Unbeknownst to her husband, Malvina had neglected to make good on a promise to a friend to give away Harlan's heirloom inkstand—the one that Chief Justice Roger B. Taney had used in 1857 to write the Court's ignominious decision in *Dred Scott*. Almost forty years later, Justice Harlan wrestled with his dissent in *Plessy v. Ferguson*—an 1896 case in which the other Justices reaffirmed the notion that blacks and whites were not equal, thus providing the legal justification for segregation that would endure for six decades. Malvina sneakily brought out the tainted inkstand to help him formulate his lone dissent. She described the ploy in her memoirs:

His dissent (which many lawyers consider to have been one of his greatest opinions) cost him several months of absorbing labour—his interest and anxiety often disturbing his sleep. Many times he would get up in the middle of the night, in order to jot down some thought or paragraph which he feared might elude him in the morning. It was a trying time for him. In point of years, he was much the youngest man on the Bench; and standing alone, as he did in regard to a decision which the whole country was anxiously awaiting, he felt that, on a question of such far-reaching importance, he must speak, not only forcibly but wisely.

In the preparation of his dissenting opinion, he had reached a stage when his thoughts refused to flow easily. He seemed to be in a quagmire of logic, precedent and law. Sunday morning came, and as the plan which had occurred to me, in my wakeful hours of the night before, had to be put into action during his absence from the house, I told him that I would not go to church with him that day. Nothing ever kept him from church.

As soon as he had left the house, I found the long-hidden Taney inkstand, gave it a good cleaning and polishing, and filled it with ink. Then taking all the other ink-wells from his study table, I put that historic, and inspiring inkstand directly before his pad of paper; and, as I looked at it, Taney's inkstand seemed to say to me, "I will help him."

I was on the look-out for his return, and met him at the front door. In as cheery a voice as I could muster (for I was beginning to feel somewhat conscience-stricken as I recalled those "evasive answers" of several months before), I said to him: "I have put a bit of inspiration on your study table. I believe it is just what you need and I am sure it will help you."

He was full of curiosity, which I refused to gratify. As soon as possible he went to his study. His eye lighting upon the little inkstand, he came running down to my room to ask where in the world I had found it. With mingled shame and joy I then "'fessed up," telling him how I had secretly hidden the inkstand . . . because I knew how much he prized and loved it, and felt sure it ought really not to go out of his possession. He laughed over my naughty act and freely forgave it.

The inkstand did prove inspirational to Harlan's dissent. After dipping his pen in it he wrote the visionary words: "Our Constitution is color-blind, and neither knows nor tolerates classes among citizens." In doing so, he made a small scratch at undoing the stain of *Dred Scott* on the Court and on the nation. According to Malvina:

> The memory of the historic part that Taney's inkstand had played in the Dred Scott decision, in temporarily tightening the shackles of slavery upon the negro race in the ante-bellum days, seemed, that morning, to act like magic in clarifying my husband's thoughts in regard to the law that had been intended by [Senator Charles] Sumner to protect the recently emancipated slaves in the enjoyment of equal "civil rights." His pen fairly flew on that day and, with the running start he then got, he soon finished his dissent.
>
> It was, I think, a bit of "poetic justice" that the small inkstand in which Taney's pen had dipped when he wrote that famous (or rather infamous) sentence in which he said that "a black man had no rights which a white man was bound to respect," should have furnished the ink for a decision in which the black man's claim to equal civil rights was as powerfully, and even passionately asserted, as it was in my husband's dissenting opinion in the famous "Civil Rights" case.

As the twentieth century arrived, Supreme Court wives and their husbands enjoyed a high social status in the nation's capital, dining at the White House, with members of Congress, and with foreign ambassadors. In 1906 David J. Brewer expressed doubts that his friend and bench-mate Henry Billings Brown would retire as promised at age seventy because Supreme Court "wives cut an important figure, and of course they are always opposed to it [their husbands retiring]."

The growing sophistication of the city of Washington rendered the social duties of a Supreme Court wife increasingly elaborate. By 1926, Milton Handler, a law clerk to Justice Harlan Fiske Stone, viewed these rituals as excessive:

> It was customary in that era in Washington for visitors to leave cards when making a call. Mrs. [Agnes] Stone, for example, would go out some days in her chauffeured car with as many as 20 to 30 cards. She would drive to the embassies, to the homes of the Supreme Court Justices and Cabinet Secretaries, and to the White House. The chauffeur would hand the Stones' card to the Butler of the establishment. Similarly, visitors would drive up to the Stones and deposit their cards, just to show that they were maintaining social relations between dinner parties, which the Stones attended practically every night.

Another Stone clerk, Warner W. Gardner, confirmed that the pace had not abated a decade later:

> The Stones in 1934–1935 carried through an appalling social calendar. My impression at the time was that they dined in company every night of the

week, month in and month out. The cost was not too great, since both were completely temperate and never left later than ten-thirty. But, neither then nor now, was the regime understandable to me. Stone, however, was a good conversationalist and enjoyed it, and Mrs. Stone seemed, too, to find a real pleasure in the social life of Washington.

But not all Justices' wives played the game. Dean Acheson, Louis D. Brandeis's law clerk from 1919 to 1921, noted that the Brandeises did not attend many social functions. Alice Brandeis kept their social life more low key, welcoming visitors from her husband's coterie of progressives in a modest and intimate way.

The Brandeises' "at home" was purposeful and austere. The hostess, erect on a black horsehair sofa, presided at the tea table. Above her, an engraved tiger couchant, gazing off over pretty dreary country, evoked depressing memories of our dentist's waiting room. Two female acolytes, often my wife and another conscripted pupil of Mrs. Brandeis's weekly seminar on child education, assisted her. The current law clerk presented new-comers. This done, disciples gathered in a semicircle around the Justice. For the most part they were young and with spouses—lawyers in government and out, writers, conservationists from Agriculture and Interior, frustrated regulators of utilities or monopolies, and, often, pilgrims to this shrine.

And what of Justices who were unmarried? Thrice-widowed Chief Justice Salmon P. Chase (1864–1873) had relied on his charming and talented daughter, Kate, to serve as his social escort and hostess. She delighted in the role and was the toast of the town. When she married a wealthy Senator, William Sprague, the couple decided to live with her father in his Washington home, where they entertained lavishly. Although the Spragues spent more than six months of the year in William's home state of Rhode Island, the Senator paid for the expansion and upkeep of Chase's house, and for his servants. This was a relief to the Chief Justice, who had a hard time reciprocating the many elegant dinners he was invited to without straining his modest budget.

Unfortunately, Sprague, a heavy drinker, also had a nasty streak. He sat on the Senate Appropriations Committee and was in the position to vote for a badly needed salary augmentation for the Justices. In 1866 Chase found himself in the position of lobbying his own son-in-law: "No judge can now live and pay his travelling expenses on his salary. . . . Its amount practically is not as large as it was at the organization of the Government. That of the Chief Justice should be at least 12,000 and that of each Associate 10,000." The Committee did raise the salaries, but only to $8,000 (Associate Justices) and $8,500 (Chief Justice). The higher figures originally requested had failed to pass by a single Senate vote—Sprague's. Kate divorced him soon after.

Lifelong bachelor James C. McReynolds (1914–1941) resorted to pressing his clerks into taking on some of the social duties of a wife. According to John Knox, his clerk in the 1936 Term, the irascible Justice found it tiresome to explain how the calling-card system worked—training he had to give every time he broke in a new clerk. A flat card meant it was delivered by a chauffeur; if the corner was bent then the sender had delivered it in person. Justice McReynolds informed his clerk:

> When all these people leave their calling cards for me here at 2400 [my apartment], it is then up to me to decide which cards I wish to acknowledge. Most of them will be ignored, as I haven't the time or the inclination to meet many people. The cards which have been acknowledged can be kept in a small pile, but the others was thrown away. And my card will almost always be sent flat—meaning that it should be delivered by Harry [Parker, his butler/chauffeur] and not by me, or else sent through the mail. I very seldom make a special trip to leave my calling card in person with anyone.

Unfortunately for Knox, he served as a clerk during the high-profile Court-packing episode, when President Franklin D. Roosevelt proposed a plan to add new Justices to the Court because it had been striking down his New Deal legislation. Snaring a Justice for one of her dinner parties was at the top of every Washington hostess's list that year as the Court was so much in the spotlight. Knox was saddled with extra work even though the Justice chose to decline these invitations:

> I soon realized that McReynolds was indeed serious about the Washington practice of receiving and sending calling cards. This was no matter which could be treated lightly, at least with him. And once his card was received, the family he had acknowledged was then free to invite the Justice to teas, dinners, receptions, and the like. However, he often declined such invitations after the Court-packing controversy burst so unexpectedly upon the nation in February 1937.

The Depression and World War II put an end to these frenetic social traditions. Chief Justice Charles Evans Hughes's daughter, Elizabeth, reported that her mother had found home-based receptions burdensome in the 1930s and was relieved when the custom ended:

> Those were the days of receptions—not cocktail parties, but afternoon teas. Wives of Cabinet officers and of other officials were "at home" on various days of the week. For example, Mondays were reserved for the Supreme Court ladies, Wednesdays for the Cabinet wives, Fridays for the embassies and legations, etc. In addition, the official wives in all categories often paid calls on others and left calling cards. Such practices fortunately were abandoned during the Second World War. Not only were those elegant teas costly; they were time-consuming and tiring.

In the postwar era, ethical standards evolved to the point that judges were generally expected to distance themselves from members of the legislative and executive branches to maintain impartiality. Fraternization between judges and the attorneys who argued cases before them was also frowned upon. By the 1960s, the social obligations of a Supreme Court Justice's wife were consequently more subdued. Dorothy Goldberg, who had been a Cabinet wife prior to her husband Arthur's appointment to the Supreme Court in 1962, compared the two roles:

> Formal social life on the Court was quieter than on the Cabinet. Justices and their wives are not expected to reciprocate invitations extended to them by others, nor do they very often accept invitations other than from their private friends. We had, however, become friendly with some of the ambassadors, and we continued to receive invitations from them and from some members of the Cabinet. We rarely accepted Thursday evening invitations, however— conference was on Friday; and we declined others if they brought the total number of our evenings out to more than one or two a week. . . .
>
> The Supreme Court is the only place in the government where wives and family are accorded a special courtesy and regarded as a group. Of course, it is easier when only nine persons are involved. The Congress has a wives' gallery, to be sure, and the President's family has the first row in the family section on opening of Congress occasions, but the Executive, to my knowledge, makes no provision for the inclusion of family during work hours and probably would prefer that wives remain at home, to emerge for picture-taking purposes only. Early in the Nixon administration, there was an effort to show how wives were included in a briefing with their husbands, but that laudable effort seemed to collapse almost immediately.
>
> On the Court, whenever a case is being argued, there is always room for Court wives in the family pews. There is also a dining room where they may gather for luncheons, though officially it is a place for entertaining visiting foreign jurists or for intimate ceremonial events, such as the presentation of a portrait by members of a Judge's family.
>
> I had not known about the family pews and was surprised to learn from Nina Warren [wife of the Chief Justice] that a wife was expected to be there when her husband delivered an important opinion. Perhaps only Nina expected that. "Dorothy, we haven't been seeing you lately." When I looked as puzzled as I felt, she explained that the wives often appeared for Monday morning opinions, particularly if their husbands were making important contributions. I had thought that Arthur could surely deliver himself of an opinion without my presence. I had never been essential previously, though I had always been present at his steel hearings [Goldberg had been Secretary of Labor], and at conventions and various meetings, but that was because he invited me, not because I was expected.

Josephine Powell apparently slipped up on this etiquette as well. Her husband, Justice Lewis F. Powell, Jr., recalled that she received a gentle teasing from his colleague not long after he joined the Court in 1972:

There is [a] custom, that we [Mrs. Powell and I] violated the first time I handed down an opinion. The wife of a justice delivering an opinion is expected to be present in the courtroom and to be seated in a particular place. I got the word and I advised Jo and she showed up about 15 minutes late, which is not unusual in the Powell family. She immediately received a note from Justice Potter Stewart, sent there by one of the pages, saying "You just missed your husband's greatest opinion."

Although spouses hold a permanent ringside seat in the section of the Courtroom reserved for family members, few other than Elizabeth Black and Dorothy Goldberg have recorded eyewitness accounts. Instead, Supreme Court wives and husbands have prized discretion. In her memoir, Goldberg recalled being struck by the emphasis wives placed on this value—and by the courteous manner in which their husbands treated them:

there is a courtliness in [the Justices'] bearing toward their wives, an observance of old-fashioned manners, at least in their publicly visible relationships. One almost never sees a Justice walking several feet ahead of a wife who is breathlessly trying to walk alongside him as he rushes to talk to another Justice or lawyer. Only rarely does one see a Justice skillfully ignoring a wife or another Justice's wife after the first routine arrival kiss. I saw the Justices and their wives through rose-colored glasses, I suppose, glimpsing only affection, devotion, loving kindness, with everyone trying to avoid the slightest bit of gossip.

In addition to being discreet, Supreme Court spouses have been expected to preserve the dignity of the institution by behaving with decorum. Hugo L. Black, who served on the Supreme Court from 1937 to 1971, made a little speech to this effect when he proposed to his second wife, Elizabeth, in 1957. He made it clear that the Court would always be his first love and that to honor the institution her behavior must always be beyond reproach. She recorded in her diary his visit to her house to pop the question:

He took me by both my hands and sat me down on the sofa next to him. Hugo Black did not speak of marriage. He spoke of love and the Supreme Court.

"Who knows what love is?" Hugo asked me musingly. "It is a chemical blend of hormones, happiness, and harmony," he went on to say. "But I have a prior love affair for almost twenty years now with an institution. It is with the Supreme Court. I have a tremendous respect for the prestige of the Court. We have to act on so many controversial matters and we are bound to make some people mad at every decision we make. Therefore, in my personal life I have had to be like Caesar's wife: above reproach. I have to know that the woman I marry is a one-man woman. The woman I marry will be around extremely attractive intellectual men. I am seventy-one years old. You are

The Justices' wives posed for their traditional formal portrait in 1961. From left are (sitting) Mary R. Clark, Elizabeth S. Black, Nina P. Warren, Mercedes H. Douglas, and Winifred Whittaker; (standing) Ethel A. Harlan, Marjorie Brennan, and Mary Ann Stewart. The elaborate social obligations historically expected of Supreme Court wives had greatly diminished by the 1960s. (Collection of the Supreme Court of the United States)

twenty-two years younger than I. In another five or ten years you may not find me as attractive as you do now. If that were to happen and you wanted a divorce, I would give you one. But I think it would finish me and hurt the prestige of the Court."

Elizabeth Black proved to be a supportive wife and a useful sounding board when her husband was wrestling with difficult cases. Apparently, Justice Black was partial to nocturnal discussions:

Almost invariably, on an opinion he thinks to be very important, Hugo awakens in the middle of the night thinking about it. Soon he pulls the chain to turn on the light. "Darling," he says to me, "are you awake?" By that time I am, of course, fully awake. "I am bothered about a case." "Tell me about it," I say. "Well this is what it is all about . . ." Then he recounts in detail and with passion the horrible injustice being perpetrated on a person because of his brethren's failure to see it his way. "I will have to write it on very narrow grounds if I want to get a Court," he says, naming those he has with him and those against.

Sometimes this unwinds him, sometimes not. If he doesn't feel he can go to sleep, he says, "Now it's three o'clock in the morning and I have just got to be fresh for the Conference tomorrow. I need sleep. What do you think I ought to do?" Then I suggest, "Why don't you take a little bourbon to make you sleepy?" (Hugo is terribly inhibited about taking liquor and usually wants me to be the one to suggest it.) And so he pours a splash of bourbon on ice, fills the glass with water, and soon is sound asleep. The next morning he awakens as bright and clear-minded as can be, and he approaches the day with his usual eager zest for life and vast good humor.

Elizabeth Black also enjoyed helping to look after each year's new crop of clerks by occasionally hosting them in her home. A clerk to Byron R. White (1962–1993) recalls that the Justice's wife, Marion, similarly adopted a nurturing role: "White took a proprietary interest in her husband's law clerks—recording marriages and births, encouraging the unmarried to settle down, and offering advice on the proper balance between career and family." To enhance clerks' year-long stay in the nation's capital, many wives have organized sightseeing expeditions for them. Dottie Blackmun, for example, arranged for clerks to visit the FBI, the White House, and accompanied them to see the cherry blossoms every spring.

Wives have traditionally had to tread carefully when participating in public life—even volunteer activities could potentially pose a conflict of interest for the Justice. If such a conflict were to occur, the Justice would have to disqualify himself, leaving only eight Court members to decide the case and introducing the possibility of a stalemate. To drive home the point, Arthur Goldberg once admonished his wife: "Listen, Do[rothy], when I took the oath of office, whether you know it or not, you did too. Get it?" For Dorothy, the hardest part of being a Supreme Court wife was being told to restrict her involvement in political activism and having to turn down all but a few charity organizations that sought her help. Nina Warren, the Chief Justice's wife, told her that she supported the Salvation Army in part because it was a safe choice. One incident in particular made Dorothy realize her position:

The code was brought home to me personally in November 1962, on the occasion of the Thanksgiving Day football match between a predominantly black Washington high school and a predominantly white school. A fracas ensued that went beyond any usual team competitiveness and was the first of the bitter racial clashes erupting publicly; It was, at least, the first of which I was aware. I thought it important to call Charles Horsky, Presidential Assistant for the District of Columbia, to tell him that it was a sign that something had better be done quickly to alleviate rising tensions. He agreed. It occurred to me to invite the high school superintendent, the administrative staff, and Mr. Henley of the Urban Service, the newly funded school-volunteer program, to meet with Mr. Horsky and the others to discuss what the schools could do to avoid similar situations and what the private sector and government might do to help. I unthinkingly sent out invitations to a meeting in the wives' dining room of the Court, since I had always had full permission from Arthur to do so in the Department of Labor.

When I phoned Nina Warren [the Chief Justice's wife] to invite her, she said, "Have you talked with Mrs. McHugh?" (Mrs. Margaret K. McHugh was secretary to the Chief.) I said no, I hadn't thought to invite her. Nina said nothing further, but that evening, at a dinner at the embassy of Israel, the Chief came up to me and said earnestly, while wagging his index finger, "Dorothy, Mrs. McHugh tells me you're planning on inviting school officials to the Court. That is impermissible. Arthur would have to disqualify himself if a case arose involving the schools."

I was vexed with my obtuseness at having to learn the hard way all the fundamental facts of everyday life. A person of my age should not have been that naïve, I realized, and now again I was marching into new areas without first having thought to ask about directions.

Many contemporary Justices now arrive at the Court with spouses, like Carolyn Agger, who have careers of their own. Conflict-of-interest concerns, particularly for wives and husbands working in the legal profession or in politics, are increasingly an issue. A spouse's job may also engender conflicts of interest in more indirect ways as well. For example, in 1997 Martin Ginsburg, a prominent tax lawyer and professor at Georgetown University Law Center, ordered his broker to sell all the stocks in his individual retirement account so that his wife, Justice Ruth Bader Ginsburg (1993–), would not have to worry about disqualifying herself when a company in the account was represented in a case before the Supreme Court. (He had earlier sold the couple's jointly held stocks when his wife became an appellate court judge.)

Despite these limitations, Martin Ginsburg dismissed any notion of personal sacrifice because of his wife's career: "I have been supportive of my wife since the beginning of time, and she has been supportive of me. It's not sacrifice; it's family." Indeed, Martin, who died in 2010, took over responsibility early in the marriage for preparing meals both for family suppers and for the gourmet dinners they hosted. On one occasion he may even have tried to be *too* supportive. When Ruth joined the Court in 1991, Martin decided to devise a unique response system to relieve his wife from the burden of answering the daily flood of correspondence that came her way. Justice Ginsburg humorously described this attempt to protect her:

During my first months on the Court I received, week after week, as I still do, literally hundreds of letters—nowadays increasingly fedexes, faxes, and emails—requesting all manner of responses. Brought up under instructions that plates must be cleaned and communications answered, I was drowning in correspondence despite the best efforts of my resourceful secretaries to contain the flood.

Early in 1994, Justice Scalia and I traveled to India for a judicial exchange. In my absence, my spouse tested his conviction that my mail could be handled more efficiently. He visited chambers, checked the incoming correspondence, grouped the requests into a dozen or so categories, and devised an all-purpose response for my secretaries' signature. When I returned, he gave me the form, which to this day, he regards as a model of utility and grace. I will read a few parts of the letter my husband composed. You may judge for yourself its usefulness and grace.

You recently wrote Justice Ginsburg. She would respond personally if she could, but (as Frederick told Mabel in Gilbert & Sullivan's Pirates of Penzance) she is not able. Incoming mail reached flood levels months ago and shows no sign of receding.

To help the Justice stay above water, we have endeavored to explain why she cannot do what you have asked her to do. Please refer to the paragraph below with the caption that best fits your request.

Favorite Recipes. The Justice was expelled from the kitchen nearly three decades ago by her food-loving children. She no longer cooks and the one recipe from her youth, tuna fish casserole, is nobody's favorite.

Photograph. Justice Ginsburg is flattered, indeed amazed, by the number of requests for her photograph. She is now 61 years of age ah, those were the days!—and understandably keeps no supply.

Are We Related? The birth names of the Justice's parents are Bader and Amster. Many who bear those names have written, giving details of origin and immigration. While the information is engrossing, you and she probably are not related within any reasonable degree of consanguinity. Justice Ginsburg knows, or knew, all of the issue of all in her family fortunate enough to make their way to the U.S.A.

I will spare you my husband's thoughts on Fund-raising, School Projects, Congratulatory Letters, Document Requests, Sundry Invitations, and proceed to one last category:

May I Visit? If you are any of the Justice's four grandchildren and wish to visit, she will be overjoyed. If you are a writer or researcher and want to observe the work of Chambers, the answer is "no." Confidentiality really matters in this workplace.

My secretaries, you will not be surprised to learn, vetoed my husband's letter, and in the ensuing years they have managed to cope with the mail flood through measures more *sympathique.*

Being the child of a Supreme Court Justice can also be a complex proposition. It has its privileges, but also its responsibilities. In the early decades of the Court, children, like their mother, had to endure long separations from their father when he left for a Supreme Court session or to ride circuit. When Chief Justice Oliver Ellsworth embarked in 1797 on the 1,800 mile southern circuit encompassing North Carolina, South Carolina, and Georgia, he made a promise to his son back in Connecticut: "Daddy is going about a thousand miles further off, where the oranges grow—and he will begin to come home & come as fast as he can, and will bring some oranges."

Charles Evans Hughes's daughter, Elizabeth, said she greatly enjoyed the privileges of being the daughter of a Justice when he was appointed in 1910. She learned, however, to be circumspect about any remarks she overheard:

> I remember well the rides in mother's electric automobile to take father to the Court and often call for him there. During that period I began to realize that my family was different and I felt a compelling need to do the best I could so as not to "let father down." There was no mention of this at home; but my brother, sisters, and I just felt it and carried on as best we could. . . . I was allowed to join the family at dinner at an unusually early age, because my parents realized that otherwise I would be alone. Thus I was fortunate enough to be allowed to listen and absorb when guests came; and distinguished ones some of them were! Children were "seen and not heard" in those days, and to me that seemed an advantage. I wouldn't have ventured a remark in any event, but I listened carefully and tried to understand what I heard. Although father never discussed cases pending before the Court, of course, he occasionally expressed a confidential opinion on current events; but he always cautioned us with the remark: "This is not to be repeated to anyone." We never did and were benefited by that early training.

Children can also be an important pipeline of information to the Justices by keeping them abreast of what is going on outside the Court's marble pillars. Sometimes, though, even solicited advice from children can be burdensome. Justice Harry A. Blackmun's youngest daughter, Susan, remembers advising her father on the issue of abortion in 1972 before he wrote the Court's opinion in *Roe v. Wade*. It was a long way from the "seen and not heard" days of Elizabeth Hughes:

> All three of us girls happened to be in Washington soon after Justice [Warren] Burger had assigned the opinion to Dad. During a family dinner, Dad brought up the issue. "What are your views on abortion?" he asked the four women at his table. Mom's answer was slightly to the right of center. She promoted choice but with some restrictions. Sally's reply was carefully thought out and middle of the road, the route she has taken all her life. Lucky girl. Nancy, a Radcliffe and Harvard graduate, sounded off with an intellectually leftish opinion. I had not yet emerged from my hippie phase and

spouted out a far-to-the-left, shake-the-old-man-up response. Dad put down his fork mid-bite and pushed down his chair. "I think I'll go lie down," he said. "I'm getting a headache."

Having a parent on the Supreme Court can impact a child's career path. Elizabeth Hughes's older brother, Charles, found this out the hard way when he was serving as Solicitor General in the 1930s. His father had stepped down from the Court in 1916 to run, unsuccessfully, for President on the Republican ticket. Facing a vacancy upon the death of Chief Justice William H. Taft, President Herbert Hoover was advised that he should offer the seat to Hughes senior, now a New York lawyer, as a courtesy. The assumption was that he would not accept the offer, as going on the bench meant that his son would have to resign as Solicitor General to avoid a conflict of interest. The hope was that Hoover then could promote Associate Justice Harlan Fiske Stone to the center chair and appoint Learned Hand, a New York judge of enormous talent and national reputation, to fill Stone's seat. This did not work out as planned.

Joseph P. Cotton, Acting Secretary of State and an old and trusted friend of President Hoover's, told his friend, Harvard law school professor Felix Frankfurter, the inside story on this father/son incident. A year later, Frankfurter related Cotton's account to Frederick Bernays Weiner, his former student. Weiner relays it here:

News of the impending Taft retirement reached the president while Mr. Cotton was with him. The latter immediately said, in substance—and the conversations that follow are, necessarily, given in substance—"That provides you with a great opportunity, Mr. President. Now you can promote Justice Stone to be Chief justice." Justice Stone was not only a member of Hoover's medicine ball cabinet [his work-out group] that met daily on the White House lawn at 7:30 A.M., but Justice and Mrs. Stone had long been close friends of the Hoovers, an intimacy reflected in their Sunday evening suppers together over many years. "And then," continued Cotton, "you can appoint Judge Learned Hand to fill Stone's place, and thus put on the Supreme Court the most distinguished judge on the bench today."

The President had his doubts. "[Promoting Associate Justice Stone] would be fine, very fine. But I feel I must offer the chief Justiceship to Governor Hughes. As a former Justice there can be no question of his qualifications, and I feel so greatly obliged to him for that splendid speech he made for me on the Sunday before the election that it would be unforgivable ingratitude on my part not to offer him this position."

"But Mr. President," said Cotton, "Hughes can't take it. His son Charles, Jr., is your Solicitor General, and in that job he handles all government litigation before the Supreme Court. That comes to about 40 percent of all the cases there. Consequently, if the father is Chief Justice, the son can't be Solicitor General. That means that Governor Hughes won't accept."

"Well," said the President "if he won't, that solves our problem. Then I can promote Stone and appoint your friend Hand. But, since the public knows Hughes and not Hand, it would be fine to announce that I had offered the post to Hughes before appointing Stone and Hand. So I really must make the offer to Hughes."

Which he proceeded to do, over the telephone. . . .

And then—here I quote Cotton as related by Frankfurter, this time verbatim—"The son-of-a-bitch never even thought of his son!" For Hughes accepted then and there.

When this story came out, Hoover denied it. The President even wrote to Hughes directly to contradict it. Frankfurter later retracted the part about Hughes accepting the offer without hesitation over the telephone and Hoover criticizing Hughes for not having given his son a second thought. Apparently, two conservative Justices already had been sent up to New York to sound out whether Hughes would take the Chief's job, if offered. Hughes thus had been afforded plenty of time to think over the offer and consult with his son before accepting.

Although this eyewitness account is thirdhand and suspect, the facts nonetheless remain. Hughes did indeed take the Chief Justice job, and his son resigned the solicitor generalship—perhaps the most prestigious job for a lawyer in America. Hughes, Jr., stepped down the day after his father was sworn in and never held federal office again. (He did hold one minor, temporary, public office in his state before predeceasing his father.)

A similar father/son episode occurred in 1967, but in reverse. President Lyndon B. Johnson wanted to remove Truman appointee Tom C. Clark (1949–1967) from the Court so he could fill the vacancy with his own pick. He seized on the idea of appointing Ramsey Clark, the Justice's son, as Attorney General, to force a conflict of interest (the Court gets many of its cases from the Department of Justice). Ramsey tried to persuade the President that as Attorney General he would not be influenced by his father, and vice versa. Unlike the Solicitor General, who argues frequently, the Attorney General usually only presents one token case before the Court. Ramsey told President Johnson that his father would not resign because, at age sixty-seven, Clark Sr. was at the peak of his powers: "I felt that . . . my dad's career had been the great pride of our family and that it was unthinkable that he would resign. I told him that and that was the extent of the discussion. It was a little comment that was made several times but I thought it was unthinkable that he would resign." He also said it would be impolitic for Johnson to force him off the Court: "In the police community and some other conservative areas Dad ranks awfully high. For you to replace him with a liberal would hurt you." But, according to Clark, Jr., Johnson was stubborn:

[I]f my judgment is that you become attorney general, [Tom Clark] would have to leave the Court. For no other reason than the public appearance of an old man sitting on his boy's case. Every taxi driver in the country, he'd tell me that the old man couldn't judge fairly what his old boy is sending up [laughter].

Much to Ramsey's surprise, Justice Clark did resign in 1967, giving up his lifetime seat so his son could serve what turned out to be two years as Attorney General. Still energetic, Clark accepted invitations to sit on federal courts in all judicial circuits in the country to help with heavy caseloads. Ramsey Clark eulogized his father in 1977 with these words:

> Tom Clark was a giver. He gave what once seemed to me too much: career, power, prestige—the work of a lifetime—cut off prematurely as he retired from the Supreme Court. He never discussed it. He never even mentioned it. Instead, he turned to things like traffic courts and for three years he labored that the good people of this land brought before municipal courts would see principle possessed there, truth found and applied in their cases.

But a son or daughter need not be a top government attorney to face conflicts of interest. For example, Eugene Scalia, one of Justice Antonin Scalia's nine children, is currently a labor-law specialist and a partner at a Washington law firm whose appellate lawyers often present cases before the Court. Federal law requires that, like other federal judges, Justice Scalia would have to disqualify himself if the outcome of a case would "substantially" affect his son's earnings. The Supreme Court has issued a written policy that Justices will remove themselves from cases when a relative is a partner in a firm handling the case, unless the firm has provided the Court with "written assurances that income from Supreme Court litigation is, on a permanent basis, excluded from our relatives' partnership shares." Eugene Scalia's firm has supplied such assurances to the Court. Accordingly, he receives a smaller paycheck than his law partners because his father sits on the high bench.

When a Justice's decisions come under criticism, his or her children are often affected. After Hugo L. Black cast his vote to desegregate schools in 1954, he was so vilified in his native Alabama that his son had to give up his law practice in Birmingham and move to Florida because he, too, was ostracized. Perhaps the most poignant description of the complexities of having a parent on the Supreme Court comes from Chief Justice Earl Warren's son, Earl, Jr. He and his five siblings found themselves being held accountable for the groundbreaking and controversial direction their father's Court was taking in the 1950s and 1960s. Under Warren, the Court overturned precedents of earlier Courts and greatly expanded constitutional rights for individuals. According to Warren, Jr., living far away from Washington did not insulate him from the repercussions of what was happening on the Court at the time:

> Then came my father's appointment to the Supreme Court, which was a turning point in all our lives. We were basically adults at the time, so only our parents moved to the District of Columbia.

Now we were separated geographically. Now we were no longer politically naive, but acutely aware of what my father had been, what he had done, what he was, and what he believed in. But none of us envisioned the controversy which would follow his appointment, nor the impact on our individual lives which would result.

We were then, and subsequently, politically divided; some Republicans, some Democrats, some Independents, some decidedly liberal, others ultra-conservative, and some middle-of-the-roaders. In this respect, I am including an "expanded family" which includes spouses and their families, for our family has always been deemed to include all involved in it. It should be emphasized that my mother was always apolitical and that my father never tried to impress any particular political philosophy on any family member.

Whereas we had previously felt some focusing of the political spotlight upon us, this was Showdown time, a period of about 20 years when we would be forced to defend or refute what the Supreme Court was doing. And it was terribly difficult—for regardless of political persuasion or personal feelings, we, as individuals, had to take stands. There was a stigma to being in the family and it took many strange turns. Friends became enemies. Enemies became friends. And, in most cases, both became skeptics. We had to explain, disavow or support, for the Court was one of the major issues of our time. And this affected our personal lives immensely. Yet through all of this, my father and mother remained the same as always—stoic, serene, totally understanding, and one-hundred-percent parents. And because of this, they became the greatest sources of earthly strength that we had, as well as symbols of what we should strive to be.

5

⚖

Yes, Mr. President

Appointment and Confirmation

"The job I have for you is just that," President Franklin D. Roosevelt explained to William O. Douglas, then chairman of the Securities and Exchange Commission. "It is one of the toughest jobs in Washington. Furthermore, it is a thankless sort of job with long hours. And it is dreary, confining, and uninteresting. The fact is this new job of yours is something like being in jail." Mused Douglas: "I then suspected that he was talking about the vacancy on the Supreme Court." President Roosevelt did manage to persuade Douglas to accept the position, which he went on to hold for a record thirty-six years. But Roosevelt was prescient: Douglas indeed found the Supreme Court cloistered and confining, and would try to maneuver his way into the White House.

When a vacancy occurs on the High Bench, Courtwatchers shift their gaze to the executive branch, bringing the relationship between the President and the Supreme Court keenly into focus. How a President decides who to nominate is an idiosyncratic process—no two appointment stories are alike. Staffing the Court is subject to the personal style of the President and prevailing political conditions. Factors such as geographic, religious, racial, or gender representation can also play a part. The President has a limitless supply of candidates: the law does not even require that a Justice be trained as a lawyer (although all have been) or be born in the United States. Would-be nominees must possess, above all else, luck. Presidents need luck too. In his single term, Jimmy Carter never got the opportunity to appoint a Justice; William Howard Taft made six appointments during his four years as President.

A President with an open Court seat is besieged by personal and political supporters lobbying for their candidates. In the nineteenth century and well into the twentieth, Presidents relied on appointment advice from the Attorney General; members of Congress also made recommendations. When President Martin Van Buren faced a vacancy in 1823, his Attorney General, William Wirt, urged him to put aside partisan considerations from his New York supporters and choose the most talented candidate:

> I have said that the appointment of a judge of the Supreme Court is a national and not a local concern: and therefore, in making the appointment, I think that instead of consulting the feelings of local factions, (whose heat . . . is always in proportion to their want of light), and instead of consulting the little and narrow views of exasperated parties, a President of the United States should look to the good of the whole country, to their great and permanent interests, and not to the ephemeral whims and exacerbations of the day. . . .
>
> I know that there must be some sacrifice to popular prejudices, even to enable the President to mitigate the rage of party itself. But the field of appointments is wide, and there is room enough for this sacrifice, without invading the bench of the Supreme Court. That bench should be set apart, and consecrated to talent and virtue, without regard to the shades of political opinion by which its members may have been or may still be distinguished.

Presidents have sometimes chosen personal friends, or rewarded political supporters for past loyalty. It is tempting to assume that such favoritism diminished the selection quality and tarnished the process. Indeed, in 1874 Associate Justice Samuel F. Miller was dismayed to learn that President Ulysses Grant was considering one of his corrupt cronies for a Court vacancy. Grant's first two picks—both friends—had fizzled out: one pulled out knowing he lacked judicial experience and the other was withdrawn in the face of opposition from the bar. Justice Miller bitterly observed:

> Who will be the next nominated no one knows. The President has said that it is only a question of which one of his friends is next to be sacrificed. If any one would have the courage to tell him, that if he would content to look out of the small coterie of his personal following, to the true friends of himself and the country, a service would be rendered to him and to his party. For there is the great difficulty. He is alarmed and he is obstinate. He will not give it to any man except as a personal favor conferred on a friend and associate. It is beginning to dawn on him that among them he may not find a man acceptable to the public. Fitness for the office has at no time been an element of his choice.

Grant would strike out three more times before finding an acceptable candidate.

Yet Grant's cronyism is the exception, not the rule. Most Presidents have appointed friends or supporters who also possessed exceptional qualifications. Abraham Lincoln understandably fretted about the public's reaction if he appointed his campaign manager, David Davis, who had helped him win the 1860 election. Leonard Swett, a mutual friend, took it upon himself to come to Washington, D.C., from Illinois in 1862 to persuade the President not to worry about appearances and to reward his devoted aide. Davis was eminently qualified, having served for fourteen years on the Illinois bench in addition to his work for the Republican Party. Swett recalled his meeting with Lincoln:

> In the morning about seven o'clock, for I knew Mr. Lincoln's habits well, [I] was at the door of his room at the White House and spent most of the forenoon with him. I tried to impress upon him that he had been brought into prominence by the circuit court lawyers of the old Eighth Circuit, headed by Judge Davis. "If Judge Davis with his tact and his force had not lived, and all other things had been as they were, I believe you would not be sitting now where you are sitting." He replied: "I guess that is so." "Now," I said, "it is the common law of mankind that one raised into prominence is expected to recognize the force that lifts him, or, if from a pinch, the force that lets him out . . . Here is Judge Davis, whom you know to be in every respect to be qualified for this position, and you ought in justice to yourself and public expectation to give him this place." We had an earnest pleasant forenoon, and I thought I had the best of the argument and I think he thought so too.

Davis was confirmed easily. He would uphold Lincoln's constitutional interpretations when they came before the Supreme Court . . . at least until the President's death.

President Lyndon B. Johnson had no qualms about appointing his personal attorney, Abe Fortas, an old pal from New Deal days. In fact he thought so highly of Fortas that he strong-armed him into taking the job in 1965. A brilliant litigator, Fortas had been content with his private practice work as head of one of Washington's most prominent law firms, and did not want to give up his high salary for a seat on the Supreme Court. Undaunted, Johnson decided to ambush him. He called up Fortas and invited him over to the White House to help put the finishing touches on a press announcement about troop escalation in the Vietnam War—less than thirty minutes before a live press conference would be televised. Fortas put down the legal brief he was working on in his law office and dutifully drove over. It was not until they were in the elevator on their way to the East Room—where hoards of reporters awaited the President—that Johnson told Fortas he was going to announce his nomination to the Supreme Court. Fortas later recalled that the President informed him his only choice was whether to walk down the hall of the

White House with him and face the cameras or to watch the announcement on television. Johnson clinched the deal over Fortas's continued
protests with these words: "Well, you know, I'm sending all these boys
to Vietnam, and they're giving their life for their country and you can do
no less. If your president asks you to do something for your country, can
you run out on him?" Fortas later recalled: "To the best of my knowledge,
and belief, I never said yes."

Once on the bench, Fortas continued to be on call unofficially to give
Johnson legal advice and write speeches. Fortas even counseled the
President on the thorniest political issues of the day, including military
strategy and race riots. When Johnson tried to elevate Fortas to be Chief
Justice three years later, Senator Sam Ervin expressed the prevailing view
about the Justice's extrajudicial role:

> I just think it is the height of impropriety for a Supreme Court Justice, no
> matter how close he may have been to the President, to advise him or consult
> with him on matters, public matters, that properly belong within the realm
> of the executive branch of the Government, and which may wind up in the
> form of litigation before the Court.

At Fortas's request, Johnson, who had decided not to seek reelection in
the face of growing unpopularity, withdrew the nomination. No president has placed a crony on the Supreme Court bench since then.

For a long time, geography was a crucial factor in selecting Court nominees. The idea was for every region to feel represented on the high bench
to help bind the country together. Presidents continued to worry about
sectional balance long past the Civil War and Reconstruction: geographic
representation was still considered a factor as late as the 1970s. Yet Presidents have also made geographic choices for purely political reasons. For
example, in the wake of the highly disputed 1876 presidential election
that brought him to power, Republican President Rutherford B. Hayes
sought a "reconciliation" candidate for the Supreme Court: a moderate
Republican who was acceptable to the South. In 1877 he solicited the
advice of Wayne MacVeigh, who was heading a commission to smooth
over political difficulties in Louisiana, a former Confederate state that
was still occupied by federal troops. MacVeigh, a Pennsylvanian, cautioned the President against choosing a Southerner from the Deep South
and suggested he pick a candidate from one of the more northern of the
Southern states. MacVeigh proposed John Marshall Harlan, an influential
Kentucky lawyer who had helped secure Hayes's presidential nomination. MacVeigh laid out his arguments:

> You will remember that you did me the kindness at one time to talk with me
> about a vacancy on the Bench of the Supreme Court, and as to the weighty

considerations of public interest which you desired to consult in filling it. I therefore venture to say that I have also endeavored to consider the subject from the same high ground; and that I cannot resist the conclusion that you are wrong in the tendency that you first expressed to fill it from one of the extreme Southern States.

I certainly need not protest that I am wholly free from prejudices against that section of our common country, or that I would have the slightest desire to keep alive the bitterness of the Civil War; but in view of the political history of the country for the thirty years preceding the Rebellion, as well as of the sixteen years since, I cannot divest myself of the conviction that if a lawyer of unquestioned ability, a statesman of comprehensive views and a thoroughly sound Republican can be found living in the more Northern States of the South, it is safer to offer him the position.

I believe General Harlan of Kentucky meets all the requirements, and that you could not possibly do a wiser or better thing for the country as well as for your Administration, than to offer him the existing position. If another vacancy occurred during your term of office, I could reconcile myself far more easily to the appointment of a gentleman from the cotton-growing States.

Harlan was quickly appointed and served with distinction for thirty-four years on the Supreme Court.

Presidents have often received advice from Justices, both solicited and unsolicited, about whom they wanted to sit with on the bench. On the strength of a letter signed by every member of the Court, President Franklin Pierce had little choice but to nominate John A. Campbell in 1853. Journeying from his hometown of Mobile, Alabama, Campbell had appeared a dozen times before the high bench as an advocate and had greatly impressed the Justices with his performances.

Four decades later, two would-be Justices managed to persuade President Benjamin Harrison to name each other to the Supreme Court. Henry Billings Brown, a district judge from Michigan, and Howell E. Jackson, a circuit judge from Tennessee, had developed a close friendship in the 1880s when Jackson stayed in Brown's home while he was presiding over the circuit court in Detroit: "I found [Jackson] the most delightful of guests. He had a fund of droll anecdotes at his disposal, which he drew upon for our amusement and told in his peculiar Southern accent." Brown's houseguest would, in turn, amply reward him for his hospitality:

One day as we were returning from court . . . [Jackson] told me that he had been informed that Mr. Justice [Stanley] Matthews was fatally ill, and that in case of his death he proposed to go to Washington, see President [Benjamin] Harrison, a former colleague of his in the Senate, and persuade him to appoint me to fill the vacancy. As my aspirations had never mounted to the Supreme Bench, and I had never dreamed of it as a possibility, I was naturally surprised, especially in view of the fact that the offer came from one who was my superior in rank and that my appointment involved a promotion over his head. . . . He made his promise good, went to Washington on my behalf, and ultimately obtained my appointment, although my classmate, Mr. Justice [David] Brewer, was chosen to fill the first vacancy. My own appointment came a year later upon the death of Mr. Justice [Samuel] Miller.

Not long after Brown joined the Court in 1891, he was able to return Howell E. Jackson's favor: "[U]pon the occurrence of the next vacancy, by the death of Mr. Justice Lamar, I was instrumental in inducing President Harrison to appoint Mr. Justice Jackson in his place." Jackson was appointed in 1893 but only shared the bench with his friend for two years before succumbing to tuberculosis.

In 1932 Associate Justice Harlan Fiske Stone advised President Herbert Hoover to appoint Benjamin Cardozo, a brainy legal scholar and an outstanding judge on the New York Court of Appeals, who Stone felt would shore up the beleaguered liberal faction of the Court. So avid was Stone that he even offered to give up his own seat to Cardozo:

> When President Hoover had under consideration the appointment of a successor to Justice [Oliver Wendell] Holmes, I was apprehensive lest a selection should be made which would emphasize the Court's conservative tendencies. . . . In a conversation with President Hoover, intended to emphasize both the importance of the appointment and Judge Cardozo's fitness, I intimated to him that if he feared criticism because of the addition of a New York man to the Court, when there were two other New Yorkers already there [Stone himself and Charles Evans Hughes], I would be willing to retire from the Court. . . . I deserve no credit for the suggestion. I had some thought of retiring at that time because I felt that mine was a voice crying in the wilderness so far as the tendencies of the Court were concerned, and I had numerous opportunities to do other worth-while things.

Stone was hardly alone in gunning for the distinguished Cardozo. The powerful leader of the Senate Foreign Relations Committee, Senator William Borah of Idaho, also urged him on Hoover, who promptly assured the Senator that Cardozo was indeed on his short list. "Your list is all right, but you handed it to me upside down," retorted Borah, on seeing Cardozo's name at the very bottom. When Hoover complained that his appointment would mean two Jews and three New Yorkers on the Court, Borah countered that Cardozo belonged as much to Idaho as to New York and that religious concerns should not be a factor. In appointing the shy but brilliant Cardozo, Hoover reluctantly trumped geographic diversity and anti-Semitism with excellence. He was approved unanimously by the Senate.

In selecting a Chief Justice, the President has the added quandary of whether to simply elevate a sitting Associate Justice. But even the slightest hint that the President might be considering such an approach has on occasion sent the Associate Justices jockeying for position. Although several Presidents considered the idea, it was not until 1910 that President William Howard Taft first moved an Associate Justice to the center chair. But Taft did not believe Associates should be promoted simply as a reward for lengthy service. (President John Adams had declined to consider elevating Associate Justices William Cushing and William Paterson in 1801 for this same reason.) When the possibility of elevating Justice John Marshall Harlan, elderly and nearing retirement, was floated, he had groused: "I'll do no such damned thing. I won't make the position of chief justice a blue ribbon for the final years of any member of the court. I want someone who will coordinate the activities of the court and who has a reasonable expectation of serving ten or twenty years on the bench."

The choice of whom Taft would elevate was subject to intense debate. The President had just placed Charles Evans Hughes on the Court and had led him to believe with these words that he would become Chief Justice when that position opened:

The salary is $12,500 and will in all probability be increased to $17,500. The chief justiceship is soon likely to be vacant and I should never regard the practice of never promoting associate justices as one to be followed. Though, of course, this suggestion is only that by accepting the present position you do not bar yourself from the other, should it fall vacant in my term.

But Taft added this postscript to the end of the letter, removing any explicit promise:

Don't misunderstand me as to the chief justice-ship. I mean that if the office were now open, I should offer it to you and it is *probable* that if it were to become vacant during my term, I should promote you to it; *but, of course, conditions change* so that it would not be right for me to say by way of a promise what I would do in the future.

When Taft asked his Attorney General to poll members of the Court, they expressed a preference for Edward Douglass White, a quiet but popular Louisianan who had been an Associate Justice for seventeen years. It did not hurt that White was already sixty-six, and therefore not likely to remain Chief Justice for too long. Despite what Taft had said about not wanting to elevate an elderly Justice for fear he might soon retire, White's advanced age secretly appealed to him. The reason: Taft's lifelong ambition was not to be Chief Executive, but Chief Justice. He would admit to this envy on signing White's nomination: "There is nothing I would have loved more than being Chief Justice of the United States . . . I cannot help seeing the irony in the fact that I, who desired that office so much should now be signing the commission of another man." Since White, only Harlan Fiske Stone and William H. Rehnquist have been elevated directly from Associate Justice to Chief Justice.

President Taft's unusual ambition to become Chief Justice was fulfilled in 1921. More common has been the opposite paradigm: Justices who coveted the Presidency—either by campaigning openly or by secretly encouraging supporters. In the mid-nineteenth century, Associate Justice John McLean and Chief Justice Salmon P. Chase were afflicted with perhaps the most serious cases of presidential ambition; both campaigned feverishly from the bench. Chase's neighbor recounted how the Chief's political designs totally eclipsed his enthusiasm for the Court during his tenure (1864–1873):

> Chase was a charming man with great faculties, enthralled by an overpowering ambition to become President of the United States. . . . He took little or no pride in the high office which he held, and its labors and duties appeared to be irksome to him. When spoken to about his exalted position he disdainfully declared that it was nothing, literally nothing.

Having seen his predecessor's restless quest for a presidential nomination, Chief Justice Morrison R. Waite (1874–1888) rightly concluded that political ambitions on the part of Justices harm the Court. Waite told a friend privately in 1875 that he thought Chase's ambitions had damaged the chief justiceship and that he would never consider being a presidential candidate himself:

> The Presidency although high is only political. In my judgment, my predecessor [Chase] detracted from his fame by permitting himself to think he wanted the Presidency. Whether true or not it was said that he permitted his ambitions in that direction to influence his judicial opinions. . . . I am not one of those who believe he did so consciously, but one who occupies his position, should keep himself above suspicion. There can't be a doubt that in these days of political-judicial questions, it is dangerous to have a judge who thinks beyond the judicial in his personal ambitions. The Court is now looked upon as the sheet anchor. Will it be so if its Chief Justice is placed in the political whirlpool? The office has come down to me covered with honor. When I accepted it, my duty was not to make it a stepping stone to something else, but to preserve its original purity. . . . No man ought to accept this place unless he takes a vow to leave it as honorable as he found it.

When Charles Evans Hughes ran for President in 1916, he heeded Waite's counsel and stepped down from the Court before mounting his campaign.

Once the President and his circle of advisors have narrowed down the potential choices for an open Supreme Court seat, the vetting process begins. White House counselors and the Attorney General's staff at the Justice Department investigate the candidates' backgrounds, writings, and legal opinions. They then invite a select few to come in for interviews so the President can assess them personally, and find out if they are willing to accept the job. Since 1948 the American Bar Association has provided ratings for the shortlisted candidates, from "well qualified" to "not qualified." During the 1950s and 1960s, the ABA's advice was used to prescreen candidates prior to their nomination, but in recent times the ABA has evaluated candidates after they are nominated and given its recommendations directly to the Senate Judiciary Committee.

The vetting process was so unintrusive in the 1950s that candidates were not necessarily aware they were under consideration for the Supreme Court. When William J. Brennan, Jr., boarded an overnight sleeper from New Jersey to meet with President Dwight D. Eisenhower in 1956, he claimed he did not even know why he was being summoned. His wife, Marjorie, recalled:

> On Friday afternoon my husband called me from the office and said there was a telegram from the Attorney General. It said something about "Come down and have breakfast with me and then we'll see the President." It was such a surprise that we even had to borrow a suitcase from a neighbor, so we could get him off in time to make the [1:00 a.m.] train.

Brennan picked up the story after getting off the sleeper train at 5:30 in the morning:

> As I approached the gates to go out, there was standing the Attorney General [Herbert Brownell], and he greeted me and said "We're going to have breakfast at our house." So I shrugged and said fine, and we got into his chauffeured limousine. I still had no idea, mind you, why I was there. Well we hadn't gone but a few blocks when Brownell said, "You know why the President wants to see you, don't you?" and I said, "If it has to do with that follow-up conference I don't see. . ." He interrupted me and said "No, no, no. He wants to ask you if you'll take the seat vacated by Justice Sherman Minton." Well, I knew we got to his house, and I knew we had breakfast, but I was utterly in a daze. Anyone would be. I had absolutely no expectation about a thing like that. I'm sure the papers at the time had been full of possible successors to Justice Minton. For example, John Foster Dulles, who was Secretary of State at that time, or any number of people very prominent in the administration were mentioned. It never dawned on me at the time that my name would be suggested, none whatsoever. In any event, we got to the White House and I was taken to the Oval Office. I thought there'd be other people, but suddenly I found myself alone in the room with him, not a soul but me and the President. It was something!

Perhaps Brennan, a Democrat, was so surprised to have been summoned because he assumed that a Republican President would be looking for an appointee from his own party. But Eisenhower informed Brennan on the spot that he would name him to the Court. (There have been twelve other instances of Presidents crossing party lines in their Supreme Court appointments, mainly Republicans appointing Democrats.)

When Harry A. Blackmun came up for consideration in 1970, he was summoned to Washington from Minnesota and knew full well he would be given a thorough scrutiny. Blackmun was especially carefully vetted because two of President Richard Nixon's previous nominees, Clement Haynesworth and G. Harrold Carswell, had just failed to be confirmed by the Senate. Embarrassed, the Nixon administration was determined to make sure his third pick went through. An FBI agent escorted him to the Justice Department to meet with Attorney General John Mitchell. Blackmun later recalled how methodical was the ordeal:

> Two others entered. One was Johnnie M. Walters, head of the Tax Division. The second was William H. Rehnquist, Jr., then chief of the Office of Legal Counsel. They and I went to another room where the two questioned me at length. We reviewed my meager investments and they inquired whether I had ever sat in a case involving a corporation in which I held shares. They asked about our daughters. That gave me an opportunity to bring out my photographs. I was asked whether I was free to stay for lunch. I had the feeling that there was not much freedom about it: I was there and was to stay. After lunch, the questioning continued. They went over my outside income. Did I have with me copies of my income tax returns? No one had suggested this. The Attorney General observed that it would be desirable for Mr. Walters to go to Rochester [Minnesota] to review my returns in detail. I had a 5:00 p.m. reservation for Minneapolis. Mr. Walters called and obtained one on a different flight that left about fifteen minutes later.
>
> It seemed to me that the three were spending a vast amount of time on me. It became apparent, however, that all three were sensitive about the Haynsworth/Carswell nominations, were especially disappointed about the Haynsworth rejection, and were annoyed by the Carswell fracas. Several references were made to the fact that the President had ordered a thorough FBI investigation of me to be completed overnight and that it was difficult to perform that substantial task in such a short time. There was newspaper speculation that an announcement would be made within the week.
>
> About 1:45 p.m., General Mitchell, two agents, and I took the small elevator down to the garage. The limousine and driver were waiting. We were taken to the southwest entrance of the White House where the presence of the Attorney General was announced to the guards. They were satisfied with his identity but looked somewhat disparagingly at me. Nonetheless, they waved us in. We were taken to the Cabinet Room off the Rose Garden. After about fifteen minutes, the Attorney General and I were escorted through the secretaries' room into the Oval Office. The President was behind his desk. He stood, came over, and shook hands. He directed me to sit in a chair on the left side of his desk and asked General Mitchell to sit across from him.

The conversation, to my surprise, was fairly formal. The President obviously wanted to see this person whose name had been suggested to him. We were there about forty-five minutes. It was clear that Mr. Nixon was irked about the Carswell event. He asked me directly: "Judge Blackmun, what are you worth?" My hackles rose at this point, and I must have shown it. I told him that, apart from our home, my net worth probably was not even $70,000. The response was: "We have reached the point where we have to put paupers on the Supreme Court." I must have flushed and indicated annoyance, for he then said: "Do not misunderstand me. What I mean is that anyone with substantial wealth is under a disadvantage from the start." He stated that when he left the vice presidency he was worth $42,000, and observed that many in subordinate positions departed from Washington with substantial means. Coffee was served. On occasion, the presidential feet went to the top of the desk. What came through to me was that Mr. Nixon was forceful, hard-nosed, and tough. Finally, he said: "Well, Mr. Attorney General, do you have a recommendation, and, if so, what is it?" The response was: "Mr. President, we recommend that Judge Blackmun be nominated as an Associate Justice of the Supreme Court."

Occasionally, those advising the President on Supreme Court nominations have ended up being selected themselves. In 1962, Byron R. White was serving in the Justice Department under Deputy Attorney General Nicholas Katzenbach when an opening occurred on the Supreme Court. Katzenbach asked him to help formulate a short list for President John Kennedy. A former pro-football player who had served with Kennedy in the navy and who had campaigned hard for his friend in his native Colorado, White soon emerged as one of Attorney General Robert Kennedy's top choices. But White was humble about his abilities when Katzenbach called to ask if he was interested in the job:

I phoned Byron, and he was somewhat ambivalent about any desire to be a candidate. "The President can do much better than that," he said. "The geography is good," I replied, meaning that a justice from Colorado would be preferable to adding a second from Massachusetts or California. He repeated, "I think the President can do much better than that, and I would rather not be put on the list." I said, "You are on the list. Do you really want me to scratch you off?" "Well, I wouldn't be happy if you scratched me off entirely. But go ahead."

Robert Kennedy, who counted on White to run the Justice Department during his absences, persuaded him to accept the nomination even if it meant that he would be losing his right-hand man:

[H]e was not very enthusiastic about it, really. . . . I don't think he liked to retire from active life so quickly. But I talked to him on the basis of the fact that who knew what was going to happen in the future? If you knew definitely that he could be around for five years and then be appointed in 1967, then that was fine. But you never knew that. The time to do it was at the time you could. It was really on that basis that he accepted the appointment.

Keeping the names of short-listed candidates a secret has become almost impossible given the extensive investigations now used to evaluate them. But when Ronald Reagan named the first woman to the Supreme Court in 1981, the headlines came as a huge surprise to most of the nation. William French Smith, the Attorney General, revealed in his memoirs how secrecy had been maintained:

[T]he confirmation of Justice O'Connor capped a four-month, undercover "talent search" for the person to replace retiring Supreme Court justice Potter Stewart. Rarely had an important secret been kept in Washington for so long. It all began on March 4, 1981, with a phone call from the vice president. George Bush was calling to advise me that his close friend, Supreme Court justice Potter Stewart, had asked him to arrange a meeting with me. I called the justice immediately, and scheduled a meeting at his home for March 26.

. . . I met with Justice Stewart at his home in the Palisades section of northwest Washington. We had a most pleasant meeting, in his solarium, during which he informed me that he planned to step down from the Court at the end of its present term. However, he did not want his decision known until he could announce his retirement, which he would do when the current Court term ended in June. We talked for a while about possible successors, and then, after promising to keep his decision a secret, I left. As I rode back to the Justice Department I thought of [a] list tucked away somewhere on my desk, for it contained the names of the top women candidates for nomination to the United States Supreme Court.

Repeatedly during the campaign, Ronald Reagan had said he would give serious consideration to naming a woman to the Supreme Court. As the car neared the Justice Department, I realized I was now about to begin, in secret, the process by which that historic event might take place. For I knew that when he made that promise, Ronald Reagan was dead serious—and the reason I knew was that not long after the election, he reminded me of it!

The very next day I directed Ken Starr, who was counselor to the attorney general, to begin to research possible candidates for the Supreme Court, just so that we would be "prepared" in case a vacancy developed. I did not, however, tell Ken anything about my visit with Justice Stewart.

As Ken was about to leave my office, I handed him the back-of-the-phone-message-slip list that contained the names of the five women candidates.

He gave it a quick glance and said, "Who's 'O'Connor'? All you've got here is a last name."

"That's Sandra Day O'Connor," I said. "She's an appeals court judge in Arizona."

Ken Starr promptly began the research necessary for compiling a list of possible candidates. The writings and judicial opinions of all of the candidates were gathered together and then analyzed by Ken and a team we put together, consisting of: F. Henry ("Hank") Habicht, special assistant to the attorney general . . . ; Emma C. Jordan, who was then serving as a White House Fellow and a special assistant to the attorney general; Solicitor General Rex E. Lee; Jonathan C. Rose, assistant attorney general, Office of Legal Policy; and Bruce E. Fein, associate deputy attorney general. A list of twenty-one men and women was compiled, with appropriate background information. The list was then given to me for review. . . . Up to this point, the process had moved along nicely, and with no media attention. All that changed on June 18 when Justice Stewart formally announced his retirement, and the process was intensified. Additional names were added to the list, and more information was gathered regarding the writings and records of individuals already identified.

On June 23, I met with the president to discuss with him the various candidates. We agreed that one of the candidates whose background clearly merited additional and in-depth review was Judge O'Connor. As a result, I sent Hank Habicht the next day to Arizona, where he spent two days obtaining (on a confidential basis) even more background and information concerning Judge O'Connor.

Although Judge O'Connor was a leading candidate at this point, other candidates were also being considered, and we were doing similar checks of the backgrounds of some of them. Although my staff was now aware of the coming vacancy, throughout the search process I had emphasized the need for confidentiality. The staff's goal in reviewing local Arizona sources was to obtain, discreetly, as much information as possible and to gain an assessment of Judge O'Connor's reputation and interests in the community.

. . . All my sources confirmed that Judge O'Connor had earned bipartisan respect and affection in Arizona, both as a professional and as a family woman. Our search turned up nothing controversial, and certainly nothing that could have disqualified her.

The next step in the process was for me to call the judge personally, which I did on Thursday, June 25. As I picked up the telephone, I hesitated slightly—not from any second thoughts, but from the realization that what I was about to do could well change history, and Judge O'Connor's life.

On the phone, I told her that I would like to consider her for a "federal position," and I asked if she would agree to be interviewed, in Phoenix, by two of my top aides. She agreed, and two days later Ken Starr and Jonathan Rose were sitting in the O'Connors' living room.

I liked what I heard about that daylong meeting, and so I called the judge again. This time I invited her to Washington for further talks. Again she agreed, even though neither one of us mentioned the identity of the court we both knew we were talking about, which is the way that dance goes.

All who met her [when she returned to Washington to meet with White House staff Ed Meese, Jim Baker, and Michael Deaver] were highly impressed, so I went ahead with the next step. I called President Reagan and told him I would like him to meet Judge O'Connor the next day.

Now I really had my work cut out for me if I wanted to keep the impending appointment secret. Meeting the president meant going to the White House—one couldn't expect the chief executive to slip over, unnoticed, to a Washington hotel, even a chief executive as accommodating as Ronald Reagan. What's more, by this point there'd been considerable speculation in the media, especially by the press, that Judge O'Connor was a "finalist," and it seemed to me that if I escorted her to the White House, any number of reporters would run with the story. So we arranged that my confidential assistant, Myra Tankersley, would be the judge's escort. . . . Shortly after 9:30, I got word that the president would meet with Judge O'Connor at 10:15. Scrambling, I told Myra to call the judge immediately. She did, and then prepared to leave. Watching Myra, I marveled at her calm.

"Where are you going to meet?" I asked her.

"In front of the People's Drug Store on DuPont Circle," replied Myra, as if she were talking about a lunch date with a friend. "Wait a minute," I said, suddenly remembering that Myra had never met the Arizona judge. "Do you know what she looks like?" "No," said Myra with a smile, "but she told me she's wearing a lavender suit."

Despite my fears, everything went smoothly, and Judge O'Connor got to the White House on time for what had to be one of the biggest moments of her life. The meeting itself went swimmingly. In addition to the president and Judge O'Connor, Baker, Deaver, Meese, and I were also present. Immediately following the meeting, President Reagan made his decision to nominate Sandra Day O'Connor to be the first woman in history to sit on the United States Supreme Court. Justice Stewart's intentions had not leaked for some four months. Following the meeting with the president, all agreed that Judge O'Connor's nomination would be kept secret until the president could officially notify her, and until other processes could be completed. However, what would later become common knowledge concerning White House leaks was well demonstrated here. True to form, on the very next day, Thursday, July 2, 1981, the *Washington Post* broke the story that Judge O'Connor was the leading candidate for the vacancy created by Justice Stewart's retirement! Deliberations continued over the next few days. On Monday, July 6, the president telephoned Judge O'Connor in Phoenix and informed her that he would like to nominate her to fill the vacancy on the United States Supreme Court. She accepted.

When candidates are brought in for interviews they try not to get their hopes up, knowing others are also being considered. John G. Roberts, Jr. was teaching a class in London in 2005 when he got a call asking him to fly back to Washington and meet with the President. George W. Bush interviewed him for more than an hour and then Roberts returned to London. No sooner had he arrived when he got another call asking him to meet again with the President in a few days time. Nearing the end of term in London, Roberts finished up his teaching duties, packed up his belongings, and got up at 3:30 in the morning to go to the airport. That's when, he said, the trouble started:

I'm passing this long line of people and I remember feeling very sorry for them, because they obviously had some difficulty that they were waiting in line and this line [was] snaking around. And then as I turned right . . . I noticed the line was turning right too, and, sure enough, it was my flight that was the problem. All the computers were down, and I got turned around and went to the end of the line.

Roberts was nervous that if he missed his flight he would be passed over for the nomination: "I was sure that things were moving and the White House was a very efficient operation and I'm sure if I wasn't there, they'd just go down the list and take whoever was next. . . . There were no promises." Roberts eventually checked in and the flight made it to Washington.

[W]e landed and I was going through customs in Dulles [airport] and on the Blackberry I got an urgent message to call the White House right away. And if you've been to Dulles customs you know every 10 feet they have a big sign saying, "If you use a cell phone, it will be confiscated immediately."

When he finally got through to the White House they told him to expect a phone call at his home at 12:30:

It was 11:40 exactly and it takes exactly that long to get from Dulles to my house. So I had just enough time. I remember diving into the first cab, yelling out where I needed to go and the cab driver turning around and saying, "This is my first day on the job. Where is this place, Chevy Chase?" . . . I was yelling directions at him the whole time and I got home at 12:30, threw a bunch of money at him that I think were English pounds. And as I walked in the door, the phone was ringing and it was the call from the White House.

Bush offered Roberts the Court appointment, which he promptly accepted. At 9:00 p.m. he brought his wife and two young children to the White House so the President could make the announcement. A jet-lagged Roberts had been awake for nearly twenty-four hours by this point.

While O'Connor and Roberts did not put themselves forward for a Supreme Court seat, other would-be Justices have lobbied intensely for the job. Some have done so directly, but most have used intermediaries to maneuver for them. Pierce Butler, a Minnesota corporate lawyer appointed to the Court in 1923, was backed by a prodigious lobbying effort by Chief Justice Taft. Butler himself had been tempted to ask powerful friends to lobby President Warren Harding on his behalf, but decided not to, in the interest of modesty. Yet he told his son he felt conflicted about *not* asking them for support:

[The President] does not know who such friends of mine [could provide helpful information]. . . . The problem of much difficulty is due to the fact that my friends who would want to help know nothing of the situation. I cannot and am not at all inclined to tell them. I will not ask anyone to do anything to promote the matter and I think you should avoid doing so. Yet I feel that there are some who would think that they ought to be told what is going on at least. So there you are. A dilemma in a sense.

Some Justices have pretended to be surprised to get the nod, despite having pushed back-channel negotiations like mad. Such was the case with Felix Frankfurter, whose nomination for a Court seat did not come as easily as he would have liked. A highly esteemed Harvard law professor, he was such an obvious choice for the Court that his old friend and mentor Franklin D. Roosevelt felt obligated to tell him directly that he was not being considered. The Court was full of Easterners, Roosevelt explained, and the President had promised that the next nominee would be from the geographically underrepresented area west of the Mississippi. While Frankfurter replied, "I perfectly understand," he proceeded to promote his candidacy among the New Deal brain trusters surrounding the President. (In later years Frankfurter would claim, quite falsely, that before receiving Roosevelt's call, "being named to the Supreme Court of the United States never crossed my mind"—a bit of disingenuousness found in several other Justices' memoirs.)

Evidently, the efforts of Frankfurter's supporters worked:

On Tuesday, January 4 [1939] . . . while I was in my BVD's, the door bell rang at 192 Brattle Street, and my wife [Marion] was going down [to greet a very punctual dinner guest]. . . . She said "Please hurry! You're always late."

Just then while I had this conjugal injunction the telephone rang . . . and there was the ebullient, the exuberant, resilient, warmth-enveloping voice of [Franklin D. Roosevelt] the President of the United States, "Hello. How are you?" . . . "You know, I told you I don't want to appoint you to the Supreme Court of the United States."

I said, "Yes." I no more expected the denouement of this conversation. You know, he was given to teasing. Some people said that it was an innocently sadistic streak in him. He just had to have an outlet for fun. "I told you I can't appoint you to the Supreme Court."

"Yes, you told me that."

"I mean this. I mean this. I don't want to appoint you to the Supreme Court." . . .

I said, "Yes, you told me that. You've made that perfectly clear. I understand that."

I was getting bored, really, when he whipped around on the telephone and said, "But unless you give me an insurmountable objection I'm going to send your name in for the Court tomorrow at twelve o'clock."—just like that, and I remember saying, and it is natural to remember this very vividly—"All I can say is that I wish my mother were alive."

The President promised to call him back the next day and tell him what kind of reception his nomination received. "I went back and continued dressing," Frankfurter continued, "I went downstairs saying to myself, 'Well, here is an event, something that has just happened which will change the course of the lives of Marion and me, and I can't tell her about it.'" Frankfurter waited impatiently for their guest, who unexpectedly lingered until midnight, to depart. "When the door shut I said, 'Marion let me tell you what your fate and mine is.'"

Once the President has made his selection, the nominee still has to be approved by the Senate, which, according to the Constitution, is expected to give its "advice and consent." When Ulysses S. Grant appointed his outspoken and independent Attorney General, Ebenezer Rockwood Hoar, in 1869, Hoar was on tenterhooks for seven weeks while the Senate debated his qualifications:

> I am not having a very agreeable time just at present; the Senate does not act on my nomination, and there is said to be some prospect that they will not confirm it. This I do not think probable, but, as they adjourn for a fortnight on Wednesday next, they may leave it undecided, which leaves me in a condition rather *afloat* . . . So that things are not altogether lovely. On the other hand, I am pretty well (intend to leave off smoking!), and have many active and excellent friends. So life is not exactly a burden, but if things work so that I cannot spend the next month at home, I shall be disgusted.

Eminently qualified and popular with the people, Hoar nonetheless had managed to alienate many Senators with his brusque manner and insistence on a merit-based civil service system. Like roughly one-fifth of all nominees to the Supreme Court, Hoar was never confirmed by the Senate and did not serve on the high bench.

It wasn't until 1925, when Harlan Fiske Stone was called to answer questions about his actions as Attorney General, that the first Supreme Court nominee agreed to testify before the Senate as part of his confirmation hearings. The next candidate to do so was Felix Frankfurter. He appeared in 1939 to answer slanderous accusations by Senator Pat McCarren of Nevada as to whether Frankfurter, born in Vienna, was truly a U.S. citizen, and whether he had links to Communist groups. According to his memoirs, Frankfurter was reluctant to attend the hearings:

> Then there was a committee hearing on my nomination, the Judiciary Committee. I asked [advisor] Dean Acheson if he would attend and hold a watching brief, sit there and see what happened. I was charged with having despoiled the Cherokee Indians of ten thousand acres of land. [Anti-Communist crusader] Elizabeth Dilling and other crackpots came and testified. One day [White House Press Secretary] Steve Early called me, and he said, "Why don't you come down? You'd better come down to Washington." They'd had these Senate hearings. I said, "Why should I? Did the Committee ask me to come?"
> "No. You ought to come."
> "Why should I?"

"Well," he said, "people are saying, 'Evidently he thinks it more important to be up there teaching at the Harvard Law School than to be in Washington while there's a hearing going on before a Senate Committee.'"

"I think it is more important."

"You're an impossible fellow to do anything with."

"I guess that's right. I just want you to know—I don't want you to be under any misapprehension—that if the committee of the Senate invites me to attend the hearing, of course I shall attend, but if they don't ask me, I shall stay right here and attend to my job."

He thought that was something! They finally did invite me. I did attend, but that's a matter of history, I had the time of my life with Senator Pat McCarran. Dean Acheson tells a story that I was really having a wonderful time, was misbehaving, playing tricks with the committee. I finally told Senator McCarran, in effect, "If I understand the philosophy of Communism and the scheme of society it represents, everything in my nature, all my view and convictions, life-long cares and concerns, are as opposed to it as anyone can possibly be. If I understand what Americanism is, I think I'm as good an American as you are," whereupon the whole place broke into terrific applause. When I thought of going before the committee, I thought that it would be just a little room where we'd sit around. I found that this was Madison Square Garden. There were hundreds of photographers, movies, everything, the whole Senate Judiciary Committee, and I finally said to the chairman of the committee, that very nice Senator [Matthew M.] Neely of West Virginia, "Don't you think we'd better get through with this business?" In fact, I took charge. It was the only thing to do. Dean Acheson said to me that it was the only time he had a client who wouldn't let him do a thing, who just took control, and he just sat there. There were [Senators William] Borah, [George] Norris, [Alexander] Wiley, etcetera, but when it came to McCarran's turn, he called me "Doctor." Well, the amount of poison he put into that term, as though "Doctor" was a contagious disease, and as for Harvard, that was a plague spot. This was in 1939. He did his damndest by all sorts of devices and schemes to prevent my confirmation. I understand that [Attorney General] Cummings fought like a Trojan against naming me because he thought that Roosevelt would have a great fight on his hands and I would open the sluices of the "Red" charges and everything else. The humor of the situation is that in the history of the Supreme Court, I'm one of the few people who was confirmed without a dissenting vote in the Senate. That was the funny thing about it. At one point Dean Acheson had a terrible time because somebody tipped McCarran off that I really wasn't a citizen in that my father obtained his citizenship through fraud. Naturalization requires a residence of five years. McCarran was reportedly tipped off that my father took the necessary oaths in order to get his naturalization in New York a year before he was eligible. Therefore, I wasn't naturalized as a minor through him; therefore, I wasn't a citizen; and therefore, I couldn't go on the Supreme Court—you know the argument. It was an awful thing to get the documents, but I knew that what was essential was to dig out when my father came here. In my experience with the United States Attorney's Office I knew that the ship's manifest had to be at least in triplicate, so that one copy could be deposited at the Custom House in New York. I told this to Dean Acheson, but alas, the Custom House had burnt down years ago, so that all the documents prior to the burning were gone. Then I said that I knew they had another copy deposited in the Treasury. Henry Morgenthau got people busy in the mucky cellars of the Treasury Department, and sure enough they found the ship's manifest. This was 1939.

Frankfurter was confirmed unanimously.

Personal appearances before the Senate Judiciary Committee were sporadic until 1955, but have since become routine. The proceedings have become lengthier and the questioning more rigorous as Congress tries to give nominees a careful scrutiny to make sure they are up to the job. Joseph Biden, chair of the Senate Judiciary Committee during Sandra Day O'Connor's confirmation hearings in 1981, put it this way: "Once a justice dons these robes, enters that inner sanctum across the road, we have no control. [A]ll bets are off."

The same sentiment could be voiced by the President. No matter how close an ally, once an appointee takes the oath, he or she is now at the top of a separate, independent branch of government. Behind every appointment is the possibility that the Justice will turn out not to toe the administration's line when making judgments on the bench. It is, of course, impossible for a President to predict how an appointee will rule on cases or even which questions will come before the Court. Some Justices have gone so far as to refrain from voting in elections in an effort to completely remove themselves from the political arena and to enhance their actual and apparent independence.

In the Supreme Court's very early days, Justices would often stop in to pay a call on the President when they rode into town to begin a session. When the Court began convening in the fall for the start of a single term, the Justices paid their annual courtesy call on the President immediately after adjourning their first session. A social observer described this custom in 1887:

> Having laid aside their robes, the Court in a body, attended by its own officers and accompanied by the Attorney General and the Solicitor General, proceed to the Executive Mansion, and, being formally announced, are received by the President in the audience parlor. The Chief Justice congratulates the President upon his appearance and good health. And the Justices in turn present their compliments, the Court retires. . . . The President never returning a call in form, except that of a sovereign ruler of a country or member of a royal family visiting Washington, does not return the call of the Court. During the [social] season, however, it is customary for him to give a state dinner in its honor.

In 1921 the Justices were photographed arriving to pay their annual call on the President. From left to right are Louis D. Brandeis, John H. Clarke, Mahlon Pitney, Willis Van Devanter, James C. McReynolds, William R. Day, Oliver Wendell Holmes, Jr., Joseph McKenna, Chief Justice William H. Taft. (Courtesy of the Library of Congress)

According to the Court's Reporter of Decisions, annual visits to the White House by the Justices continued to be perfunctory under President Woodrow Wilson: "Exactly five minutes after we had entered the portals of the Executive Mansion, we were on our way out." The annual ritual of the Justices parading down Pennsylvania Avenue together to pay a call on the President died out in the 1960s. Contemporary Justices are often invited to state dinners or other White House functions, but individually.

Intimate friendships between Presidents and sitting Justices were common in the nineteenth century. Malvina Harlan, for example, wrote that she and her husband, John Marshall Harlan, remained close friends with President Rutherford Hayes and his wife, Lucy, after Harlan's appointment to the Court in 1877:

> On Sunday evening after church, we often "stopped in" at the White House and found our way to the "Green Room" on the second floor, where, with perhaps eight or ten other visitors, we would spend the rest of the evening in singing the old-fashioned hymns, my oldest daughter, Edith, playing the accompaniments and adding to the pleasure of the occasion by the beauty of her rare voice.

In the twentieth century, however, only a few sitting Justices, notably Felix Frankfurter, Tom C. Clark, Fred Vinson, and Abe Fortas, have main-

In 1953 President Dwight D. Eisenhower greeted the Justices as they arrived for their White House visit. Pictured in the front row are William O. Douglas, Felix Frankfurter, Hugo L. Black, Eisenhower, Earl Warren, and Stanley F. Reed. Robert H. Jackson, Tom C. Clark, John Marshall Harlan, Sherman Minton, and Harold H. Burton are in the background. (Courtesy of the Library of Congress)

tained close social relationships with Presidents. Franklin D. Roosevelt did continue to invite Justice William O. Douglas regularly to the White House after appointing him to the Court in 1939. But, according to Douglas's diary, they were neither singing hymns nor talking business:

> Attended another poker party at the White House tonight. These are held half a dozen times or so a year. The President gets a lot of relaxation out of them. Usually the same gang. . . . I dubbed one game—a mean one with lots of cards wild—Charles the Baptist, after [Chief Justice Charles Evans Hughes]. The President roared. And another similar one, tho a little dirtier, Mr. Justice McReynolds. These sessions start at dinner & end at 1 A.M. I am usually a loser. . . . The President has not been doing so well this season. Stakes are not high. A poker party is rollicking fun when the President is there. No serious word is spoken from 7, when the President mixes the dry martinis, to 1 AM when we finish. Anyone who tries to get the President's ear on business is never invited again.

And what happens when a President who is no longer in power finds himself in the Supreme Court arguing a case before Justices he himself appointed? Only Grover Cleveland and Benjamin Harrison have had this experience (former President John Quincy Adams's lone appointee was long gone in 1841 when he argued the famous *Amistad* case.) Cleveland appeared in 1891 before two of his appointees—Chief Justice Melville W. Fuller and Justice Lucius Q. C. Lamar—and, according to the Reporter of Decisions who chronicled secondhand how he fared, the former President was politely refused any special favor:

> Speaking of the punctuality of the Court in regard to adjournment, Marshal [John Montgomery] Wright, my chief source of supply of Court anecdotes, did tell me this story. Chief Justice Fuller was an appointee of President Cleveland. Mr. Cleveland never appeared before the Court but once. That was during his interregnum, and while he was a member of a well-known firm of New York lawyers. His name appeared on the upper left hand corner of their letterheads as "Counsel."
>
> At his single appearance before the Court, one afternoon, Mr. Cleveland having the last word, while finishing his argument at about two minutes before closing time, looked up at the clock. He remarked to the Court that he noticed it was closing time, but added that he would detain them for only a very few minutes to complete his argument.
>
> Thereupon . . . the Chief Justice [Fuller], bowing with great courtesy, replied: "Mr. Cleveland, we will hear you tomorrow morning."
>
> It takes more than an ex-President to have the Court sit over-time, even if that ex-President has himself appointed the presiding officer.

Cleveland's two appointees ruled against him and he lost the case.

President Harry S Truman learned the hard way about the complex nature of relationships between Presidents and their Supreme Court appointees. He made four appointments to the Court: all political, professional, and personal friends. Two of his appointees joined the majority in ruling that Truman's seizure of steels mills in the 1952 case of *Youngstown Sheet and Tube Co. v. Sawyer* was an unconstitutional overreach of presidential power. Chief Justice Fred Vinson, with whom he played poker and attended ballgames, and Sherman Minton, his last appointee, did dissent in his favor. Truman nonetheless complained: "[P]acking the Supreme Court [with allies] simply can't be done. . . . I've tried it and it won't work. . . . Whenever you put a man on the Supreme Court, he ceases to be your friend."

6

⚖

Learning the Ropes
A Rookie Arrives

When Earl Warren arrived in Washington in 1953 to take his seat as the new Chief Justice, he was nervous. Although he had been governing the state of California with great skill, Warren had not been in a courtroom for a long time. His discomfort at being new to the job could not have been helped by his very public stumble as he literally took his seat in the center chair for the first time. He was given an old robe that had belonged to a much taller Justice so he could quickly take the Constitutional Oath in the privacy of the Conference room with only his new brethren as witnesses. Later that day, the Clerk of Court administered the Judicial Oath in the public Courtroom. It was the opening day of the 1953 Term and the room was packed with spectators. Warren later recalled his gaffe:

> I was then conducted to the seat of the Chief Justice, a high-backed chair in the center of the raised bench. It was here that I almost created a major incident by stepping on the overlength robe. Thrown off balance, I tripped over the step up to the bench. It was enough to be noted and commented on by the press, so I suppose it could be said that I literally stumbled onto the bench.

Being the rookie on the bench can be daunting. "It's quite a frightening experience to come here for the first time," Justice William J. Brennan, Jr., confessed to Justice Tom C. Clark's daughter in reminiscing about how kind her father had been to him as a newcomer in 1956. At the time of his arrival, he had modestly characterized himself as "the mule entered in the Kentucky Derby—I don't expect to distinguish myself, but I do expect to benefit from the association."

Newly appointed Justice Elena Kagan signed the judicial oath under the guidance of Chief Justice John G. Roberts in 2010, filling the seat vacated by John Paul Stevens. (Collection of the Supreme Court of the United States, photograph by Steve Petteway)

For lawyers in private practice, accepting an appointment to the Supreme Court has meant taking a substantially reduced salary. When Joseph Story, for example, consented to President James Madison's appointment to the Court in 1812 his pay was cut from the $5,000–6,000 he was making in fees as a Massachusetts lawyer to the $3,500 salary that the Justices then received. But, as he told a friend, there were side benefits:

> Notwithstanding [that] the emoluments of my present business exceed the salary, I have determined to accept the office. The high honor attached to it, the permanence of the tenure, the respectability, if I may so say, of the salary, and the opportunity it will allow me to pursue, what of all things I admire, juridical studies, have combined to urge me to this result. It is also no unpleasant thing to be able to look out upon the political world without being engaged in it. . . . The opportunity also . . . of meeting with the great men of the nation, will be, I am persuaded, of great benefit to my social feelings, as well as intellectual improvement.

Appointees coming from lower courts, on the other hand, have viewed Supreme Court salaries as a step up. Henry Billings Brown nevertheless had mixed feelings about leaving his position as a Michigan district judge in 1890:

My appointment to the Supreme Bench necessitated my removal to Washington and the severance of family and social relations which had been the growth of thirty years. While I had been much attached to Detroit and its people, there was much to compensate me in my new sphere of activity. If the duties of the new office were not so congenial to my taste as those of district judge, it was a position of far more dignity, was better paid and was infinitely more gratifying to one's ambition.

When he took his seat in 1862, Samuel F. Miller had harbored a more substantive worry than leaving friends behind. Miller was deeply apprehensive about meeting his Chief Justice, of whom he disapproved. And with reason: Roger Taney had written the notorious *Dred Scott* opinion five years earlier, holding that blacks were property and not citizens of the United States. And as Secretary of the Treasury, Taney had earlier sided with states' rights proponents against the formation of a federal bank.

When I came to Washington, I had never looked upon the face of judge Taney, but I knew of him. I remembered that he had attempted to throttle the Bank of the United States, and I hated him for it. I remembered that he took his seat upon the Bench, as I believed, in reward for what he had done in that connection, and I hated him for that. He had been the chief Spokesman of the Court in the Dred Scott case, and I hated him for that. But from my first acquaintance with him, I realized that these feelings toward him were but the suggestions of the worst elements of our nature; for before the first term of my service in the Court had passed, I more than liked him; I loved him. And after all that has been said of that great, good man, I stand always ready to say that conscience was his guide and sense of duty his principle.

Taney had evidently been just as nervous about the arrival of the new Justice from Iowa. He confessed at the end of term:

My brother Miller, I am an old and broken man. I may not be here when you return. I can not let you go without expressing to you my great gratification that you have come among us. At the beginning of the term I feared that the unhappy condition of the country would cause collisions among us. On the other hand, this has proved one of the pleasantest terms I have ever attended. I owe it greatly to your courtesy. Your learning, zeal, and powers of mind assure me that you will maintain and advance the high traditions of the Court. I predict for you a career of great usefulness and honor.

Miller did prove to be an extremely prolific and influential Justice, although not a particularly cordial or humble one. He did not consider many of his brethren to be up to caliber . . . sometimes with reason.

When Morrison R. Waite was named Chief Justice in 1874, Miller, who had coveted the chief justiceship for himself, looked down his nose at Waite's undistinguished credentials. President Ulysses Grant's seventh choice, Waite had one main quality: he was not a crony of the President and was untainted by the corruption scandals embroiling the administration. But Miller was not alone in showing his disdain. The obscure lawyer from Ohio was greeted skeptically by the Associate Justices because he was an unknown. But good-humored Waite wrote to his wife, Amelia, still back home in Ohio, that he was managing to bear up under the strain of scrutiny during his first few weeks:

> Saturday I went through my severest ordeal. It was to meet the Judges in consultation for the first time and when as a matter of course severe criticism would be in order. I got through with it very successfully I think. At any rate there was nothing to cause any uneasiness or discomfort on my part. It was a pretty easy time and my nerves were as cool as it is possible to be for a wonder, and so it has been all the time since I have been here. I have been perfectly self-possessed and have made very few mistakes. . . . Won't it be good to see you, and how many there are who want to get a first look at you. You will have to be prepared for a long look, a strong look, and a look altogether. All I have got to say—keep cool—take it & it will not be found very hard to take. I cant write about my sensations as to the gown or otherwise. I will tell you all at some time. They were strange sometimes, but yet I seem to take to them naturally.

Four days later, Waite continued his report:

> We live to learn, darlings, & if we keep our eyes & ears open we do learn. Come here with that feeling. You are the best of any of them. Feel that you are so, and everybody will acknowledge it to be true. I have learned a heap since I have been here. The result is, take the place that belongs to you, not offensively, but let everybody feel that it is yours.

This last bit of advice to his wife doubled as his own strategy for winning acceptance. Waite coolly grabbed the reins of leadership, having told Amelia: "I am going to drive and those gentlemen know it." He proved to be a natural manager who won over his brethren's skepticism about his abilities with friendliness and humility.

The work itself, however, proved more difficult. Waite's letter to his wife after five weeks as Chief Justice tried too hard to be reassuring:

> Every day in Court hard at work and harder at work outside of the Courtroom. It is all new and I have adopted the plan of going to the bottom of all new questions so that when I once understand it fully, I shall not have to look it up again. . . . I have as yet read no opinions, in Court, and have prepared none. When I pass this test successfully I shall put myself where I have nothing more to fear, if I keep up to my standards. It has been in some respect an anxious five weeks since I left you, and yet not so much so as when I left you I supposed it would be. Some how I have found myself equal to taking everything as it comes and not being overcome. . . . Everything is "rose color"

now, and while I cannot ask that shall continue always, I do hope I may be able to keep it about me until I feel at home where I am.

When Melville W. Fuller succeeded Waite as Chief Justice in 1888, his wife, Mary Ellen, and seven of his nine children were in attendance to witness Fuller take the oath of office. So was a Bowdoin College fraternity brother, William P. Drew, who recorded a firsthand account of the ceremony for his former classmate:

> A small white-walled room . . . a long massive desk, behind which, seated in their massive chairs ranged side by side, sit eight figures . . . clothed to their feet in flowing robes of "solemn black," apparently unmovable with stern fixed glaze, and seemingly almost as emotionless as effigies of departed greatness which are clustered in Statuary Hall not too far distant . . . Then from the "robing room" at one side of the courtroom, a small lithe and graceful figure, which his rich bench robe rather accentuates than conceals, steps lightly and quickly forth unattended and stands for a moment, as if in prayerful invocation just below and in front of the bench. . . . Then holding raised before him the Holy Bible in his right hand he [recites] . . . in a voice clear and steady at first, but toward the close somewhat shaken, as if by overmastering emotion that simple yet comprehensive "oath of office" which completes and sanctifies this great office to which he thus consecrates himself.

After taking the judicial oath, Fuller took his seat on the bench and got right down to business, starting with swearing in attorneys to become members of the Supreme Court bar. According to Drew, the regime change was now complete: "A tremor as of reviving consciousness seems to pass through the other Justices, who during the entire ceremony have sat unmoved, and more than one of them is seen to cast an almost startled look upon their new chief, as though some new 'force' had suddenly invaded their quiet ranks."

Once sworn in, a newcomer has to learn quickly the many customs and traditions that govern Supreme Court procedure. When Charles Evans Hughes was appointed Associate Justice in 1910, a huge backlog of cases awaited him, in part because Justice William Moody was ill and the Court had been operating a man short. According to Hughes, he narrowly avoided a protocol blunder when taking his seat on the bench:

> During the first three months of my service on the bench, there were only seven Justices. Chief Justice Fuller died in July 1910, and Justice Moody was incapacitated by illness which soon led to his retirement under a special Act of Congress. Thus, I never sat in the last seat on the extreme left of the Chief Justice. But took my place in the last seat on the right. Adjoining was the vacant seat of Justice Moody and next to that sat Justice [Oliver Wendell]

Holmes. The very first day I sat, Justice Holmes leaned over and beckoned me to move up and take Justice Moody's place. I knew enough of the traditions not to make such a faux pas, and I tremble to think what might have happened if I had been innocent enough to follow Justice Holmes's kindly but rather thoughtless suggestion. The other Justices would have regarded me as a fresh and bumptious newcomer, and even the Chief Justices in their marble busts might have raised their eyebrows.

Hughes was quickly made to feel at home, but the job nonetheless proved challenging:

> I found the work very difficult. At that time the Court was far behind in its calendar and it was the practice to advance important cases to be heard at the beginning of each session. It was generally about January before the Court reached the regular call, and if at the end of the Term in June we had left only 150 unheard cases (which could have been argued if reached) we thought we were doing well. That was before the reform made by the Act of 1925, which gave the Court in large measure, through the certiorari practice, the right to determine in advance whether cases were of such a character as to justify their being heard. In after years, the Court was able, by virtue of this reform, to close its term every year with the record of having heard all cases that were ready for argument. . . .
>
> In my very first week, with the advanced cases bunched for argument, I had a heavy load. I thought, as the arguments went on, that in a month or so I might be ready to vote, and I was amazed to find that, save for some special reason for delay, it was expected that the cases heard during the week would be voted on at the Conference on Saturday. I plunged into the work and it was not long before I was able fairly well to keep up with it.

But it is not simply the sheer volume of the work that can be daunting. Figuring out how to write opinions and dispose of cases well and efficiently can take years for a rookie Justice to master. "It takes three or four years to find oneself easily in the movements of the Court . . . and it went hard with me," confessed Justice Louis D. Brandeis to Felix Frankfurter in 1923, when the latter was still a law professor. Charles Evans Hughes later reflected on why the period of adjustment was so lengthy:

> A new Justice is not at ease in his seat until he has made a thorough study of lines of cases, so that when a case is argued he at once recognizes, or by looking at a key case brings back to his memory, the jurisprudence of the Court upon the general subject and can address his mind to the particular variant now presented. That is the explanation of the ability of experienced justices to dispose rapidly of their work, and also of the difficulties the new justice encounters in going over ground which is more familiar to his seniors on the bench.

Freshman Justices are usually cautioned by a wise veteran to be pre-pared for the lengthy breaking-in cycle. William O. Douglas recalled that it was Stone who advised him in 1939:

> As Justice Harlan F. Stone said, it takes some years "to get around the track," meaning that since there are so many new fields of law that come into focus through our cases, it takes time for the newcomer to get on speaking terms with them. And so it does.

Byron R. White (1962–1993) counseled newcomers that it would take as many as five years to get fully adjusted. According to Justice Clarence Thomas, who was appointed in 1991, White's prediction proved to be accurate:

> Justice White would often say that it takes about [five years] to go around the full horn of all the cases, the kinds of cases that we get. . . . That doesn't mean you can't do your work. It just means that things are still new for the first five years. You may not have had as many original jurisdiction cases involving water rights or boundaries. You may not have had a lot of admiralty cases. So you get all of that. It was Chief Justice [William H.] Rehnquist, when I was complaining, "Oh my goodness, what am I doing here?" It was my first year. I would look around me and see people like him who had been here, at that time, for three decades. I would see Justice White, who was legendary; Justice [Sandra Day] O'Connor. And [Justice White] said: "Well, Clarence, in your first five years you wonder how you got here. After that you wonder how your colleagues got here." I don't know whether that is true, exactly, but it certainly is an indication that that five-year period was fairly well accepted as the break-in period.

The adjustment to the Supreme Court can be especially challenging for those who have not previously sat as a judge. Appointees coming from the rough-and-tumble of political jobs in Congress or the Cabinet have not always had an easy time adapting to the quiet, contemplative life of a judge. When Harold Burton left the Senate to join the Court in 1945, he likened it to going "direct from a circus to a monastery." Justice Arthur J. Goldberg (1962–1965) was candid and amusing about the merits and drawbacks of transitioning from the Cabinet to the cloistered, delibera-tive Court. As President John F. Kennedy's Secretary of Labor, Goldberg had arbitrated high-profile labor disputes. He describes the change from "peripatetic" Cabinet member to "sitting" Associate Justice:

> One is "elevated" to the Court and consequently, in socially conscious Wash-ington, eats higher on the hog, but the Secretary, though outranked at the table, is driven to the dinner in a government Cadillac, whereas the Justice

steers and parks his own car. Who gains by the exchange depends on a value judgment—whether a good chef is to be preferred to a competent chauffeur. The Secretary's phone never stops ringing; the Justice's phone never rings—even his best friends won't call him.

The Secretary continually worries about what the President and the unpredictable Congress will do to his carefully formulated legislative proposals; the President, the Congress and the Secretary wonder what the Justice will do to theirs. . . . The Secretary numbers among his several thousand employees doorkeepers to guard his privacy; the newest Justice is, himself, the doorkeeper to protect the Court's.

This "doorkeeper" reference alludes to the function that new Justices perform in ensuring complete secrecy during the private Conferences where the Justices discuss and vote on cases. The last-appointed sits near the door, answers any knocks, and receives messages and documents from the outside. This practice was instituted in 1910 after a leak in an important economic case caused a panic on Wall Street. Before that incident, attendants served drinks in the Conference room and fetched documents.

Goldberg only served three terms before Kennedy's successor, Lyndon B. Johnson, persuaded him to transfer back to the executive branch to be Ambassador to the United Nations, overpromising that he would be an influential voice in helping broker an end to the Vietnam War. His successor, Abe Fortas, was dismayed to find himself isolated—as Goldberg had been—from his wide circle of Washington friends once he joined the Supreme Court:

The greatest fear of Justices on the Supreme Court is of dying on the Court. I would come into a room and there would be a roomful of people and there would be lively conversations. They would be talking about everything and it was very exciting. Then I would hit the threshold of that room and there would be utter silence. No one would talk. . . . Even my own friends would not talk to me anymore. There were people I had been talking to throughout my life. People I had been doing things with for years. But now they didn't know what they could say to me. They didn't know how far they could go. So they wouldn't say a thing to me. You just cannot understand the isolation of being on the Court.

But even nominees who are already serving as judges find being elevated to the High Court a significant change. After three weeks as Associate Justice, Oliver Wendell Holmes, Jr., who had spent twenty distinguished years on the Supreme Judicial Court of Massachusetts before his appointment in 1902, described the transition to his friend back home:

Yes—here I am—and more absorbed, interested and impressed than ever I dreamed I might be. The work of the past seems a finished book—locked up far away, and a new and solemn volume opens. The variety and novelty to me of the questions, the remote spaces from which they come, the amount of work they require, all help the effect. I have written on the constitutionality of part of the Constitution of California, on the powers of the Railroad Commissioners of Arkansas, on the question of whether a law of Wisconsin impairs the obligation of the plaintiff's contract. I have to consider a question between a grant of the U.S. in aid of a military road and an Indian reservation on the Pacific coast. I have heard conflicting mining claims in Arizona and whether a granite quarry is "Minerals" within an exception in a Railway land grant and fifty other things as remote from each other as these.

Despite having served for a decade as an appeals court judge, Harry A. Blackmun was anxious that he would not measure up when he joined the Court in 1970. He confessed to his former circuit court bench-mate: "In my few short days in Washington, it is very apparent that the technique and the pace and the attitudes are different. I don't know if I shall be able to survive." Another former appeals court judge, Stephen G. Breyer, also felt the stakes were raised when he ascended the High Court in 1994:

I think psychologically it is a different world from the Court of Appeals, because I know, as does everyone, that we are making a final decision on a matter that is . . . very important . . . to people. . . . And moreover, it's, in a sense, a fishbowl: it is not secret, people follow very closely what goes on.

When Earl Warren (1953–1969) was appointed Chief Justice, he came not from the Cabinet, the private sector, or the judiciary, but from the state of California, where he was governor. But his lack of familiarity with the ways of Washington, and the long gap since he had worked as a lawyer, made him apprehensive about his transition to the Supreme Court:

The day of my induction as Chief Justice of the United States was for me at once the most awesome and the loneliest day of my public career. . . . I approached the high office with a reverential regard and with a profound recognition of my unpreparedness to assume its obligations in such an abrupt manner.

It was completely different from the other offices I had held. Before becoming a district attorney, I had had four years of grooming in that office and had definite ideas as to how it could be improved. On becoming state attorney general, I had many years' background of law enforcement locally, statewide, and nationally. I also knew county government and its relation to the state, and felt prepared to plunge into both the civil and criminal aspects of the job. As governor, my experience in these earlier positions had acquainted me with many of the problems of the state and with ways of tackling them in the best interest of the public. I also knew the personalities involved and the atmosphere in which I must work, and while I did not feel that I had answers to all the issues of growth and war that confronted me, I had a solid background of experience for approaching them.

With the Chief Justiceship, it was quite different. I was not acquainted with Washington or even with members of the Supreme Court. . . . In addition to this disadvantage of not knowing many of the justices personally, there was my long absence from the courtroom. Since becoming governor, I had not been engaged in handling legal matters except to study contracts of the state with other parties to see that they were consistent with my policies and to study all bills passed by the Legislature to determine, among other things, if they conformed to the state and federal constitutions.

Coming to the Court as Chief Justice can be doubly daunting because one is also tasked with administrating the entire institution. Although Warren brought considerable management experience, he was fortunate to be able to retain Margaret McHugh, the executive secretary of his recently deceased predecessor, Fred Vinson. Warren also kept on the three clerks who had worked under Chief Justice Vinson:

I told them they were welcome to remain with me, and they all consented to do so, aiding in the transition for me. But it was a painful transition. Among my duties were the management of the Supreme Court building and the administration of the Court itself. It was difficult to find out anything from official records about the offices of the Clerk, the Marshal, the Librarian, or the Reporter of Decisions. When I made my inquiry about practices or procedures from the officers, I was told there was nothing in writing. Their predecessors had told them it had always been done in a certain way, and they had continued to do so in a certain way, and they had continued to do it in like manner. Thank goodness Mrs. McHugh had been with Chief Justice Vinson throughout his tenure, and she knew every facet of staff relationships. As a consequence, the two of us handle all the personnel problems without outside help. . . .

After visiting with staff members for a few minutes, I had Mrs. McHugh take me to the chambers of Mr. Justice Hugo L. Black, the Senior Associate Justice. He welcomed me heartily, and explained to me the procedure in the Conference Room as well as the fact that there were several hundred new cases, some of the gravest importance, which had accumulated during the summer to be preliminarily considered immediately after I was inducted. I, of course, had no knowledge of the records or issues involved in any of them, and no idea of conduct in the Conference Room. I asked Mr. Justice Black if he would manage a few of the conferences until I could familiarize myself with procedures. He graciously agreed to do this.

Despite his judicial inexperience, Warren proved to be an effective manager who was successful at steering the Court to expand civil rights and constitutional protections of individual rights. He was aided greatly by William J. Brennan, Jr. (1956–1990), who shared Warren's judicial philosophy and became his informal advisor and sounding board. Their first meeting was, however, inauspicious. As Brennan remembered it, on his first day at the Court the Chief Justice took him up to the third floor to meet his new colleagues:

> In a small room, my seven new colleagues were sitting around a table having sandwiches. The room was dark, and he put on the light, and there they all were, watching the opening game of the 1956 World Series. I was introduced by the Chief to each of them and someone said "Put out the light." They put out the light and they went on watching the game.

Brennan was an avid Brooklyn Dodgers fan and they were playing the Yankees so he completely understood the terseness of his reception.

In 1967 Brennan was joined by Thurgood Marshall, who became a reliable ally in supporting his expansive view of the Constitution and individual rights. Elizabeth Black, the wife of Senior Associate Justice Hugo L. Black, excitedly recorded in her diary the details of Marshall's historic swearing-in as the first African American member of the Supreme Court:

> Hugo told me there was a possibility that Thurgood Marshall would be sworn in today and for me to keep in touch. I arrived at the Court about 2:30 and found the Supreme Court Marshal, Perry Lippitt, sitting in the guard's box in the driveway. He didn't know when Marshall was due to come in and he didn't intend to miss him. Perry escorted the Marshalls—his wife Cissy, Thurgood, Jr., age eleven, and John, age eight—to Hugo's office. Hugo called Bill Brennan, the only other Justice in the building at the time. Hugo asked Thurgood if he had a favorite chapter in the Bible, and Thurgood said he couldn't think of one, so Hugo said "What about I Corinthians 13: 'And now abideth faith, hope, charity, these three; but the greatest of these is charity.'" Thurgood loved it, and Hugo swore him in on his white Gideon Bible bearing an insert saying it was from the U.S.S. Arizona. I suggested that Hugo present the Bible to Thurgood. We all wrote our names in the margin of the page of I Corinthians 13. Thurgood wished his daddy could have been there, but said he knew he was on some street corner in heaven shaking his finger and saying, "I knew my boy would do it."

(Marshall's father, the son of a freed slave, had worked as a dining car waiter and then as chief steward at a private club.)

Warren's successor as Chief Justice, Warren Burger, recommended his old childhood friend from Minnesota, appeals court judge Harry A. Blackmun, to President Richard Nixon in 1970. Two previous nominees having been rejected by the Senate, the President and the rest of the country were greatly relieved when Blackmun's nomination was finally approved. "Good Old Number Three," as Blackmun called himself in his self-deprecating fashion, hastily joined the Court in June, with the term almost over. But there was still just enough time to give him a quick taste of the work and to make acquaintance with the staff so he could ready

Justice Hugo L. Black (right) swore in Thurgood Marshall as Solicitor General in 1965 as President Lyndon B. Johnson, Marshall's wife, Cecilia, and sons Thurgood Jr. and John looked on. Two years later, Marshall would once again take the oath of office from Black when Johnson appointed him to the Supreme Court. (Courtesy of LBJ Library)

himself for the next term. Blackmun drily recalled the sequence of events surrounding his appointment:

> On Tuesday, May 5, word came that the Judiciary Committee had voted 17 to 0 to approve. This unanimous vote was gratifying, of course. I was told that the matter would come up on the Senate floor May 12. That day came along, and I was concerned to see photographers out in the hall near the room in the Rochester hotel where I was having lunch. I told them I would meet them near my chambers, a few blocks away. They accepted this suggestion and were there equipped with tapes and cameras. We entered and went upstairs. One of the local reporters called shortly to say that the Senate had voted and that it was 94 to 0 to confirm. The President called. That conversation was brief but to the point. He seemed relieved that it was over. I told the press I had no oral observation to make, but I did distribute a short written statement. They took photographs of [my wife] Dottie and me and she made a brief comment. That night and the next day, the calls and correspondence continued. The Chief Justice [Warren Burger] telephoned and indicated that it would be desirable for me to examine some twenty pending certiorari petitions that the Court had been "holding for nine" and were to be voted upon before the end of the Term. I therefore should come to the Court, [be] sworn

in and . . . participate in the vote on those matters. I was to be concerned about pending Eighth Circuit cases that had been assigned to me. He said that I should assign them out to others. I did so in an effort to get those responsibilities off my desk. Everyone was gracious about relieving me. There was another call from the Chief Justice. He suggested that I be sworn in on June 8 or 9. He indicated that he thought the Court would finish within the week. June 9 was chosen. . . .

The next morning everyone was driven to the garage in the Court building. We were taken to what were to be my Chambers. At 9:30 a.m., we were escorted to the courtyard where photographers were present.

The Chief Justice, the Governor of Minnesota, and Congressmen [Albert Harold] Quie and [Clark] MacGregor appeared. Eventually, the Marshal took me into the Courtroom to be seated near the Clerk's desk on the "John Marshall chair." I was surprised to see how full the room was. The proceedings were brief. I took the judicial oath at the center of the bench. I was then robed and sat down at the far left, and that was it. Good old Number Three.

On Blackmun's first day on the bench he was looked after by a solicitous colleague:

I had taken my seat, and was examining things. I pulled open a drawer in the bench, and found some cough drops. And a copy of the Constitution, stamped "O.W. Holmes" and signed by Justice [Felix] Frankfurter, a successor in this seat. The Marshal brought me a Bible to sign—presented by the first Justice Harlan and signed by all the Justices since. Suddenly Byron White was leaning over to me, whispering "Harry! Harry, where's your spittoon?" He snapped a finger—softly—for a page. "Get the Justice his spittoon!"

Once used by nineteenth-century Justices and oral advocates, who had no time limits on their arguments and chewed tobacco to keep themselves going for hours and hours, the spittoons now serve as wastepaper baskets.

The Court, like the rest of the judiciary, is organized by a rigid seniority system, and the newest member starts on the bottom rung of the ladder. Publically, this means sitting on the extreme left of the bench and standing last in line at official functions. More substantively, in the Justices' private Conference the junior waits to speak last when the Justices are discussing and voting on cases. According to William H. Rehnquist, who came aboard as the junior Justice in 1972, this can be frustrating:

When I first went on the Court, I was both surprised and disappointed at how little interplay there was between the various justices during the process of conferring on a case. Each would state his views, and a junior justice could express agreement or disagreement with views expressed by a justice senior to him earlier in the discussion, but the converse did not apply; a junior justice's views were seldom commented upon, because votes had already been cast up the line. Like most junior justices before me must have felt, I thought I had some very significant contributions to make, and was disappointed that they hardly ever seemed to influence anyone because people did not change their votes in response to their contrary views. I thought it would be desirable to have more of a round-table discussion of the matter after each of us had expressed our views.

Rehnquist presumably struggled harder to persuade his brethren than previous junior Justices because he was often in the minority on the Burger Court and wrote many lone dissents. By the time he was elevated to Chief Justice in 1986, Rehnquist had, however, come to accept the hierarchical system and recognized its practicality. Of course if the Justices are split four to four on a case, what the junior Justice has to say is listened to very carefully by the others members of the Conference. "[B]y the time they got to me, I was either irrelevant or I was very important, depending on how the vote had come out," remarked Samuel Alito on being the junior in 2006. It also helps that, since Warren Burger became Chief Justice in 1969, there has been an unwritten rule that no Justice speaks twice in Conference until everyone has had a turn to speak.

When a Justice joins the Court, the staff of the Court pulls together to teach the newcomer how things operate. Often a new Justice will be given a secretary who worked for another Justice and who already knows the ropes. Justice Ruth Bader Ginsburg was grateful to her predecessor, Byron R. White, for sharing his operating manual with her when he retired in 1993: "It was Justice White who gave me his chambers manual, the operating procedures that he had written for his chambers early on and gave it over to his law clerks." Ginsburg perpetuated the tradition of passing down the chambers manual in 2009: "The day that Sonia [Sotomayor] was sworn in, I was away . . . but I had delivered to her that chambers manual."

Seeking the guidance of an experienced Justice can help a rookie get acclimated. Sandra Day O'Connor, for example, was mentored by Lewis F. Powell, Jr., a courtly Southerner who took her under his wing when she took her seat in 1981:

No one did more than Lewis Powell to help me get settled as a new Justice. He found us a place to live. He allowed me to hire one of his two secretaries as my chambers' secretary. Most important, he was willing to talk about cases and the issues. His door was always open.

When Ginsburg joined the Court twelve years later, O'Connor in turn went out of her way to give her a helping hand:

Justice O'Connor's welcome when I became junior Justice is characteristic [of her personality]. The Court has customs and habits one cannot find in the official Rules or in Stern & Gressman [Supreme Court practice manual]. Justice O'Connor knew what it was like to learn the ropes on one's own. She told me what I needed to know when I came on board for the Court's 1993 Term—not in an intimidating dose, just enough to enable me to navigate safely for my first days and weeks.

In keeping with tradition, Ginsburg expected to be given an easy, unanimous, case for her initial writing assignment. But the Chief Justice had other plans:

> I eagerly awaited my first opinion assignment, expecting—as the legend goes—that the brand-new Justice would be slated for an uncontroversial, unanimous opinion. When the list came round, I was dismayed. The Chief [Rehnquist] had given me an intricate, not at all easy, ERISA [Employment Retirement Income Security Act of 1974] case, on which the Court had divided six to three.

Justice O'Connor offered this advice: "Just do it . . . and, if you can, circulate your draft before [the Chief Justice] makes the next set of assignments. Otherwise, you will risk receiving another tedious case." When Ginsburg read her first bench announcement summarizing the Court's decision, a Marshal Office attendant slipped her an encouraging note from O'Connor (who dissented in the case) that read: "This is your first opinion for the Court, it is a fine one, I look forward to many more."

Unlike Ginsburg, Samuel Alito was assigned a straightforward, unanimous case when he joined the Court in 2006. But that didn't make him any less nervous:

> My first opinion was an opinion in which we were unanimous. I think it's a good practice. I remember when I sent it around and I had gotten back approvals from everybody with a few changes. Somebody said, "Don't think it's going to be this easy all the time in the future," and that certainly has proven to be the case. I distinctly remember drafting that opinion. Before I came here I had been a court of appeals judge for fifteen years. I had written hundreds of opinions, and I thought I had done my best on all of those. But when I drafted that first opinion, realizing where I was now, I went back over it, and over it. I have never revised an opinion as many times as I did before I sent that out.

Alito took his seat in the middle of a term and did not have the benefit of the summer to get himself up to speed. He has characterized his first term as "baptism by fire" or "learn as you go."

While it may take years to become comfortable as one of the final arbiters of the Constitution, the rituals of the Supreme Court become habit quickly. Sometimes the customs even become too ingrained. Breyer served as the junior Justice for eleven years—the second longest stretch in Court history without turnover—before passing the baton to Alito. According to Alito, Breyer had held the job so long he had difficulty relinquishing it:

> It took him a while to adjust to not being the junior justice. I remember very distinctly at the first conference there was a knock at the door and I was processing this: "Someone is knocking at the door; it's my job now to get up and answer the door." And before I could even start to get out of the chair, Justice Breyer was out of his chair and headed for the door. The chief justice had to say, "Steve, sit down, that's not your job anymore."

How do the veteran Justices feel when it is time to rearrange themselves on the bench and make room for a rookie? It can be hard for the other members of the Court to say goodbye to a friend and absorb a new member. According to Justice Thomas: "As far as the composition of the Court, you're bringing in basically . . . a family member. It changes the whole family. . . . I have to admit, you grow very fond of the Court that you spent a long time on. . . . You have to start all over. The chemistry is different."

Lyle Denniston, a news reporter who has covered the Court for more than fifty years, has observed that the introduction of a new member always affects the Court as a whole:

> A new Justice comes into the Court and brings a personality, brings a history, brings a style of judging, a style of writing, and because there is this constantly changing internal dynamic, the addition of a new ingredient in that dynamic changes the whole. Now, it doesn't cause other Justices necessarily to change their views, but it does open up the possibility of shifting majorities, shifting blocs within the Court.

7

⚖️

Inside the Courtroom

Views of the Bench

The deaths of some of our most talented jurists have been attributed to this location of the Courtroom; and it would be but common justice in Congress to provide better accommodation for its sittings," urged architect Robert Mills in 1850, referring to the Supreme Court's dungeon-like room in the Capitol building. It was not simply that the working space was inadequate. Housing the Supreme Court in Congress's basement also sent the message that legislation was superior to justice. Justice John Catron (1837–1865) complained of this slight: "[I was] grievously annoyed by the dampness, darkness, and want of ventilation of the old basement room; into which, I have always supposed, the Supreme Court was thrust in a spirit of hostility to it, by the Political Department."

Accommodations for the Justices improved in 1860 as the Senate was given its own wing of the Capitol. The room it vacated was remodeled for the Supreme Court, finally providing the Justices with a more dignified chamber befitting their status atop a coequal branch of government. The Vice President's old office was turned into their Conference room. Journalist E. V. Smalley gave his readers a virtual tour of this new Courtroom in 1882:

> Midway in the rather dingy and ill-lighted passage that leads from the great rotunda of the Capitol to the Senate wing sits a colored man holding a cord attached to the handle of a closed door. If you pause, as if desirous of entering, he pulls the cord; the door opens and you are in a narrow vestibule. Another door swings inward silently, and another colored man politely motions you to a seat on the crimson cushions of a big sofa. A high screen in front of the door hides the room from you when you first enter, but once on

When the Senate was given its own wing in the Capitol building in 1860, the Supreme Court moved upstairs to the Old Senate Chamber. This early photograph shows the Courtroom scene before the Justices made their appearance: pages fidget behind the Justices' chairs, the Clerk of the Court stands at his desk, and spectators are seated. (The white vases on the ground are spittoons.) (Collection of the Supreme Court of the United States)

the sofa you find that you are in the Supreme Court chamber. Suppose it to be a few moments before noon. The long row of big, easy-chairs, on a high platform back of a desk of equal length, are still vacant, for the court meets at twelve. You have time to study the room. Its form is that of a semi-circle, with a half-dome for the ceiling, pierced by sky-windows, through which a mild light falls on crimson curtains and upholstery, and on the pleasant gray tint of the walls. A small gallery over the judges' seats is supported by pillars of the peculiar mottled gray and black stone called Potomac marble, and pilasters of the same stone relieve the circling sweep of the wall. Behind the pillars and under the gallery there are heavily curtained windows, and a screened passage leading to the retiring-room of the judges on one hand, and to the marshal's office on the other. Upon the wall are busts of the six Chief-Justices who preceded the present incumbent,—Jay, Rutledge, Ellsworth, Marshall, Taney, and Chase. The greater part of the floor-space is railed off for the members of the bar. Outside of this are the sofas for spectators—the only really comfortable seats for public use to be found in the Capitol.

But the Supreme Court's ever-expanding judicial and administrative work made it outgrow its new lodging all too quickly. An adjacent room

Spectators crowded into the Old Senate Chamber to hear arguments in the 1895 case deciding the constitutionality of a national income tax. (Collection of the Supreme Court of the United States)

for a Clerk's office was initially lacking, so advocates arriving to argue cases had to prepare themselves in the corridor. Absent chambers, the Justices worked out of their homes, isolated from one another. They nonetheless held sessions in this old Senate chamber for seventy-five years.

By 1912, Chief Justice William Howard Taft had decided to take matters into his own hands. He vigorously lobbied Congress for funds to construct new quarters for the Court so the Justices would cease being Congress's tenant and finally get their own edifice. (He oversaw the building's initial planning, but died before construction was complete.) Taft's successor, Charles Evans Hughes, took over the project, having long viewed the Court's accommodations to be inadequate:

> The facilities afforded to the Court were then very slender. The old court room in the Capitol, though inadequate in size, gave the Court a worthy setting and was rich in memories. Across a hall was the robing room where the Justices robed and took their lunch during sessions. Below was the conference room and library, small and cluttered, where we crowded about the conference table. As some of the Justices objected to open windows, the room became overheated and the air foul during our long conferences, not conducive to good humor. . . . The Clerk's office was also most inadequate.

Its entrance room and the corridor outside the courtroom were the only places where the members of the bar could congregate and smoke, awaiting the call of their cases. I suppose that no high court in the country had fewer conveniences.

The new building opened to great fanfare in 1935. But the Justices were apprehensive about the move. They were curiously attached to their old quarters, particularly to their chairs (the notion of sitting on a bench having long been a figurative one). Smalley had noted in 1882 that "Each justice of the Supreme Court has a chair to suit his own notions of what constitutes a comfortable seat. Some of the chairs have high backs to rest the head, some have low backs; some have horse-hair cushions, some velvet, some no cushions at all." Reporting on the grand opening of the new building, a reporter was bemused by the Justices' insistence on dragging their cherished chairs along with them:

> But behind the massive bench, in dignified isolation, the justices will survey classic marble columns and costly rose drapes from favorite old chairs brought over from their abandoned quarters in the Capitol. An odd assortment, weirdly incongruous in so luxurious a chamber, the chairs may be replaced later. But among some Court attaches the betting is at least even that the old ones will be retained. There is the story of Justice [Benjamin] Cardozo, for example. A frail figure, he appeared uncomfortable in his high upholstered seat. He was asked if he desired a new chair. "No," he replied slowly, "if Justice Holmes sat in this for twenty years, I can sit in it for a while." Justices [Owen J.] Roberts and [George] Sutherland have chairs with curved thin backs. Justice [James C.] McReynolds has a swivel chair. The other chairs are alike, thickly upholstered.

The old chairs did not survive the first term. When Justice Roberts leaned back, his chair leg cracked, forcing him to grab the bench to balance himself. The Court promptly sold the chairs to a furniture dealer for thirty-five dollars.

Journalists Drew Pearson and Robert S. Allen witnessed the first session of the Court in its new dwelling a block east of the Capitol. They likened the excitement to the opening of a Broadway play:

> The stage is a long dais of carefully polished mahogany. The curtain is of red velvet, just beyond. And as the hands of the great gold clock, suspended above, come together at noon, a hushed silence falls over the throng. Behind the velvet curtains nine aged actors wait their cue. They stand abreast, gowned in black. In front of them is a little boy in knee breeches. At a nod from the leading man—a bearded gentleman of stately mien—the boy pushes a buzzer and the Nine Old Men advance abreast through the curtains.
>
> The audience rises.

"The Honorable, the Chief Justice and the Associate Justices of the Supreme Court!" calls the court crier.

The justices take their seats; the Supreme Court of the United States, most powerful judicial body in the world, is now in session.

Smalley had described this same ritual when it took place in the old chambers, but apparently in that era there was also bowing:

> At the head walks the Chief-Justice, and the others follow in the order of their length of service in the court. They stand a moment in front of their chairs, and all bow at once to the bar. The lawyers return the salute; then the judges sit down, the Associates being careful, however, not to occupy their chairs before the Chief-Justice is settled in his.

The new building was built for magnificence, not humans. The naked white marble felt cold; there were drafts. Two journalists unkindly compared the new Courtroom chamber to "the interior of a classical icebox decorated for some surrealist reason by an insane upholsterer." The lighting in the Courtroom was dark. The Justices complained that they could not see well and were given desk lamps. According to Justice William O. Douglas, sounds bounced off the marble:

> We had difficulty with the acoustics in the new Courtroom, and though the ceiling was lowered and softer material used, that did not seem to help. Heavy red curtains were placed behind and on the two sides of the bench in an effort to stop the echo and re-echo of voices. This helped some, but it did not greatly improve the situation. It was still difficult for a Justice who sat on one side of the bench to hear a question asked by a Justice on the opposite end.

Sixteen years after the Courtroom's unveiling, Justice Robert H. Jackson felt obliged to warn attorneys that the acoustics continued to be "wretched": "If your voice is low, it burdens the hearing, and parts of what you say may be missed. On the other hand, no judge likes to be shouted at as if he were an ox. I know of nothing you can do except to bear the difficulty in mind, watch the bench, and adapt your delivery to avoid causing apparent strain."

Two Justices insisted on working from home in the 1930s and never occupied their offices in the new building. According to his law clerk, Louis D. Brandeis "was strongly opposed and never moved into the offices set aside for him. He found more than symbolic importance in having the Supreme Court midway between the Senate and the House, almost directly under the dome of the Capitol, accessible to the main flow of life through the old building." Brandeis's grandson, Frank J. Gilbert, has explained that the Justice worried that the grandiosity of the Marble Palace, as it was quickly called, would make his brethren more pompous:

> He thought the plans were too grand. He liked the intimate chambers which existed from the nineteenth century into the twentieth century in the Capitol building. He thought the new proposed building would not contribute to the Justices' humility, which they needed. . . . Grandfather . . . never set foot inside the chambers, and continued to do the work at home in his apartment. Actually, I am told that staff of the Supreme Court used . . . the suite in the 1930s to point out what Justices' offices would look like with his empty office.

But by 1941 all of the Justices were regularly using their chambers, with one holdout: Chief Justice Harlan Fiske Stone. "The place is almost bombastically pretentious," he grumbled, "and thus seems to me wholly inappropriate for a quiet group of old boys such as the Supreme Court of the United States."

The Justices finally got their own building in 1935, and the new Courtroom was unveiled to great fanfare. Calling the edifice "almost bombastically pretentious," Justice Harlan Fiske Stone refused to move into his new Chambers and continued working from home. (Collection of the Supreme Court of the United States, photograph by Underwood and Underwood)

The Courtroom now boasts good lighting and exquisite sound. To address the auditory problems, in 1972 Chief Justice Warren Burger arranged for the bench to be reconstituted into a crescent shape. (By then, however, the use of microphones had already made it much easier for the Justices to hear one another, prompting Justice Douglas to deride the new bench "as useless and unnecessary as a man's sixth Cadillac.") To modern eyes, the chamber seems both intimate and majestic. In 2009 Justice David Souter praised the room's dimensions:

> One of the amazing things about the courtroom, despite its splendor, is the intimacy of it. On the one hand, it's not that big a room, but the real intimacy comes in the relationship between the lawyer who is arguing at the podium and the Court that he's arguing to. And if you stop to think of it when you go in there, I would tell a visitor, you would see that if one of us leaned over the bench as far as we could lean, and the lawyer arguing at the podium leaned toward us, we could almost shake hands. And that is a very important thing because it means that when arguments take place, you are physically and psychologically close enough to each other so that there is possibility for real engagement.

The business conducted inside the Courtroom is straightforward: admissions of new members to the Supreme Court bar, oral arguments, and announcements of written opinions. This is how Smalley described the proceedings in the old Courtroom in the 1880s:

> Business begins promptly and is dispatched rapidly. First, motions [to admit attorneys to the Supreme Court bar] are heard, then the docket is taken up. The Chief-Justice calls the case in order in a quiet tone, and a lawyer is on the floor making an argument, while you are still expecting that there will be some further formality attending the opening of so august a tribunal. The proceedings are impressive only for their simplicity. Usually the arguments of counsel are delivered in low, conversational tones. Often the judges interrupt to ask questions.

Shortly after the new building opened for business, two journalists offered a snapshot of a day in which the Justices announced opinions in the morning and heard arguments in the afternoon:

> Chief Justice Hughes nods to Justice [Benjamin] Cardozo at the extreme left, and Justice Cardozo launches a long opinion on building-and-loan associations. Newsmen stuff messages into pneumatic tubes to be carried to the telegraph room on the floor below. No scurrying messenger boys disturb the supreme serenity.
> Like a schoolmaster calling on his pupils, the stately Chief Justice nods to one, then another, of his colleagues. They recite. Audience attention, which lagged during Cardozo's dreary dissertation on mortgages, suddenly snaps

back. At the other end of the bench, Owen Roberts, square-jawed and deep-voiced, begins to speak. . . . He speaks with full, resonant tones, not once referring to his notes. He is a superb actor, with poor lines. Chief Justice Hughes is the same. But their colleagues mumble into their papers with feeble chords.

Opinion after opinion drones on: Indian property, workmen's compensation, mortgages, garbage disposal. The expectant audience is bored. It is now one-thirty. Suddenly the Court recesses. The first act has been slow. But, as if with a sense of the dramatic, the nine aged actors have kept their best show for the end.

Crackers and milk in the robing room. Justice [Louis D.] Brandeis eats two sandwiches, put up in a small box by his wife before he leaves home. Justice [James C.] McReynolds departs abruptly, seeking solitude and more solid food.

Once again the justices march out on their stage. This time, Stanley Reed, Solicitor General of the Justice Department, stands before them in morning coat and gray-striped trousers. Senator Smith cups one hand behind a large ear. [The Marshal of the Court] Frank B. Kellogg forgets that he has been bored. Newsmen shoot their messages faster through the pneumatic tubes.

Although Courtwatchers attend Court sessions primarily to hear the substantive business of oral argument (see chapter 8), closely observing the behavior of the Justices on the bench is also part of the show. John Knox, a young clerk hired by Justice James C. McReynolds in 1936, recorded his irreverent impressions of the Justices during their second term hearing cases in the new Courtroom:

After studying . . . Chief Justice [Charles Evans Hughes], I glanced at Justice McReynolds. His thoughts seemed to be far away as he gazed out over the crowded Courtroom. Proud and never-changing he sat, mysterious and strange: lonely, yet possessing the rewards of life withheld from so many of his fellow men. Like a gloomy Caesar he appeared—the Romanesque features of his granite-like expression conveying something forbidding and almost sinister. Here indeed was the man forever doomed to imperial isolation and yet somehow a vibrant and puzzling part of life. And on that day I was proud to be his law clerk, and my loyalty to him was undiminished.

I next looked at Justice [Willis] Van Devanter. He seemed stern and forbidding—staring straight ahead with his thin lips tightly compressed. His bald head almost matched the color of the marble pillar near where he sat. And I could scarcely believe that one with his generous character and instinctive friendliness could seem so austere when sitting on the nation's highest tribunal and garbed in his robes of office. He appeared to be even more reserved than McReynolds.

At that moment Justice [Louis D.] Brandeis began to fidget, and he slowly turned his swivel chair to the left until he was almost facing Van Devanter. Brandeis appeared more ascetic than any of the other Justices, with the exception of [Benjamin] Cardozo, who sat quietly at one end of the bench, looking straight ahead, not moving a muscle and reminding me of Little Jack Horner. Or perhaps of teacher's pet at school. He had an almost imperceptible smile on his lips and was making no attempt to be a person of immense dignity. Unlike Cardozo, however, Brandeis appeared to be somewhat bored by the admission of so many attorneys. He continued for several minutes to look at Van Devanter with a rather cold and appraising eye. That Justice, however, gave no indication of awareness that he was being stared at.

Owen J. Roberts, at the far end from Cardozo, was busily looking at a sheet of paper. Pierce Butler leaned over toward Roberts as if to see whether the junior Justice was merely doodling with his pencil. Butler exhibited a forbidding scowl while on the bench that day, and he seemed very displeased with the world. Whether he had the same lovable character of a Van Devanter remained to be seen. I then noticed that McReynolds had just slipped on a pair of horn-rimmed glasses, and that he and Butler were the only Justices wearing them. Even Cardozo, who had used his eyes so strenuously over the years, had no need of glasses while in the Courtroom that day.

My attention was then directed to Harlan F. Stone and George Sutherland. To my surprise both men appeared rather colorless. Justice Stone, stocky and perhaps even stodgy, sat in an informal and unconcerned fashion in his chair. He looked like a bored Wall Street executive patiently waiting for a business meeting to commence. Now and then he would shift his position as if he were not quite comfortable. No one studying him that day could have guessed the warmth of Stone's personality or the greatness of his heart. He appeared almost ill at ease.

Justice Sutherland looked exactly like the photographs I had seen of him, but despite his gray hair and rather striking beard, he did not exhibit any trace of the commanding presence that Hughes possessed. "But, of course, he might be impressive too if he were sitting in the middle chair and doing all the talking," I mused.

Little did I realize that Justice Stone would be stricken with a serious illness within a few days, and that he would be unable to attend to any court work until the following February. Perhaps he was already ill. Nor did I suspect that Justice Brandeis would die exactly five years later—on October 5, 1941. But on that October day in 1936 they all sat before me—Nine Old Men—an incredible mirage of a million wonderful hopes.

I then glanced at one of the attorneys, who was busily engaged in sponsoring another candidate for admission. He appeared ill at ease, and his voice had begun to falter. I also noticed that he spoke with a marked Southern accent. A gentleman seated next to me leaned over and whispered, "A Georgia cracker! He's nervous and scared!" I nodded my head but said nothing. Harry [Parker, Justice McReynolds' messenger/driver] had told me that even whispering was strictly forbidden while the Court was in session.

During tedious arguments, some Courtwatchers have found themselves scrutinizing the habits and mannerisms of individual Justices on the bench. Oliver Wendell Holmes, Jr. (1902–1932), who rated oral advocates as "kitchen-knifes, razors, and stings," was occasionally seen drifting off if a dull "kitchen-knife" was at the podium. He once confessed to a friend that he felt justified writing him a letter during oral argument because some advocates were simply unworthy of his time: "[W]e don't shut up bores, one has to listen to discourses dragging slowly along after one has seen the point and made up one's mind. That is what is happening now and I take the chance to write as I sit with my brethren. I hope I shall be supposed to taking notes."

When oral arguments inconveniently conflict with baseball games, pages and clerks have been spotted sending notes to Justices with the latest scores. Justice Potter Stewart (1958–1991), a rabid Cincinnati Reds fan who kept a newspaper article in his wallet explaining the mathematical probabilities of scoring runs in each inning, asked his clerks to keep him apprised on the bench—on an inning-by-inning basis—of the runs scored during the 1972 Reds-Mets National League playoff games. One of Stewart's clerks recounted this anecdote about the final playoff game:

> [B]efore the final game began, [Stewart] asked for scores "every half-inning." And as it was played, he wanted a report on each batter. At 2:35 P.M., the game was interrupted by the surprising news of Vice-President [Spiro] Agnew's resignation. The clerks dutifully sent Stewart a note: "[Mets hitter Ed] Kranepool flies to right. Agnew resigns."

Elderly Justices have occasionally been observed snoozing through oral argument. This happened particularly in the mid- and late 1800s, when the Court was swamped with mundane cases it would not have accepted if the Justices had enjoyed better control over the docket. Most noticeably, Justice Robert Grier (1846–1870) had a habit of keeping his eyes closed on the bench, causing the bar to think the elderly Justice was dozing. Not necessarily so. One attorney, Philip Phillips, was stunned when Grier later complimented him on his performance. A friend relayed the anecdote as Phillips told it to him:

> On one occasion Judge Grier complimented Mr. Phillips on an argument he made. "But," said Mr. Phillips, "I thought you were asleep, Judge." "Oh," said the Judge, partly excusing himself, "you see, Phillips, when I have seen where you go in, I know where you are coming out; but with some of these fellows I have to keep awake and watch them all the time."

Justices Noah Swayne (1862–1881) and David Davis (1862–1877) broke the tedium of long hours on the bench by sending out for sweets (which did not help their very large waistlines). According to Walter H. Smith, an attorney who argued frequently before them:

They both loved candy, and it was no unusual thing for one or the other of them to send a page out for a dime's worth of the old-fashioned stick candy and the two to munch it while listening to the argument. They frequently grew tired and would stand for a long time, leaning against one of the heavy pillars back of the seats of the court. Swayne was perhaps the heavier of the two.

Smith also noticed that some Justices appeared less bored when the Courtroom filled up with spectators. Justice Nathan Clifford (1858–1881) liked to draw the crowd's attention by asking questions from the bench:

> Clifford was, in avoirdupois, the largest one of the justices. His mouth was of a rather peculiar shape, as if he were ready to dispute with some one. When the lobby was approximately empty he would sit leaning back in his chair, looking as if he were taking little interest in the proceedings. But let the lobby fill up and then would come a marked change. Leaning forward, he would fire a question at the attorney who was speaking, and, hardly waiting for an answer, would shoot at him another, and then turn toward the lobby with a broad smile, as if to say, "Did you see how I got him?"
>
> As long as the lobby remained full this by-play would go on, but when the lobby emptied Clifford would sink back in his seat as if no longer interested in what was going on.

Justice Stephen J. Field (1863–1897) apparently also became more animated when the Courtroom was full:

> With an empty lobby he usually sat back in his chair, with an appearance of listening to the argument of the attorney, but let the lobby fill up and a change would come. He was sure to grow nervous and fidgety. Seizing a pad of paper and a pencil, he would make out a list of books and send a page to the library. On the return of the page with arms full of books, Mr. Field would seize upon them, turn the pages rapidly, and frequently with considerable noise throw the books on the floor, and then make out another long list. This would keep up until the lobby became apparently empty, when he would once more lean back in his chair and resume attention to the speaker.

After oral arguments have been heard, the Justices meet (usually within three days) in their private Conference room to discuss and vote on cases. They then set to work at the slow task of writing opinions, which, once completed, are simultaneously published and announced orally from the bench. Until the 1970s, the Justices read aloud their full written opinions. Hearing a Justice read his own words could be dramatic, especially if he deviated from the text and extemporized. Spoken dissents could sound harsh. A clerk to Justice Holmes, who was unflinching in his dissents, recalled his tone in a 1928 case: "I sat in the courtroom and heard the old man read his dissent. His words and voice and manner were disdainful. It seemed as though he were obliged to hold something unpleasant in his hands."

Yet the practice of delivering decisions orally took up a lot of Courtroom time. The announcements were often perfunctory, dull even, and the Courtroom half-empty. Justice Douglas noted that the ritual was controversial from the day he took his seat on the bench in 1939:

> Opinions were announced on Mondays; and when I first took my seat it was customary to read the opinions in some detail. One week we read opinions all of Monday and all of Tuesday and part of Wednesday before we finished. It seemed to some of us that this was a needless expenditure of time and that reading opinions should be abandoned. [Justice Hugo L.] Black and I proposed that the Chief Justice simply announce the result in each case—who wrote for the Court, who concurred, who dissented, and so on—and of course at that time all opinions would be released to the press and to interested members of the bar. That aroused Felix Frankfurter's vehement opposition. He maintained that the oral announcements put the public on a wavelength with the Justices and gave them a better idea what kind of persons the Justices were. The arguments on this were long and passionate, and a majority took Frankfurter's view.
>
> But the factor of time weighed heavily on us; besides, the oral announcements often had little relevancy to the written opinion. For example, one day [Justice James C.] McReynolds, who had written a rather prosaic dissent [in 1935], announced it with heat and vigor. Hitting the bench with his fist, he shouted, "The Constitution is gone!" and proceeded to explain why he felt so. But none of that was in the written dissent. All of us, I suppose, deviated at times from the text. Once Frankfurter, speaking for the Court, ad-libbed at length, giving reasons for the decision that had no resemblance to the opinion. As we walked out, Harlan Fiske Stone said, "By God, Felix, if you had put all that stuff in the opinion, never in my life would I have agreed to it."
>
> These excesses had a long-range effect. As the years passed, the announcements became more and more summary.

Others maintained a more favorable view of the practice. A Court-watcher in the 1950s praised the ritual:

> This is a remarkable proceeding; a busy institution interrupts pressing work in order to tell a handful of persons in the courtroom what everyone else in the country necessarily learns by reading. On opinion days, which during the regular term are commonly three Mondays in each month, from thirty minutes to four hours may sometimes be taken in making these announcements. In the extreme case this means that as much as twenty percent of the courtroom time for a week may go into these statements, all of which would be as effective if the Justices simply handed them to the official reporter.
>
> Nonetheless, this ceremony is deeply gratifying to those who see it. Clearly it is expendable but in the various adjustments to the pressures of

time, it should be among the last to go. The tradition of announcing opinions orally is old, and while the announcements are sometimes a bore when a case is not particularly interesting or the opinion is poorly announced, they are sometimes lively and exciting. The Justices themselves sometimes control tedium by giving extremely short statements with some verve. Variances between the oral statements and the written statements occasionally provide color, although the variations are of no practical importance.

But as opinions grew lengthier in the twentieth century, patience was tested. At the end of the 1963 Term, for example, William O. Douglas grew weary of listening to Tom C. Clark recite his extensive Court opinion in a case that questioned whether state-sanctioned Bible reading should be permitted in public schools. To let off steam, Douglas passed a note to Black that read: "Is he going to read all of it? He told me he was only going to say a few words—he is on p. 20 now—58 more to go. Perhaps we need an antifilibuster rule as badly as some say the Senate does."

In 1971 Chief Justice Warren Burger persuaded the brethren to abandon the time-consuming practice of reading their full opinions (including footnotes) in open Court. Since then, the Justices have simply announced the result after a brief summary—except in major rulings. Many Courtwatchers still pay close attention when opinions are handed down, hoping a Justice will ad-lib or throw in a phrase with a bit of color or humor. Joan Biskupic, a reporter who currently covers the Supreme Court, admits she makes a point of being in the Courtroom to witness the announcements:

> I personally do go up and want to hear the opinion announced from the bench. I like the pageantry of that. I like to hear the justice himself or herself announce what's in the opinion and also to potentially hear a dissenting justice explain why he or she does not like that majority opinion. Then I race down the stairs to the Court press area where we all have our laptops set up. I write a first version of that story so it can go on our Internet site.

A few Justices, notably Hugo L. Black and John Marshall Harlan, opposed eliminating the tradition of reading opinions in full voice— especially dissents. Just before he stepped down in 1971, Harlan urged his colleague Potter Stewart to keep the custom alive. According to John Paul Stevens, who joined the Court a few terms later: "Potter [Stewart] . . . is the Justice who told me that John Harlan had asked him to make sure to preserve the tradition of making at least one oral announcement of a dissenting opinion each Term." Stewart evidently chose to carry out Harlan's request. In the 1978 Term a newspaper reporter recorded this Courtroom scene:

> In recent years, dissenters only infrequently have given opinions from the bench. Yesterday, however, Potter Stewart read aloud almost a five-page

dissent. . . . Chief Justice Warren E. Burger, one of the majority, was at Stewart's right as the dissenter spoke in a strong, controlled voice. As one cutting phrase tumbled on another, Burger's face reddened. Other Justices also appeared to be uncomfortable. The tension struck observers as almost palpable.

Anthony Lewis, who covered the Supreme Court for the *New York Times* from 1969 to 2001, chronicled an even more highly charged episode in 1958 involving Justice Felix Frankfurter, who had a habit of extemporizing at length in his oral dissents. Only a reporter sitting in the Courtroom that day could have recorded such a rebuke: other spectators are not permitted to take notes. The case involved a prisoner on death row whose lawyers claimed that he was insane and therefore could not be executed under California law. He disagreed with the assessment of a state-appointed psychiatrist—who found him sane—and demanded the right to be diagnosed by a psychiatrist of his choosing. The Supreme Court rejected his claim. Lewis recalls:

> Chief Justice [Earl] Warren announced the decision in a few sentences on opinion day. Justice Frankfurter had filed a brief dissent. But in the courtroom that day he went way beyond the printed version and spoke passionately about the unfairness—the inhumanity—of executing someone on the basis of a mental finding by the prosecution's doctor. When he finally finished, Chief Justice Warren told the courtroom that what they had just heard was not in Frankfurter's formal dissent. Warren [formerly the governor of California] added, with feeling, that California's criminal justice system was not as brutal as Frankfurter's words made it seem. "Neither the judgment of this court nor that of California is quite as savage as this dissent would indicate," said Warren.

Nowadays, Justices extemporize in dissents fairly often to call attention to majority opinions they feel are particularly wrong-headed.

If modern Justices and advocates no longer pander to the audience as some may have in the nineteenth century, spectators in the Courtroom are still treated to a show. As recently as the 1960s, society women continued to enjoy attending arguments. Justice Hugo L. Black's wife, Elizabeth, recounted a typical outing:

> I took two friends into the Court to hear the Connecticut Contraceptive case [*Griswold v. Connecticut*, (1965)]. When we arrived, they were arguing the case where a man named Brown had been elected an officer of a labor union and was an admitted member of the Communist Party. The Solicitor General, Archibald Cox, argued it, and afterward his wife, Phyllis, went to lunch with us. She said Archie has three nightmares: (1) he would be late to Court; (2) he would forget his argument in the middle; and (3) he would look down someday and discover he was in his BVD's with no pants on! When Phyllis

went back to Court, Archie told her he had had a hassle with Justice Black. We had heard Hugo question him keenly on several points.

The Contraceptive case started at about 1:00, and Ethel and Joan Kennedy came in and sat next to us. Thomas Emerson, a professor at Yale Law School, opened the arguments. The bench, already lively, really came to life, leaning forward, all asking questions 'til the poor man said he had tried to reach their points but couldn't.

Yet modern Courtwatchers increasingly find it difficult to snag a seat to witness a particularly exciting case being argued. When the Court heard arguments on the impeachment of President Richard Nixon in 1974, for example, a seat in the small (192-seat) Courtroom was the hottest ticket in the world. The Court's Public Information Office had the impossible job of deciding how to allot seating between the Justices (for friends and family), members of the Supreme Court bar, and Congress and the Senate—all the while keeping some seats set aside for the walk-in public, a long-standing custom. According to Barrett McGurn, who was the Public Information Officer at the time, there were only nineteen regular seats for the press (including sketch artists and foreign press), but staff managed to remove "a dozen or so comfortable upholstered chairs" and squeeze in eighty folding ones, "quadrupling the media's usual allotment." More than 1,500 people attended at least part of the argument. A proposal to pipe in the hearings to adjacent large conference rooms was rejected by the Court. McGurn explained, "The Supreme Court, regardless of what the ladies of the early nineteenth century might have thought . . . is not a theater. Its hearings occur inside the Courtroom and nowhere else, neither on TV nor radio nor in other rooms of the Court building."

Nowadays live audio is piped into the Lawyer's Lounge for the benefit of members of the Supreme Court bar during important cases when space is at a premium. Oral arguments are also routinely audiotaped and the recordings made available to the public. But cameras are still forbidden. The debate over whether to permit cameras in the Courtroom has intensified in recent years. Most of the Justices have raised specific objections to the prospect of televising oral arguments. Justice Antonin Scalia views it this way:

I wouldn't mind having the proceedings of the court, not just audioed, but televised, if I thought it would only go out on a channel that everyone would watch gavel-to-gavel. But if you send it out on C-SPAN, what will happen is, for every one person who sees it . . . gavel-to-gavel . . . 10,000 will see 15-second takeouts on the network news, which I guarantee you will be uncharacteristic of what the Court does. . . . So, I have come to the conclusion that it will misinform the public rather than inform the public to have our proceedings televised. They want "man bites dog" stories. They don't want people to watch what the Supreme Court does over the course of a whole hour of argument. People aren't going to do that.

Justice Anthony Kennedy offered a different objection when he testified on the subject before the House Appropriations Committee in 2007:

> The discussions that the Justices have with the attorneys during oral arguments is a splendid dynamic. If you introduce cameras it is human nature for me to suspect that one of my colleagues is saying something for a soundbite. Please don't introduce that insidious dynamic into what is now a collegial Court. Our Court works. . . . We teach, by having no cameras, that we are different. We are judged by what we write. We are judged over a much longer term.

Yet Courtwatchers always emphasize how the experience of being in the Courtroom is irreplaceable. Even reporters whose job it is to cover the Supreme Court day in and day out are not immune to its spell. In the words of seasoned reporter Lyle Denniston:

> The aura of the place is always present. If you go into that room, it doesn't make any difference how badly the lawyer is doing . . . there is something about the feel of the place that tells you that something important is going on here. And to my mind, it's very much different from watching, let's say, a debate on the House and Senate, where you realize that what may be going on on the floor in any given moment really doesn't have anything to do with the legislative process. . . . Everything that goes on in the Supreme Court is related to something important, and it's a part of a process that is working from beginning to end and will result in a subsequent outcome. It's all meaningful.

And veterans like Denniston always know when they are witnessing something particularly historic: "When you go in for a big case, what we in the press think of as a big case, one with high visibility, where the stakes are really large, where you can feel the tectonic plates of the Constitution potentially beginning to shift . . . you would be brutish if you didn't have a high level of sensitivity to the importance of that moment."

8

⚖️

Silver Tongues and Quill Pens

Oral Argument

Every lawyer who has argued a case before the Justices has a story to tell. In this unusual recent account, the advocate was representing pro bono a democratic activist who had fled Cameroon fearing for his life and was now contesting a deportation order from the U.S. government. She had had only eight weeks to prepare his emergency appeal:

> After I took my place at the podium, I could hear the Court fill with specta-
> tors behind me. My heart started to beat faster, but I tried not to turn around.
> When the Justices walked in, they sat just five feet away. I felt starstruck, but
> they smiled at everyone. I read one sentence from my notes, but after that I
> found myself just talking to them as if they were interested colleagues. They
> interrupted with rapid-fire questions, but it actually felt like the ten of us
> were figuring out the answer to a puzzle. I kept telling myself that if I could
> convince the Justices I was right, I could potentially save a man's life.

Although the Marshall Court era is considered the golden age of Supreme Court advocacy when the likes of William Wirt and Daniel Webster extemporized for days on end (see chapter 2), gifted orators with
silver tongues have addressed the bench in every term. In the post–Civil
War era, transportation and accommodations were too expensive for
provincial attorneys to bring their cases from regional appellate courts
to Washington. Instead, most of the advocates hired to argue Supreme
Court cases were U.S. Senators who lived in Washington during Congressional sessions. (To argue before the Court one must first be admitted
to the Supreme Court bar, on motion of two current bar members who

swear that the applicant has been a member in good standing of the bar of the highest court in their state for at least three years.)

Justice Samuel F. Miller's praise for Matthew Carpenter, a Senator from Wisconsin, was typical of the accolades heaped on the best advocates of the late nineteenth century:

> He was beyond any one whom I have known—in fact he is the only man whom I recall, to whom I would apply the old fashioned phrase—"a man of genius." Take his will, his manner, his command of language and his skill in argument. I think he is the foremost orator of his day. As a lawyer, he stood in the front rank deservedly. This was founded on all the elements which go to make up a great lawyer. In addition to his eloquence, his logic was close, his judgment sound, and his perception of the legal principles involved in a case both quick and accurate. With all this he spent as much labor on the case which he argued as if he had just entered the profession. . . . He delighted in the dress and swagger of the bar room. In his loftiest flight of eloquence, or closest train of logic, if a funny ridiculous illustration struck him he would have it out then without regard to its fitness. He had the finest private library both legal and miscellaneous, of any man west of the Allegheny Mountains and he was familiar with its contents.

Texas lawyer William Pitt Ballinger (Justice Miller's brother-in-law) had a similarly high opinion of Carpenter according to an entry he scrawled in his diary after watching the Senator argue a case in 1877. Apparently the fact that Carpenter was drunk did not diminish his performance: "Carpenter concluded, occupying about an hour and a half in a most lawyerlike speech delivered in an admirable manner—He struggled on the wrong side apparently and against the strong prepossession of the court but did it to the best advantage—I admire him extremely—Looks to be full of liquor though."

Late-nineteenth-century oral advocates continued the tradition of theatrical performances of the Marshall and Taney Court eras. They, too, relished arguing in front of full houses. Former Attorney General Jeremiah S. Black, a frequent and colorful advocate in the 1860s and 1870s, even tried to manipulate the docket so as to ensure a robust audience. Samuel W. Pennypacker, who made a living writing up his own reports of Supreme Court cases, said that Justice Miller once told him that the Court let Black get away with this vanity:

> Black, as a man, was simply abominable, but there was no one who appeared before the court to whom it was so agreeable to listen. In hearing him you felt that you did not care a damn whether he was talking about his case or about any other case but there was a wealth of illustration, a knowledge of the Bible and of Shakespeare wrought into his arguments which made you feel that you would like him to go on forever. . . . He never was a sound lawyer. When

he first came down to Washington, he had only been in the habit of getting ten and fifteen dollar fees, but he soon found that he could get almost any sum and he afterwards charged enormous fees.

Toward the latter part of the time he used to argue for the listeners and pay less attention to the law and would maneuver so as to postpone his cases until there were hearers. We humored him, more or less, in the matter.

Attorney Walter H. Smith made regular appearances in the Courtroom in the 1870s and 1880s. He evaluated the performance quality of his competitors:

When [Jeremiah S. Black] was to speak he always chose a spot nearest to where the great South Carolinian, John C. Calhoun, occupied a seat when a member of the Senate, while Reverdy Johnson's favorite position when addressing the court was where it was said [Daniel] Webster stood. . . . In all his arguments Black quoted freely from Shakespeare and the Bible . . . Black was rather tall of figure, and . . . his hair was always black and shiny. He had a round, full voice, speaking, it was said, as if he had "mush in his mouth." . . . [Benjamin] Curtis had the sweetest voice I ever heard in a public speaker. It was so musical and the diction was so clear that he could make the driest legal argument a delight to hear. [Reverdy] Johnson's voice was full, like Black, but his annunciation was much more distinct.

In the early nineteenth century the Justices heard arguments from roughly eleven to five. They would break up the tedium of day-long sessions by retiring behind the curtain to eat lunch—while oratory continued. According to a Court staffer, one advocate told him that at times this practice made it difficult to ascertain if there was a quorum present:

There was a space back of the Bench wide enough to accommodate small tables on which the messengers of the Justices would serve them luncheon from the kitchen of the Senate Restaurant. As not more than two Justices usually took luncheon at the same time, there would always be a quorum on the Bench. While the partition between the rear of the Bench and the space in which the luncheon tables stood . . . prevented the audience in the Court Room from seeing what was going on behind the screen, the rattle of the knives and forks, and sometimes the directions of the Justices to their messengers could be heard very distinctly.

The Judicial Code requires at least six members to constitute a quorum. Shortly before my appearance on the scene [in 1902] a case was being argued before only seven Justices, as inclement weather had kept two of them at home. During the argument two of the Justices retired behind the screen for luncheon. Mr. Frank Hackett, who told me the story himself, stopped his argument. Asked by the Chief Justice to proceed, he said:

"If it please your Honor, there does not seem to be a quorum of the Court present."

To this the Chief Justice returned: "Although you may not see them, Mr. Hackett, there are two Justices present who can hear the argument, and you may proceed."

Faced with a burgeoning workload, in 1849 the Court began to require written briefs and ordered that no counsel should be permitted to speak for more than two hours (with two counsel allowed per side this meant eight hours total per case). As the Justices became more familiar with each case before hearing it argued, they would ask the advocates questions during arguments. In 1871, the Court again cut down argument time to two hours total per side. With shorter time allotted to each case, the Justices questioned advocates more aggressively in order to get straight to the essentials.

Despite these measures, by 1880 the Supreme Court had developed a crushing backlog of cases with more than three years passing between the time a case was accepted for review and the date it was argued. The problem was that before the creation of circuit courts in 1891 the Court was obliged to hear every case on appeal involving a federal question. Not surprisingly, when one advocate, former Attorney General Augustus Garland, asked for a case to be reheard, he found himself mercilessly rebuffed by the overworked Justices:

I arose and offered to present a motion for a rehearing of the case, and was about to proceed to make a few "brief remarks" when Justice [Joseph P.] Bradley started as if powder had exploded under his seat, and with much spirit said: "What is that?" I repeated what I was seeking to do, and then he turned somewhat pale and remonstrated with much spirit, and told how hard the court labored at cases—how closely the judges consulted—how wearied they were with these applications for rehearing after all their intense work to arrive at conclusions—how the [British] House of Lords disposed of such things, and growing warmer and warmer, how inappropriate it was in lawyers to be asking the Court to travel over all this work again, and many other things not well remembered, as my mind just at these utterances was not as clear as the often alluded to noonday sun. What astonished me more was that Justice Bradley had not delivered the opinion of the Court, but Justice [Samuel] Miller had, and as I thought the storm was lulling and almost lulled, Justice Miller with his usual scratch over his right ear, when he was getting ready to charge, came to Justice Bradley's aid, and really it occurred to me it was superfluous as Justice Bradley then needed no aid;—he was not the suffering one;—then Justice [Stephen] Field, with more moderation gave me a lecture upon the error of such a course. . . . I looked in vain for a friend at Court. The Chief Justice [Melville Fuller] looked as if he would say something consoling to me—sympathetic as it were, but he had not been there very long and probably he did not wish to appear too [precious], and he did not say it. I thought, too, Justice [John Marshall] Harlan once looked like he would help me, but he fell back and sent out a note to someone else. I fought nobly I thought, but it was uphill and against decided odds, and I was somewhat routed and driven back almost in dismay, and the lawyers present did enjoy it;—it did them good as it always does, notwithstanding their so-called clannishness, to see the Court pounce down upon and shake up a brother lawyer.

Garland further complained that the clogged condition of the docket was causing the impatient Justices to jump in with questions so as to get to the crux of the matter more quickly:

> Very often I have seen lawyers high up in their profession, but not used to the ways and manners of this court in this respect, frightened, so to speak, out of their wits into forgetfulness of the entire case, when suddenly pulled up by the court to know this or that before they had time to tell anything of it, and when they were getting ready to tell it.

Not long after chronicling these incidents, Garland "was stricken with apoplexy" while arguing a case and "died within ten minutes"—inside the Courtroom.

Even after legislation enabled them to gain better control of the docket, the Justices continued to strategize over how to reduce argument time in order to expedite cases. While serving as Reporter of Decisions at the Supreme Court from 1902 to 1916, Charles Henry Butler heard them express conflicting views on this issue:

> In respect to time allowed for argument, there has also been a great modification of the rules. Based on their own remarks, made in my hearing, Chief Justice [Melville W.] Fuller and Justices [John Marshall] Harlan and [David J.] Brewer considered that counsel should have ample time to present the cases of their clients and constantly opposed any effort to limit them.
>
> Mr. Justice [Oliver Wendell] Holmes was all for cutting the time down, and more than once told me that he was never influenced by oral arguments, but considered the cases wholly on the briefs. In nearly every case counsel were allowed two hours a side, which, if availed of, would take a full day for each case. Frequently extra time was given. In some of the anti-trust cases, such as those involving the United States Steel Company, the Standard Oil Company, and the International Harvester Company, each case was allowed six hours. Thus a single case occupied three entire days.
>
> The two-hours a side Court rule applied to cases that came up on writ of error or appeal based on a Federal question being involved. To these cases the full time was permitted, even if the writs or the appeals were founded on very doubtful grounds. So long as the cases could not be affirmed or dismissed on motion for lack of Federal question, no matter how ephemeral the basis might be, full time had to be granted if counsel so desired, as counsel generally did.

In the 1920s the Court decided to divide cases into "regular"—allotted one hour and two counsel per side—and "summary"—allotted only one-half hour and only one counsel per side. This speeded things up, but apparently not enough. In 1933 a young lawyer named Erwin Griswold was working in the Office of the Solicitor General, the section of the Justice Department responsible for arguing the government's cases before the high court. Griswold (who later was appointed Solicitor General) reported that Chief Justice Hughes, trying to save time, occasionally did not permit the respondent's side of the case to be argued because the case was insubstantial or because he knew that the Justices had already made up their minds. But in one such case the attorney denied his argument time apparently would not give up so easily:

> In all cases before the Court, each side was allotted an hour for oral argument. Some cases took the full time, while others used less time, sometimes considerably less. In some cases, after the petitioner or appellant had finished argument, the Chief Justice, after a quick glance at his fellow judges, would say, "The Court does not care to hear further argument," This, meant of course, that the "bottom side"—the respondent or appellee—had won the case.
>
> In one case which I heard, Chief Justice Hughes said that "The Court does not care to hear further argument." Nevertheless, counsel for the respondent arose and started to address the Court. The Chief Justice repeated his statement, in a stronger voice. Respondent's counsel continued his argument. In a very loud voice, apparently having understood the Chief Justice to say that he should speak louder. At this point the Chief Justice turned to the already defeated counsel for the petitioner, and said: "Won't you please tell counsel that the Court does not care to hear further argument." Counsel for the petitioner rose, turned to counsel for the respondent, and said, in a loud, clear voice, "They say they would rather give you the case than listen to you."

In 1970, with his brethren's consent, Chief Justice Warren Burger further limited argument time to thirty minutes per side (eliminating the summary docket). It has always been the discretion of the Chief Justice to determine how tightly to set the parameters for oral arguments. Drew Days III, who served as Solicitor General in the 1990s, has noted that some Chief Justices have been more of a stickler for time limits than others:

> I remember . . . there was the different rhythm of oral arguments when Chief Justice [Warren] Burger headed the Court. They were fairly relaxed. One had the full 30 minutes. Justices held off on the questioning for a while, at least let you get in maybe five or so minutes of your argument and then the questions began to fly. When I argued under Chief Justice [William H.] Rehnquist's tenure, the rhythm was quite different. He ran it in a military way, where you got thirty minutes. When you get to the end of your time, if you were

The nature of oral argument has changed considerably since the Court's inception as the time allotted to each side has shrunk from unlimited to thirty minutes. The contemporary Court usually barrages advocates with questions to get at the crux of the question as quickly as possible. This is a sketch of the bench in 2006, composed of Stephen G. Breyer, Clarence Thomas, Anthony Kennedy, John Paul Stevens, John G. Roberts, Jr., Antonin Scalia, David Souter, Ruth Bader Ginsburg, and Samuel Alito. (Artwork by Wm. Hennessy, CourtroomArt.com)

mid-syllable, he would say, "Thank you, General Days," and that was the end of the story. I had to get accustomed to that difference in rhythm. Now, under Chief Justice [John G.] Roberts, we are back to a more relaxed sense in the Court, I think largely because Chief Justice Roberts was an advocate before the Court a number of times. I think to the extent that he is allowed, he identifies with those who are standing up and arguing cases, and thinks that maybe they should be allowed to finish their sentences before they are told to sit down.

As the time allotted for oral argument shortened, counsel's carefully memorized speeches repeating facts and arguments already found in the briefs were no longer viable. Members of the Supreme Court bar had a hard time adjusting to this new reality in the early twentieth century. In 1928 former Associate Justice Charles Evans Hughes felt obliged to defend the Justices' interruptions by explaining that asking questions was a valuable way for them "to be able more quickly to separate the wheat from the chaff" in deciding cases:

> The judges of the Supreme Court are quite free in addressing questions to counsel during argument. The Bar is divided as to the wisdom of this practice in courts of last resort. Some think that as a rule that the court will get at the case more quickly if counsel are permitted to present it in their own way. Well-prepared and experienced counsel, however, do not object to inquiries from the bench, if the time allowed for argument is not unduly curtailed, as they would much prefer to have the opportunity of knowing the difficulties in the minds of the court and of attempting to meet them rather than to have them concealed and presented in conference when counsel are not present. They prefer an open attack to a masked battery. From the standpoint of the bench, the desirability of questions is quite obvious as the judges are not there to listen to speeches but to decide the case. They have an irrepressible desire for immediate knowledge as to the points to be determined.

Gifted advocates armed with useful information continued, however, to hold the Supreme Court's attention and manage to get in a full argument without much interruption. For instance, when attorney Louis D. Brandeis argued a case in 1914, a Courtroom spectator said the Justices were riveted:

> I have just heard Mr. Brandeis make one of the greatest arguments I have ever listened to. . . . When [he] began to speak, the Court showed all the inertia and elemental hostility which courts cherish for a new thought, or a new right, or even a new remedy for an old wrong, but he visibly lifted all this burden, and without orationizing or chewing of the rag he reached them all and held even [Justice Mahlon] Pitney.

Weaker advocates often simply ignored questions from the bench and plowed ahead with their prepared speeches. When Brandeis became a Justice in 1916, one of his law clerks noted that he particularly frowned upon counsel who dodged questions:

> No skill[ed advocate] can, or should try to, avoid questions here. Whether at this point or earlier, however, a question means a puzzled mind which will not be listening until its problem is settled. So it should be answered at once, not postponed. "Never say," . . . Justice [Brandeis] would admonish, "Your Honor, I am coming to that in a moment." One will have lost the attention of the questioner until his problem has been met. Furthermore, pert and overconfident answers seemed to him to suggest lack of candor on the part of counsel or lack of intelligence on the part of the questioner. In every case worthy of the Court's attention, lurk difficult questions for both sides. These should be dealt with seriously for what they are, either questions arising out of the technical complexities of the subject matter, and, hence, subject to

explanation, or the question demanding decision—or close to it—and, hence, requiring persuasion. In neither case does cockiness help.

Years ago a gifted Solicitor General, now a judge, demonstrated his mastery of this branch of advocacy. Interrupted by a deeply disturbing question, he paused to give his full mind to the problem, then said, "Ah, your Honor, how often I have asked myself that question; and more and more seek its answer along this way." From then on counsel and Justice joined in a common search for truth and light.

Some Justices have proven more unnerving than others in their manner of posing questions. Felix Frankfurter (1939–1962), a former law professor known for treating lawyers—and sometimes fellow Justices—as if they were his students, was notorious for his curveballs. He could throw inexperienced advocates so off track in their arguments that they could not get out a full statement about the case. Frankfurter once interrupted ninety-three times during 120 minutes of oral argument, prompting his rival, Justice William O. Douglas, to come repeatedly to the aid of the hapless advocate. Annoyed, Frankfurter snapped: "I thought *you* were arguing this case?" "I am," replied the attorney, "but I can use all the help I can get." Even someone as experienced as Solicitor General Francis Biddle feared Frankfurter's questions. Biddle recalled his experience in the 1940 Term:

> on the average I argued a case every two weeks. I had to work through long evenings to master the records. To be ready to answer Mr. Justice Frankfurter's questions—he had the ability to swallow records like oysters. . . . [He] liked to pick out some obscure morsel not referred to in the briefs—which became horribly relevant if the Solicitor General missed it—darting down into the record apparently at random and pulling out and holding up a telling bit. A suspended and involuted question would then emerge, as if Henry James had been dictating *The Wings of a Dove* to a new amanuensis. Do you see what I mean, Mr. Solicitor? The answer need not be simple, he seemed to indicate, sitting back to watch the government lawyer's reaction.

Not surprisingly, there have been several fainting episodes. In the nineteenth century a father and son both lost consciousness on separate occasions, perhaps indicating that the cause was less intimidation by the Justices than a particular genetic disposition. Senator Thomas Ewing of Ohio collapsed in mid-argument before the bench in 1869; his son, General Thomas Ewing, fainted before a different set of Justices twenty-five years later. A reporter in the Courtroom made the family connection:

> An extraordinary coincidence that was brought to the mind of one of the ancient Supreme Court employees, and that was amply verified in the course of the day, was the fact that about [twenty-five] years ago, Hon. Thomas

Ewing, father of Gen. Ewing, who was twice a United States Senator from Ohio, Secretary of the Treasury under President Taylor, had precisely such a mishap, affecting him in a very similar way, and under exactly the same conditions. While making an argument before the Supreme Court he fell faint to the floor, in about three feet of the spot where his son sunk on the carpet yesterday.

In 1935 Solicitor General Stanley F. Reed famously fainted while arguing for a key piece of New Deal legislation in front of an unsympathetic Court. The *New York Times* reported, "Reed faltered this afternoon and sat down, physically unable to continue. His collapse as he defended the Bankhead [Cotton Control Law] was in the midst of a barrage of technical questions from the nine judges." But Reed got back in the saddle quickly and was able to persuade the Court to uphold other New Deal initiatives in a manner so impressive that President Franklin D. Roosevelt appointed him to the Supreme Court in 1938. Another hapless advocate who fainted after "very searching" questioning from the bench in the 1950s was also able to redeem himself. Justice Douglas recounted the dramatic incident:

The critical document [in the case] was an affidavit; and I asked the attorney, "Who prepared this affidavit?" He instantly fainted, falling to the floor and hitting his head against a table as he went down. Chief Justice Stone recessed the Court while attendants and a doctor administered to the stricken lawyer. In due course the Court reconvened, and the lawyer, now recovered, though a bit shaky, turned to me and said, "In answer to your question, I drafted the affidavit." I admired him for his frankness and his guts.

Rattled advocates can provide opportunities for humor from the bench. For instance, when a government lawyer realized he had confused Justice David Souter with Justice Antonin Scalia during a 2005 argument, he quickly apologized. "Thank you," replied the self-effacing Souter, "but apologize to him." But when advocates themselves try to dispel tension with humor, their attempts have usually failed. It is considered smarter to be the straight man and let the Justices make the jokes. During a 1995 argument on the issue of whether schools can require athletes to submit urine samples for drug testing, however, the subject matter made it practically impossible for counsel to avoid a wisecrack. According to a *Washington Post* reporter who was in the Courtroom:

Justice Stephen G. Breyer said he did not see why providing a urine sample to a school official was so intrusive since urination is a fact of life. It "isn't really a tremendously private thing," he said. Thomas M. Christ, representing the Oregon student [the plaintiff], conceded that everyone urinates. Then the advocate, who was under heavy questioning, added, "In fact, I might do so here."[*No laughter*]

For most of the twentieth century the quality of oral argument was uneven. Attorneys who specialized in specific areas of the law—taxes, bankruptcy, patents—tended to be consistently useful to the Justices in their presentations. Government attorneys from the Office of the Solicitor General almost always excelled. Robert H. Jackson, appointed Solicitor General in 1938, was so good that Justice Brandeis declared he should be made Solicitor General for life. But often counsel was an attorney who had shepherded the case from the trial level and would appear before the Justices only once in a lifetime. These attorneys—often first-rate in their own specialties but inexperienced in federal appellate litigation—occasionally faltered, finding themselves unable to answer direct questions posed by the Justices. A clerk to Chief Justice Earl Warren in the 1961 Term eavesdropped on a conversation involving a particularly lackluster advocate who clearly didn't understand how oral argument worked:

> My principle recollection of Justice [Hugo L.] Black turns on a case heard during our Term involving the zoning regulations in the town of Hempstead, New York. The operator of a gravel pit claimed that the regulations effectively expropriated his property and, therefore, was "unconstitutional." During oral argument in the case, Justice Black had asked counsel to identify the provision of the Constitution on which he rested his claim. He replied with some consternation "Why? The entire Constitution." While we later both stood in line to buy lunch in the Court cafeteria, I overheard the lawyer tell a companion, "Can you imagine that? After all these years on the Court, Justice Black was asking me on what provision of the Constitution we relied!"

Yet, according to a clerk in the 1934 Term, Harlan Fiske Stone, for one, was forgiving of novices:

> [Stone] was persistently bitter at the incompetence of many of the lawyers who appeared before him. Not the unknown attorney from a distant town whom the chances of litigation had brought before the Court, but the richly paid or highly honored attorney who Stone thought should do better than he did. He bewailed, in one case of monetary substance, that the successful attorney would be paid at least $50,000 for winning the case on a ground which had never occurred to him. . . . When he praised an argument, as he often did, it was invariably the work of a very young man.

In 1951 Justice Robert H. Jackson nonetheless advised first-timers not to confess their inexperience . . . and not to grovel:

> On your first appearance before the Court, do not waste your time, or ours, telling us so. We are likely to discover for ourselves that you are a novice but will think none the less of you for it. Every famous lawyer had his first day

at our bar and perhaps a sad one. It is not ingratiating to tell us you think it is an overwhelming honor to appear, for we think of the case as the important thing before us, not the counsel. . . . Be respectful, of course, but also be self-respectful, and neither disparage yourself nor flatter the Justices. We think well enough of ourselves already.

Justices like Jackson who have argued cases before the Supreme Court earlier in their careers are presumably more understanding about how nerve-wracking oral advocacy can be. Justice Ruth Bader Ginsburg was barely able to master her jitters when she presented her first case in 1972:

> The first time I argued a case here I didn't have lunch . . . because I didn't know whether I could keep it down. I was initially terribly nervous, and after about two minutes into the argument I looked up at these guys and said, "I have a captive audience. They have no place to go for the next half hour. They must listen to me."

She proceeded to argue five more sex-discrimination cases before being appointed to the Court in 1993. Chief Justice John G. Roberts, Jr., who argued in the Supreme Court a remarkable thirty-nine times before his own appointment in 2005, has confessed that fear is not just for novices: "I was very nervous [my first time]. But I was very nervous when I did my last oral argument as well. I think if you are a lawyer appearing before the Supreme Court and you are not very nervous you don't really understand what is going on." Roberts's extensive experience has allowed him to weigh in on what it's like to be on either side of the bench. "It's a lot easier to ask questions than answer them," he admits.

Sitting on the high bench for more than thirty years, William H. Rehnquist (1972–2005) witnessed thousands of arguments, dismissing many advocates as mediocre. He praised the best ones, whom he termed "All-Americans," but categorized weak attorneys according to their unhelpful style of advocacy:

> The first is the lector, and he does just what his name implies: He reads his argument. The worst case of the lector is the lawyer who actually reads the brief itself; this behavior is so egregious that it is rarely seen. But milder cases read paraphrases of the brief, although they train themselves to look up from their script occasionally to meet the judges' eyes. Questions from the judges, instead of being used as an opportunity to advance one's own arguments by response, are looked upon as an interruption in the advocate's delivery of his "speech," and the lawyer after answering the question returns to the printed page at exactly where he left off; returns, one often feels, with the phrase "as I was saying" implied if not expressed. One feels on occasion that at the conclusion of his argument the lector will say, "Thus endeth the lesson for today."

The lector is very seldom a good oral advocate. It would be foolish for a lawyer to stand before an appellate court with *nothing* written out to guide his presentation, but the use of notes for reference conveys a far different effect from the reading of a series of typed pages. The ultimate purpose of oral argument, from the point of view of the advocate, is to work his way into the judge's consciousness and make the judge think about the things that the advocate wishes him to think about. One of the best ways to begin this process is to establish eye contact with as many of the judges as possible, and this simply can't be done while you are reading your presentation.

An oral advocate should welcome questions from the bench, because a question shows that at least one judge is inviting him to say what he thinks about a particular aspect of the case. A question also has the valuable psychological effect of bringing a second voice into the performance, so that the minds of judges, which may have momentarily strayed from the lawyer's presentation, are brought back simply by this different sound. But the lector is apt to receive fewer questions than a better advocate just because he seems less willing than other lawyers to take the trouble to carefully answer the questions. When he has finished reading a presentation to the Court, all he has done is to state a logical and reasoned basis for the position he has taken on behalf of his client before the Court; but this much should have been accomplished in his briefs. If oral argument provides nothing more than a summary of the brief in monologue, it is of very little value to the Court.

A second "species" of advocate Rehnquist called "the debating champion":

He has an excellent grasp of his theory of the case and the arguments supporting it, and with the aid of a few notes and memorization can depart from the printed page at will. But he is so full of his subject, and so desirous of demonstrating this to others, that he doesn't listen carefully to questions. He is the authority, and every question from the bench is presumed to call for one of several stock answers, none of which may be particularly helpful to the inquiring judge. He pulls out all the stops, welcomes questions, and exudes confidence; when he has finished and sat down, one judge may turn to another and say, "Boy, he certainly knows his subject." But simply showing how well you know your subject is not the same as convincing doubters by first carefully listening to their questions and then carefully answering them.

A third type, whom Rehnquist nicknamed "Casey Jones," he considered flawed but an improvement over the others:

This lawyer has a complete grasp of his subject matter, *does* listen to questions, tries to answer them carefully, and does not read from any prepared text. He is a good oral advocate, but falls short of being a top-notch oral advocate because he forgets about the limitations of those he is trying to convince. The reason I call him Casey Jones is because he is like an engineer on a nonstop train—he will not stop to pick up passengers along the way.

He knows the complexities of his subject, and knows that if he were permitted to do so he could easily spend an hour and a half arguing this particular case without ever repeating himself. He is probably right. For this reason, in order to get as much as possible of his argument into half an hour, he speaks very rapidly, without realizing that when he is arguing before a bench of nine people, each of them will require a little time to assimilate what he is saying. If the lawyer goes nonstop throughout the thirty minutes without even a pause, except for questions, even able and well-prepared judges are going to be left behind. To become a truly first-rate oral advocate, this lawyer must simply learn to leave the secondary points to the brief, to slow down his pace of speaking, and to remember that the lawyer who makes six points, of which three are remembered by the judges, is a better lawyer than a lawyer who makes twelve points, of which only one is remembered by the judges.

Courtwatchers say the quality of oral advocacy has steadily improved since the 1980s as the number of cases the Supreme Court agrees to review has fallen from 120 in the 1980 Term to fewer than 80 in recent terms. The shrinking docket has coincided with the re-emergence of a cadre of experienced appellate lawyers who appear frequently before the Supreme Court. These specialists are usually former Supreme Court clerks or former members of the Solicitor General's staff who are prized for their familiarity with the workings of the Court. They actively try to position cases in lower courts for possible Supreme Court appeals and give strategic advice to less experienced advocates and to outside groups filing supplementary briefs. With fewer cases being argued, the competition among them has become fiercer and the prestige of being hired to present a case even greater.

Experience and intellectual agility are in high demand as oral argument has come to be completely dominated by the thrust and parry of question and answer. With a smaller docket, the Justices can devote more time to preparing for oral argument. Having completely mastered the details of the case, they come to the bench brimming with difficult questions and expect counsel to be able to answer them quickly and succinctly. In their inquiries, the Justices try to ferret out issues that counsel has omitted from the written briefs because they might weaken the case. Lengthy hypothetical questions about situations that are comparable to the one at issue, and are logical extensions of the case, pop up frequently as well. Veteran advocate Drew Days III understands why the Justices must push the parameters beyond the individual case, but has admitted that hypothetical questions can be challenging for counsel:

> One of the things the Justices do is take your argument and to move it to the next level and the next level after that, because the Court is concerned with resolving not only the case before it but thinking about how their decision

will affect similar cases or related cases down the road. What will be the impact of precedent? And so, one of the answers that is often given—though is not helpful to the Court—but you can't restrain yourself from saying, "But that's not this case." And usually one of the Justices will say, "We know that; that's why we asked the question."

During oral argument, the Justices are also having a conversation among themselves, signaling which issues interest them. Each Justice is trying to frame the conversation for the discussion that will take place later in Conference; some may be lobbying for votes. Chief Justice Roberts elucidates:

> We come to [oral argument] cold as far as knowing what everybody thinks. So through the questioning we're learning for the first time what other justices' views are of the case. And that can alter how you view it, right on the spot. If they're raising questions about an issue that you hadn't thought were important, you can start looking into that issue during the questioning a little bit. It's a very dynamic and very exciting part of the job.

The Justices also communicate indirectly with each other through questions to counsel. A contemporary advocate describes this triangular method:

> There are some questions that are real questions. Justices want to know the answer to the question, something that's been [preying] on their minds. Other times they are talking to a fellow justice through you. You are kind of a ventriloquist dummy. The Justices have already gotten to know something about their fellow Justices' views on the issue. Then there will be back and forth, and you will be pushed.

Although being spoken through and bombarded with questions makes it tougher to get through an argument, counsel appreciate that the Justices' questions ultimately help them to present their cases more effectively. To win the case for their clients, they must assist the Justices in finding the best reasoning on which to rest their judgments. As one Supreme Court specialist sees it:

> [T]hrough the modern practice of questioning counsel, the Court is able to get the substance of argument with greater speed. If a point is obvious or repetitious, the Court can move the discussion ahead without loss of time. If a point is irrelevant, it can be cut off. If weaknesses have been obscured by a mass of detail in the briefs, the Court can expose those weaknesses through questions and answers. The Court can, in short, break down problems into manageable components and focus light where it is most needed.

On rare occasions a Justice will make a comment that is more an exposition than a question. For instance, in a 2003 case dealing with the legality of modern-day cross burning by the Ku Klux Klan, Justice Clarence

Thomas, a descendant of Georgia slaves, interrupted the petitioner to emphasize how the Klan historically used lynchings of blacks to impose a reign of terror. The burning of crosses, he reminded, continues to symbolize that brutality and elicits fear. Opposing counsel recalled the reaction in the Courtroom:

> In all my life as an advocate and an observer of legal proceedings, I have never seen the mood in a courtroom change so suddenly and dramatically. The impact of Justice Thomas's remarks was palpable and physical. Justice [Stephen] Breyer, who sat next to Thomas on the bench, drew closer to him, putting an arm on his back in a gesture of collegial respect and good will. Justice [Antonin] Scalia, who sat on the opposite side of Thomas but nearly facing him (because of the curvature of the bench), seemed to viscerally connect with his fellow justice, nodding in agreement as he spoke.

Justice Thomas no longer asks questions from the bench. He says he prefers to listen:

> When I first came to the Court [in 1991], the Court was much quieter than it is now . . . I liked it that way because it left big gaps so you could actually have a conversation. I think it's hard to have a conversation when nobody is listening, when you can't complete sentences or answers. Perhaps that's a southern thing. . . . I find that coherence that you get from a conversation far more helpful than the rapid-fire questions. I don't see how you can learn a whole lot when there are fifty questions in an hour.

Thomas's bench-mate, Samuel Alito, who joined the Court in 2006 from a three-member appeals court, agrees that the current Court is extremely active. Jumping in to ask a question is not always easy, he says:

> I learned when I got here that it's a lot harder to get in a question on a bench of nine than it is on a bench of three. It had been my practice on the court of appeals to try to wait for the end of the lawyer's paragraph before interrupting with a question. And here I learned if, in a hot case, if you wait until the end of the sentence, you will never get a question in. You have to interrupt to make your voice heard.

But probing questions from the bench may be giving renewed vigor to what some Courtwatchers worried was in danger of becoming an outdated tradition. Critics perennially asked whether oral argument had outlived its usefulness. They contended that by the time a Justice has digested the written briefs, his or her mind is already made up about a case.

But the Justices have defended the relevancy of oral argument. In 1967 Justice William J. Brennan insisted: "Often my whole notion of what a case is about crystallizes at oral argument. This happens even though I read the briefs before oral argument." In 1980 Chief Justice Rehnquist affirmed that oral argument had occasionally changed his mind about a case:

> I think that in a significant minority of the cases in which I have heard oral argument, I have left the bench feeling different about the case than I did when I came on the bench. The change is seldom a full one-hundred-and-eighty-degree swing, and I find that it is most likely to occur in cases involving areas of law which I am least familiar.

Thirty years later, Antonin Scalia continues to praise the practice's utility:

> [I]t is probably quite rare, although not unheard of, that oral argument will change my mind. But it is quite common that I go in with my mind not made up. A lot of these cases are very close, and you go in on a knife's edge. Persuasive counsel can make the difference. There are things you can do with oral argument that cannot be done in a brief. You can convey the relative importance of your various points. . . . The brief cannot answer back when I write "nonsense" in the margin. [In the oral argument, though] you can ask, "Counsel, is there some reason why this point is not nonsense?" And sometimes they can tell you. So, I am a big proponent of oral argument. I think it's very important and you would be surprised how much probing can be done within half an hour—an awful lot.

Justice Stephen G. Breyer estimates that after oral argument he only changes his mind about which side should win in five to ten percent of cases. But, he says, he "think[s] differently about a case" after hearing it argued roughly one-third of the time.

The key to an effective oral argument has always been preparation. Justice Robert H. Jackson (1941–1954), whose oratorical gifts had made him a particularly effective Solicitor General, suggested rehearsing as much as possible with whoever could be pressed into service:

> [If] you have an associate, try out different approaches and thrash out every point with him. Answer the questions that occur to another mind. See what sequence of facts is most effective. Accustom yourself to the materials in different arrangements. Argue the case to yourself, your client, your secretary, your friend, and your wife if she is patient. Use every available anvil on which to hammer out your argument.

Nowadays, advocates routinely engage in formal practice sessions—called moot courts—where other attorneys and former judges stand in for the Justices and pummel them with every possible question they think might arise during argument. Counsel must be ready to change course quickly to respond to whichever issues seem important to individual Justices, as revealed by their questions. According to Justice

Alito, "The best advocates understand exactly where they want to go and have in mind alternative routes to get there. And they can evaluate based on the questions whether route A is going to work and if it isn't then they will be open to talk about route B, route C, route D. They're not rigid." Attorney Maureen Mahoney, who has argued more than twenty cases before the Court, emphasizes how much effort goes into preparing for the day of the argument:

> You have to be extremely well prepared if you are going to do well. You have to know [the case] backward and forward, inside and out, you have to know it better than anyone in the Courtroom. And you have to be able to recall it very quickly and weave it into a narrative that you are giving to the Court. . . . You can get questions from any Justice at any time and your job is to answer the questions. Most of the time that I spend preparing for argument is spent anticipating the questions and preparing answers that I think I would like to give to those questions. Sometimes that involves thinking of hundreds of questions that they might ask, even though they will probably not ask more than fifty or so [in the course of half an hour].

On the actual day of the argument, some attorneys heed this ruthless advice given by Justice Jackson in 1951:

> When the day arrives, shut out every influence that might distract your mind. An interview with an emotional client in difficulty may be upsetting. Friends who bear bad news may unintentionally disturb your poise. Hear nothing but your case, see nothing but your case, talk nothing but your case. If making an argument is not a great day in your life, don't make it: and if it is, give it everything in you.
>
> By all means leave at home the associate who feels constantly impelled to tug at your coattails, to push briefs in front of you, or to pass up unasked-for suggestions while you are speaking. These well-meant but ill-conceived offerings distract the attention of the Court, but they are even more embarrassing and confusing to counsel. The offender is an unmitigated pest, and even if he is the attorney who employed you, suppress him.

When counsel arrive at Court the morning of their argument, they traditionally gather in the Lawyer's Lounge, where the Clerk of the Court preps them before they proceed to the Courtroom. The Clerk gives practical pointers, tries to put everyone at ease, and introduces opposing counsel if they don't already know each other. When they get to their counsel tables (only a few feet from the Justices' bench) they find two quill pens—a memento from the Court and a reminder of the distinguished tradition of the art which they are about to practice. The first words out of each advocate's mouth are: "Mr. Chief Justice and May it Please the Court . . ."

A Courtroom artist sketched oral advocate Maureen Mahoney delivering an argument before the high bench (only Justice John Paul Stevens is pictured) in 1998. Courtroom sessions are not allowed to be photographed or videotaped. (Courtesy of Dana Verkouteren)

In keeping with the theatricality of oral argument, wardrobe has always been an important element of the show. In the late nineteenth century, formal cutaways and gray pinstriped trousers became the dress code for advocates. The Marshal, the Clerk, and other Courtroom staff donned formal attire as well. Justice Horace Gray was reportedly the sartorial dictator of the Court in the 1890s; he even kept several old frock coats in a closet in case counsel showed up to argue in less formal attire. But when Charles Henry Butler was hired as Court Reporter in 1902 he noted that wardrobe standards were relaxing . . . up to a point:

> For some time after the decease of Justice [Horace] Gray, counsel continued to appear either in frock coats or cutaways. The Attorney General's office still adheres to the latter dress. Other counsel generally wear dark clothes, though very often of much shorter length than the old-time frock coat or the present cutaway. In late years, however, counsel have appeared in much lighter garb than ever was known in the olden days. In one case, counsel appeared in an olive-yellow tweed suit, tan shoes, pink shirt and no vest. He

was permitted to address the Court, however, because he came from Kansas and had an important message to deliver. In another case, by the direction of Chief Justice [William Howard] Taft, the Clerk, during the luncheon hour, requested an Assistant State Attorney General, either to put on a vest or else button up his coat so as not to expose quite so much of his shirt to view.

According to a page who worked at the Supreme Court in the 1920s, cutaways continued to be strongly preferred by Court members. He overheard two Justices disparaging a provincial attorney who deviated from the dress code:

> One young red-haired lawyer from Oklahoma didn't get the word or didn't have the money to rent [formal cutaways]. He appeared in a brown suit with a vast expanse of white shirt and loud tie. I heard [Justice] Owen Roberts say to [Justice] Pierce Butler, "Where does the SOB think he is, police court?"

Women advocates wore prim dresses until Mabel Walker Willebrandt was named Assistant Attorney General in 1923 and decided to pair a skirt made out of pinstripe material with a black coat to "[call] the attention of her gentlemen colleagues of the bar to her ability to conform to the regulations of what a well-dressed lawyer should wear before the Supreme Court." When women began joining the Office of the Solicitor General in the 1970s, a few followed Willebrandt's lead but others opted for simple dresses or suits. The first female Solicitor General, Elena Kagan, made her debut before the Court in 2009 wearing a dark suit, having checked with the Justices beforehand and been told they would not take offense if she did not wear the Solicitor General's traditional morning suit.

Now only male attorneys from the Department of Justice and senior Court staff (both men and women) appear in formal cutaways. Most advocates wear sleek dark suits. But even this simple requirement was a struggle for one young lawyer from Kansas. In 1953 Paul Wilson, an assistant attorney general with no appellate experience, was sent to Washington to argue Kansas's case in *Brown v. Board of Education of Topeka*. No one higher up in the Kansas Attorney General's office wanted to take on the highly controversial case for keeping schools segregated, especially as the state was expected to lose. But Wilson performed his part with dignity, as befitting the importance of the landmark case, and had done his best to prepare:

> Along with my substantive preparation, I undertook to learn something of Supreme Court procedure and protocol. I read Stern and Gressman ['s book] *Supreme Court Practice*, then a single, not-very-thick, volume. I read about Courtroom decorum—where I should sit, when I should stand, how I should address the court, what I should wear. It was the matter of proper garb that gave me pause. I was pleased to learn that the traditional formal dress was

no longer required but a little disturbed to read that the acceptable alternative was a conservative business suit "in a dark color in keeping with the dignity of the court." My dark suit had been purchased several years before and no longer fit. My more recent purchases had been a tan gabardine, a pepper and salt tweed, and miscellaneous sport jackets and trousers. These served well in Kansas, but I had a date in the Supreme Court and nothing to wear. Seeking assistance, I went to the Palace Clothing Store, then the Topeka counterpart of Brooks Brothers, where I found a midnight-blue suit of worsted wool; a perfect fit. I was assured by the salesman that a garment of that quality was a bargain at forty-five dollars. But this only partially solved the problem. In 1951 the state of Kansas was not a lavish paymaster. With house payments, a car payment, a wife, three children, and a household, I could ill-afford an unplanned-for expenditure of forty-five dollars. The era of the credit card had not yet arrived. Hence, this solution. With a five dollar deposit, the suit was removed from the display rack and laid away to be picked up and paid for when I needed it. Eventually I wore the suit during the argument.

Wilson's blue suit now hangs in the Kansas Museum of History as part of an exhibit on *Brown*, in which the Court unanimously held segregation in schools to be unconstitutional.

9

⚖

Nine Justices, One Bench

Building Consensus

W hen you are going to serve on a court . . . for the rest of your pro-
ductive days," Chief Justice Earl Warren reflected after he retired in
1969, "you accustom yourself to the institution like you do to the institution of marriage, and you realize that you can't be in a brawl every day
and still get any satisfaction out of life." Indeed, the Justices have always
had a strong incentive to compromise and be collegial because their work
requires collaboration. They decide collectively which cases to select for
review and how they then will come together to forge a majority holding
for each argued case. The purpose of their private Conference is thus to
discover the consensus.

Exactly how this is accomplished is somewhat of a mystery. Vivid
firsthand accounts of these secret internal deliberations are few. Only
the Justices themselves are present and not many of them have recorded
their impressions beyond keeping track in their docket books of others'
viewpoints and votes on specific cases. Fortunately, Justice John McLean
(1830–1844) recorded an early insider account of the Conference under
Chief Justice Roger B. Taney (1836–1864). In that era, the Justices deliberated after dinner in a private room in a boardinghouse which was pleas-
anter and more conveniently located than the dingy Conference room
given them in the Capitol building:

> Before any opinion is formed by the Court, the case after being argued at the
> Bar is thoroughly discussed in consultation. Night after night, this is done,
> in a case of difficulty, until the mind of every judge is satisfied, and then
> each judge gives his views of the whole case, embracing every point of it. In
> this way the opinion of the judges is expressed, and then the Chief Justice

requests a particular judge to write, not his opinion, but the opinion of the Court. And after the opinion is read, it is read to all of the judges, and if it does not embrace the views of the judges, it is modified and corrected.

Chief Justice Taney strove to maintain the high level of unanimity that the Court had enjoyed under his predecessor, John Marshall. But the increased size of the Court—as many as ten Justices by the end of his tenure—and political divisions over slavery made it more of a struggle. Justice John A. Campbell (1853–1861) nonetheless painted a congenial portrait of Conferences in the Taney Court's later period:

> The Chief Justice presided, the deliberations were usually frank and candid. It was a rare incident in the whole of this period the slightest disturbance from irritation, excitement, passion, or impatience. There was habitually courtesy, good breeding, self control [and] mutual deference. . . . There was nothing of cabal, combination, or exorbitant desire to carry questions or cases. Their aims were honorable and all the arts employed to attain them were manly arts. The venerable age of the Chief Justice, his gentleness, refinement, and feminine sense of propriety, were felt and realized in the privacy and confidence of these consultations. . . . The discussion was free and open among all the Justices till all were satisfied.

Campbell's account is curiously rosy given that he delivered it at a memorial service for his friend and former colleague Benjamin R. Curtis. After sharply disagreeing with Taney over the content of the Chief Justice's majority opinion in the *Dred Scott* case and accusing him of being underhanded in the way it was released, Curtis had resigned abruptly from the Supreme Court in 1857.

By the time Melville W. Fuller became Chief Justice (1888–1910), the days of communal living were long gone: by then, the Justices lived in Washington and worked out of their own homes. They seldom saw each other when they were not attending oral arguments or Conferences in the Capitol building. Unhappy with the poorly ventilated Conference room, Fuller initially invited his brethren to meet instead at his home on Saturday evenings. He decided to enhance cordiality by having all the Justices shake hands with one another at the start of every Conference (and also before sitting down to a session of the Court).

A tiny man with shaggy white hair and a flowing mustache, Fuller presided over men who were robust both in size and ability. Newcomer David J. Brewer reported, however, that they did not compromise easily in Conference:

> There is a long table, and we all sit down at the side except Justice [Joseph P.] Bradley, who takes the end because his legs are too long to sit sideways.

In 1888 Chief Justice Melville W. Fuller (seated, center) inaugurated the tradition of the Justices shaking hands with one another at the beginning of each Conference and before sitting for oral argument. Fuller was effective at enhancing cordiality on the bench during his tenure. From left to right are (seated) Associate Justices David J. Brewer, John Marshall Harlan, Horace Gray, Henry B. Brown, and (standing) Rufus W. Peckham, George Shiras, Jr., Edward Douglass White, and Joseph McKenna. (Courtesy of the Collection of the Supreme Court of the United States)

. . . When they all get settled, the tug of war commences. They are all strong men, and do not waste a word. They lock horns and the fight is stubborn; arguments are hurled against each other, the discussion grows animated and continues so for hours. But we always think that justice is triumphant—except the dissenters.

A Courtroom observer confirmed the battle-weary state of the Justices after these sessions: "Often and often in coming out of the conference or consultation room they look worn and fatigued, and as if they had been on rides on bicycles, or had just returned from participating in a game of football in the most approved modern style."

As junior Justice, Brewer found it difficult to make much headway in negotiating with these "strong men." After a particularly frustrating Conference, he complained: "I have been fighting all day to make my associates accept some elemental propositions of law and I could not budge one of them. They are the most obstinate men I ever saw."

During his twenty-two years as Chief, Fuller gently set about deploying his courtesy and charm to mediate among his considerably larger

brethren. Fuller's leadership qualities made such an impression on Justice
Oliver Wendell Holmes, Jr., (1902–1932) that he evidently sang his praises
to Felix Frankfurter (who would join the Court long after Fuller had died):

> I have the authority of Mr. Justice Holmes, who sat under four Chief Justices in Massachusetts before he came down to Washington, and under four (Fuller, White, Taft, Hughes) in Washington, that there was never a better presiding officer, or rather, and more important in some ways, a better moderator inside the conference chamber, than this quiet gentleman from Illinois.

Holmes had also lauded Fuller to another friend: "I think he was extraordinary. He had the business of court at his fingers' end; he was perfectly courageous, prompt, decided. He turned off the matters that daily call for action easily, swiftly, with the least possible friction, with imperturbable good humor, and with humor that relieved any tension with a laugh."

During Conferences, Fuller allowed each Justice to speak in order of seniority without being interrupted by interjections from fellow Justices. His inspired managerial skills were displayed in an episode in which he deftly used humor to avert a clash between newly appointed Holmes and Justice John Marshall Harlan. Holmes, a brilliant Boston blue blood, had usurped the Kentuckian's intellectual leadership on the Court and criticized him for being long-winded. Frankfurter, to whom Holmes later related the incident, told the story secondhand many years later:

> Justice Harlan, who was oratorical while Justice Holmes was pithy, said something during one of the Court's conferences that seemed to Holmes not ultimate wisdom. Justice Holmes said he then did something that ordinarily isn't done in the conference room of the Supreme Court. Each man speaks in order and there are no interruptions, because if you had that you would soon have a Donnybrook Fair instead of orderly discussion. But Holmes afterward said, "I did lose my temper at something that Harlan said and sharply remarked, "That won't wash. That won't wash." Tempers flared and something might have happened. But when Holmes said, "That won't wash," the silver-haired, gentle little Chief Justice said, "Well I'm scrubbing away. I'm scrubbing away."

The Justices laughed at the sight of the diminutive Chief rubbing his hands together and the tension was defused.

In 1958 Justice James F. Byrnes reflected on the handshaking tradition Fuller had inaugurated in 1888, now ingrained:

> When members gather for a conference or for a session of court, it has been the custom for more than half a century that upon entering the room each should shake hands with all his colleagues, who are referred to as "breth-

ren." On my first day I regarded this as rather superfluous, for I had greeted each of the brethren elsewhere that morning. Later there were times when it reminded me of the usual instruction of the referee in the prize ring, "Shake hands, go to your corner and come out fighting." But I soon realized that it was a useful reminder of the courtesy and mutual respect that the justices seek to preserve no matter how heated their debates.

A half-century later, Justice Sandra Day O'Connor confirmed that the ritual, which requires thirty-six handshakes total, continued to be vital: "I think that's a great custom. Not all courts do that. I think it's wonderful. If you take someone's hand and shake it, you're much less likely, I think, to hold a grudge. There's something about human contact that matters." In addition to being effective, Justice Ruth Bader Ginsburg recently characterized the group handshake before entering the Courtroom as having broader significance:

[It's] a symbol of the work we do as a collegial body. That is, you may be temporarily miffed because you receive a spicy dissenting opinion from a colleague, but when we go to sit on the bench, we look at each other, shake hands, and it's a way of saying, "We're all in this together." We care about this institution more than our individual egos, and we are all devoted to keeping the Supreme Court in the place that it is—as a co-equal third branch of government and I think a model for the world in collegiality and independence of judges.

After the mutual greeting, the action in Conference begins. The Justices now face their toughest audience: each other. According to Justice Anthony Kennedy, he and some of his colleagues on the current Court are nervous going into the Conference because of the pressure to perform:

It's like being an attorney once again. You're arguing your case. I have eight colleagues who have studied very hard on the case, who may have some very fixed views, they may be tentative depending on how they have thought the case through, and I have to give my point of view and hopefully persuade them. And I feel a sense of anticipation, whether it's an adrenalin rush or I don't know what they call it, but this is a big, big day for us. We sometimes have as many as six cases and I have to present the argument—well, usually four—and I have to be professional and accurate and fair. And each of my colleagues feels the same way so there is a little tension and excitement in the room, but we love it. We're lawyers, we're designed to do that. The job is no good if you can't argue.

But it is the Chief Justice whose skill as a moderator is most tested behind those closed doors. In a private room adjacent to his chambers, the Chief Justice presides at the head of a long table around which the Associate

Justices are seated according to seniority. He presents his views first on the case being reviewed and is thus able to frame the debate. But the Chief's vote counts no more than that of an Associate Justice. And his authority over his brethren is limited, as William H. Rehnquist emphasized when he was still an Associate Justice:

> The power to calm . . . naturally troubled waters is usually beyond the capacity of any mortal chief justice. He presides over a conference not of eight subordinates, whom he may direct or instruct, but of eight associates who, like him, have tenure during good behavior, and who are as independent as hogs on ice. He may at most persuade or cajole them.

Like Melville W. Fuller, Chief Justice Charles Evans Hughes (1930–1941) was praised by his peers for being an extremely effective Conference manager. A patrician New Yorker, Hughes benefited from having served as an Associate Justice (1910–1916) and of already knowing the ropes. He tightly controlled the discussions during Conferences and did most of the speaking. Like a strict classroom teacher, he made sure Conferences did not exceed four hours and he firmly enforced the protocol of having each Justice speak in turn according to seniority. Impatient with discussion and debate, Hughes succeeded in increasing the number of cases being decided each term. At William O. Douglas's first Conference as a new member of the Court in 1939 he marveled at Hughes's management skills:

> The C.J. certainly handles the conference in a masterful manner. He states the cases which have been argued & those coming up by certiorari [petition] & appeal most meticulously and carefully. He sets them up in a very grand Olympian manner. And the way he puts the facts tells you the place he is headed for. He is most skilled and adroit & for the most part fair in presentation. Yet he is nonetheless crafty and overbearing. . . . [In two cases being] discussed & voted upon. . . . [t]he judges were hopelessly split not on the conclusion so much as on the reasons. At the end the C.J. said, "I will take the opinion & resolve all the differences and harmonize the points of view."

Drawing on his photographic memory, Hughes presented cases in such a thorough way that the other Justices knew they had to come to Conference well prepared or risk embarrassment. According to Douglas, Hughes was also fastidious about punctuality:

> [Hughes] accomplished in four hours what it would take the average judge eight hours or more to do. He was very meticulous in every respect and most punctilious in the affairs of the Court. At that time the Court met at twelve noon [on Saturdays] and we always walked in not thirty seconds late or

ten seconds late—but exactly at twelve. Hughes would be in his robe in the Conference Room by five minutes to twelve, and if one of the Brethren had not appeared by three minutes or two minutes to twelve, he would send a messenger down the hall to get him.

Felix Frankfurter, who had joined the Court a few months before Douglas, only served under Hughes for two full terms before the Chief retired. But he, too, quickly came to admire Hughes's executive talents:

Chief Justice Hughes radiated authority, not through any other quality than the intrinsic moral power that was his. He was master of the business. He could disembowel a brief and a record. He had an extraordinary memory and vast experience in the conduct of litigation, and of course he had been on the Court six years, from 1910 to 1916. And he had intimate and warm relations with some of the men he found on the Court. He was a great admirer of, that greatest intellect, in my judgment, who ever sat on the Court, Mr. Justice Holmes. He was an old friend at the bar of Mr. Justice [Louis D.] Brandeis. He had been one year in the cabinet with [Harlan Fiske] Stone. So he not only felt at home in the courtroom, he felt at home with his colleagues.

I have often used a word which for me best expresses the atmosphere that Hughes generated; it was taut. Everything was taut. He infected and affected counsel that way. Everybody was better because of Toscanini Hughes, the leader of the orchestra.

Harlan Fiske Stone, who succeeded Hughes as Chief Justice in 1941, exhibited a very different style of management. A former law professor who enjoyed debating every point, Stone preferred the give-and-take of a college seminar to the seniority-based style of speaking in turn. He may have adopted an easygoing manner as Chief Justice precisely because he had chafed under Hughes's strict hand when Stone, appointed in 1925, served under him as Associate Justice. Just before Hughes retired and Stone became Chief Justice, Justice Douglas reported in his diary:

[Associate Justice] Stone harbors a deep resentment at Hughes. That also goes back a long way. I do not know what is [its] origin. But it is manifest in a myriad of ways. I think it relates to the early treatment Stone got as a member of the Court. According to Stone, Hughes ran the Court with a high hand when he was made C.J. Stone has told me many times how the Chief would whisk a case around the table, intolerant of opposition etc. Stone says that it was not profitable to express your views at Conference, so he & Cardozo & Brandeis would keep silent & later produce their dissents. It is not that way any more. There are long, frank, give-and-take discussions in Conference. And that is the way it should be. By the Constitution at most the C.J. is entitled only to one vote.

But while Stone saw debate being stifled, Frankfurter saw extraneous chatter being eliminated:

> It has been said that there wasn't free and easy talk in Hughes' day in the conference room. Nothing could be further from the truth. There was less wasteful talk. There was less repetitious talk. There was less foolish talk. You just didn't like to talk unless you were dead sure of your ground, because that gimlet mind of his was there ahead of you.

Stone's relaxed management style eventually had a deleterious effect on Court business. In 1945 Frankfurter complained to Justice Wiley Rutledge of "an increasing tendency on the part of members of this Court to behave like little school boys and throw spitballs at one another." What Frankfurter did not acknowledge was that he himself was guilty of throwing spitballs too.

An effective Chief can make the day-to-day functioning of the institution smooth enough that personal clashes and jurisprudential antagonisms stay in check. Current Justices report that under both William H. Rehnquist and John G. Roberts, Jr., the atmosphere in the Conference has generally been marked by decorum and collegiality. Despite frequent five-to-four splits, Clarence Thomas, appointed in 1991, says that the Justices remain cordial:

> To see people who are trying their best to decide hard things and feel strongly about their view of it, is fascinating. And the thing that's been great is, I just finished my eighteenth term, and I still haven't heard the first unkind word in that [Conference] room. You think what we've decided—life and death, abortion, execution, war and peace, financial ruin, government's relationship with citizens. You name it. We've decided it. And I still have not heard the first ad hominem [insult] in that room.

But it is not always the Chief Justice who proves to be the most gifted of the nine at Conference deliberations. Wyoming-born Willis Van Devanter (1911–1937) is a prime example of an Associate Justice whose leadership ability made him a Conference stalwart. Nearly incapable of writing opinions, Van Devanter nonetheless shone in oral discussions and proved invaluable to the Chief Justices with whom he served. When Chief Justice William Howard Taft took ill in 1924, he relied on Van Devanter to run the Conference. Observed Charles Evans Hughes: "[Van Devanter's] careful and elaborate statements in conference, with his accurate review of authorities, were of the greatest value. If these statements had been taken down stenographically, they would have served with but little editing as excellent opinions. His perspicacity and common sense made him a trusted advisor in all sorts of matters. Chief Justice [Edward Douglass] White leaned heavily upon him and so did Chief Justice Taft."

The nature of Conferences has changed considerably since Van Devanter's era. Until the 1940s the Justices fully discussed each case in descending order of seniority before voting, a method that promoted debate. The junior Justice would then cast his vote first and the others would vote in order of ascending seniority. This system gave the Chief Justice the advantage of voting last, and of having the option of joining the majority and retaining control over the assignment of the opinion. Now the line between discussion and voting is blurred: the Justices' initial comments indicate how they will vote as well.

As the number of cases taken up for review each term increased in the 1970s, there was not enough time to hammer out agreements face to face in each Conference. Instead, deliberation began taking place after the Conference sessions—usually in formal, written communications. Contemporary Conferences are thus less a forum for the Justices to persuade each other through impassioned speeches than for declaring individual positions and determining what is the view of the majority. Justice Antonin Scalia described the function of the Conference in 1988, when Chief Justice Rehnquist ran an exceptionally tight ship: "Not very

Deliberations inside the Conference room are secret; there are no recording devices and each Justice takes notes. It is the task of the junior Justice to serve as doorkeeper—receiving documents and messages from the outside—and to keep a careful tally of Conference votes in order to report afterward to the Clerk of Court which cases the Justices have chosen to be briefed and argued. (Collection of the Supreme Court of the United States, photograph by Steve Petteway)

much conferencing goes on. In fact, to call our discussion of a case in conference a 'conference' is really something of a misnomer. It's much more a statement of the views of each of the nine Justices, after which the totals are added and the case is assigned." More recently, Justice Thomas has characterized Conference discussions under Chief Justice Roberts as being a bit looser:

> And people are engaged; they actually talk about the case. They actually tell you what they think and why. You record the votes. And there's some back-and-forth; there's more now. When Chief Justice Rehnquist was here, he moved it along very quickly. Now there's more back-and-forth, more discussion. We normally have one break, and there's more discussion off to the sides, about cases.

The Justices all take notes about what the others say in Conference so that if they are assigned to write the majority opinion, they will, in Scalia's words, "know how to write it in a way that will get at least four other votes besides your own." But the votes are tentative; anything can change until the Court actually hands down its decision. There is plenty of room post-Conference for bargaining, vote shifting, and coalition building. With a particularly complex case, discussion may be inconclusive the first go-round and the case will be brought up again in the next Conference.

Once a tentative vote is recorded, establishing which Justices are in the majority and which will dissent, it is then the responsibility of the Chief Justice to assign the writing of the majority opinion to a particular Justice. If the Chief Justice is in the minority, the task falls to the most senior Associate Justice in the majority. Matching Justices with cases is a delicate task and requires finesse and good leadership. Historically, Justices have often been assigned cases that fall into their area of special expertise. Fairness is also a consideration: some cases are more interesting and prestigious than others and each Justice wants a share of the plums.

When Fred Vinson became Chief Justice in 1946, he decided to distribute the opinions equitably to ensure that no Justice fell behind in his assignments and that decisions were handed down in a timely fashion. Subsequent Chief Justices have followed suit to prevent workload bottleneck. If different views are expressed in preliminary Conference discussions about how to reach a result in a case, the Chief Justice may decide to assign the case to a Justice who is skilled at mediating consensus. On occasion, a Chief Justice or Senior Associate Justice has selflessly given up the glory of writing a landmark decision in order to secure a shaky majority by assigning it to a wavering Justice.

In instances when an Associate Justice suffering from failing health has no longer been able to write reliable opinions, it has been up to the Chief Justice to handle the situation. This has usually meant assigning only relatively easy, unanimous opinions to the enfeebled Justice. In the 1870s, for example, Chief Justice Morrison R. Waite was obliged to manage Nathan Clifford, who had become increasingly erratic and fussy as his mental and physical capacities declined. Clifford frequently rejected opinion-writing assignments; Waite ended up quietly writing them himself. Yet he still managed to politely respond to Clifford after the grouchy Justice rejected yet another assignment:

> I regret that my assignment of cases to you last evening was not satisfactory. I gave you [case #] 93 because you were familiar with the law of copyright, and although the case was a simple one, I thought it might be made the foundation of one of your useful opinions. In looking over the cases again, since your note came, I can now see where I might have pleased you better, and in respect to one in particular some things have occurred to me that I overlooked before, which make it apparent that there would have been great propriety in giving it to you. I regret that it is now beyond my control. If you still think you do not want 93, I will keep it and announce the decision stating simply that the grounds on which it is placed without more. I wanted to give you the two important land cases which [Justice Samuel] Miller has, but you said expressly in the conference that you did not want them.

Bennett Boskey, who clerked for Chief Justice Stone in the 1941 and 1942 Terms, was privy to how his boss made decisions about opinion-writing assignments. Stone, like some others who have occupied the center chair, kept for himself perhaps more than his fair share of the plum assignments. Yet Boskey also witnessed his Chief make a particularly strategic assignment to an Associate Justice to give the ruling more weight. The case was *Taylor v. Georgia,* and the Justices had unanimously decided in Conference to reverse the conviction of a manual laborer because certain provisions of the Georgia statute violated the prohibition against peonage in the Thirteenth Amendment and in the implementing federal statute. Stone decided to assign the case to Justice James F. Byrnes, a new member of the Court. Boskey explained the Chief's strategy: "As is well known, Byrnes was a southerner, having most recently served in the U.S. Senate from South Carolina, and was generally looked upon as a conservative. . . . It was thought that an opinion from such a source on such a subject would be good for Justice Byrnes' image and good for the Court."

After serving with four Chief Justices, Felix Frankfurter (1939–1962) summed up the intricacies and challenges of the opinion-assignment function:

> You can see the important function that rests with the Chief Justice in determining who should be the spokesman of the Court in expressing the decision reached, because the manner in which a case is stated, the grounds on which a decision is rested—one ground rather than another, or one ground

rather than two grounds—how much is said and how it is said, what kind of phrasing will give least trouble in the future in a system of law in which as far as possible you are to decide the concrete issue and not embarrass the future too much—all these things matter a great deal. The deployment of his judicial force by the Chief Justice is his single most influential function. Some do that with ease. Some do it with great anguish. Some do it with great wisdom. Some have done it with less than great wisdom. . . . Some cases are more interesting than others, and it is the prerogative of the Chief Justice not only to be kindly and fair and generous in the distribution of cases, but also to appear to be so. The task calls for qualities of tact, of understanding, and for skill in the effective utilization of the particular qualities that are available. Should one man become a specialist in a subject? Or is it important not to place too much reliance on one man because he's a great authority in the field? Should you pick the man who will write in the narrowest possible way? Or should you take the chance of putting a few seeds in the earth for future flowering? Those are all very difficult, very delicate, very responsible questions.

Justice Henry Billings Brown (1891–1906) gave an earlier glimpse of how opinions were assigned. In those days, a Justice's expertise in a specific area of law drew considerable weight:

My colleagues upon the Supreme Bench were all men of distinction and ability in their several specialities. Chief Justice [Melville W.] Fuller was specially happy in his executive duties and his assignments of cases to us for the preparation of opinions constantly had in mind our previous experiences in particular branches of the law, the circuits from which the cases arose, as well as any interest a justice may have taken in an individual case. Each member of the Court was given his share of constitutional cases. To Justices [Stephen] Field, [John Marshall] Harlan, [Lucius Q. C.] Lamar and [David] Brewer were usually assigned the land cases, to [Horace] Gray most of the commercial cases, to [Joseph P.] Bradley, [Samuel] Blatchford and myself the patent and admiralty cases, while those turning upon questions of practice were by immemorial custom disposed of by the Chief Justice. . . . By reason of his previous experience as Secretary of the Interior, Justice Lamar's assignments were chiefly confined to land cases. He had practised law but a few years, and that early in life, and always lamented his lack of special equipment for judicial labour.

When Chief Justice Roberts describes the current thought process behind making assignments, however, he says he believes that Justices should be given a variety of different types of cases:

If I'm in the majority, I get to determine who will write the opinion in that case. And that's a very important responsibility because you want to make sure that the assignment is given to the justice whose view commands the most support on the Court. You want to make sure the work gets done on time, so if some-one's a little slower than the others, you make sure that person gets . . . heavy assignments, earlier on. Some cases are more interesting than others. You want to make sure those are fairly distributed. Some cases are harder than others. You want to make sure that's fairly distributed. We get all sorts of different issues. You want to make sure each justice has a nice mix. You don't want one justice just doing criminal cases or something like that.

Whether a case is considered a plum or a dog can, of course, be highly subjective. Justice Scalia, for example, has admitted that he did not always see eye-to-eye with Chief Justice Rehnquist on his assignments:

> Of course, sometimes what they think is a good opinion is not what you think is a good opinion. Chief Justice Rehnquist used to love Fourth Amend-ment cases involving searches and seizures, and I just hate Fourth Amend-ment cases. I think it's almost a jury question—whether this variation is an unreasonable search and seizure; variation 3,542. Yes, I'll write the opinion, but I don't consider it a plum, and if he gave you that [assignment], he thought he was entitled to give you a dog. I didn't much like that.

After a Justice receives the assignment, comes the hard work. An au-thor cannot simply craft an opinion to his or her own satisfaction. (Con-currences and dissents are, of course, another matter.) Nor can the writer count on a Justice who voted with the majority in Conference not to have a change of mind as informal discussions continue and the drafts are circulated. At least four other Justices must be persuaded to sign onto a circulated draft for the opinion to become law. The opinion that is eventu-ally handed down is often as much an institutional product, a collective judgment, as the position of the Justice who wrote it.

Communication is now done in writing—rarely orally—because even the smallest details matter when the legal language is so precise. Before computers were introduced in the 1970s, there was more face-to-face lobbying, but the ease with which drafts are circulated electronically has greatly eliminated one-on-one discussions. After serving six years on the Court, Justice Sandra Day O'Connor, appointed in 1981, said she devel-oped an appreciation for written memoranda:

> You know the real persuasion around here isn't so much done at our oral conference discussion as it is in the writing. . . . Having been here a while I understand why that's so. Because I think when you have time to sit down with pen in hand and reflect on these things and spell out in writing with all the authorities mustered and set out, then you can be more persuasive than you could just giving oral thought off the top of your head at the oral conference.

The practice of circulating draft opinions for comment began around the turn of the twentieth century. But Justices in the majority were expected then to be deferential to the author of the opinion of the Court and they seldom wrote critical comments on the draft. Milton Handler, Associate Justice Stone's law clerk in the 1926 Term, recalled that it "was rare in those days for the Justices to comment on each other's draft opinions, unlike the practice of later Courts to circulate elaborate memoranda of their views." He went on to explain the procedure for circulating the page proofs of a proposed opinion:

> The proofs were folded four times and on top of the fold he would write (for example), "To Holmes, J. from Stone, J." If the Justice receiving the draft agreed with it, he would return the proofs, writing the word "yes" followed by his initials. If the draft was not returned, that meant that the nonresponding Justice was dissenting and that his dissenting opinion would be circulated in due course. Most of the Justices merely returned the page proofs with the word "yes."

The practice in that era was to return comments within twenty-four hours of receiving a draft, which also effectively reduced the scope of commentary. Given this culture of deference, Handler was understandably irked when Justice Van Devanter insisted on rewriting his boss's opinions. But, according to Handler, Stone quickly set his young clerk straight:

> Van Devanter . . . whose productivity ebbed as he grew older, produced very little of his own, but he would take a Stone opinion and virtually rewrite it from beginning to end. This, as a brash youngster, infuriated me. When I exploded one day and said to Stone "I don't know why he doesn't attend to his own assignments, rather than messing up your opinions," Stone turned to me and said, "Have you ever read the first line of a Supreme Court opinion?" He then pointed to it and read aloud, "Mr. Justice Stone delivered the opinion of the Court" (emphasizing the word "Court").

Of course in simple, noncontentious cases, members of the Court continued to sign on easily. Justice Byrnes (1941–1942) admitted that he found it especially gratifying when his brethren would add words of praise:

> If a justice is impressed with the opinion, frequently he will amplify the customary "I agree." In fact, when recently I looked over some of my opinions, with the notations by the justices, I was considerably amused. One notation is "Neat and complete. I verily believe that you say more by saying less—and what you say is truly good." Another, and this is from the Chief Justice [Stone], "I agree. It makes the stump speech of your opponent seem quite unnecessary."

But in complex or difficult cases, extensive comments on draft opinions gradually came to be the norm. Justice Tom C. Clark (1949–1967) noted that when a Justice first circulated a draft opinion it was merely an opener, an invitation for comment:

> When an author concludes that he has an unanswerable document, it is printed in the print shop in the Supreme Court building and circulated to each of the Justices. Then the fur begins to fly. Returns come in, some favorable and many otherwise. In controversial cases, and all have some touches of controversy, the process often takes months. . . . There will be, as always, some heat.

Lewis F. Powell, Jr. (1972–1987), described to his clerks how nerve-wracking it feels to wait for comments on one's own draft opinion:

> After an opinion is circulated, we anxiously await responses from other Chambers. The happiest word is simply a note saying "Please join me." Less welcome communications include advice that "I will await circulation of the dissent," or a long memorandum suggesting major changes in our draft. Perhaps the most disquieting situation is to circulate an opinion, and receive no response at all. This means that even the Justices who voted with me in Conference do not like my draft. In this situation, negotiations may take place or the opinion may be reassigned to another Justice.

Powell was far from alone in sweating his negotiations with fellow Justices. Hugo L. Black's wife, Elizabeth, who had served as his secretary for several years, said her husband always "ran scared":

> Although the Judge was confident of his views, his confidence in vote-getting among the other Justices was never absolute. He always "ran scared." In some cases, everything would go smoothly and the votes would come in quickly, often indicated by a line written on the back of the Judge's circulated opinion. "Hugo, count me in" was a typical notation. In order to iron out a case, one or another of "the brethren" (as they called each other) would come into the Judge's office to go over an opinion—line by line, word by word—until there was a meeting of the minds. If there could be no agreement, then the other Justice might decide to write a dissenting or a concurring opinion. Sometimes it happened that the Judge would lose his Court, and his opinion would turn out to be a dissent or a concurring opinion.

According to Harry A. Blackmun (1970–1994), the pressure could be especially intense when the vote was close:

> I think this job is very competitive among the nine of us. . . . If a vote goes 5–4 on a given case—a tentative vote—and one is assigned the opinion to write, he circulates it. And somebody on the down side, on the four, is preparing

a dissent. You're locked in combat. It's competitive to that degree. You're struggling for the fifth vote.

And conversely, when a majority is solid, there is less enthusiasm for complying with requested changes. Chief Justice Roberts recently explained: "When you get eight votes and the ninth one comes in, saying 'Change this or that,' you often say, 'Well, you know . . .'"

Changes to the text of an opinion can be negotiated more or less graciously. The following reply from Chief Justice Hughes to comments from Justice Frankfurter on his draft opinion in 1940 is an example of good-natured compromise:

> I am surprised that exception should be taken to the statements in the paragraphs you mentioned in your letter. I thought that they gave the true milk of the word. While I think the opinion will not be as complete and well rounded without them, I am willing in the interest of harmony to make the omission you suggest. Justice [Oliver Wendell] Holmes used to say, when we asked him to excise portions of his opinions which he thought pretty good, that he was willing to be "reasonably raped." I feel the same way.

Apparently Holmes had developed many other colorful expressions for protesting edits to his opinions because he was frequently under pressure to rein in his sweeping language. In 1920 he complained that one of his drafts "had a tiny pair of testicles but the scruples of my brethren have caused their removal and it sings in a very soft voice now, but whether I shall be told to let it be heard remains to be seen."

One way to gain a colleague's support is to flatter him by citing one of his earlier opinions. Justice William O. Douglas noted in a 1940 diary entry that this tactic worked particularly well with Justice Harlan Fiske Stone:

> When you write an opinion it will be well to cite opinions which Stone has written on or near the point. If you don't he will always suggest it. F.F. [Justice Felix Frankfurter] calls it "Stone's disease." When F.F. suggested to me that I might cite in one of my opinions an earlier one by F.F. I told him "I will gladly do so. But it is interesting to me how Stone's disease is spreading." F.F. who has a keen sense of humor was highly entertained.

Another strategy for finding common ground is to deploy one's law clerks to ascertain the positions of other Justices by talking to their clerks. Justice Powell explicitly told his clerks that they should make themselves useful in this regard:

> Negotiations often occur at two levels: (i) by me with respect to proposed major changes, although the clerk will work with me in Chambers; and (ii) by my clerk directly with his opposite number. The latter situation occurs frequently with respect to editorial-type changes. For this, and other profes-

sional and personal reasons, it is helpful to maintain warm and cordial relations with the clerks in other Chambers.

Perhaps the greatest master of the art of coalition building was Justice
William J. Brennan, Jr. (1956–1990). His clerks often complained that they
did not understand why he was so willing to modify his drafts—deleting
bits or adding new language—in order to persuade one more Justice to
sign on to it. "Five votes. Five votes can do anything around here," Brennan would explain, stretching open his hand and fingers. An elfin presence with a perpetual twinkle in his eye, Brennan was immensely likeable
and could use his charm to great effect. He greeted even the sternest of
his brethren with a "Hiya, pal," linking arms as they walked together to
Conference. David Souter, who replaced Brennan on the Court in 1990,
described his predecessor's gift for flattery:

> He made us members of a huge family by adoption, and when we were with
> him every one of us always felt like the favorite child. That was how it was
> with me. I'd stick my head in his chamber door [Brennan kept an office in
> the Court during his retirement] and he'd look up and say, "Get in here, pal,"
> and when I was ready to go he'd call me pal again. He wouldn't just shake
> my hand; he'd grab it in both of his and squeeze it and look me right in the
> eye and repeat my name. If he thought I'd stayed away too long, he'd give
> me one of his bear hugs to let me know that I'd been missed. While I was
> with him, he might tell me some things that were true, like how to count to
> five. And he might tell me a few things that were patently false, which he
> thought I might enjoy hearing anyway. He'd bring up some pedestrian opin-
> ion that I'd delivered, and he'd tell me it was not just a very good opinion
> but a truly great one. Then, a minute later, he'd go on and tell me it wasn't
> just great but a genuine classic of the judge's art. And I'd sit there and listen
> to him, and start to think that maybe he was right. Maybe it was pretty good.
> And when, inevitably, I'd realize again that it wasn't, I'd still feel great my-
> self. I always felt great when I'd been with Bill.

But Brennan squarely rejected the notion that personal charisma or
flattery can persuade other Court members to sign onto an opinion. He
claimed his effectiveness came instead from knowing how to appeal to
the other Justices' professional and jurisprudential concerns and in finding common ground:

> I am not a playmaker. I don't go around cajoling and importuning my col-
> leagues to go along with my point of view. When I have been able to draw
> a consensus, I have done it by the drafts circulated among my colleagues.
> Rather than try to talk something out with another Justice, I sit down and
> recite concrete suggestions as to what I don't like about what he has done or
> what I do like about it. I suggest changes in their drafts, and other Justices
> will suggest changes in what I've written. Every Justice of this Court admits
> that holding on to a majority can be a very difficult thing, and what we all

do is try to persuade each other in what we write to each other. From time to time, when I think I'm going to have a five-person majority, one of the four will write to me and say, "I'll be happy to join with you if you delete this and this." If you can, you do it. But there are times when I have to write back and say "I don't think I should, because then it wouldn't be what I wanted to say." It's quite important to get these differences out by written changes.

Of course it was also a lot easier for Brennan to persuade others to vote with him on the Warren Court, where as many as seven members shared his liberal jurisprudence, than on the more conservative Burger Court, where he increasingly found himself in the minority.

Although Justices do come together to form alliances, these coalitions are often fleeting and hatched over individual cases. Justice Breyer recently explained that when a case is decided he, like his colleagues, does not look back and moves on to the next one:

> [A] rule which is absolute is what I call, "Tomorrow is another day." You and I, we're the greatest allies in the world on this case. We think, "We are 100 percent right, and those who disagree with us are completely wrong." And we are going to convince them; so we are complete allies. Now the case is over. On the next case, we're on totally opposite sides. The fact that you were my ally in case one has nothing to do with how I will decide or you will decide case two. There is no linkage as there is sometimes in the political system. That's good, too. It also produces good human relations because when you disagree, you know that tomorrow you may agree.

In other words, the Court is no place for grudges.

When Justices disagree with the majority they can either fight back by writing a dissent, or by writing a separate or concurring opinion. (The latter agrees with the majority holding but expresses a different reasoning for doing so, and, unlike a separate opinion, does not join the majority opinion.) Although every member of the Court prefers unanimity, dissents are not seen as harmful. Charles Evans Hughes once sanguinely described a dissenter's intention: "A dissent in a court of last resort is an appeal to the brooding spirit of the law, to the intelligence of a future day, when a later decision may possibly correct the error into which the dissenting judge believes the court to have been betrayed."

Indeed, a dissent, or even the threat of a dissent, can make the majority opinion stronger. "Dissents keep the boys on their toes," insisted Hugo L. Black. Sometimes for strategic reasons Justices will choose, however, to suppress their opposition and acquiesce to the majority. When a Justice disagrees with an opinion he has signed, it is called a "graveyard dissent." Brandeis, who often dissented, once explained to Holmes that he had decided not to dissent in a particular case because "it would only aggravate the harm." In another case, Brandeis amplified on his reason for joining the majority: "I think this case . . . is wrongly decided. . . . But you have restricted the opinion so closely to the facts of this case, that I am inclined to think it will do less harm to let it pass unnoticed by dissent."

Occasionally, dissents express emotion, but seldom are they pointed enough to descend to the level of personal attacks. The formalism of written dissents and the tradition of not mentioning an opponent's name have traditionally kept clashes impersonal. The ever-courteous Justice Powell described the dispassionate nature of dissents in 1975:

> News stories sometime portray a picture of discord among the justices. A strong dissenting opinion is often characterized as "bitter," and a five-four decision is said to reflect deep-seated personal animosities among the justices. These stories are wide of the mark. They result perhaps from failure to understand that judges, like lawyers, may disagree strongly without personal rancor or ill will. The fact is that genuine cordiality exists among the justices.

Justice Scalia recently confirmed that even when the Justices strongly disagree with one another, they are careful to keep their differences from becoming openly personal: "You criticize the argument and not the person, that's all. . . . I feel quite justified in whacking the argument as hard as it deserves. That's not impugning the individual that made the argument."

Of course not every case engenders a dissent. Although the modern Court does not prize institutional decisions nearly as highly as it did in the nineteenth century, the Justices have agreed unanimously in more than a third of cases in the past fifty years. Since the 1960s, separate, concurring, and dissenting opinions have, however, become increasingly common.

Members of the Court have always had a huge incentive to get along because they often sit together for many years. Given the intellectual wattage of most Justices, mutual respect has rarely been difficult to muster. Indeed, the privilege of sharing the bench with a more brilliant member is a common refrain in Justices' memoirs. But overt fawning is not always appreciated. Justice Harlan Fiske Stone's son, Marshall, once overheard his father try to flatter retired Justice Oliver Wendell Holmes, Jr.—perhaps the cleverest writer to sit on the high bench. Marshall recalled that his father regaled Holmes, age ninety-two, with an account of hearing prodigy Yehudi Menuhin, age seventeen, play violin:

> "Ah," said Holmes with a sigh . . . "What a triumph! I sometimes think I would give ten years of my life to be able to play like that."
>
> "Yes," replied Justice Stone, "but some of us would give ten years of our lives to write opinions like yours."
>
> Justice Holmes brightened, showed that he enjoyed the praise, then, with a twinkle in his eye, he said, "My boy,"—Stone was then sixty-two—"God sees through all this modesty."

10

⚖

(Not So) Good Behavior
Discord and Feuds

In 1922 Oliver Wendell Holmes, Jr., took a break from a heated Conference discussion to write a note to Felix Frankfurter, then a law professor at Harvard. His missive concluded with these words: "I stepped out of a cloud of biting mosquitoes for a word of freedom with you. Now I go back to the swamp."

Getting along with eight colleagues over long periods of time would be challenging in any small, tight-knit organization, but when weighty constitutional issues are at stake tension may be unavoidable. Sixty-five years after Holmes admitted to Frankfurter that he needed a breather, Harry A. Blackmun told a reporter that he, too, sought an occasional respite from his fellow Justices:

> Well, I like to get away. As a matter of fact, I think I have to get away from Washington and this building, once in awhile, just to maintain my sanity. This is a very close intimate association that the nine of us have. We're working constantly with each other under conditions of a certain amount of agreement, and a very definite amount of disagreement.

Relationships between Justices have tended toward polite respect, although there have been some important friendships as well. But the Supreme Court has also weathered some miserable periods of feuding among the Justices. These clashes have sometimes stemmed from ideological differences, but were exacerbated by the abrasive personalities and rude behavior of individual members. "Nothing is more distressing on any bench than the exhibition of a captious, impatient, querulous spirit," admonished Charles Evans Hughes in 1927. "Independence does not mean cantankerousness and a judge may be a strong judge without being an impossible person."

The first Justice to exhibit disruptive behavior on the bench, Samuel Chase, nearly got himself thrown off the Court in 1804. A pro-Federalist political firebrand, he was boorish and made insulting comments to Republican attorneys arguing before him. Chase was also unabashed at showing his irritation when counsel spoke too long or argued at length on the merits of a point which he considered already settled. On one occasion, Chase kept interrupting the speech of a prominent advocate, Jared Ingersoll, to tell him that the point was made and that he needn't waste the Court's time arguing it further. After Chase's third interruption, an indignant Ingersoll simply abandoned his argument and sat down. According to a spectator in the Courtroom, Chief Justice Oliver Ellsworth expressed annoyance with Chase for his impertinence:

> The Chief Justice had now borne with his Associate as long as respect for himself and the Court would allow; and taking out his snuff-box, and as his custom was, tapping it on the side preparatory to abstracting a pinch, said to Mr. Ingersoll, with an emphatic manner and meaning not misunderstood by his Associate, "The Court has expressed no opinion, Sir, upon these points, and when it does, you will hear it from the proper organ of the Court [i.e., the Chief Justice]. You will proceed, Sir, and I pledge you my word you shall not be interrupted again;" then turned his face towards Judge Chase with a withering look of rebuke, under which the judge, with all his nerve and daring, fairly quailed.

Although the Constitution provides that judges "shall hold their Offices during good Behaviour," the Senate did not, of course, initiate impeachment charges against Chase for being rude. The House of Representatives impeached him for sedition—in the form of partisan attacks on President Thomas Jefferson and the Republicans. Chase was saved by the Senate, however, where enough Jeffersonians joined the Federalists in acquitting him, thereby protecting political speech for future Supreme Court Justices.

Since Chase, the Court has seen its share of ornery Justices who were unpleasant to work with. But these traits were usually brought on by physical and mental decline due to old age or illness. Justice James C. McReynolds (1914–1941) of Tennessee, however, deserves singling out because he was a curmudgeon from the start. McReynolds had been so abrasive as Attorney General that President Woodrow Wilson allegedly kicked him upstairs to the Supreme Court after barely a year on the job. Not long after William H. Taft became Chief Justice in 1921, he pronounced him a troublemaker: "[McReynolds is] selfish to the last degree

. . . one who delights in making others uncomfortable. He has no sense of duty. . . . He is a continual grouch; and . . . really seems to have less of a loyal spirit to the Court than anybody."

McReynolds targeted a few of his brethren for particular scorn. He was cruel to Justice Mahlon Pitney because he disliked his voice, and to Justice John H. Clarke because he thought he voted with his heart, not his head. Clarke wearily resigned from the Court in 1922 after six years of being subjected to McReynolds's steady torment. When Harlan Fiske Stone complained about a long-winded attorney's brief—"[That] was the dullest argument I ever heard in my life"—McReynolds, who shared the bench with Stone for more than fifteen years, retorted: "The only duller thing I can think of is to hear you read one of your opinions."

One of McReynolds's most disruptive traits was that he liked to shirk his work. He would play hooky from the Court to golf with his buddies or to duck hunt on the Eastern shore of Maryland. On one occasion this meant not finishing a dissent and preventing a furious Chief Justice Taft from handing down the Court's decision. "An imperious voice has called me out of town. I don't think my sudden illness will prove fatal, but strange things some time happen around Thanksgiving," McReynolds mischievously informed Chief Justice Taft to explain another such unannounced absence.

Oliver Wendell Holmes, Jr., who sat with McReynolds from 1914 to 1932, once described him as "a savage, with all the irrational impulses of a savage." Among these base impulses were misogyny (he would leave the bench in disgust if counsel was female), racism, and ethnic hatred of German Americans. But his greatest bigotry was directed toward Jews. An avowed anti-Semite, McReynolds refused to eat with, shake hands with, or talk to Jews. Accordingly, he did not speak to Louis D. Brandeis, the Court's first Jewish Justice, for three years following Brandeis's appointment in 1916, and barely much after. He would also leave the room when Brandeis spoke in Conference (but left the door enough ajar so he knew when to come back in). No official group photo of the Justices could be taken in 1924 because McReynolds refused to sit next to Brandeis, whom he immediately preceded in seniority. "The difficulty is with me and me alone," McReynolds admitted to Taft, "I have absolutely refused to go through the bore of picture-taking again until there is a change in the Court, and maybe not even then." When Benjamin Cardozo took the oath of office in 1932, McReynolds, who had reportedly implored Herbert Hoover not to "afflict the Court with another Jew," expressed his opposition by reading a newspaper ostentatiously during the ceremony. He later would hold briefs in front of his face when Cardozo delivered an opinion from the bench.

Brandeis ignored McReynolds' rudeness and tried to maintain civility. One of his clerks, Dean Acheson, even managed to get along with the vitriolic Justice:

> Mr. Justice James Clark McReynolds of Tennessee was a different kettle of fish. The ogre of the liberals, a deplorable judge, an outrageous old curmudgeon, or, to put it in another's supreme understatement, "a man of numerous and abrasive personal idiosyncrasies," he remained my friend until death. . . . Before my arrival on the scene, McReynolds had ceased speaking to his brethren Brandeis and [John H.] Clarke because of some imagined slight on their part. This bothered Justice Holmes, who was most sensitive to personal friction near him and rendered acutely unhappy by rudeness. He struggled to mend matters, but McReynolds would neither explain nor forget. Knowing this, though not from my chief, I undertook with some trepidation my first mission to McReynolds's chambers in the Rochambeau (now demolished) on Connecticut Avenue between H and I Streets. But apprehension was unwarranted by the event. The Justice received me courteously, explained with complete frankness that he was not on speaking terms with my employer, but that this had nothing to do with me. He would treat me with consideration and would expect the same treatment from me. Furthermore, he added, I was not to smoke in his apartment (which I had no intention of doing) or before coming to it, since he could only readily detect the repulsive odor which hung about a smoker. At first, our easy and friendly relations produced a sense of disloyalty, which I confessed to Justice Brandeis's amusement. He assured me that any ease of strain had its blessing.

Harriet Griswold, the wife of Solicitor General Erwin Griswold, witnessed the inconvenience McReynolds's bad behavior caused Chief Justice Hughes in the 1930s:

> Justice McReynolds, a cantankerous bachelor, had us to one of his famous breakfasts. He was a pleasant host, a contrast to the expression of displeasure as he sat on the Supreme Court. He showed his intolerance by turning his back on Justice Brandeis and Justice Cardozo and any woman, such as Assistant Attorney General Mabel Walker Willebrandt, who argued cases before the Supreme Court. Mindful of this, Chief Justice and Mrs. Hughes had two separate judicial dinners, dividing the Justices to avoid embarrassment.

The need for separate dinners also underscored the fundamental political differences on the Supreme Court during the Great Depression. A deep ideological schism divided the four ultraconservatives—McReynolds, Willis Van Devanter, Pierce Butler, and George Sutherland—from the three liberals—Brandeis, Stone, and Cardozo—and caused serious antipathy. According to Joseph L. Rauh, Jr., who clerked for Justice Cardozo in 1936:

Hostility between the two blocs was inevitable and open; they even held intra-bloc "skull practice" regularly. The four conservative Justices rode in the same automobile to and from the Supreme Court building for oral arguments and for the Saturday conferences of all nine Justices at which the Justices decided cases (in those days the Justices' offices were in their homes). To compete with these regular get-togethers of the conservatives, the liberals began to meet at Brandeis's home on Friday evenings to plan their strategies for the Saturday conferences. I always waited until Justice Cardozo returned to his apartment so I could get a full report on the liberal warm-up. I never found the Justice more unhappy than on the few occasions when Brandeis or Stone announced that they were not going to join his dissent in a particular case the following day despite their belief that the majority was going to make a wrong decision.

The balance of power, of course, lay with the other two Justices, Chief Justice Charles Evans Hughes and Associate Justice Owen Roberts. . . . Justice Roberts quickly became a fellow-traveler of the conservative four, with the Chief Justice swinging back and forth sufficiently to earn the sobriquet: "the man on the flying trapeze."

Van Devanter retired in 1937 and Roberts and Hughes began siding with the liberal coalition, giving it the necessary votes to uphold New Deal legislation. The rift on the high bench cooled.

But the Supreme Court would once again find itself in deep discord during World War II. This time the frictions were based as much on personality clashes and power struggles as on ideology. The results were bitter, unprecedented feuds that would hamper the Court for more than two decades. The main antagonism was between two of history's most intriguing and obstinate Justices—Felix Frankfurter and William O. Douglas—who were both appointed by President Franklin D. Roosevelt in 1939. A reporter for the *New York Times* revealed the entrenched hostilities that had engulfed the Court by the end of the 1945 Term:

As it is told in the cocktail parties and congressional corridors, personal antagonisms were never more accentuated among the black-robed justices than in the term now closing. The hidden fires have not flamed to the surface in sharp dissents as in past days, but they are smouldering in the closed conference room, so it is said.

One of the high jurists, who cannot be named here, is accused of rigidity which, on one occasion, it is reported, enraged another sufficiently for a violent clash of words. On the other hand, Justice Whosit, well-known figure in the national capital, is credited with almost a hatred for Justice Thatso, and Justice Thatso is said to entertain an utter contempt for his critic. So it goes.

Reports such as these fly thick and fast. Of course, many are exaggerations, but the very multitude of the rumors make for conviction that harmony has flown out the window. Moreover, individual likes and dislikes of the high jurists are not concealed, as in other years. Their friends know these situations and pass them on to eager listeners.

Justice Frankfurter was a short, spectacled former Harvard law professor who had emigrated from Austria at age twelve with his Jewish family. According to a contemporary, he "was inexhaustible in his energy and his curiosity, giving off sparks like an overcharged electric battery." Never at a shortage for words, Frankfurter wrote copious diary entries, letters, and memoirs, all of which unwittingly document his meddling and proselytizing on the Court. Douglas was an avid outdoorsman from a small town in Washington State. He had been recruited by Roosevelt to head up the Securities and Exchange Commission after teaching commercial law at Yale University. Douglas divulged his experiences on the Court in a bestselling autobiography, but his penchant for inventing biographical details to make himself more sympathetic render him an unreliable eyewitness.

William O. Douglas was only forty when Franklin D. Roosevelt appointed him to the Supreme Court in 1939. He served for thirty-six years and seven months—a record. (Courtesy of the Library of Congress)

An influential legal thinker who was better versed in constitutional history than his brethren on the Court, Frankfurter had expected to become their intellectual leader. When first appointed, he did manage briefly to lead the other Roosevelt appointees. Greatly influenced by the war effort in Europe, the Justices joined Frankfurter in ruling in *Minersville v. Gobitas* that students could be lawfully compelled to salute the American flag even if it violated their religious beliefs. Douglas described how he and two others reluctantly went along with Frankfurter in the 1940 case:

> It has been a most difficult one to decide. I had grave doubts about F.F.'s decision, as did Hugo [Black] & Frank [Murphy]. We decided to go along, tho it was very very close in our minds. I talked it over with Brandeis. He was very clear that F.F. was right—he had no doubts. That influenced me. One thing influencing F.F., I suspect, is his early experience as an immigrant. He has told me with what exhilaration he as a lad used to salute the flag in his school in N.Y.C. It was a symbol of a new life to him.

But Frankfurter's didactic professorial airs rubbed his bench-mates the wrong way. He liked to quote from memory the words of his heroes Holmes and Brandeis to his brethren, whom he treated as if they were his law students. Frankfurter was particularly condescending to Justice Stanley F. Reed (1938–1957), a "uniformly gracious, uniformly courteous, uniformly polite" Kentuckian whom Frankfurter considered his intellectual inferior and whom he tried to mentor and control. He confided to a friend: "Reed is largely vegetable—he has managed to give himself a nimbus of reasonableness but is as unjudicial-minded, as flagrantly moved, at times, by irrelevant considerations for adjudication, as any of them. He has a reasonable voice in the service of a dogmatic, worldly, timid mind."

Reed admired Frankfurter's intellect and did not get angry when the former professor patronized him. Nor did he submit. One of his clerks witnessed this scene in 1950, when a frustrated Frankfurter failed yet again to dominate Reed:

> Felix would come all hotted up and charge in to talk with Stanley Reed and to lobby him and try to persuade him of something or other. Felix would have seventeen arguments and be talking like a machine gun and just brandishing his intellectuality and his citations and his European rhetoric and his epigrams. And it was like talking to a Buddha. And I've watched this happen so often and Felix was tiny, small, whirring around like a hornet or like a bee, whirling around this sort of Buddha-like figure [Reed] . . . watching, listening, with a kind of bemused tolerance smile. At the end of which, he would say "Thank you very much Felix. I appreciate your spending the time with me." And he would never, really, engage or respond to any of this and it just drove Felix crazy.

Frankfurter's leadership—and the flag-salute holding—did not endure. He could be extravagant in his flattery of new Justices when they voted his way. But when they didn't, he would turn vindictive and blithely announce that their appointment to the Court had been a mistake. Frankfurter felt especially betrayed by Douglas, whom he had expected to be his disciple. He denounced Douglas for using flattery in a strategic way (an assessment riddled with hypocrisy given that Frankfurter was not above using the same tactic):

> Except in cases where he knows it is useless or in cases where he knows or suspects that people are on to him, he is the most systematic exploiter of flattery I have ever encountered in my life. He tried it on me when he first came on the Court—every opinion of mine that he returned, he returned with the most extravagant praise, all of which ceased after I left him in no doubt that I did not come on to the Court to play politics on the Court but to vote in each case as my poor lights guided me.

But Douglas, who tended to be aloof, had quickly chafed at Frankfurter's relentless and overbearing manner:

> [Frankfurter] was . . . a proselytizer, and every waking hour vigorously promoted the ideas he espoused. Up and down the halls he went, pleading, needling, nudging, probing. He never stopped trying to change the votes on a case until the decision came down. . . . [H]e also indulged in histrionics in Conference. He often came in with piles of books, and on his turn to talk, would pound the table, read from the books, throw them around and create a great disturbance. His purpose was never aimless. His act was designed to get a particular Justice's vote or at least create doubts in the mind of a Justice who was thinking the other way. At times, when another was talking, he would break in, make a derisive comment and shout down the speaker.

To retaliate against Frankfurter, Douglas developed an array of tactics to needle him. He would insult him on the bench:

> When some incompetent soul was wasting our time trying to present a case, I often sent a note to Felix Frankfurter. Sometimes it read: "I understand this chap led your class at Harvard Law School." Sometimes it read: "Rumor has it that this lawyer got the highest grade at Harvard Law School you ever awarded a student." Almost always Felix would be ignited, just like a match.

He was also merciless at undermining him in Conference, where Frankfurter would lecture his brethren to show off his professorial erudition. Justice Potter Stewart (1958–1981) witnessed Douglas's spiteful behavior:

> [A]fter Felix spoke in order of seniority, then it was Bill Douglas' turn, and often, I remember, Bill was absolutely devastating after one of those fifty minute lectures. Bill would say, in a quiet voice, "When I came into this

Roosevelt had appointed Harvard law school professor Felix Frankfurter to the Court a few months before Douglas took his seat. A chronic proselytizer, Frankfurter expected Douglas to be his disciple, but instead the two Justices feuded for decades. (Courtesy of the Library of Congress)

conference, I agreed with the conclusion Felix has just announced; but he's talked me out of it"—which used to drive Felix Frankfurter crazy.

Douglas also borrowed a trick from Justice McReynolds and would absent himself from the table during Frankfurter's long-winded speeches (which, legend has it, usually lasted fifty minutes, the exact length of a

Harvard Law School lecture). Frankfurter's former law student, Justice William J. Brennan, Jr., recalled that Frankfurter just kept talking: "When [Frankfurter] took more time than Bill thought justified, he, on occasions, would rise from his seat, approach the Chief Justice and say, 'When Felix finishes, Chief, I'll be back,' and leave the conference. Justice Frankfurter would be furious but nevertheless would continue until he had fully expressed his view."

But their antipathy was not merely a schoolboy rivalry or a battle of outsized egos. Its roots were substantive. Frankfurter grew more rigid and more conservative during his tenure and became fixated with preserving the social order. This put him at odds with Douglas and the other increasingly liberal Justices who were intent on expanding civil liberties. They also had different work styles: Douglas was one of the Court's all-time fastest workers and was very impatient when his brethren, especially Frankfurter, took their time getting out their opinions. Taking another page from McReynolds, Douglas would often leave for his summer vacation—mountain-climbing and horseback-riding adventures—once he had finished his individual writing assignments, but before the term was over and the Court had handed down all its opinions.

Another bone of contention was Frankfurter's suspicion that Douglas was using the Court as a springboard to get elected to the White House. In his diary, Frankfurter recorded the views he expressed to a fellow Justice explaining why Douglas would be violating the Court's sanctity if he tried for a presidential run in 1944:

> When a priest enters a monastery, he must leave—or ought to leave—all sorts of worldly desires behind him. And this Court has no excuse for being unless it's a monastery. And this isn't idle, high-flown talk. We are all poor human creatures and it's difficult enough to be wholly intellectually and morally disinterested when one has no other motive except that of being a judge according to one's full conscience. And the returns are all in on judges of the Court who, while on the Court, have had conflicting political ambitions. We know all the instances and the experience is unedifying and disastrous.

Douglas, who did indeed feel that the Court did not provide an adequate forum for his abilities, came very close to being named to the 1944 Democratic ticket as the vice-presidential candidate. Four years later, he turned down President Truman's offer of the vice-presidential nomination because he thought Truman would lose the race.

Douglas allied himself with Hugo L. Black, a folksy Senator from Alabama, who had also been appointed by President Roosevelt. Justice Black's growing insistence that the First Amendment be given a "preferred" position in the Bill of Rights and that the abridgment of speech be prohibited as much as possible, increasingly infuriated Frankfurter.

As Black's judicial views drew support on the Court, Frankfurter, a proponent of judicial restraint, complained to a friend about what he saw as Black's radicalism: "Hugo is a self-righteous, self-deluded part fanatic, part demagogue, who really disbelieves in law, thinks it essentially manipulation of language. Intrinsically, the best brain in the lot, but undisciplined and 'functional' in its employment, an instrument for supporting a predetermined result, not a means for responsible inquiry."

After two particularly long and trying Conferences in 1943, Frankfurter received a visit in his chambers from another Justice who resented Black's activism and growing power. Writing in his diary, Frankfurter approvingly recorded the words he said a "tired and dispirited" Owen J. Roberts (1930–1945) used to criticize Black and his allies: "we tear up law with complete indifference to the precedents or the consequences. Black with his vehemence and vitality and lack of savoir faire and ruthlessness and unflagging industry will before long absolutely control the Court."

Indeed, Black's persuasive style, honed as a politician, made him an effective advocate for his judicial philosophy. His son, Hugo Black, Jr., later explained why ultimately Frankfurter was no match for him:

> With all his brilliance, charm and stratagems, however, FF [Felix Frankfurter] could not really match Daddy in picking up converts. Even though their passionate conviction of the righteousness of their positions was equal, there was one important difference that gave Hugo the edge. FF had gained his reputation in an academic system, where he was mainly concerned with instructing, not persuading. But Hugo had gotten ahead by convincing ordinary citizens—juries, voters—as well as congressmen and judges, that his view was right. When out to persuade, FF was likely to try to instruct his brethren by presenting an intellectual tour de force, often in language that was more a display of his exceptional vocabulary than a means of communication. FF tended to believe that he was a member of an intellectual elite, and before long some of his colleagues came to believe that FF did not consider them to be of this elite and may have resented his attitude. Hugo, on the other hand, believed in no elite of any kind. If he thought he was brighter than any of the brethren, he never admitted it. Whenever he wished to make a point, he tried to persuade the other Justices with the same sample rhetoric he used with juries and political audiences, employing among other things his sound logic, acting and storytelling abilities, and quotations from great men of the past.

As if Douglas and Black were not enough, Frankfurter faced a third opponent on the Court: Frank Murphy. (He referred to the three of them belligerently as "the Axis.") Murphy had joined the Court in 1940 with reluctance. Having served as governor of Michigan and as Attorney General, he preferred the active life of a politician to the contemplative life on the Court. As a Justice, Murphy was unabashed about siding with the downtrodden and expressed a desire to write compassion into the law. He was more interested in results than legal craftsmanship. This infuriated Frankfurter, who nonetheless admired Murphy, a devout Catholic, for being a man of conscience. But Frankfurter did not respect Murphy's legal mind. Douglas later revealed the pettiness of Frankfurter's scorn:

> Murphy was a special target of Frankfurter, who made fun of him behind his back. Murphy had a disease that caused poor blood circulation in his extremities. So he spent the hours in Conference rubbing his hands, massaging his fingers, and the like. Frankfurter pilloried Murphy for the habit, whispering that Murphy was so distraught that he was trying to solve legal problems by wringing his hands.

The divisions on the Court in the 1940s were exacerbated by Chief Justice Harlan Fiske Stone's disinclination to lead with a firm hand. The attributes that had made Stone an exemplary legal scholar and Associate Justice did not translate well to being Chief Justice. He liked to engage in lengthy intellectual debates when an Associate Justice expressed an opposing viewpoint. He enjoyed freewheeling discussions where every possible aspect of a case was considered and debated as if in a college seminar. Conferences dragged on and on without conclusion. Frankfurter once noted in his diary that a single Conference session had lasted nearly eight hours. "We have [Conferences] all the time these days and they seem eternally long—and often dull," complained Douglas. Stone's penchant for allowing open-ended and heated debate, instead of keeping discussions to the point, permitted personal hostilities to flourish. Stone wearily confided to a friend: "I have had much difficulty herding my collection of fleas."

The fractured Court sometimes resulted in murky or inconsistent law that was hard for lower court judges to interpret. A startling example of this was the turnabout in 1943 from the 1940 case compelling schoolchildren to salute the flag even if their religion opposed such action. The Justices reversed themselves, this time holding that First Amendment rights outweigh political concerns. Prominent New York circuit court judge Learned Hand, who found himself trying to interpret a growing number of precedent-toppling Supreme Court decisions in his lower court, complained to his friend Frankfurter about "the Axis":

> [T]hey are sowing the wind, those reforming colleagues of yours. As soon as they convince the people that they can do what they want, the people will demand of them that they do what the people want. I wonder whether in times of bland reaction—[and] they are coming—Hillbilly Hugo, Good Old Bill, and Jesus lover of my Soul [Murphy] will like that.

Chief Justice Stone's sudden death in 1946 did not improve matters. His successor, Fred M. Vinson (1946–1953), was a close friend of President Harry S Truman, who admired his political acumen and negotiating skills and thought he could heal the rifts on the Court. After Vinson's first Conference in 1946, however, the ever-critical Frankfurter zeroed in on the new Chief's weakness at presenting cases:

> He is confident and easy-going and sure and shallow. Of course it is a heavy burden that he is taking on and one must give him ample time to show his qualities, but he seems to me to have the confident air of a man who does not see all the complexities of problems and blithely hits the obvious points. He does it all in good temper and with dispatch. He evidently has been told that Stone used to fumble over things and allow talk to be too loose.

A few weeks later, Frankfurter confirmed that Vinson lacked depth: "Vinson conducts the Conference with ease and good humor, disposing of each case rather briefly, by choosing, as it were, to float merely on the surface of the problems raised by the cases." Frankfurter's colleagues soon came to agree with this assessment of the new Chief as an intellectual lightweight. According to William K. Bachelder, a law clerk to Justice Sherman Minton in the 1952 Term, Vinson by then had lost the respect of the Associate Justices. Bachelder recalled that they "would discuss in his presence the view that the Chief's job should rotate annually and . . . made no bones about regarding him—correctly—as their intellectual inferior."

Unanimity in deciding cases plunged to a new low under Vinson. And a sideshow feud—between Justice Black and Justice Robert H. Jackson, who had been appointed in 1941—heated up. A master prose stylist and a judicial pragmatist, Jackson was ambitious. He had his eye on either the chief justiceship or the presidency. When President Truman passed him over in favor of Vinson, Justice Jackson, who at the time was absent from the Court to serve in Germany as the chief prosecutor at the Nuremburg trials of Nazi war criminals, was furious. He suspected that Black had torpedoed his promotion to Chief Justice by threatening to resign if the President nominated him. "If war is declared on me, I propose to wage it with the weapons of the open warrior, not those of the stealthy assassin," Jackson warned Truman.

Jackson's weapon of choice was a 1,500-word cable to Congress denouncing Black. At issue was a 1945 labor case, decided five to four, in which Black had refused to disqualify himself despite Jackson's insistence he do so because his former law partner was counsel to the plaintiffs. The ensuing publicity did much to damage the Court's prestige. Newspapers called for both the resignation of Black and Jackson. One prominent lawyer, Charles C. Burlingham, lamented the fallout:

> We are all shocked by Jackson's statement—foolish and worse! . . . It is hard to see how he can sit on the same bench with Black . . . Black himself is smart and hard working, but he is a skunk and I can prove it—but I won't trouble to do that now. He will never resign! These quarrels have lowered the prestige of the Court greatly. Our people are not much interested in courts or judges, but the Supreme Court is an exception as it represents the third estate.

The fact that Jackson went on to join Frankfurter and Vinson in forming a conservative coalition would only further drive a wedge between him and Black.

As the Cold War escalated in the 1950s, and security issues permeated Supreme Court cases, Frankfurter's conservative bloc became dominant. Jackson died in 1954, but other Justices, notably John Marshall Harlan, stepped in to follow Frankfurter's lead. Yet the gentlemanly Harlan emerged as a cool counterweight to some of the hotheads he served with. One of his law clerks in the 1957 Term was amazed at how diplomatic Harlan managed to remain amongst all the backbiting:

> An unusual aspect of the Justice's civility was that, to the best of my recollection, in our entire year together he never personally criticized another Justice or anyone else. To be sure, he often objected, sometimes strenuously to certain legal conclusions or reasoning. And on occasion he would signal perplexity or disapproval by the quizzical lifting of an eyebrow. But I never heard him say a disparaging word about anyone's capacity or motivation, even though he sometimes was provoked, as when he received a proposed opinion from another Justice in a complex federal jurisdiction case that, to put it kindly, was difficult to comprehend.

Vinson died in 1953, and was succeeded by Earl Warren, who, like his predecessor, was neither an intellectual nor a legal scholar. But Warren, who had served as governor of California, was a gifted administrator. Justice Stewart later praised him for adapting his managerial talents to lead the splintered Court: "I think he came to realize very early, certainly long before I came here [1958] that this group of nine rather prima donnaish people could not be led, could not be told, in the way that the Governor of California can tell a subordinate, do this or do that."

Indeed Chief Justice Warren pulled off a remarkable feat in 1954 when he persuaded all nine Justices to sign onto the *Brown v. Board of Education* opinion striking down segregation in schools, leaving lower courts no choice but to comply. He would continue to find ways to muster majorities and pulled the Court in a liberal direction in the 1960s.

Despite Warren's competent leadership, Frankfurter and Douglas's feud continued unabated until Frankfurter retired in 1962 because of ill health.

Douglas had grown more openly disdainful of Frankfurter as the years rolled by. In 1954 Frankfurter had complained to his friend Learned Hand: "Bill [Douglas] is the most cynical, shamelessly immoral character I've ever known. With him I have no more relation than the necessities of court work require. He is too unscrupulous for any unavoidable entanglement."

By the end of his tenure, Frankfurter's behavior had grown increasingly volatile. In one telling episode in the 1960 Term, he erupted in Conference over the majority's consensus in a landmark case requiring state police officers to comply with Fourth Amendment standards when making searches. A shaken Justice Brennan went back to Chambers and confided to his clerk, Richard S. Arnold, about the blow up. Arnold relayed his boss's account in his diary:

> In conference, Frankfurter became violent. He shook, almost cried—it is "a death blow for federalism." He demanded reargument—which was voted down, five to four. Most of the tirade was aimed straight at the boss [Brennan], who said "I've had things said to me today that haven't been said since I was a child."

Frankfurter's behavior had worsened to the point that Douglas had even felt compelled to write—but did not send—this memo to his brethren announcing he would cease attending Conferences so as to avoid his nemesis's wrath:

> The continuous violent outbursts against me [in Conference] by my Brother Frankfurter give me great concern. They do not bother me. For I have been on the hustings too long.
>
> But he's an ill man; and these violent outbursts create a fear in my heart that one of them may be his end.
>
> I do not consciously do anything to annoy him. But twenty-odd years have shown that I am a disturbing symbol in his life. His outbursts against me are increasing in intensity. In the interest of his health and long life I have reluctantly concluded to participate in no more conferences while he is on the Court.

Although Douglas was the only Justice not to attend Frankfurter's funeral in 1965, he later insisted that there was no personal animosity between them, but that they simply had "clashed often at the ideological level." This attempt to downplay their feud was clearly aimed at posterity. But by then Douglas had also gained a better understanding of what he thought motivated his rival's behavior:

> Frankfurter had a basic weakness. I think he had deep inside him a feeling of inadequacy. He was a man of short stature. Perhaps that was part of it. He longed to be accepted. He was an artist at teasing and taunting the Establishment and its advocates. . . . But he also needed to be accepted by them

and honored and admired by them. While he wanted the Establishment to be decent and civilized, his basic positions were ultimately aligned with it.

And Douglas himself, while brilliant, had never been a paragon. He stayed aloof from his colleagues. His clerks feared his temper. He divorced three of his four wives. Douglas officially retired from the Court after thirty-six years (a record) in 1975 following an incapacitating stroke, but he quickly changed his mind and refused to let go. He tried to vote in cases that had been accepted prior to his resignation—an unprecedented action and one that Chief Justice Warren Burger asked staff to ignore. "Bill is like an old firehouse dog, too old to run along with the trucks, but his ears prick up just the same," Burger told a clerk.

11

⚖

A Peek Inside Chambers

Clerk Stories

Dean Acheson was horrified to realize that he had committed a grave error while clerking for Justice Louis D. Brandeis in the 1919 Term. While researching a Prohibition case questioning whether beer with 3.4 percent alcohol was intoxicating, he had cited to the wrong cases in the footnotes of Brandeis's opinion. Acheson, who would later go on to become Secretary of State, recounted the embarrassing episode:

> On the Monday when the opinion was due to come down, I courted displeasure by knocking off work to listen in Court. While other opinions were being announced, a page kept bringing Justice Brandeis volumes of reports. This seemed strange and vaguely ominous. At length, when the Chief Justice nodded to him . . . he shook his head. Something was very wrong. Back at the office, I waited. When he came, the Justice put two volumes of state reports on my desk. "Did you read all the cases you cited in the footnotes?" he asked. I answered that I had. "Suppose you read these two again," he said and went into his study.
>
> The cases had nothing whatever to do with the propositions for which they were cited. Plainly, having made from the digests a list of cases to look up, I had checked two wrong ones for what some other cases had held. The explanation was too stupid to bother making. When I expressed chagrin and regret, he dismissed the matter with a sentence—"Please remember that your function is to correct my errors, not to introduce errors of your own." I remembered.

The fear of making a mistake has always weighed heavily on clerks. Indeed, clerking for a Supreme Court Justice can be as arduous and stressful as it is prestigious and exhilarating. "This job of being a law clerk is a pretty mean one," Justice William O. Douglas once warned, "It entails tremendously long hours and is very exacting. As you can imagine, fumbles are costly."

The first law clerk, Thomas A. Russell, was hired in 1882 by Justice Horace Gray, who paid him out of his own pocket. Four years later, Congress began providing funds for each Justice to hire a "stenographic clerk" to take dictation, copy out opinions, and perform other administrative tasks. This was in response to the Justices' cries for help as they were drowning in work in that era. Some of these clerks stayed on for many years.

Initially, only Horace Gray gave his clerks substantive duties (such as performing legal research) in addition to stenographic work. Gray's half-brother, a professor at Harvard Law School, was tasked with recruiting the school's best students to clerk for him. Some needed persuading. Samuel Williston, for one, later confessed his reluctance at accepting an offer from Gray: "Though I had some doubt as to the wisdom of postponing my entrance into practice, I finally accepted the offer." As all the Justices worked at home into the 1930s, so did their clerks. The only contact clerks then had with each other was in the Supreme Court library or in the Courtroom—if they managed to steal time to attend oral arguments.

Williston's memories of the duties he performed during the 1888 Term emphasized the apprenticeship aspect of the job:

> My employer's method for dealing with me was quite according to the Law School tradition, if he had been trying to instruct me rather than get help for himself. When he returned from court each day he would hand me the records and the briefs of any cases in which arguments had been completed, and he would tell me to look over these "novelettes" as he called them, and see what I thought of them. This I would do, often being compelled to work in the evening in order to be prepared to make my reports. When I made them, the Judge would question me to bring out the essential points, and I rarely learned what he thought of a case until I had been thoroughly cross-examined. I would also frequently be asked to write an opinion on the cases that had been assigned to the Judge. I do not wish, however, to give the impression that my work served for more than a stimulus for the judge's own mind. He was a careful man and examined cases for himself, and wrote his own opinions; my work served only as a suggestion.

Williston stayed with the Justice for only one term before starting his own legal career, becoming a legendary professor at Harvard Law School and the century's leading expert on contract law.

Another clerk in that era, Edgar R. Rombauer, recorded similar memories of his experience. After completing law school in 1890, he was hired as a "private secretary" to Justice John Marshall Harlan while waiting to turn twenty-one and take the bar exam. Rombauer had been working in a Chicago law office with Justice Harlan's son, who recommended him to his father. His duties were a mix of secretarial and legal; he found the non-stenographic work "very interesting":

> My work consisted in part of taking letters for the Judge in shorthand and transcribing them on the typewriter, in part of reading records in cases and stating the facts from them, in part of examining authorities in briefs filed in cases pending before the court, and in doing the odds and ends always attendant upon a position involving close personal employer and employee.

The clerkship position slowly evolved when Congress appropriated funds in 1919 to allow each Justice to employ one law clerk in addition to a secretary—a perquisite that became permanent in 1924. Charles Evans Hughes, who served as Associate Justice from 1910 to 1916, described the unsettled state of clerking before this transition took place:

> Most of the Justices had secretaries who were lawyers, but these spent the greater part of their time in stenographic work and typewriting correspondence, memoranda and opinions. My secretaries (while Associate Justice I had three, in succession) were fine young men who had been admitted to the bar, but as I kept them busy with dictation, hating to write in longhand, they had little or no time to devote to research and whatever was necessary in that line I did myself. Occasionally, the question of providing law clerks in addition to secretaries would be raised but nothing would be done. Some suggested that if we had experienced law clerks, it might be thought that they were writing our opinions. An exception was Chief Justice [Edward Douglass] White who hired a law clerk and paid him out of his own pocket. Justice [Oliver Wendell] Holmes who wrote his letters and opinions in his own hand and did not need a stenographer took each year as his secretary a brilliant graduate of the Harvard Law School and made a companion of him.

Despite the luxury of being permitted two assistants, some Justices chose not to hire a second clerk to perform legal research. And the clerks who were hired as legal researchers still had to do a fair amount of transcribing in the days before word processing and photocopiers. When Milton Handler was engaged as a clerk in 1926, Justice Harlan Fiske Stone made it very clear that he must be a good typist. He was also inquisitive about his marital status:

> Stone interviewed me in the dean's office of Columbia Law School for possible appointment as law secretary (as it was then called) for the 1926 Term, his second on the Court. When I walked into this office, I noted that the lower part of the window had been opened full length. There was a gale raging in the room. There he sat with his jacket wide open, oblivious to the wind and the cold. It was bad enough to be quaking with nervousness, but to be shivering also from the cold was hardly conducive to a satisfactory

interview. He put me at ease, asking me some pertinent questions about the courses I had taken, what I thought of the law school, and probing my qualifications for the clerkship. He then told me that the work was very heavy and that he felt it necessary to impose two requirements. One was that I not marry during the period of my clerkship and, second, that I must be able to type. I had to confess that typing was not one of my talents, but I was very emphatic that there was no prospect whatsoever of my getting married that year. He made it clear that the reason for the unusual condition of not marrying was that the work of a clerk was very exacting and time consuming, and he didn't feel that it would be fair to a young bride to spend a year in Washington, never seeing or having the company of her spouse. Thus reassured, he offered the job to me.

Yet Arthur E. Sutherland, who clerked for Justice Holmes the following term, recalled that his impending marriage was not a deal-breaker:

During my second year out of law school, I was grubbing away one day, wishing I could get enough free time for a trip to Northampton to see a girl I was to marry next fall, when I had a telegram from Felix Frankfurter [his professor at Harvard Law School] suggesting that I might be Holmes' secretary the next year. Excitement was crossed with doubt—I vaguely remembered a tradition that the secretary mustn't be engaged. A horrid alternative! I went to Cambridge (via Northampton) to see Frankfurter. He expressed doubt but said he'd see the Justice. Finally I had a telegram in Rochester from Felix Frankfurter saying I could have the job and the lady too.

The most substantive task asked of clerks in the 1920s was to write memos summarizing petitions for certiorari (petitions asking the Supreme Court to take up a case for review). But, according to Handler, Justice Stone took only a cursory look at his clerk's memos before going into Conference to discuss with his brethren which petitions should be granted:

On Saturday, the day of the conference, Stone would amble in after 10:00. Even though the conference was scheduled for 12:00 at the Capitol, he would begin by reading his mail and dictating responses. It was not until sometime after 11:00 that he started preparing for the conference. The agenda normally included about seventy-five matters, including eighteen argued cases, several submitted cases on which I prepared memos, certiorari petitions and motions. Each of the twenty-five certiorari memos that I had done during the week was normally about one-page long: he would read them in about one half hour—approximately one minute for each.

When it was time for the Justice to write opinions in cases assigned to him, Handler, like other clerks, provided research assistance, checked the accuracy of citations, and contributed footnotes. But Stone did not allow him to prepare drafts:

Stone would tackle the hardest case first, leaving to the last the simpler ones. With his experience as an appellate lawyer, he could digest records and briefs with phenomenal speed. Before long, he would begin to write. His first draft was written in pencil on yellow sheets of paper, in a scrawl notorious for illegibility. After he wrote two or three pages, he would summon Miss [Gertrude] Jenkins and immediately dictate what he had written. If he waited too long, neither he nor any other human being could decipher his writing. . . . At this stage, Stone's sole objective was to get his thoughts on paper; he was not yet striving for literary perfection. He explained to me that he never paid the slightest attention to organization, wording, punctuation, or any of the elements of writing. He said the important thing was to get his ideas down on paper. If he did that, he would have plenty of time to reorganize, to rewrite, and to polish.

Once the opinion was drafted, Handler helped to revise it. This could be a manually laborious process in the days of cutting and pasting with scissors and glue:

When Stone had completed the draft, he would turn it over to me for revision. That was the clerk's main role in the process. I would then work on the opinion, chewing it up, tearing it to pieces and reorganizing it. What I did constituted the second draft. We would argue about the validity and cogency of the opinion's reasoning. We might even fight about the result, although there was little chance that the Justice would go counter to the vote of the Court, although, to be sure, this sometimes happened. Then the two of us would sit together, sometimes for days, rewriting and reorganizing, dealing first with structure and organization.

Another Stone clerk, this one from the 1931 Term, summed up the nature of their working relationship: "He made one feel a co-worker—a very junior and subordinate co-worker, to be sure, but nevertheless one whose opinion counted and whose assistance was valuable."

Dean Acheson, Brandeis's clerk who committed the error during the 1919 Term, also reported that he and the Justice had a collaborative working style, revising each other's drafts:

From the assignment slip, the Justice would indicate the cases on which he would start drafting and those on which I was to start. If there was a dissenting opinion to be written, he would give instructions about that. He drafted in longhand; I, on a typewriter. When he reached a point where he wanted his draft checked, he would give it to me and take mine from me in whatever state it was; sometimes using parts of it, sometimes not. My instructions regarding his work were to look with suspicion on every statement of fact until it was proved from the record of the case, and on every statement of law until I had exhausted the authorities. If additional points should be made, I was to develop them thoroughly. Sometimes my work took the form of a revision of his; sometimes of a memorandum of suggestions to him. He was remarkably tolerant of physical alteration and often dissection of his sheets.

When, at length, the time came for a fair copy, the court printer made it from the nearly undecipherable manuscript put together with the aid of scissors and paste. The printer's proof was, in turn, subjected to further revision. When we were both satisfied, the final proof was circulated among the Justices for their editing, suggestions, and concurrence or dissent. A touching part of our relationship was the Justice's insistence that nothing should go out unless we were *both* satisfied with the product. His patience and generosity were inexhaustible.

When the Supreme Court got its own building in 1935, the clerks became more integrated into the institution. But some of the Justices dragged their feet about moving into their new Chambers. John Knox, clerk to the ill-tempered James C. McReynolds, endured an "extremely lonely" year working in isolation at the Justice's apartment. His description of preparing a dissenting opinion with McReynolds reveals how tedious a clerkship could be:

Following this latest conference with the three other conservatives, the "paste and shears" method of writing was to be resorted to. In other words, McReynolds now announced that we were to quote verbatim the three opinions of the lower courts instead of summarizing them in his own language . . . dictated changes in other paragraphs, and gradually a new draft of the opinion was developed. I merely typed his dictation and contributed nothing to the substance of the opinion. Nor did I attempt to.

As the days went by, McReynolds continued to labor on the dissent—dictating, revising my typing, dictating again, and revising again. And I was, as far as I knew, still operating as an efficient secretary and law clerk—despite the late hours I had been keeping. The duties of the job had now become so routine that I almost never made an error either in taking dictation or in transcribing my shorthand notes . . . I was also never late to work in the morning, and I never left early at the end of the day . . . I did not leave the apartment without permission unless McReynolds happened to be away, too, and I always tried to be back before his expected return. . . .

Despite all this effort, however, the gradual deterioration in my position as a law clerk continued. It was as if the very floor were slowly slipping out from under me—try as I might to prevent it. . . . But the difficulty was that I had by now simply lost all interest in the Justice as a man. I had finally come to realize that we were light years apart in our ways of thinking and in reacting to people—even though we worked together each day in close surroundings and in ostensible harmony.

McReynolds did ask Knox once to draft an opinion, providing him with the enjoyable prospect of performing an interesting task. But it turned out to be an academic assignment. "[H]e quietly reached across the desk and silently, almost gently let my opinion glide downward into his wastebasket," recalled the disappointed clerk.

Gradually, the Justices began to allow their clerks to take a crack at drafting opinions. This was more a reward for a year of heavy toil than because the Justices needed their help. For example, John P. Frank, who clerked for Hugo L. Black in the 1942 Term, was allowed to try his hand at drafting an opinion—but only at the end of the term and in a dissent of little importance:

> In the early 1940's at least, Justice Black wrote the first draft of all his opinions, except that toward the end of the year he would let the youngster try his hand at one first draft of something extremely unimportant. In my own case, the day of glory came when I did the first draft of a lone dissent on a minor point of statutory construction, which the Justice then revised and which no one has ever noticed since.

Law clerk Bennett Boskey drove Chief Justice Harlan Fiske Stone to the Supreme Court for the opening day of the October Term in 1941 (C. Roger Nelson, Stone's other law clerk, took the back seat). (Courtesy of Bennett Boskey)

Frank described the primary duty of a clerk in his day as performing research, but that there could be ancillary social duties:

> The tasks of the clerks are also very much the product of the whims of their Justices. In general, it is the job of the clerk to be the eyes and legs for his judge, finding and bringing in useful materials. This can involve an immense amount of work depending upon how curious the Justice is. . . . The clerks may also have semi-social duties, like those who visited with Holmes or took walks with Stone or played tennis with Black, or superintended the circulation of guests at the Brandeis Sunday teas. All of this is in the spirit of an amiable relationship between a wise, elderly man and a young cub at the bar.

In the 1940s clerks were still being selected in a somewhat haphazard fashion. Nepotism had been a factor in the early days of clerking: both Justices William Rufus Day (1903–1922) and John Marshall Harlan (1877–1911) had hired their own sons to clerk for them. Justice Gray's half-brother, John Chipman Gray, recruited the best graduates from Harvard Law School and sent them for one-year stints to Gray, and then to his successor, Oliver Wendell Holmes, Jr. Before being appointed to the Court in 1939, Felix Frankfurter, a Harvard law school professor, had taken over the selection of clerks for Holmes, whom he greatly admired. Justice Brandeis, who also entrusted Frankfurter with selecting his clerks, once explained why this "feeder" method suited him:

> There isn't one chance in a thousand for any graduate of the Harvard Law School to come to the Court these days without Professor Frankfurter's approval. . . . Of course a Justice can appoint a law clerk if he wishes. It is more convenient, however, for some of us to have a professor make the choice because he knows many of the students and associates with them for several years. Down here in Washington I don't get to see any students—from Harvard or from any other school.

Other Justices have chosen clerks from their own alma maters, also relying on trusted law professors and law school deans to help make the selections. Justice Stone, for example, predominantly hired clerks from Columbia Law School, where he had been dean. Potter Stewart liked Yale Law School graduates, as did Black—but usually on the condition that, like him, they were born in the South. Many other Justices have favored clerks from their own geographic area or from their assigned circuits. For example, Frank Murphy and Lewis F. Powell, Jr. picked some graduates from the state law schools in Michigan and Virginia, respectively. The first female clerk, Lucille Lomen, was recruited in 1944 by William O. Douglas, who was stymied by a shortage of stellar male candidates due to the war effort. The next female clerk was not hired until twenty-two years later.

In recent decades, a few Justices have sought out clerks from lesser-known law schools. Others rotate the schools from which they select their clerks. Ivy League Schools still dominate but no longer hold a monopoly. Deans and professors at law schools with whom the Justice has a close relationship often make the initial recommendation. So do lower court judges who have already employed the clerk for one term. Nowadays, committees composed of a Justice's former clerks usually manage the selection process, prescreening or even interviewing candidates. Service on the school's law review and top grades are crucial to getting the job. Yet Justices are also looking for good character. Justice Clarence Thomas once compared choosing clerks to "selecting mates in a foxhole." In a similar spirit, William H. Rehnquist explained how he liked to evaluate potential clerks:

> Naturally I want law clerks who will get along with me and with whom I will get along, but this is not much of a problem; very few employees would fail to get along with their boss when the job lasts only one year. I also want law clerks who will get along with my secretaries and messenger, since the total population of our chambers is eight, and we all have to work together to be productive. I like law clerks who seem to have a sense of humor, and who do not give the impression of being too sold upon themselves.

Those lucky enough to be granted a formal interview by a Justice come to Washington at their own expense. One clerk candidate described his revealing interview with the self-effacing Harry A. Blackmun in 1988:

> From across a broad, nearly bare desk, the Justice began his questioning, the talk of family and upbringing and general interests of which I had been warned. The purpose by now was clear. Rather than a grilling, he wanted simply to see how we'd get along for forty-five minutes or so—and how, together with three other clerks, two secretaries, and a messenger, we might get along for what, if he hired me, promised to be the most arduous year of my life.
>
> Much of the time it sounded as if he were trying to talk me out of the job. More than once he alluded to the hard work and long hours. And with a self-deprecation hard to imagine (or believe) in a Supreme Court Justice, he insisted that his was the least desirable clerkship at the Court, in part because his colleagues were more intelligent and better teachers than he.

In 1941 the Justices had been authorized to hire two clerks to meet the increasing demands of the workload. The number of petitions that the Justices were asked to review each term began to surge in the second half of the twentieth century—from a stable one thousand until 1950, climbing to five thousand in 1980, to more than ten thousand in 2010. To cope with this explosion, the Justices were permitted to add a third clerk in 1970;

four years later Congress increased the allotment to four. When John Paul Stevens was appointed in 1975, however, he decided to stick with only three, a policy he continued until his retirement in 2010. The Chief Justice may employ a fifth clerk to help with administrative tasks, but John G. Roberts, Jr., says he only needs four and his predecessor, William H. Rehnquist, only employed three.

Once hired, clerks must be shown the ropes. Justice Rehnquist explained how he indoctrinated new arrivals: "I ask the new clerks to begin work about the first of July, just at the time the Court will have recessed for the summer. I ask one of the old law clerks to stay for ten days to help break in the new ones, and the Court also conducts orientation sessions for the new law clerks." There is a formal welcoming party for clerks held several weeks before the term opens. But one clerk described it as not much of an icebreaker:

> Aside from chance encounters, clerks did not meet Justices other than their own until a welcoming cocktail party near the end of the summer recess. I remember a dazzling but awkward event, thirty-six clerks mingling (sort of) with most of the Justices and much of the upper echelon Court staff. For a while, the clerks from each Chambers tended to congregate among themselves, diplomats from nine separate nation-states, wine cups in hand, appraising their counterparts around the chandeliered room.

Training new law clerks each year is hard work. "It's good for me. It keeps me from getting lazy," Brandeis once admitted. One of Stanley F. Reed's clerks highlighted the value of introducing fresh minds each year: "[Clerks] bring a continual infusion of the latest thinking of the law schools to the bench and bring the enthusiasm and the new perspectives of younger people to judges who, in many ways, are quite isolated from what's maybe going on at the universities, etc. So, I think it's a uniquely valuable function in that regard."

Of the incoming new work, certiorari petitions are by far the most numerous (original jurisdiction claims and other applications make up the balance). "Certs," as they are informally called, are requests to the Supreme Court to hear and decide a case that the petitioner has lost in a federal court of appeals or a state supreme court. The unwritten rule is for certiorari to be granted if four out of the nine Justices agree to review the case. The Supreme Court most often will review cases where there have been different decisions in lower courts in a similar question to be decided or when it believes a lower court has incorrectly applied a Supreme Court precedent. Clerks learn to evaluate cert petitions with these criteria in mind. They then write concise memoranda—usually a page or at most two—that disclose the nature of the case, the questions presented, how the issues have been raised, and whether or not the law clerk thinks the case is "certworthy" and why—that is, whether the law clerk recommends that certiorari should be granted or should be denied. When John Knox arrived in August 1936 to clerk for Justice McReynolds, he was faced with a pile of petitions to plow through all by himself:

> The floor of the entire room was literally filled to a depth of more than a foot with hundreds of statements of fact, briefs, answers, etc.—all comprising what seemed to be countless petitions for certiorari. There were at the time approximately five hundred petitions piled on the floor of that room. All of these would have to be read before the opening of Court in October, and a page referring to each petition would then have to be typed. I had five weeks and two days in which to do this work.

But Knox's experience was atypical in that era: the other Justices routinely helped their clerks handle the certiorari petitions. With the exception of Brandeis, Frankfurter, and Brennan—who resisted having their clerks summarize petitions—the cert work was shared to varying degrees between clerk and Justice until the late 1960s, when the overworked Justices finally had to relinquish the task entirely. After three decades on the Court, Justice Douglas neatly explained to his clerks exactly how he used their cert memos during the term:

> The purpose of the cert memo is to prepare an accurate summary of the issues in the case which can be used three months or a year from the time it is written so as to give a rather complete conception of what the case involves without going back to the original briefs and records.
> The flow of cases is so great that it is difficult to carry in mind even during one term the precise issues raised in each case. Some of the cases in which you prepare cert memos will be discussed that very week but others will go over from Conference to Conference and a final vote and discussion may not be had until some months later. In that time the case may very well become dim in the memories of everyone in the office. . . .
> During the summer I go over the cases in the Far West and merely send back my votes attached to each numbered case. I make no separate votes. During the winter, while I am here, I go over each case separately from the law clerks' memos.

Until 1935, the Justices formally considered in Conference every cert petition the Court received. But then, in the interest of efficiency, Chief Justice Charles Evans Hughes decided to put the cases he thought were frivolous or unimportant on what came to be called the "dead list"—indicating they would not be discussed in Conference unless a Justice specifically requested it. This effectively gave the clerks more power, as the Justices came to rely heavily on their cert memos to determine if a worthy case was being overlooked. A clerk to Chief Justice Earl Warren in the 1961 Term recalled the crucial role of clerks in performing the initial triage:

> With regard to each of these requests to be heard, we could suggest "grant"—almost never suggested; "discuss"—more liberally suggested by us than acted upon by him; or "X-deny"—suggesting that the Chief not even include the case on a list he circulated to the Court weekly of petitions to be discussed at the Justice's next conference. Of course, any Justice could request a full discussion of any such petition; not even the Chief's recommendations were dispositive. Nevertheless, our routing of the cert petitions to the "X-deny" list was probably the most significant (and virtually unreviewed) aspect of our work at the Court.

By the 1960s, the Justices felt increasingly burdened by the rising number of certiorari petitions—now numbering in the thousands—which each Chamber was expected to read and summarize each year. In 1972 the Justices decided to pool collectively their clerks and divvy up the incoming cases. Clerks in the "cert pool" began writing summary memoranda that were then shared among all the Justices. But not all members of the Court agreed to participate in the cert pool: Douglas, Brennan, Potter Stewart, and Thurgood Marshall declined. Douglas explained his hesitation to Chief Justice Warren Burger:

> I like to go over these petitions personally. They are interesting and absorbing, and for me much more meaningful than when they are reduced to a memorandum written by someone else . . . I think that the more Justices who look at these petitions, the better the end product will be. Different eyes see different things, and the merits of these petitions obviously cannot be routed through a computer. The law clerks are fine. Most of them are sharp and able. But after all, they have never been confirmed by the Senate and the job here is so highly personal, depending upon the judgment, discretion, experience and point of view of each of the nine of us that in my view the fewer obstacles put in our way, the better.

Before the advent of the cert pool, clerks had learned to tailor cert memos to their particular Justice's needs. For example, a 1955 clerk recalled how his boss, Justice Stanley Reed, preferred them written:

> Reed was not as interested in full-blown, thorough analyses of cert petitions as some of the other justices were. He wanted you to, in as few words as possible, tell him what the turning issues were. He really wanted you to synthesize them as much as possible to give him a sense of how important it was or wasn't. He was more interested in learning how important the matter was than whether or not it had been decided correctly below. As a consequence our cert memos were significantly less long than almost any other clerk's. And he could go through those very, very quickly. And then he would end

up with a much smaller group and then he'd want broader, longer, analytical memos. I always thought that it was exactly what he should be doing, exactly the focus he should give to you, and as a consequence we had much more time to spend with him on his opinions. And we even had a lot of time to go to oral arguments. A lot of clerks never would show up in court because they were constantly researching on all these cert petitions.

By contrast, writing for the cert pool meant that all the pros and cons had to be carefully laid out in an objective fashion, no matter how meritless the case. A clerk to Potter Stewart, who did not join the pool, acknowledged it was more efficient for clerks to write for their own Justice than for a collective audience:

> On the cert petitions we had to learn what his views were about whether the cases were certworthy or not and you tried to do recommendations to reflect his views. You knew if it was an obscenity case he would want to have this recommendation or if it was another kind of case you would have to go this way. Since it was only to one justice, we didn't have to spend the time the cert pool did. You could write a cert memo very short. Just by seeing the issue you knew he would say that he wasn't interested.

Clerk bias was also a big concern. A Blackmun clerk described the prevailing unease when the pool was inaugurated in 1973:

> [T]he cert pool was controversial because of the danger that one clerk preparing the pool memo could, inadvertently or not, have too much influence of the Court's decision to accept a case for review. Many clerks felt that it was important that at least a few chambers not participate in the cert pool in order to serve as a check on the process by having at least one or two other clerks look at all of the petitions independently.

Another Blackmun clerk recalled that during the 1979 Term the Justice continued to be suspicious of bias creeping into cert pool memos:

> In our day, HAB [Justice Blackmun] would mark up the pool memos with strange hieroglyphs—indicating some secret coded commentary about the court or specific judges who authored the opinions below, and sometimes—we theorized—on the author of the pool memo from another Chambers, as in "this law clerk is not to be trusted on this sort of issue." We never really cracked the code.

But Blackmun and the other participating Justices quickly deemed the pool an overall success. And as non-participating Justices retired, they were usually replaced by ones who opted in. John Paul Stevens (1975–2010), however, chose not to participate in the cert pool. He recently explained: "I thought I could handle the cases more efficiently independently than as part of the cert pool. The memos they prepare are very thorough and very carefully written, but they're a lot longer than I thought was necessary in order to make a decision on whether to vote or grant or to deny." As of 2010, Samuel Alito is the only Justice not participating in the pool.

The cert pool did serve to free up clerks' time, which they then were able to devote to other duties. Once the Justices have selected a list of cases to be argued that term, it becomes the clerks' duty to research and analyze them so they can help prepare their Justices for hearing oral arguments. To accomplish this, the clerks review the lower court records, research relevant precedents, and summarize the essential information. Unlike the cert pool, these "bench memos" are written specifically for a clerk's own Justice and reflect special interests and needs. Sometimes clerks are asked to delve very deeply into a particular aspect of a case. Justices discuss the cases openly and informally with clerks before hearing arguments in the Courtroom. Some clerks like to play devil's advocate but most simply chime in with their ideas on specific points. One Blackmun clerk recalled how bench memos were prepared:

> In Justice Blackmun's chambers, a bench memo was prepared by a clerk (the clerks tended to divvy up the memos, too) for each case to be argued during the term. The only exceptions were tax cases, which the Justice took on himself without a clerk's memo, or with only a brief memo. Tax law had been a large part of his practice, and he was rightly respected by his fellow Justices as the tax expert on the Court. Our memos followed a general form, but varied in length and content depending on the complexity of the case or its importance. The memos included a summary of the arguments made by the parties and then an independent analysis based on research conducted by the clerk, pointing out weaknesses in the case, problems that might arise because the facts did not present the issue well, and the forms of reasoning or doctrine that would need to be applied to decide the case and the implications of such reasoning in light of prior and, as important, future cases. A clerk would often offer his or her own recommendation in a separate section of the memo.

Not all Justices have required their clerks to write formal bench memos. Brandeis even refused to allow his clerks to provide them, preferring to make up his mind unaided. According to his clerk, "To Justice Brandeis [bench memos were] a profanation of advocacy. He owed it to counsel . . . to present them with a judicial mind unscratched by the scribbling of clerks."

William H. Rehnquist chose a more informal method of preparing for oral argument—which included getting out of the building for fresh air:

Several of my colleagues get what are called bench memos from their law clerks on the cases . . . I do not do this simply because it does not suit my own style of working. When I start to prepare for a case that will be orally argued, I begin by reading the opinion of the lower court which is to be reviewed. . . . I then read the petitioner's brief, then the respondent's brief. Meanwhile, I have asked one of my clerks to do the same thing, with a view to our discussing the case. . . .

When the law clerk and I are both ready to talk about the case, we do just that—sometimes walking around the neighborhood of the Court building, sometimes sitting in my chambers. I tell the law clerk some of my reactions to the arguments of the parties, and am interested in getting the clerk's reactions to those same arguments. If there is some point of law involved in the case that doesn't appear to be adequately covered by the briefs, I may ask the law clerk to write me a memorandum on that particular point.

And Justice Ginsburg only asks her clerks to write bench memoranda in the more complex cases. She says these memos are designed "to be a road map to everything that I have to read [in the case] and to bring the case to the front of my mind just before oral argument."

Clerks try to find time to attend oral arguments and hear skilled advocates argue the points that the clerks have carefully researched themselves. But at least one Justice did not permit his clerks this perquisite. William O. Douglas was so strict about his clerks' time that if they wanted to attend a historic oral argument, they would secretly stand behind "The Douglas Pillar"—so named because the Justice could not see members of the audience in that section of the courtroom from his vantage point on the bench. One Douglas clerk explained the consequences of getting caught:

Douglas clerks had to do this because their presence in Court during argument always seemed to pose a challenge to him. It meant that the clerk had run out of work and, since that was intolerable, a note with a research project would shortly arrive by one of the messengers.

After arguments, the cases are discussed privately in Conference by the Justices, votes cast, and then the opinions are assigned to specific Justices to write. Clerks wait with great curiosity for their Justice to return to chambers and brief them on how things played out in Conference. A Blackmun clerk recalled the excitement of hearing the results:

One of the highlights of our work occurred when we all gathered in Justice Blackmun's office after the Court's Friday conferences to hear about the Court's action on certs and jurisdictional statements and on the votes cast by the Justices after oral argument in accepted cases. Justice Blackmun would report to us on the discussion among the Justices, the tentative vote, the reasoning, the likely opinion assignment, and whether the Justice would likely write the opinion (assignments were formally announced the next Monday, as a rule) or would otherwise want to write a dissent if the conference vote held. These Friday meetings gave the clerks a true glimpse into the judgment-formation process of the Court and the intellectual preferences and habits of all the Justices. But more than anything else, they gave us a sense of Justice Blackmun's values and judgments.

A few Justices—particularly Brandeis and Douglas—did not share much, however, with their clerks about what happened behind closed doors.

After the writing assignments have been doled out, comes the clerks' next big task: helping their Justice to write opinions. The extent to which clerks have contributed to the finished opinions has always been a subject of enormous interest to Courtwatchers. There has never been one formula for clerk usage: each Justice has deployed clerks in different ways at different times depending on a complex matrix involving the size of the workload that term, the Justice's experience and stamina on the bench, the subject matter of the case, and the relative ability of clerks that term.

Although the Justices began to allow their clerks to help with opinion writing in the 1940s, there was a broad disparity in clerk input. According to a 1942 Term clerk to Hugo L. Black:

> The function of the clerks in relation to the writing of the opinions . . . varies widely. . . . Sometimes a Justice writes the first draft of one opinion while the clerk writes the first draft of another, and the opinions are then exchanged and the clerk writes a second draft of his Justice's opinion while the Justice writes a second draft of the clerk's. Sometimes clerks are allowed to do the bulk of the serious writing for the Justice . . .
>
> Even on those rare occasions when the clerk does the writing, the judge does the deciding. The ultimate matters of yes or no, affirm or reverse, the judges invariably keep in their own hands. . . . [I]n my own year as a law clerk, my Justice made approximately one thousand decisions, and I had precisely no influence on any of them.

By the 1950s, most Justices were asking clerks to help draft opinions on a more regular basis. (One Justice only delegated first drafts of concurring or dissenting opinions to his clerks, keeping majority opinions entirely to himself.) Clerks' draft opinions were then revised by the Justices to a greater or lesser extent. While serving as his clerk in 1953, William H. Rehnquist described how Justice Robert H. Jackson, for example, edited his drafts:

> On a couple of occasions each term, Justice Jackson would ask each clerk to draft an opinion for him along lines which he suggested. If the clerk were

reasonably diligent in his work, the Justice would be quite charitable with his black pencil and paste pot. The result reached in these opinions was no less the product of Justice Jackson than those he drafted himself; in literary style, these opinions generally suffered by comparison with those which he had drafted.

Despite openly struggling with writing opinions, Justice Stanley F. Reed retained complete control, asserted a 1951 Term clerk:

> And some opinions he would ask us to do a draft on, and sometimes he would do a draft and ask us to revise or comment. Mutual ways of mutual work. . . . He used us, but he was very much in control, even though he always knew that the clerks were always conspiring to influence the justice and . . . to write the opinions. And he was very aware of that and his eyes would twinkle and so forth.

Aside from whatever writing duties they performed, clerks have also served as sounding boards. But advice from clerks has not always been graciously accepted. When a clerk objected to the lack of clarity in an opinion drafted by Holmes in 1930, the Justice famously and ferociously responded: "What the hell do you mean—not clear! Give it to me. Well, if you don't understand it, there may be some other damn fool who won't. So I would better change it."

Most Justices, however, have encouraged clerk feedback. Felix Frankfurter especially enjoyed having his clerks challenge him intellectually. Justice Black's wife, Elizabeth, described how the clerks gave him "mental exercise" in the 1960s:

> Hugo has certain steps to warm up for writing either an opinion or a dissent. First he reads the record of the case exhaustively and painstakingly. Then he talks it over with his law clerks for hours—searchingly and argumentatively. Often he has the clerks come to the house and spend the day. It's exciting to hear the give and take that goes on. Hugo always tries his best to convince them he's right. Sometimes he does, but once in a while he doesn't. If he feels pretty hopeless about it, he might say, "I'll dictate the first draft myself." Sometimes he has the objectors to his ideas write the first draft of the opinion, and then, when they have to use Hugo's reasoning, they become convinced he's right. Sometimes the law clerks put a doubt in his mind, but I think they would agree with me that this has been very rare.

One of Black's clerks, Daniel J. Meador, completed the picture:

> The draft is then turned over to the clerks, and with all the confidence of youth, they work it over. Then the fun begins. The two clerks and Black gather around his large desk and start through the draft, word by word, line by line. This may go on for hours. When the Judge has an opinion in the mill,

he does not drop it for anything else. The discussion, often turning into lively debate, will sometimes be transferred to the study in his 18th century house in Alexandria and last until midnight.

By contrast, Douglas preferred to keep his clerks at arm's length. A 1972 Term clerk recalled one occasion when Douglas stubbornly held his ground even when all his clerks opposed him. The case involved a small Florida tax exemption to widows—but not widowers—and the clerks all agreed that the law discriminated on the basis of sex:

> We made our legal arguments to the Justice, and pointed out that in our day and age this sex-based difference should not be sustained. He listened—briefly. Perhaps he was thinking of his own mother, for he had at the time been working on his autobiography, *Go East, Young Man*. In any event, he looked squarely at us and said: "I've known a lot of starving widows." The Justice was voting to uphold the statute—no doubts, no second thoughts, no more discussion.

By the 1970s the Justices had come to depend heavily on their clerks in the opinion-writing process. This was a consequence of both the burgeoning docket and of the workload being spread among the Justices more evenly. Some of the slower, more methodical, writers struggled to keep up and turned to their clerks for help, especially as the end of term drew near and assignments came due. Even Justice Powell complained in 1973 that he had felt pinched for time at the end of the previous term:

> One of the problems which we encountered last term was that I became the "bottleneck" the last week in May, when several draft opinions hit my desk at about the same time. This makes it a bit difficult for me to do the type of reviewing, revising, rewriting and—above all—careful thinking about each opinion, which I wish to be free always to undertake, a task which varies with the case for all the obvious reasons.

The delegation of opinion writing continued to differ from chamber to chamber. A clerk to Potter Stewart (1958–1981), for example, described how his Justice loosely controlled the process, if not the outcome:

> He would tell you to go start the opinion and sometimes he would tell you what the opinion should say, I mean he would tell you how it should come out, and sort of generally about what the reasoning was but basically not a lot. . . . He might say, "Write an opinion following the lines we talked about yesterday," or it might be, "write an opinion along the lines of the United States brief," or "the petitioner's brief." It might be as short as that.

Clerks to Harry A. Blackmun (1970–1994) during the Justice's first few terms noted that his reliance on clerks was even more limited. Apparently, Blackmun even liked to do his own cite checking, which often made him late in circulating his opinions:

> Justice Blackmun's opinions were very much his own. He would write them surrounded by books in the Justice's library on the second floor, to which he might disappear for days. Clerks would often prepare a draft of the statement of facts, which HAB [Blackmun] would often change. Clerks would review and edit his opinions after the first draft, occasionally seeing with satisfaction that something they had written in the bench memo had found its way into an opinion (although this was often wishful thinking in a strictly textual sense, as HAB had his own style and form of writing opinions). Occasionally a clerk would be asked to offer a draft opinion, and some of it might be reflected in the final opinion after Justice Blackmun had added and subtracted. Justice Blackmun also, at least in the 1972 Term, did his own cite-checking, not as a separate exercise but instead as part of his very thorough manner of writing with all of the material before him. The effort HAB put into opinions may well be one reason that he tended to take a great deal of time and, thus, be very late in circulating his opinions.

According to later clerks, however, Blackmun came to delegate more heavily as the years went by and he grew comfortable in the job—a common progression for Justices.

Some Courtwatchers have expressed alarm about undue clerk influence. In 1980 Chief Justice Rehnquist drily conceded that drafting opinions gave the clerks "considerable responsibility." But he also emphasized that the task was done under his strict guidance:

> The law clerk is given, as best I can, a summary of the conference discussion, a description of the result reached by the majority in that discussion, and my views as to how a written opinion can best be prepared embodying that reasoning. The law clerk is not off on a frolic of his own, but is instead engaged in a highly structured task which has been largely mapped out for him by the conference discussion and my suggestions to him. This is not to say that the clerk who prepares a first draft does not have a considerable responsibility in the matter. The discussion in conference has been entirely oral . . . nine oral statements of position suffice to convey the broad outlines of the views of the justices but do not invariably settle exactly how the opinion will be reasoned through.

In explaining her opinion-writing procedure, Justice Ginsburg makes it clear that clerk draft opinions are simply that—drafts. The best require heavy editing; most undergo a complete rewrite:

> I read over everything . . . I start with the opinion below, I re-read the briefs, the bench memo—if I had one—and then I write the opening. It will be anywhere from one to three paragraphs. It's kind of a press release, and it will

tell you what the issue was and how it was resolved. After the opening, I will make a detailed outline of how I think the opinion should go. I give that outline to the law clerk. Sometimes, to my delight, they will give me a draft that I can make my own version through heavy editing, but I don't have to re-do it. I'd say it's a good year if I have two law clerks that have that skill. In most cases, what they do is always valuable to me—sometimes I see that my organization was not right and should be done another way. So their draft is always of use to me, but in most cases I can't simply take it over.

Former Blackmun clerk Harold Koh has argued that clerks often over-estimate their influence during their service and only later realize how much their Justice actually molded their thinking:

> Clerks rarely appreciate until much later in life just how much a Justice really set the tone for his or her chambers. The clerks operate within that atmo-sphere, and adopt that tone, and therefore every law clerk's work product strongly takes on the Justice's voice. To me, the best image is the School of Michelangelo. As we all know, the myriad students in Michelangelo's school of painting produced marvelous works of Renaissance art, many of which can barely be distinguished from the master's own work. Michelangelo himself did not personally put paintbrush to canvas on all of these works, but they nevertheless all look like the work of Michelangelo for the simple reason that he set the tone; he was the guiding intelligence behind the work of the entire school.

At the beginning of each term, clerks are lectured by the Chief Justice on the importance of keeping secret the work that goes on in chambers from family, friends and, above all, reporters. As Brandeis warned his new clerk in 1932: "Here you shall see a good deal and hear a good deal that is highly confidential. There have been no leaks from this office in the past, and I mean that there shall be none in the future." Leaks about the outcome of cases before the opinions are formally announced are the main concern. But the Court also does not want it revealed how the Justices arrived at their decision in a case—about the behind-the-scenes negotiations—because such knowledge might weaken the decision's authority. Leaks could also choke the free interchange of ideas if Justices have to worry about what they say during Conference negotiations. "You will learn things, hear things, know things that you will take to your grave with you," Chief Justice Earl Warren admonished incoming clerks in the 1960 Term.

But clerks can and do talk to each other. They even have a private din-ing room where they freely discuss cases with clerks from other Cham-bers over lunch. This back-channel network can be very useful to the Justices when they want to gain information about the positions of their colleagues and form coalitions. When a Justice's draft opinion is circulated, it is the clerk's job to manage the process of negotiation and compromise with clerks from other Chambers in order to come up with a final product that their Justices can sign onto. One Rehnquist clerk explained why this aspect of the job, forging coalitions, is so crucial: "Eight out of nine opinions were written by another justice, so [a] major part of [the] job was whether and how to join other opinions, request changes to others' opinions, etc. Here, [a] clerk's input was of influence." An example of a helpful memo to a Justice relaying information gleaned through the clerk network is the following one from a Blackmun clerk in 1973 regarding a circulated opinion by the Justice:

> The vote in the case presently stands at 4–2 with the CJ [Chief Justice Warren Burger], PS [Potter Stewart] and TM [Thurgood Marshall] having not yet voted. J Stewart has not read the opinion, but his clerks think that he is inclined toward the dissent. J. Marshall's clerks feel that he will join if some changes are made or that he will write a concurrence. The objections of J Marshall's clerks and J. [William J.] Brennan's clerks are the same. . . . Most of J. [William O.] Douglas' dissent is not too bad. . . . I think that he is wrong . . . where he states that we have erred. . . . I have spoken to J Douglas' clerks about this.

While clerks definitely serve as ambassadors to other chambers, there is some question as to whether they are also lobbyists. A clerk to Justice Tom C. Clark in the 1950s insisted that lobbying was indeed a key aspect of the job:

> When you need five votes and you only have four, you go to somebody who you think you can win over and say, "What's it going to take?" That's a very important part of the process. To some extent this is a political process of course. Consensus always is. You talk to the other clerks about the drafts they had sent around and say "You know I have trouble with that," or "explain this to me," or whatever. It's a collegial process.

But some Court members have been wary of the clerk network out of concern it could promote activism. Chief Justice Warren, especially, did not like having his clerks "talking out of school." Brandeis had also cautioned his clerks not to reveal much to the other clerks. But he slyly did not object to their picking up useful information: "Of course you can listen to what they tell you about their Justices . . ." By contrast, in the 1980s Justice Powell encouraged his clerks to network, but with this caveat:

> While sharing views on pending cases may be constructive, it is prudent not to become clerk "politicians" who try to lobby the clerks of other Chambers. The line between lawyer-like discussion and "lobbying" is a fine one and not easy to draw. It becomes a matter of judgment. Another caveat, of course, is

never speak *for* your Justice or *argue* for a view you know your Justice probably does not share.

To offset the grueling pace and long hours, clerks are rewarded with a
few perquisites. Justices and outside dignitaries are often invited to address
the clerks' luncheons. J. Harvie Wilkinson III remarked on how much he
enjoyed this respite while clerking during the 1971 and 1972 Terms:

> There were points of relief in a day of clerking to which I looked forward
> to with great relish. One was lunch, where clerks from various chambers
> would generally get together. We were provided a small and separate din-
> ing room—several long tables pushed together—in which no outsiders, not
> even spouses, were normally permitted. Occasionally, there was an invited
> guest, Senators Phil Hart and Edward Kennedy, acting FBI director Patrick
> Gray, Solicitor General Erwin Griswold, and Dan Rather of CBS News were
> among those I remember. Each of the Justices also ate with us once a term,
> and took questions afterward on an informal and confidential basis. Mostly,
> however, it was just clerks, and conversation flowed freely, a mixture of shop
> talk with lots of very warm air about politics, sports, and other handy topics.

Another way to break the stress of overwork has traditionally been to
play basketball on the court on the third floor of the building—dubbed
"the highest court in the land." Again, Wilkinson:

> But the greatest of all clerking sidelines was basketball, which eight or ten
> of us played about twice a week late in the afternoon in the Court's small
> gymnasium. . . . Our games were not unlike any pickup match at a public
> park, a melee of free-verse talent and clumsiness, known in the vernacular as
> jungle ball. We refereed our own struggles, played under a loose and shifting
> set of rules, and in "uniforms" of different colors, shapes, sizes, and states
> of cleanliness. Once every so often an "All Star" team of clerks challenged
> the Court's police force or the night maintenance crew, with mixed success.
> Occasionally, too, Justice [Byron] White would participate; he is a talented
> hoopster who once demolished me in a game of "horse" with a series of left-
> handed set and hook shots.

Justice White, a former professional football player, apparently had such
sharp elbows that more than one clerk needed to get new glasses after
playing on the court with him.

Almost all the Justices have found a way to socialize with their clerks
outside of chambers, if only by inviting them for cocktails with their
spouses. Both Black and Rehnquist were avid tennis players who also liked
to press their clerks into service across the net. Blackmun hosted a regular
breakfast for his clerks, but Court business was evidently not on the menu:

> With Justice Blackmun, breakfast was the ritual through which the nearly fa-
> milial bond between judge and clerk, elder and neophyte, was formed. Every

weekday from September to July, at approximately 8:10, Blackmun, flanked by my co-clerks and me, would . . . head into the public cafeteria for the first meal of the day. By this time the Justice would have been at work for the better part of an hour. We would still be rubbing sleep from our eyes. Despite occasional mornings of excruciating silence, these breakfasts were one of the great rewards of a Blackmun clerkship. Breakfast was personal time, largely unencumbered by Court business, the time when we learned that the Justice had worked at a dude ranch to help put himself through Harvard College, that he loved junk mysteries, that he could sing the fight song of rival Dartmouth—perfectly on pitch.

Some clerks have been privileged to develop close relationships with their Justices. For example, Charles A. Reich, who clerked in the 1953 Term, had an exceptionally tight bond with Justice Black because he and his co-clerk lived with him:

> David [J. Vann] and I lived with Justice Black in his Alexandria, Virginia home all year and spent the entire day with him seven days a week starting with breakfast cooked by the Judge and served at the kitchen table, continuing with the drive to Washington and a day at the Court, and ending with dinner and an evening of discussion in the Judge's study upstairs. Justice Black had recently lost his wife [Josephine] and his children were grown and had left home, so David and I were "family" as well as law clerks.

But not all Justices have encouraged intimacy. William O. Douglas, especially, was known for working his clerks hard and keeping his distance. According to Richard L. Jacobson, many Douglas clerks feared their boss: "It is common knowledge that clerking for [Douglas] could be like 52 weeks of boot camp. It is difficult to convey, unless you went through it, the absolute terror that a Douglas clerk felt at the thought of making a mistake." Douglas's long-time secretary, Fay Aull Deusterman, agreed: "Ten thousand dollars a year did not seem enough for what those boys had to put up with. We all thought they, and we, for that matter, should get combat pay in addition."

Clerks often feel a letdown after leaving the Supreme Court. Some even consider their clerkship to be the high point in their careers. Justice John Paul Stevens, who clerked for Wiley Rutledge in 1947, once joked, "You get an inappropriate idea of your importance in the world for a year, and then you're out doing mortgage foreclosures. After you leave, there's a real letdown." Future Justice William H. Rehnquist reflected more seriously on what his 1953 Supreme Court clerkship taught him in a letter to his former boss, Justice Robert H. Jackson. Rehnquist had returned to Arizona and was working in private practice:

> I have occasionally reflected on the experience which I got while working for you; I think there is a tendency when one first leaves a job like that and

turns to the details of a general law practice, to feel "Why, hell, that didn't teach me anything about practicing law." In a sense it didn't, and in that regard I am sure you would be the first to agree that there is no substitute for actually practicing. But I can't help feel that, in addition to the enjoyment from the personal contacts, one does pick up from a clerkship some sort of intuition about the nature of the judicial process. It is so intangible I will not attempt to describe it further, but I think it is valuable especially in appellate brief-writing.

Clerks stay in contact with their Justice and serve as a kind of extended family, getting together for reunions and offering support to the Justice as needed. Antonin Scalia says he delights in the annual clerk reunion:

It's one of the most enjoyable parts of the job. . . . You work very closely with four young people every year. There are new ones every year. They are full of vim and vigor. They are not jaded . . . it's all new to them. Their enthusiasm rubs off on you. . . . You really become very close and then they go off. It's like acquiring four new nieces and nephews every year, none of whom will be a failure. They all go off to do very significant things and it's fun to follow their later careers.

When a Justice dies, the casket is traditionally displayed in the Great Hall so the public can pay its respects. And it is the role of former clerks to carry the casket up the steps of the Supreme Court building. They then stand vigil in shifts for the duration of the lying-in-state.

12

"Welcome to the Chain Gang"

Managing the Workload

Chief Justice Edward Douglass White (1910–1921) anguished over thorny cases and liked to put off deciding them as long as possible. According to one of his brethren: "Sometimes the Chief Justice would bring to the conference cases on which he could reach no decision. Here is a difficult case, he would say with a gesture of despair. 'God help us!'" Deciding the toughest cases—ones lower courts have not been able to resolve definitively—is indeed a daunting task. Justice William J. Brennan, Jr., keenly felt the weight of judging, which he viewed as "a lonely, troubling experience for fallible human beings conscious that their best may not be adequate to the challenge." He humbly added: "The notion that we're awesome men is wrong. What is awesome is the responsibility."

The workload of a Supreme Court Justice has also at times been very demanding—although there have been considerable fluctuations in the size of the docket and the length of the term. In 1910 a veteran Justice warned Charles Evans Hughes at his induction ceremony that he was "entering upon a life of slavery." "Yes, I know," Hughes reassured him, "I have experienced freedom and even it has its illusions." Nearly three decades later, Justice Harlan Fiske Stone congratulated William O. Douglas on his nomination to the Supreme Court with these ominous words: "Welcome to the chain gang."

How does a Justice handle the demands of the job? According to Felix Frankfurter, the secret is to stay focused:

First and foremost, complete absorption in the work of the Court is demanded. That is not as easy to attain as you might think, because this is a

203

very foolish and distracting town. Secondly, he must have great industry because . . . for about nine months of the year it is a steady grind. Further, he must have the capacity to learn, he must be alert to the range and complexities of the problems that come before this Court . . .

Originally, the Court held two sessions a year and each lasted only a few days or weeks. Without the additional burden of circuit riding, being a member of the Supreme Court was more like holding a seasonal job. But the length of the term kept expanding in response to rising caseloads. In 1917 the Supreme Court began opening its term the first Monday in October. That is still the day the Court holds its first public session and hears its first arguments.

To cope with the ever-increasing volume of business, however, the Justices decided in 1975 to move their first Conference to the last week of September. Now they meet every day that week to catch up with appeals and petitions that have come in over the summer and leftover matters that have not been disposed of during the preceding term. In 1993 the Justices began announcing after this September Conference some of the cases they had voted to put on the calendar. Each Term lasts nine months, and ends when action has been taken on the last argued case, usually by the end of June. Clarence Thomas has explained how he approaches the workload that greets him each new term:

> When I first got here Justice [Byron] White said that you have to get a system. So you develop a system to approach every case, because there is nobody to tell you when to start. There's no game plan that's sent out by anyone. There's no timeline. You know when the sittings [for oral argument] are, you know what cases are going to be dealt with, you know when we're going to have our conferences. . . . I usually divide the work into three categories: you have to decide which cases come here; you decide those cases; and then you write opinions. And you agree or disagree with opinions. That's it.

The Supreme Court is asked to pass judgment on a huge range of subjects. When he clerked during the early 1970s, J. Harvie Wilkinson III marveled at the variety of issues that the Justices were expected to understand:

> Reading and summarizing literally hundreds upon hundreds of petitions for certiorari was at times the most tedious of jobs, but it provided me with a frontline, rapid-fire view of all the diverse and multitudinous problems people expect the Supreme Court to hear. So many different matters come before the Court that no single lawyer, however brilliant or versatile, could possibly be knowledgeable on all of them. Antitrust, tax, labor, admiralty, securities, patent, bankruptcy, and an inexhaustible variety of criminal and constitutional claims press upon it. Justices are asked to rule on welfare systems, environmental regulations, school desegregation, legislative reap-

portionment, sex discrimination, educational finance, prison administration, abortion practice, and other equally far-flung and disparate subjects. For the Supreme Court is one institution that has not been allowed to specialize.

William O. Douglas emphasized the broad skills required to answer such a range of questions: "The electronics industry—resourceful as it is—will never produce a machine to handle these problems. They are delicate and imponderable, complex and tangled. They require at times the economist's understanding, the poet's insight, the executive's experience, the political scientist's understanding, the historian's perspective."

It is not just the breadth of scope but the quantity of petitions that taxes the Justices. And the number of petitions the Court receives each year has risen exponentially. Only fifty-one petitions were filed in 1803, but that number doubled in the 1810s. In 1837 Congress added two new seats (increasing the size of the bench to nine) and added two new circuits to cope with the mounting influx of business before the Court. In 1860 the Court docketed 310 cases, prompting Congress to authorize more circuit judges in 1869 to ease the Justices' burden. They were now sitting on the High Bench for seven months of the year (as opposed to three months in 1850). "I am worked almost to death and have hardly time to breathe," Chief Justice Morrison R. Waite wrote his brother shortly after taking his seat in 1877.

This 1885 cartoon pokes fun at the overworked Supreme Court, which was then nearly four years behind in its work. Until 1891, the Justices had to hear every appeal involving a federal question and were flooded with cases on subjects like admiralty and patent law that often lacked constitutional implications. (Courtesy of the Library of Congress)

By the time Congress finally passed legislation in 1891 relieving the overburdened Justices entirely of their obligation to sit on circuit courts, the docket had ballooned to an unmanageable 1,816. There was more than a three-year wait for an accepted case to be argued in the Courtroom. The creation of a system of circuit courts did help shrink the number of cases being appealed to the Supreme Court and in the next few years the Justices saw a huge drop in new business (the docket shrank to 275 cases in 1892). But the numbers would rise again in the 1910s after Congress passed new regulatory laws resulting from industrialization that needed judicial interpretation.

The Judiciary Act of 1925 provided a measure of relief by giving the Supreme Court more discretion over which cases it could agree to review. For the first time the Justices could hear or reject most cases at will. Nevertheless, the docket climbed from 1,039 in 1930 to 2,296 in 1960. Congress passed a host of regulatory laws in the 1960s on the environment, consumer safety, as well as civil rights and social welfare acts, all of which eventually came before the Court. By 1970 the Court was receiving more than four thousand petitions a term.

A large part of the swelled docket was due to petitions filed *in forma pauperis*: by those too poor to afford the fee (currently $300) for docketing a case. These types of petitions grew from 517 in 1951 to more than 6,000 in 2010. Half are petitions from prison inmates. Many don't have attorneys and some even handwrite their own petitions. Clerk of the Court William Suter has been in charge of receiving all petitions, analyzing them for correctness and legality, and entering them into the electronic docket since 1991. He has explained that, however numerous, the Court treats all incoming petitions with care:

> On the front of this building in marble it says "Equal Justice Under Law," so we really believe that here. Some of these petitions might be frivolous, but each one is looked at and reviewed very carefully. . . . One of our jobs in the Clerk's office is to make it as easy as we can for a person to file a document here. Don't hide the ball, the rules of the Court are written in plain English so they can be understood.

Yet fewer than one percent of *in forma pauperis* petitions are granted review.

To keep up with the volume, the Justices review certiorari petitions almost continually. Justice Thomas has explained how he manages them:

> We receive about nine thousand requests a year. In the last few years we've taken around eighty cases. Now there's a process of sorting through that. I like to go through all of those requests. . . . You do that almost every day. During the year, I like to have that done on the weekend before the Conference, which is normally on Friday. So, that's a part of your workday that you

don't normally think about. It's routine; it's like brushing your teeth. And it's continuous.

Yet Thomas, like all contemporary Justices, only reads the brief summaries of these petitions which are provided by clerks. Ones that stand out as being important get a deeper look. "You develop a pretty good eye for what kind [of petitions] you ought to look at more carefully," says Chief Justice Roberts.

The last Justice to tackle the petitions without letting his clerks screen them was William J. Brennan, Jr. (1956–1990). He was particularly concerned about giving *in forma pauperis* filings a close scrutiny for fear of overlooking an important question. "I read the rich man's *and* the poor man's. Reading them myself saves time; I know what I'm looking for and I can readily detect new trends coming our way," explained Brennan. But sometimes the incessant workload got the better of him:

> I try not to delegate any of the screening function to my law clerks and to do the complete task myself. I make exceptions during the summer recess when their initial screening of petitions is invaluable training for next term's new law clerks. And I also must make some few exceptions during the Term on occasion when opinion work must take precedence.

If a Justice wants a petition to be taken up by the Court then the case is placed on the "discuss list" circulated several days prior to each Conference. If at least four Justices vote in Conference that the case is worthy of being put on the docket, it is placed on the "orders list" and scheduled for oral argument. Nowadays, it takes less than three months before the case is argued.

To prepare for argument, the Justices read the written briefs supplied by counsel and by amicus curiae—outside groups with special expertise that file "friend of the court" briefs. This can amount to an avalanche of paper. When the Court prepared to hear the *University of California Regents v. Bakke* case in 1978, which upheld the constitutionality of affirmative action programs, the briefs were at least a foot deep. "Reading all of it you wouldn't have time to sleep," Chief Justice Warren Burger complained. But, he continued, "An experienced Judge can skim. He doesn't have to read every word. Sometime whole statutes are included when only a small part applies." Eventually, the Court began limiting briefs to fifty pages.

In the nineteenth century, oral arguments were heard on all five weekdays. Conferences were held on Saturdays because the Senate was not in session and the Justices could borrow a room from one of the Senate Committees. In the 1920s Louis D. Brandeis reportedly pushed back against Conferences cutting too deeply into his weekend. According to his law clerk: "The inhuman practice of those days was to hold the conference on Saturdays beginning at noon. . . . The Justice's mild protest was to rise at five o'clock and say, 'Chief Justice, your jurisdiction has now expired and Mrs. Brandeis's has begun.' With that he would leave for home."

In 1955 Chief Justice Earl Warren moved the Conference to Friday, instituting a much-appreciated five-day week. He accomplished this by adding a week of arguments in the fall and two weeks in the spring. Arguments are now heard on Monday, Tuesday, and Wednesday for seven two-week sessions ending around the first of May. To relieve the workload of Friday Conferences, the Court holds Conference on Wednesday afternoons after oral arguments as well. After oral arguments are finished for the term, in May, the Justices meet only once in Conference, on Thursdays.

In the early nineteenth century, the Justices held Court sessions from eleven until three, with no break for lunch. Business continued uninterrupted as the Justices would retreat behind the curtains to satisfy their hunger. Former Attorney General Augustus Garland suggested a better policy in 1898, when arguments began at noon:

> The hour of the meeting of the court does not seem to me to be a good one. I should rather think it should commence at ten and one-half A.M. and sit till one P.M. and then take a recess for an hour for refreshments and rest, and then sit from two till four:—this brings in four and one-half hours of hearing and doing court business, and this would be sufficient. There is no peculiar force or enchantment in four hours, and four and one-half hours could . . . well be substituted. Meeting as the court does now at twelve M., in the course of an hour the judges show signs of weariness and fatigue, and commence one by one to retire to lunch and sometimes barely a quorum is left. . . . And it is true that at the hour from one to two sometimes we do find some of the judges unavoidably "Napping, napping, only this And nothing more."
>
> The lunch they manage to snatch the way they are now situated cannot be very satisfactory. Behind their seats, where persons are passing to and fro, a sort of ad interim or pro tempore restaurant is in progress, and counsel is arguing in front and hears the rattle of dishes, knives and forks, and the judges eating are in a state of unrest, to eat and get back. Of all things eating should be allowed full time and ease. To meet at ten and one-half when the system is comparatively fresh, alive, and active, and not yet vexed by work or study, much work can be done till one. And then all may go and recreate and refresh themselves decently and in order, and resume work, not in a doze or half awake and half asleep condition, but invigorated and reinforced. There is plenty of time in the meanwhile, with Saturdays entirely given to that purpose, for conference and consultation.

Garland was prescient. The Court soon did institute a proper lunch break at two, but it did not assemble earlier than noon until 1961. In exchange for doing away with the Saturday Conference, Court sessions began earlier—at ten. Since 1961, oral arguments have been scheduled from ten to noon and one to three.

The lunch break is both a pause in the action and a chance for collegiality. The Justices usually eat lunch together on argument days and Conference days in the Justices' Dining Room, where food is brought up from the cafeteria. Sometimes they will invite a distinguished guest as a speaker. In the 1920s, when the Court met in the Capitol building, messengers brought the Justices' lunches from home and they ate in the Conference room during the half-hour break. A former Supreme Court page from that era was struck by two of the Justices' divergent appetites:

> Chief Justice Taft could inhale the better part of a whole roasted chicken with accompaniments from a domed silver tray during the break. The only other luncheon ingredients I recall were those of Louis Brandeis. He was a pioneer of today's health frenzy. His was a spinach sandwich—two slices of plain wheat bread with spinach between.

Taking a page from Brandeis, health-conscious Justice David Souter (1990–2009) ate only an apple and yogurt every day for his lunch.

A renowned gourmand, Harlan Fiske Stone (1925–1946) liked to bring a collection of cheeses from home. This predilection was once thrown in his face by Felix Frankfurter during a long-winded presentation by Stone in Conference. According to notes made by Justice Frank Murphy, Frankfurter taunted the Chief Justice:

> *Frankfurter:* I suppose you know more than those who drafted the Constitution.
>
> *Stone:* I know some things better than those who drafted the Constitution
>
> *Frankfurter:* Yes, on wine and cheese [*laughter*].

How much business gets conducted in each Conference session depends on how many items are on the list that day and how efficiently the Chief Justice moves things along. In 1953 Justice Robert H. Jackson tracked how time was spent in Conference under Chief Justice Fred Vinson:

> The largest conference list during the October 1953 term contained 145 items, the shortest 24, the average 70. A little computation will show that the average list would permit, at the average conference, an average of five minutes of deliberation per item, or about 33 seconds of discussion per item by each of the nine Justices, assuming, of course, that each is an average Justice who does the average amount of talking.

Three years later, Justice Tom C. Clark did a similar assessment with Earl Warren as Chief Justice. The volume of cases had increased considerably:

> The Court decided over 1800 questions last term. There was an average of 71 cases on each list covering the twenty-six conferences held during the term; the longest list included 331 cases, the shortest 38. Our conference lasts an average of 6 hours, so this would allow on the average about five minutes to each item on the list or half a minute to each Justice.

But neither of these calculations take into account the fact that discussions of cert petitions are not nearly as thorough as for argued cases (some get disposed of with almost no discussion).

In order to keep Conference lengths manageable, discussions of individual cases grew shorter in the 1950s. Justice Jackson (1941–1954) worried about the deleterious effects of this trend:

> The pressure of time may induce an attitude that discussion in conference is futile and thereby contributes to the multiplicity of individual opinions. It is often easier to write out one's own view than for nine men in such short time to explore their doubts and difficulties together, or to reach a reconciliation of viewpoints. The fact is that the Court functions less as one deliberative body than as nine, each Justice working largely in isolation except as he chooses to seek consultation with others. These working methods tend to cultivate a highly individualistic rather than a group viewpoint.

In practice, however, "discussion" among the Justices increasingly occurred in the back-and-forth of written revisions.

In terms of each Justice's individual caseload, Chief Justice Vinson (1946–1953) strove to make opinion-writing assignments fairer, so that everyone shouldered the same amount of work. Instead of waiting for a Justice to finish an opinion before assigning a new one, he tried to spread the work evenly among the Justices throughout each term. Justice Douglas reported on this change, but mistakenly remembered it as having been inaugurated by Earl Warren, who indeed did carry on with it:

> Hughes had a custom of never assigning an opinion to a man who already had an opinion that was unwritten. He made his assignments to those who had nothing to do. As a result, those who turned out work like Stone and Black and myself . . . each of us got more than a ninth of the load. And I think Stone continued that practice and I think Vinson did. . . . When Earl Warren came on as Chief Justice he instituted a different system. He decided that every member of the Court should pull the same size oar and row as hard as anybody else. And so he has roughly allotted the opinions one-ninth to each judge and he has tried to level out so if a judge gets a big, complicated case the next time around he gets a simple case. He's tried to even out the workload.

The Court has since adopted a load-sharing system that makes opinion-writing assignments even more equitably distributed and ensures that work can be completed by the end of each term. Justice Stephen G. Breyer recently described the practice: "The rule basically is that everyone writes one majority [opinion], and then everyone writes two and then everyone writes three, so the need to have the same number of majorities across the year is a constraint on how they are assigned."

Once a Justice receives an opinion assignment, how much time is spent writing the finished opinion varies enormously. In simple cases where the points of law at issue are few, an opinion can be wrapped up in a couple of weeks. The first opinions announced in the Term usually start being handed down in early December. Cases that are complex or engender several concurring or dissenting opinions can take many months. The toughest cases often come right down to the wire and the judgments are issued at the end of June. Lengthier waits for opinions may indicate that the opinion writer needed many drafts (sometimes more than a dozen) to satisfy the other Justices and to persuade them to sign on. A shorter turnaround may mean the author has chosen to take a more restricted approach to the decision as opposed to a broader, expansive one.

Some Justices possess the talent to write quickly and lucidly. Oliver Wendell Holmes, Jr., renowned for his witty aphorisms and short, pungent opinions, liked to pen his opinions standing up. "There is nothing so conducive to brevity as a caving in at the knees," he quipped. Holmes elaborated on his penchant for concision: "The art of writing legal decisions, is to omit all but the essentials—'The point of contact' is the formula—the place where the boy got his fingers pinched. The rest of the machinery doesn't matter."

Hugo L. Black prided himself on making his opinions understandable to the public. According to a clerk, he read widely before sitting down to write so could produce readable prose without lots of time-consuming editing: "Only a few naturally write a lean prose. Some can boil out the fat on redraft; others do not really care to try. . . . Black has an impression that some people other than lawyers may actually read the Supreme Court Reports. When a paragraph is turned to his satisfaction, he has a way of saying with gusto: 'Now they'll understand that.'"

William O. Douglas also had a bold style that appealed to non-lawyers. He was quick to get his opinions written because he was impatient. His clerk described the Justice's work habits during his first term on the Court in 1939:

When [Douglas] was in the office and in the room, he worked. . . . He got at it. And did it. He put pencil to paper. And he started writing right away; just as soon as he had finished [reading] the record of the case. Or he called me

Oliver Wendell Holmes, Jr., an unusually witty and pungent writer, liked to pen his opinions standing up. "There is nothing so conducive to brevity as a caving in at the knees," he quipped. (Courtesy of the Library of Congress)

and said I want a memo on this subject. He didn't tell you enough to [figure it out]. You would have to guess at it. . . . And he had his yellow tablets and sent it to [his secretary] Edith [Waters] to get it typed. I always had the feeling of "get it done." . . . Any undone job was just hovering at him. He had to get it finished.

But Douglas did not always polish his written opinions. Later in his tenure, he put much of his effort into earning outside income from writing books about his life and travels in order to pay his alimony and child support from three failed marriages.

Perhaps the most talented writer to grace the high bench was Robert H. Jackson, whose writing style and wit are still revered and recited. But James M. Marsh, his clerk from 1947 to 1949, has emphasized how much time Jackson put into crafting these graceful opinions:

> The Justice's writing was so good because he worked at it, day and night. Certainly he had a gift, he knew the law, and he had a wealth of legal experience both in and out of government; but one of the principal ingredients of his clear, concise and understandable judicial opinions was plain hard work. For example, when the Justice gave me a draft of an opinion to critique, I gave it back to him with my suggestions at the end of the day. I knew that the next version would be back on my desk as soon as he arrived at the office the next morning. He did not waste any time; he just bore down constantly to produce clear language and compelling reasoning.

Interestingly, Justice Jackson did not have a college degree. He, like many of his predecessors in the nineteenth century, learned the law through apprenticeship (and then he briefly attended Albany Law School).

Jackson shared the bench with Wiley Rutledge (1943–1949), one of many able Justices whose writing styles lacked crispness. A former law professor and law school dean, Rutledge tended to write long opinions that were painstaking and time-consuming. In 1943 one of Justice Black's clerks (John P. Frank) even wagered with a Rutledge clerk (Victor Brudney) over the predicted length of one of his boss's opinions:

> Justices Rutledge and Black were of like mind on matters of policy. Rutledge was, however, less rapidly decisive, thinking longer before getting to the common result. This kindly and scrupulous man suffered from his own fairmindedness. All of his doubts, byways, and self-torturings cropped up in bulky opinions. Rutledge had a gift for phrase and his prose was extremely readable, but there was a lot of it.
>
> Early in Rutledge's career he was assigned an opinion on a simple point. His clerk and I (then a clerk myself) agreed that a concise Justice would use two pages. We also agreed to give Rutledge a handicap. A dinner was wagered, the Rutledge clerk betting that his Justice could write the opinion in four pages. The Rutledge clerk paid for dinner.

Rutledge was a particularly indefatigable worker, who stayed up late into the night agonizing over every petition for certiorari. He also felt compelled to answer every question raised in the briefs, not just the legal ones, rendering his opinions both laborious and comprehensive. Rutledge, who liked to say that a losing litigant never complained that the Court's opinion was too long, defended his dedication: "By the time the lawyer and litigant get to the Supreme Court, they have lived years with the case, and the lawyer has put a big piece of himself into it. . . . [h]owever foolish or trivial his arguments, I want them to know that I heard him."

Many Justices have been workaholics. Benjamin Cardozo (1932–1938), who lived alone in an apartment, devoted himself to the law. Chief Justice Hughes usually arranged for opinion assignments to be delivered to Associate Justices on Saturdays after the Conference ended at five. But he knew that Cardozo, who had a "frail body and weak heart," would start writing his opinion immediately and would not rest until it was finished on Monday. So Hughes sent Cardozo his assignments on Sunday (he did the same for Willis Van Devanter because he lived in Cardozo's building). As the number of argued cases increased in the Warren and Burger Court years, assignments were made after two-week sessions—not overnight—so that the overall workload could be evaluated and the assignments smoothed out.

William J. Brennan, Jr. was also known for his prodigious work ethic. His daughter, Nancy Brennan, described his relentless schedule:

> Dad would come in every night with a full briefcase and spend time before dinner talking with my mother and listening to the news. We almost invariably ate between 6 and 6:30 and then one of two things happened. Either he'd go up to the den and sit at this old desk that was falling apart. Or, more commonly he'd set up a green card table in the middle of the living room and spread all these piles of papers within arm's reach on the rug. He'd work until he was just too tired, until 9:30 or 10. On the weekend Dad would get up for his walk, make breakfast and be at the card table by 8:30 or 9, working through most of the day.

When Brennan's wife, Marjorie, became ill with recurring throat cancer in 1969, the Justice cut out all social and extrajudicial activities to take care of his family, in addition to managing his full workload. Hugo L. Black, Brennan's ally on the Court, once had to advise him to take a break from working so hard. Brennan had become so angry at Black for making last-minute changes to an opinion over the phone that Black was compelled to walk into Brennan's chamber and tell him: "This place can become like a pressure cooker and it can beat the strongest of men. You should get out of here and forget it for a few days."

Outside the constraints of attending oral arguments and Conferences, the Justices are free to use their time as they please. Before they moved into the new Supreme Court building (all nine did not work there full time until 1946) the Justices had idiosyncratic work habits that were unmonitored by their peers. The Supreme Court still continues in many ways to operate as nine separate little law firms. Each Justice hires his or her own law clerks, secretaries, and messenger. Until they all became computer literate, members of the Court communicated the old-fashioned way—by having messengers hand-deliver written communications.

This can be a bit isolating. Confessed Lewis F. Powell, Jr., shortly after taking his seat in 1972:

> I had thought of the Court, in institutional terms, as a collegial body in which the most characteristic activities would be consultation and coopera- tive deliberation, aided by a strong supporting staff. I was in for more than a little surprise. The Court does have strong institutional characteristics, but it is perhaps one of the last citadels of jealously preserved individualism. . . . Indeed a justice may go through an entire term without being once in the chambers of all of the other eight members of the Court.

Echoed Powell's bench-mate, Potter Stewart: "One characteristic of this place, is that one is not his brother's keeper. At times, except for the con- ferences, I hardly know what the others do."

But Justice Breyer recently dismissed this notion of complete self-suffi- ciency as an exaggeration: "The suggestion . . . that we don't talk to each other or try to figure out what the others are thinking . . . [is an overstate- ment]. We do talk to each other. We have ways of finding out—mostly by memo but sometimes directly—what other judges are thinking." And retired Justice David Souter has indicated that some of his colleagues sought out pre-Conference discussions with one another. In praising his former colleague John Paul Stevens for his original thinking, Souter said that Stevens preferred to come to Conference "thinking fresh":

> He doesn't live his life reacting to the way others live theirs, any more than he ever felt a need to know how someone else on the Court viewed a case before he decided what to do on it himself. You could see it in the way he worked over the years. Justices range all over the spectrum of inclination (or not) to talk about the argued cases in the couple of days between coming off the bench and sitting down at conference. John's door was always open to anyone who wanted to bat something around, but he was hardly ever (maybe never) the one to ask about a colleague's take on an issue before all nine of us were sitting down together, ready for the first pass at it. He thought the Court would do its best thinking if we brought our own thinking fresh to the table; the singular insight was less likely to get lost in hasty con- sensus, and any homogenizing could be done just as well after conference. He didn't reach out for the comfort of pre-agreement.

In terms of daily schedules, some Justices have been night owls. A clerk to John Marshall Harlan in the 1890s found that in order to accommodate the Justice's social life, pulling all-nighters was routinely expected:

> It was my duty to report at Justice Harlan's house at nine o'clock in the morning. He would then dispose of his morning mail, which usually took about one hour, and when his work was disposed of would give me direc- tions for my day's work. Shortly before eleven o'clock each morning he left

the house and walked to the capitol building, a distance of about three miles. The dinner hour in Washington was 5 p.m., and during the social season which begins January 1 and ends with the beginning of Lent in each year, there are so many entertainments each evening that a man in high public life must attend that the Judge seldom found time for any work between the hour of adjournment of court and ten, eleven or even twelve o'clock at night. It was therefore our practice during the winter season to resume work in the Judge's study late at night. Then the letters he had dictated in the morning were read and signed, my report of the day's work was made, and the Judge would dictate opinions in cases assigned to him to me. It was not an infrequent occurrence that we began to work as late as midnight and many times we did not cease working until four or five o'clock in the morning. On these occasions I seldom went to bed before breakfast.

Chief Justice Charles Evans Hughes also burned the midnight oil before adopting a more virtuous regime in the 1910s:

Giving up smoking changed entirely my method of work. After breakfast, instead of sitting with my cigar and morning paper, I started out for a walk of half an hour. I soon found that I came back full of ideas and eager to get to my desk. In the evening, instead of indulging in a last cigar in the late hours, I went to bed. Instead of working late at night, I found that I was at my best in the morning.

Like Hughes, William O. Douglas says he took advantage of the morning hours to accomplish work when he joined the Court in 1939:

When I came to the Court there were many traditional habits and ways of doing things that were in time to be changed. In those days we sat from twelve noon until two o'clock, adjourning for thirty minutes for lunch. Then we returned to the Bench, sitting from two-thirty to four-thirty. . . . These hours were ideal for me, as I discovered they were with Hughes. We were both early risers; and prior to noon one could get a day's work done.

When Supreme Court sessions were advanced to ten in 1961, some Justices began arriving very early. For instance, Brennan liked to take walks at 5:30 a.m. and was in his chambers by 7:30. When she joined the Court in 1981 Sandra Day O'Connor established a morning aerobics class for Court staff, explaining, "I think physical fitness is enormously important to your capacity to do mental fitness work." Chief Justice Roberts says he arrives a little earlier on argument days—7:30—to go over the briefs and bounce last-minute ideas off his clerks.

During the weekend, Justices usually conduct work either at home or in their chambers, at least part of the time. Antonin Scalia has described his typical weekly schedule:

One of the nice things about the job—or one of the not nice things about the job—is that you don't have to be here to be working. I could, and I think some judges on the courts of appeals do, only come into court when there's oral argument. I could do this job from home. The main thing it would deprive me of is consultation with my law clerks and it would deprive them of my company, too. So I do like to come in, but that has no relationship to how many hours I'm putting in. I've never counted the hours in the week, but I almost always work weekends—not all weekend, every weekend, but some of the weekend every weekend.

Clerks must show up for duty on weekends as well. This did not deter John Marshall Harlan from hiring a law clerk who was an Orthodox Jew. Nathan Lewin tells the story of how Harlan accommodated his schedule in 1961, so he could observe the Sabbath:

When I came to Washington to meet the Justice, I unburdened myself of the concern that had been gnawing at me round-the-clock: "I have to tell you, Mr. Justice, that I'm an Orthodox Jew, and when winter comes, I have to leave by sundown on Fridays and I can't come in at all on Saturdays." I expected the kind of grilling I had received from law-firm recruiters. They had demanded to know why I couldn't get a dispensation for essential litigation deadlines. A Supreme Court Justice, I thought, would surely tell me how important the Court's work is and request that I find some way to bend the rule.

The Justice did none of that. He smiled and said, "Are you ready to work on Sundays?" I told him I definitely was, and that I was planning to take an apartment a few blocks from the Court so that I could walk home on Friday afternoons if an emergency kept me at the Court until the last minute before sundown. He replied "Well, I've got two clerks, and if your colleague is ready to take the Saturday shift and you're here on Sundays, that's fine with me." My co-clerk was John Rhinelander, scion of a family renowned in the Episcopal Church, and he graciously accommodated this schedule.

On weeks when the Court heard oral argument, the Justices met in conference on Friday mornings. Justice Harlan would swing straight out of these conferences into meetings with his clerks. Then winter came and the sun was going down as early as 4:30 p.m. During several postconference Friday meetings, the Justice spontaneously turned to me and said, "Nat, the sun's going down soon. It's time for you to be on your way home."

The Justices accomplish their duties not only with the help of extraordinarily hard-working clerks but also with the small (currently about 325 employees) but dedicated Supreme Court staff. One little-heralded collaborator is the Reporter of Decisions, who is responsible for editing the Justices' opinions—checking citations, correcting errors—and supervising their printing and official publication. The Court Reporter's usefulness to the Justices has improved significantly over time. Early Reporters sometimes butchered the Justice's opinions and injected political comments into the headnotes (brief summaries of what the case is about that appear at the top of published opinions). Not surprisingly, some Justices insisted in writing their own headnotes. Charles Henry Butler, who served as Reporter of Decisions from 1902 to 1916, described the unsettled state of headnote writing during his tenure:

> As a matter of fact most of [the headnotes] were my own productions. Some were submitted to the Justices delivering the opinions, and some—most of them—were not. In a few cases the author of the opinion would send me the headnote. Every Justice had the opportunity, which was not seldom availed of, to make corrections in the advance sheets and the headnote would appear amended accordingly in the bound volume. Several of the Justices wanted the headnote submitted before the opinion appeared. Numerous letters in my files contain suggestions or corrections—some of them rather drastic—in regard to my first drafts sent to them for their approval. Or disapproval.
>
> My publishers told me that Justice [Horace] Gray always wrote the headnotes of his opinions himself and sent a copy to the reporter and each of the publishers of the unofficial series. He evidently had no faith in the ability of anyone to digest and report his opinions properly. Some of the Justices, however, were averse even to pass on the headnotes because they wished to avoid all responsibility for them.

Nowadays it is the Reporter and his staff who write the summaries of the opinions, called syllabi, which include a breakdown of how the Justices voted. Until 1970, syllabi only appeared at the top of Court opinions when they were published in bound volumes—a year after the release of the decision. But the Justices grew weary of newspaper and radio reporters inaccurately explaining their rulings. Writers of morning newspapers had enough time to read the decisions and break them down, but TV, wire, radio, and evening papers had to translate them so fast that their descriptions often shortchanged their complexity. Chief Justice Warren Burger lobbied his brethren for permission to publish the syllabi at the same time as the Court's official opinions so as to give journalists a better chance at understanding what the decision meant. According to the Court's press officer, this proposal met with resistance:

> There was an immediate argument against the idea, sufficient to kill it so far as some of the veterans [Justices] were concerned: It had never been done in the previous seventeen decades of the Court's existence. . . . Justices around the table had other weapons with which to shoot down the proposal. The Reporter of Decisions, Henry Putzel, was one of the army of people who were denied access to the Court secrets as judgments are hammered out. Henry would have to be cut into the know a day or two before the announcement of the Court verdict. Why widen the circle of the informed? Could Henry be trusted? Burger tried a quick answer: "If Henry can't, then no one around here can be." That still did not satisfy the dubious.

"Why do anything for those reporters?" asked one Justice who had painful memories of past headlines.

"I feel the same as you do," The Chief assured him, "but this is not for the reporters, it is for the Court."

Chief Justice Burger eventually prevailed. For a while some Justices continued to read over the syllabi and suggest changes; others left the entire responsibility to the Court Reporter. Burger then made another change to accommodate the media: instead of announcing all opinions and orders on Monday mornings, he spaced them out throughout the week so reporters could provide better coverage of them.

For all the expertise and dedication of Court staff, the institution is run on a modest government budget. Lewis F. Powell, Jr., who had agreed to serve on the Court with some reluctance, complained publicly after his arrival in 1972 that the institution's support services compared unfavorably with that of a private law firm:

> I have an office suite of only three rooms. I have one secretary, who serves as a file clerk, receptionist, as well as a highly confidential personal secretary. . . . My three law clerks are crowded into a single small room, each doing his own typing in the absence of secretarial help. . . . There is no permanent legal staff available on the Court; no experienced lawyers to call on; and no one to do protracted and scholarly research—beyond the basic legal research— under the direction of a Justice. In short, each Justice is on his own, with resources—both physical and in personnel—far less adequate than those of a partner in a well-organized law firm.

Powell asked that the Court hire a permanent staff of legal experts with deep knowledge of specialized subjects like labor law, taxation, patent law, and bankruptcy. The response: "My brothers gently rejected my proposal, reminding me that I was being paid to render personal judgments even if they were devoid of *expertise.*"

Undaunted, Powell became the first Justice to use a computer for word processing in his Chamber. Historically, the Court has been slow to adopt new technology. A 1972 Term clerk described the primitive work conditions in Chambers in the pre-computer days:

> All of the memos and certs were typed on the "new" Smith Corona electric typewriters that the Court had just purchased. The paper used had one or two carbon copy sheets behind the front page so that there was always a copy for the file. Justice Blackmun called the copies "flimsies." Typing errors would be corrected with whiteout, but the flimsies were always pretty messy. If a sentence were to be changed, it would often be X=d out and replaced with another in the margin. The Smith Coronas were very loud typewriters, and even more so because of the flimsy copies attached to each

sheet. When all of the clerks were typing, it sounded like being trapped in the middle of enemy crossfire. Since the Justice's clerks all worked in one room in my Term, the capacity to concentrate amidst the noise was a finely honed skill that we quickly learned.

Today, the Justices write, revise, and circulate drafts on a secure computer network designed especially for them.

The budget for the Justices' salaries is set by Congress. In the early 1800s they received the highest government salary after the President and Vice President, but their remuneration quickly slipped below that of Cabinet members. The Associate Justices' salary began at $3,500 a year in 1789 and they did not get a raise until 1819. It was not for lack of asking. In 1816 Joseph Story pleaded unsuccessfully to Congress:

> The necessaries and comforts of life, the manner of living and the habits of ordinary expenses, in the same rank of society, have, between 1789 and 1815, increased in price from one hundred to two hundred per cent. The business of the Judges of the Supreme Court, both at the Law Term in February and on the Circuits, has during the same period increased in more than a quadruple ratio and is increasing annually.

To provide a salary benchmark, the most talented members of the Supreme Court bar, such as Daniel Webster, were earning more than $20,000 per year.

In 1857 Justice Benjamin R. Curtis chose to resign from the Supreme Court at the young age of 48 to return to his profitable practice in Boston. Curtis was angry over Chief Justice Roger B. Taney's handling of the *Dred Scott* decision, but he also complained that the low judicial salary had made it hard to support his family:

> The expenses of living have so largely increased, that I do not find it practicable to live on my salary, even now; and, as my younger children will soon call for much increased expenses of education, I shall soon find it difficult to meet my expenses by my entire income. Indeed, I do not think I can do so without changing, in important particulars, my mode of life. Added to this, I cannot have a house in Washington, and I must either live apart from my family from four to six months every year while I go there, or subject them to a kind of vagrant life in boarding-houses, neither congenial nor useful. I had hoped it would prove otherwise, and looked forward to being able to have a house there for six months in a year. But what with the increase of luxury and the greatly enhanced prices there, I have now no hope of being able to do this. I can add something to my means by making books, but at the expense of all my vacations, when perhaps I ought not to labor hard. The constant labor of the summer has told on my health during the last two years.

Nine years later, Chief Justice Salmon P. Chase proposed that three seats on the Supreme Court be eliminated so that the rest of its members could receive raises. He thought it unfair that the Justices earned only one-third of the salaries of military leaders (albeit recently victorious in the Civil War): "It is very important—if it is important that adequate salaries should be paid to the Judges of the Supreme Court—that the number of Judges should be reduced proportionately as vacancies may occur, to seven. I think that the salaries of the highest Judicial Officers of the nation ought not to be less than that of the highest Military officers." Congress did reduce the size of the Court to seven for political reasons as it feared that President Andrew Johnson's nominees might not support its Reconstruction program (it went back to nine a few years later). But Congress did not raise the Justices' salaries until 1871.

Members of the Court who did not receive outside income from investments felt pinched. For instance, in 1877 Chief Justice Morrison R. Waite could not afford to pay for his daughter's trip to Europe. He expressed his embarrassment to a physician friend who had offered to foot Nany's travel expenses:

> The truth is Dr., I might have been rich, but am poor. I have reached the height of my ambition . . . but the government compels me substantially to pay my own expenses. For the first time in my life, I really have been made to feel that I must count the cost of everything. It always gives me the greatest pleasure to gratify the wishes of Nany and her mother, but I must sometimes say no.

The meager salary and costly social obligations of being Chief Justice—such as hosting dinners at his home for foreign judges—depleted whatever savings Waite had accumulated before his appointment. (The top lawyer of the Supreme Court Bar was then billing about $35,000 a year compared to the Chief's $10,500 salary.) Waite was nearly bankrupt when he died in 1888, and a collection had to be raised for his widow.

Congress gradually increased the Justices' salaries by increments of roughly $2,000 and then $5,000 every decade until the 1960s. In 1964, Congress authorized a pay increase for federal employees but designated $3,000 less for the Justices than for other top-level government employees. The reason: Congress's unhappiness with the Court's recent ruling on reapportionment, which affected their political base.

In 1969 the Associate Justices got a big raise hike: from $39,500 to $60,000. But by 1989 Chief Justice William H. Rehnquist felt compelled to lobby Congress vigorously to fund raises for all federal judges, whose salaries had fallen way behind their counterparts in other areas of the legal profession—including senior law professors and law school deans.

The Justices were given a 25 percent raise and the promise of regular cost-of-living increases. But because their pay is pegged to the salaries of members of Congress, in the years when Congress decides it is politically unpalatable to raise their own pay, members of the Court suffer the consequences.

In 2009 the Justices' remuneration was $213,900 for the Associates and $223,500 for the Chief Justice. Yet the boom in private-sector law pay since the 1980s makes these figures strikingly uncompetitive. (Chief Justice Roberts, for example, earned more than $1 million in salary at his firm.) When top law firms recruit Supreme Court clerks, they now typically offer them almost as much in salary their first year as a Justice makes. On top of that, some firms give former clerks as much as a $250,000 bonus to induce them to sign on as an associate.

From 1789 to 1969, the Chief Justice earned only $500 more annually than the Associate Justices. This augmented salary was intended to cover the extra duties of administering the Court as an institution. In the Courtroom, the Chief Justice's job entails opening and closing Court sessions, making announcements, admitting lawyers to the Supreme Court bar, enforcing etiquette, and keeping the proceedings flowing. As institutional head, the Chief is expected to manage the Court's bureaucracy, staff, building, and budget. The larger salary was also intended to compensate for the extrajudicial assignments Congress or the President gave the Chief Justice in the early years of the Court. He was then seen as an all-purpose public servant who could be called upon to perform extrajudicial duties, including leading foreign missions and international arbitrations. (If called upon, the Chief Justice is also required by the Constitution to preside over the Senate when the president is tried for impeachment, but only Salmon P. Chase and William H. Rehnquist have had to do so.)

Associate Justice Samuel F. Miller's eyes were opened to what it was like to carry these extra administrative burdens when he presided over the Court during Chief Justice Waite's temporary breakdown in 1885. As Senior Associate Justice he filled in for six months, giving the overworked and exhausted Chief a break:

> In consequence of the illness of the Chief Justice [Waite] I have had to be acting Chief Justice in his place. I always knew that he did a great deal more work than I, and had many apparently unimportant, matters to look after to which the other judges gave no time and very little attention. I find now that what I had suspected hardly came up to the draft on his time as he performed these duties. . . . [I]n his way of doing it [the chief-justiceship is] a heavy load on his time and on his mind. It is this which caused his illness. He is much broken down and if [he] does not diminish his excessive labors, he will not be capable of any work in a year or two more.

Since Miller's day, the chief justiceship has acquired even more administrative functions. In 1922 Congress established the Judicial Conference of the United States to coordinate all of the federal courts and to recommend and draft legislation governing the federal judiciary, and made the Chief Justice (then William H. Taft) chairman of the conference. Since 1939 the Chief Justice has also been tasked with supervising the Administrative Office of the United States Courts, which performs most of the support functions—budget, accounting, statistical analysis—for the federal court system.

Chief Justice Harlan Fiske Stone felt overwhelmed by this increase in administrative duties. In 1946 he protested to President Harry S Truman: "Few are aware that neither my predecessor nor I . . . , have been able to meet the daily demands upon us without working nights and holidays and Sundays." Stone would die of a stroke shortly thereafter. Passed over in favor of Fred Vinson to replace Stone as Chief Justice, Hugo L. Black consoled himself in a letter to his colleague, Sherman Minton: "The administrative work of the Chief Justice is a very heavy burden, and while I could perform it if I were compelled to do so, it is not the kind of task which adds glamour to the position."

In 1953 Vinson argued that, with the increase in his outside duties, the $500 differential was too small a compensation for the Chief Justice. The Senate introduced a bill that would have raised the Chief's salary to be on level with the Vice President and the Speaker of the House—an increase of $5,000 over the Associate Justices' pay. This led to a fierce discussion in the Justices' weekly Conference. According to William O. Douglas, "The debate was long and heated. Black and Frankfurter took the lead in opposing Vinson, and I shared their views. On May 18 Frankfurter sent each of us a strong letter containing his opinion, with which I am sure a majority of the Court agreed. And as I reread it years later, the bitterness of the 1953 conference was relived." Vinson promoted the proposal anyway, but it never passed in Congress.

In 1967 Chief Justice Earl Warren asked Congress to open the Federal Judicial Center to be the research and training arm of the federal judiciary. By mandate, the Chief serves as chairman of its board. The following year a Commission on Federal Salaries recommended paying the Chief Justice $3,500 more than the Associates (who would also be given a raise). In his memoirs, Justice Douglas recounted why the Chief Justice chose to torpedo the plan:

Warren brought the proposal to Conference, saying he had opposed an increase for the Chief Justice greater than what the Justices received, but that the commission overruled him. Warren's point was that in the sweep of history, when tensions are great on the Court and personal animosities flare up, the salary difference is almost certain to be an additional irritant. In 1968 the Conference shared that view.

But in 1969, the year Warren Burger became Chief Justice, Congress authorized the Chief Justice's salary be bumped to $2,500 more than the Associates. Burger took it upon himself to act more vigorously to publicize the Supreme Court's work and to oversee the federal judiciary. He once estimated that one-third of his time was consumed with duties that the Associate Justices did not share. Barrett McGurn, the Court's press officer in that era, recalled that Burger took the extra burden in stride: "Asked about his bruisingly long work weeks, clocked by his Court secretary at up to eighty hours, Burger said of his evening meal: 'Often it is at eleven. My wife's used to it. I did the same when I practiced law.'"

In 1972 Congress authorized the Chief Justice to hire an Administrative Assistant to relieve some of his burden. The Administrative Assistant helps draft the Chief's speeches, prepares the Court's budget, and oversees developments in the administration of the judiciary.

All the members of the Court catch a break in the summer when they are free to take time off to travel, lecture, or simply relax. But during the summer recess the Justices continue to receive new cases to review; about one-fourth of applications are read by the Justices and their clerks during this time. Very rarely, the Court convenes for special sessions during the summer to hear a particularly urgent case or delays adjournment of the regular term to squeeze one more case in. Justice Scalia has described his sense of relief when the term ends:

> [T]he summertime is a break. We clean our plates before we leave at the end of June, so it really is a summer without guilt. The only work we have to do over the summer is stay on top of cert petitions because there is a monster conference at the end of the summer to vote on all of the cert petitions that have accumulated over the summer. So you have to stay on top of them, but that's a manageable job. For the rest of it, we have continued to function the way all branches of the federal government used to function. This town used to be deserted in July and August: there was nobody here. Now we are generally not around in July and August and come back in September to get ready for the arguments in October. During the summer you have time to do some of the reading that you didn't have time to do during the Court term and to regenerate your batteries.

In the interest of efficiency, Chief Justice Taft tried in 1921 to cut down the summer recess from seventeen weeks to twelve. The Associate Justices objected, especially Louis D. Brandeis, who argued eloquently for the necessity of a long summer break. Reported his clerk:

The Justice worked long and hard, but he insisted that it be with a fresh mind and at top efficiency. As soon as he felt the let-down of fatigue, he stopped and either took his morning drive, or stretched out on the couch in his study and napped for exactly twenty minutes. When he found himself reading sentences over again, he knew that, worse than wasting time, he was missing the point of what he read. "More men," he would say, "have gotten into trouble by the inability to say no, and the failure to take vacations than by more familiar vices." And again, "A year's work can be done in eleven months, but not in twelve months." In short, he worked with intensity, or recharged his reserve of energy until he could.

Taft decided to reduce the number of weeks designated for oral argument instead. Brandeis asked Charles Evans Hughes, who had returned to private practice in a New York law firm, whether he was envious of his summer off. "Not at the price you have to pay for it," was the former Justice's reply.

In 1970 the Court decided to halve oral argument time to thirty minutes per side, and the number of cases put on the argument schedule promptly doubled. From 1971 to 1988 the Court heard roughly 150 cases a term—a number that came to be considered the norm. During a Conference in 1973, Chief Justice Burger bet the Associate Justices that they were producing "up to forty Opinions each"—including concurrences and dissents—per Term. The Justices refused to believe their output was that heavy. Press officer Barrett McGurn described the nature of the wager as told to him by Burger:

> All at the table knew that the annual workload was heavy, but some thought the Chief was overstating it. "Do you have $5 to back up what you say?" asked one. "No," was the rejoinder. "But I'll buy you a bottle of wine if I am wrong, and you can get me one if I'm not." . . . There was no report on who won, but it was clear that a score or more Opinions, three or more a month from each chamber, was being produced.

But 150 cases per term proved unduly burdensome. In 1981 Justice O'Connor proposed in the interest of efficiency to allow the Justices to opt out of hearing a case argued and instead choosing to rely on the written briefs. Justice Powell cautioned his fellow Justices: "My only concern is that we might abuse this privilege. I believe in the utility of oral argument, and also in the symbolism it portrays for the public. Accordingly, if the rule is changed as suggested, I would hope that we would use this option sparingly." The proposal died amidst strong objections from Justice Brennan based on his experience on the New Jersey Supreme Court in deciding cases without oral arguments—and the lower quality of opinions that he said resulted.

When William H. Rehnquist became Chief Justice in 1986, he urged the Associate Justices to ease the workload burden by only taking appeals of important, unresolved issues. The number of cases granted review declined to seventy-five in 2005—the end of his tenure—and has not rebounded since then. There are many explanations for this shrunken docket. The main one is that a 1988 act of Congress virtually eliminated mandatory appeals to the Supreme Court. Another is that the Office of the Solicitor General, which argues cases on behalf of the federal government and is the Court's biggest patron, has been filing fewer petitions for certiorari. It tries to economize staff time by only filing the ones it believes will be successful. Some also hypothesize that a split Court in the past two decades has decreased cert activity from advocacy groups wary of establishing an unfavorable precedent and has increased denials of cert petitions from Justices uncertain of a case's outcome. Others see a reticence from clerks in the cert pool to recommend grant for anything except cases involving significant inter-circuit conflicts involving more than two out of the thirteen federal appellate courts. No clerk wants to recommend a grant of any case that is then denied by the Justices.

Chief Justice Roberts has speculated that a lack of major federal legislation passed by Congress in recent years that requires constitutional interpretation may also be a culprit:

> The court's docket tends to increase when there is major legislation enacted, particularly if the legislation is complex and the stakes are high and it affects a broad segment of the population. The relative lack of major legislation in recent years, I think, can account to some extent to the corresponding decline in the court's docket.

He has also theorized that technology allows information about current rulings in other circuits to be disseminated quickly, which presumably lessens the tendency for circuit courts to dissent from one another and require the Supreme Court to resolve the issue.

Some Justices, such as Samuel Alito, are puzzled by the persistently small number of cases accepted for review. "It's a real mystery to me. Applying the usual criteria, I just haven't seen many cases denied that really were good candidates for review. If I had the time, I'd like to take a term where they were taking the [150] cases and see whether they are cases we would grant today. But I don't have the time." Justice Antonin Scalia believes the Court could handle more cases: "I think we could do more than seventy-five; we could do one hundred well. I don't think we can do what we were doing when I first came on the Court: 150. I don't think we can do 150 well."

Do the Justices do less work? On occasion an oral argument slot has been cancelled for lack of business. Certainly, the job is no longer quite the "chain gang" of Stone's day, but the Justices and their clerks still have to plow through the ever-increasing number of cert petitions to decide which cases to accept. Similarly, amicus curiae filings, briefs by outside parties giving their expert advice on specific legal issues in a case, have increased 40 percent in the last twenty-five years and make for important, but voluminous, reading. Accepting fewer cases may also mean that the Justices spend more time researching and writing each opinion. And opinions have grown much longer and more complex. Concurring opinions and dissents are more plentiful and lengthier as well. In short, the Justices may be deciding less but writing more.

The Justices know that errors made at the Supreme Court level are enormously costly. Deciding it is wiser to allow lower courts and the political branches to try to resolve an issue is a crucial aspect of the job. As Justice Brandeis once put it: "The most important thing we do is not doing."

13

⚖

Timing It Right
Stepping Down

"I won't be down tomorrow," Oliver Wendell Holmes, Jr., quietly told the attendant who helped him on with his overcoat before he exited the Supreme Court building for the last time as an Associate Justice. Unbeknownst to spectators who listened to Holmes announce his opinion in a hoarse, faltering voice in the Courtroom that day in 1932, he had already posted a letter to President Herbert Hoover, informing him that, after twenty-nine years: "The time has come and I bow to the inevitable." Holmes was ninety and in failing health. The Chief Justice had visited him at home the day before to tell him it was time to go.

Deciding when to leave the Supreme Court can be as difficult as gaining appointment to it. Before the advent of judicial pensions in 1869, most Justices simply avoided the decision by staying on the bench until death came to call. Modern Justices usually retire because of old age or disability. For them, timing is everything. The ideal is to resign before declining health makes it too difficult to decide whether one is still capable of functioning at the extremely high level required of the job. As Justice Lewis F. Powell, Jr.'s son advised him: "It's a whole lot better to go out when some people may be sorry than it is to wait until when you decide to go out, and people say, 'Thank God we got rid of the old gent.'" Powell heeded this suggestion in 1987 and left at the height of his ability.

A few have resigned in their prime to pursue political ambitions. In the nineteenth century, some Justices had no qualms about campaigning for political office—either secretly or openly—while still on the bench. Chief Justice John Jay set a precedent in 1795 when he, as a sitting Court member, was elected governor of New York. Justice David Davis resigned in 1877 to become a U.S. Senator for Illinois, although he was elected by the state legislature and had not even sought the position. In the twentieth century, Charles Evans Hughes felt obliged to step down from the Court before campaigning for President (unsuccessfully) in 1916 on the Republican ticket.

Other Justices have resigned their seat in the quest of peace. John H. Clarke quit in 1922 to take up the fight to persuade the United States to join the League of Nations. After only six years, the Court's work had grown tiresome to Clarke, who preferred speaking out about international cooperation and the formation of a World Court. He confided to his colleague Louis D. Brandeis: "I should die happier if I should do all that is possible to promote the entrance of our government into the League of Nations than if I continued to devote my time to determining whether a drunken Indian had been deprived of his land before he died or whether the digging of a ditch in Iowa was constitutional or not."

During World War II, Justice James F. Byrnes (1941–1942) returned to the executive branch to assist his mentor, President Franklin D. Roosevelt, in running the government's domestic affairs. The Vietnam War similarly drew Justice Arthur Goldberg away from the bench in 1965. President Lyndon Johnson had appointed him Ambassador to the United Nations in hopes that he could apply his considerable negotiating skills to bring about an end to that conflict. But Goldberg bitterly came to regret his premature departure from the Court and later tried to rejoin it. He realized belatedly that his UN position carried no real power and that Johnson had wanted to get him off the Court so he could appoint his crony, Abe Fortas. Goldberg's wife, Dorothy, did not, however, come to view his decision to give up life tenure on the Court as a mistake:

> Although I finally concurred with Arthur's ultimate decision [to leave the Court], my own opposition was shared by everyone in the family, particularly the children, who were incensed about Art's even being forced to make such a choice. . . . Later, after seeing the way the United Nations functions and the work that Arthur was called on to perform, I gradually ceased to feel a sense of numbness over his having left the Court. Indeed, before we left the UN for private life, I had completely changed my mind about the decision he had made. When people ask me which office I had liked the best, I honestly say the United Nations, for the reason that nothing a person does before arriving there, and nothing one may do afterward, is commensurate with the feeling of exhilaration in the hope that maybe, just maybe, it is possible to work for a better world.

In the nineteenth century, the death of a sitting Justice was a common occurrence. When Justice Philip Barbour was taken ill in 1841, he died not on the bench, but in the boardinghouse where the Justices resided together and deliberated cases. Justice Joseph Story's moving account of Barbour's demise shows how intimate death could be at a time when the brethren served as surrogate family to one another:

> [T]he death of Mr. Justice Barbour . . . has spread a great gloom over the Court and almost disabled us from doing any business. His death was indeed awfully sudden. He was in good health and attended Court all Wednesday, and heard the extraordinary argument of Mr. [John Quincy] Adams in the case of the Amistad; extraordinary, I say, for its power, for its bitter sarcasm, and its dealing with topics far beyond the record and points of discussion. He dined heartily, and remained with the Judges in conference until after ten o'clock in the evening, and then in a most cheerful humor. The next morning the servant went into his room between six and seven o'clock and made his fire, perceiving nothing unusual and supposing him to be asleep. About one hour afterwards the messenger with letters knocked at his door, and hearing no answer went in softly, supposing him asleep, and laid a letter upon his table and withdrew. At nine o'clock the servant called us all to breakfast, and upon going into his room, finding him still in bed, he went to him and found he could not awaken him. He was frightened, and ran into my room and told me he feared Judge Barbour was dead. I went immediately and found him lying on his left side and lifeless. His eyes were closed, his feet stretched out, and his arms in a natural position. His forehead, hands, feet and limbs were perfectly cold, but upon feeling his breast, I discovered it was still warm. We sent for Dr. Sewall, who came and said that he was indeed dead, and that he must have died of angina pectoris. Probably he breathed his last about daylight, and while he was yet asleep. From all appearances, he must have died without any struggle and instantaneously. We are all thrown into utter confusion, and I sat down to a most melancholy breakfast, seeing on my side the deserted chair in which he used to sit. We went to the Court at eleven o'clock, where the Chief Justice announced the event, and the Court was at once adjourned until Monday.

The compassion shown by Story (1812–1845) is all the more touching considering that he was often at odds with Barbour (1836–1841) with respect to cases.

As they aged, some nineteenth-century Justices suffered from infirmities that greatly diminished their effectiveness. Perhaps the most notorious example was Gabriel Duvall (1811–1835), who, according to an 1827 observer, was "the oldest looking man on the bench. His head was as white as a snow-bank, with a long white cue, hanging down to his waist. He did not impress me at the time as being even up to the mediocrity on the Bench." Seven years later, another observer reported: "Judge [Duvall] is eighty-two years old, and so deaf as to be unable to participate in conversation." Indeed, during his last decade on the Court, he was unable to hear oral arguments, despite using an ear trumpet. Yet Duvall refused to resign until 1835, at age eighty-three. President Andrew Jackson finally got him off the Court by leaking the name of the man he planned to nominate as his successor, a fellow Marylander whom Duvall found a politically acceptable candidate.

Declining eyesight has also been an issue on the Court. Henry Billings Brown (1891–1906) suffered from a degenerative eye condition that forced him to dictate all his work to stenographers and to ask family members to read briefs to him. Despite this severe handicap he hung on an extra two years so he could draw a full pension. Brown explained to a friend:

> I much fear I shall lose my sight completely, but I am taking encouragement from the fact that good work has been done by blind men, and that some distinguished judges have been forced to rely upon the sight of others to prepare their opinions. Of course, it is a terrible affliction, but if I can avoid a nervous collapse for the next sixty or ninety days I hope I may succeed in reconciling myself to the situation, and perhaps take some further pleasure out of life. Of course, I would resign if I could do so and draw my pay; but after nearly thirty years' service upon the Bench I do not feel called upon to do when I am within a little over two years of completing my term.

When Brown finally resigned in 1906, he was both wistful and relieved:

> While it involves a good deal of a wrench to break up the habits of thirty years, and turn my back upon the genial and accomplished gentlemen who for more than fifteen years have been my daily associates, and wander in the land of the lotus eater where it is always afternoon, I feel there is at least some compensation awaiting me in the absolute freedom from all cares not voluntarily assumed. There is no one to say, and no inner conscience even to suggest, that it is your duty to be in Court at twelve o'clock; to keep your ears, if not your eyes, open, howevermuch you may prefer a stealthy nap, until four thirty; to listen to arguments for four hours, when in fact, you made up your mind in four minutes; and to be prepared at the next Saturday's Conference to give an opinion, which your Associates will probably overrule.

Far more damaging to the Court than physical infirmity, though, has been mental incapacity. A sad and extreme example of this problem occurred when Henry Baldwin (1830–1844) joined the Court. He suffered from mental illness and liked to pick fights with his colleagues. The Court's Reporter, Richard Peters, witnessed with distress Baldwin's disruptive influence on the other Justices:

> I venture the assertion without fear of contradiction . . . that no one who visits the court or has an opportunity of seeing [Baldwin] speaks of him with respect. It is the opinion of more than the proportion I mention that *his mind is out of order*. I have heard in one day not less than five persons . . . say "he

is crazy" . . . I know that some laugh at him and one of the persons whom I have named asked Dr. Hunt "if he was not out of his senses." He sits in his room for three or four hours in the dark—jumps up and runs down into the judges' consultation room in his stocking feet, and remains in that condition while they are deliberating.

Justices are appointed to life tenure and the only remedy Congress has for removing them is impeachment. A few Justices have been the subjects of congressional investigations, but none have led to expulsion. In the 1860s Congress was determined to design a gentler method for removing them from the bench: namely, the inducement of pensions. Edward Bates, the Attorney General, was able to observe up close the sorry state of some of the Justices and was convinced that a pension bill would give them incentive to resign. He reported in his diary:

> In Sup[rem]e Court today, I argue two revenue cases. . . . All the Judges were present except Mr. Justice Grier, who has gone home sick. The 4 seniors, [Roger B.] Taney, [James Moore] Wayne, [John] Catron and [Robert] Grier, are evidently failing, being, obviously, less active in mind and body, than at the last term. I think all four of them would gladly retire, if Congress would pass the proposed bill—to enable the justices to resign, upon an adequate pension . . . I might perhaps, as well said 5, as 4; for Mr. Justice [Samuel] Nelson shews as plainly as the other 4 signs of decay. He walks with a firmer step it is true, but I do not see that his <u>mind</u> stands more erect than theirs, or moves onward with a steadier gait.

Attorney General Bates dismissed a pension bill Congress proposed in 1864 as not inclusive enough because it did not provide for ailing Justices, merely aged ones:

> A proposition has been introduced into the Senate by Mr. Harlan of Iowa, to create a <u>retired list</u> (similar to that in the Army and Navy) of Judges of the Supreme Court, under which a judge, over 70 may withdraw from active duty, on a scale of pay according to his length of service.
> The principle is right, but the details all wrong. 70 years is no proper time; for a Judge may be much younger than that, yet, mentally or physically incapable of the duties, and still too poor to give up his salary. There ought to be no <u>retired list</u> of <u>Judges</u>; but worn out Judges ought to be respectably provided for, by allowing them to <u>resign</u>, upon a competent pension.

Congress finally passed a Judiciary Act in 1869 providing that any judge who had served on any federal court for at least ten years and had reached the age of seventy could retire from the bench and continue to receive a full salary for the rest of his life. There was still no provision for Bates's "worn-out" judges.

Despite this new inducement, the Supreme Court in the 1870s was burdened by several cases of infirmity, decrepitude, and incompetence. The best eyewitness to this unfortunate period was Justice Samuel F. Miller (1862–1890), who, having trained as a doctor, did not let any of his colleagues' symptoms go unexamined or unremarked. Miller wrote to a friend in 1877 regarding the possible appointment of a new Justice, John A. Campbell, who had served previously on the Court before the Civil War and at age seventy-five was, in his view, now over the hill:

> There is no man on the bench of the Supreme Court more interested in the character and efficiency of its personel than I am. If I live so long, it will still be nine years before I can retire with the salary. I have already been there longer than any man but two both of whom are over seventy.
>
> Within five years from this time three other of the present Judges will be over seventy. [William] Strong is now in his sixty ninth, [Ward] Hunt in his sixty eighth, and broken down with gout, and [Joseph P.] Bradley in feeble health and in his sixty sixth year.
>
> In the name of God what do I and [Morrison R.] Waite and [Stephen J.] Field all men in our sixty first year want with another old, old man on the Bench. . . . Campbell [will be] seventy five some time this year, and Judge [Nathan] Clifford thinks that when they served together they were about the same age and he is near seventy four. Campbell looks five years the older. I have already told the Attorney General that if an old man was appointed we should have within five years a majority of old imbeciles on the bench, for in the hard work we have to do no man ought to be there after he is seventy. But they will not resign. Neither [Noah] Swayne nor Clifford whose mental failure is obvious to all the Court, who have come to do nothing but write garrulous opinions and clamor for more of that work have any thought of resigning.

(Campbell was not reappointed.)

Justice Nathan Clifford (1858–1881) was arguably the worst off of the lot. He was quarrelsome with his colleagues and wrote turgid opinions. His mental capacities declined precipitously after a stroke. Miller described his colleague's sad mental state during his final Term:

> Judge Clifford reached Washington on the 8th October. . . . I saw him within three hours after his arrival, and he did not know me or any thing, and though his tongue framed words there was no sense in them. An effort was made . . . to call it paralysis because he was taken suddenly between Boston and Washington, but there was no paralysis in the case. He remains yet about in the same condition. His general health good as usual. Able to ride out and walk about the house, but his mind is a wreck and no one believes that he will ever try another case, though the one idea which he seems to have is a desire to get to his seat in the capitol. I have seen him twice and

other judges have also. It is doubtful if he knew any of us. His wife thought I could do more to persuade him to return home than any one else and sent for me. But when I saw him I saw also that it was no use to try it for he introduced me to his wife twice in ten minutes, though I have known her for eighteen years quite intimately. His work is ended though he may live for several years.

Clifford did in fact hold on for another nine months after his stroke, despite having been eligible for retirement with full salary for nearly eight years. As the last remaining Democrat appointee on the bench, he had felt obligated to hold on until a Democratic president could appoint his successor. (Republican James Garfield's election as President in 1880 squashed this hope.) Although an extreme example, Clifford's stubborn commitment reflected a tendency in the nineteenth century for Justices to remain on the Court as long as possible out of loyalty to their party and ideology.

Having been passed over for Chief Justice in 1874, Miller was especially sour about his colleagues' abilities. He outlined their shortcomings, and complained that they increased the burdens on able Justices like himself.

> If I had been made Chief Justice I think I should never have tired in this effort. And I may be more affected by the fact that I was not than I am conscious of. But I certainly strove very hard last term to have things go right and to get all the good out of our Chief and my brethren that could be had.
>
> But I feel like taking it easy now. I can't make a silk purse out of a sow's ear. I can't make a great Chief Justice out of a small man. I can't make Clifford and Swayne, who are too old to resign, nor keep the Chief Justice [Waite] from giving them cases to write opinions in which their garrulity is often mixed with mischief. I can't hinder [David] Davis from governing every act of his life by his hope of the Presidency, though I admit him to be as honest a man as I ever knew. But the best of us cannot prevent ardent wishes from coloring and warping our inner judgment.

John W. Wallace, a former Reporter of Decisions, agreed with Miller. But he thought the incapacity of Noah Swayne (1862–1881) and Clifford actually benefited the Court:

> The "shorter handed" the Court is—while the observation comes from the absence of such judges as Clifford & Swayne, the more business it will do, and the better. I often used to wonder whether in the history of the whole world there ever was such a man as the first named one, in *such a place.*
> . . . Swayne was no worse than some other cases, but bad enough no doubt.

The saving grace of that dark period was that the mediocre Justices were generally the senile ones, while the able minority (Miller, Bradley,

Members of the Supreme Court were photographed in 1865, in one of the earliest group portraits. Justice Samuel F. Miller (second from right), appointed three years earlier, would emerge as a dominant force on the Court but would complain about the mediocrity and infirmity of some of his brethren. From left to right are David Davis, Noah Swayne, Robert Grier, James M. Wayne, Chief Justice Salmon P. Chase, Samuel Nelson, Nathan Clifford, Miller, and Stephen J. Field. (Collection of the Supreme Court of the United States)

Strong,) enjoyed good health, shouldered the others' work, and were able to keep the Court functioning.

Justice William Strong (1870–1880), though still quite competent, decided to set an example for his ailing brethren by stepping down after a decade on the Court in hopes that others would follow suit. His cousin, Theron G. Strong, explained the Justice's strategy and its effect on at least one of his colleagues:

> Having reached the age of Seventy-three years, and although remarkably well preserved physically and mentally, and quite capable of efficient service as any of the other justices, he became convinced that it would be for the interest of the court if one or two of the justices who had become enfeebled by age were to retire and their places be filled by more vigorous men. He enjoyed the position and its duties, and would not have retired at that time if the retirement of other justices could have been effected without his setting an example. This conviction led him to say to Mr. Justice Swayne, who had been on the bench a long time and was quite enfeebled, that he had had

in mind the strengthening of the bench by resigning, and as they had both reached the period in life when they could retire with the continuance of their salaries during life, he would offer his resignation if Mr. Justice Swayne would follow him in so doing. Justice Swayne assented to this.

Swayne was evidently so pleased with his decision to step down that he took it upon himself to tout the joys of retirement to his former colleague, the masterful Justice Joseph P. Bradley (1870–1892), who was one year shy of retirement age:

I have no doubt you will resign at the close of your seventieth year or very soon afterwards & I think you ought to. You need have no apprehension that you will not find enough to do—constantly and agreeably to employ you— nor that a moment of your time will necessarily be attended with a sense of tedium or ennui. You will be brighter & happier than you have been for the last five years or will be in the future while you remain on the bench.

By 1881 Samuel Miller had become "very tired of the labour and indifferent to the honors" of being a Justice. But when Miller turned seventy and could finally retire, he changed his tune: "I do not believe a healthy man of seventy years accustomed to any kind of work, mental or physical, ought to quit it suddenly." Of course by that time the Court had also renewed itself and was now stacked with skilled justices. Miller died suddenly of a stroke in 1890 while still on the Court and still in full possession of his faculties. Having witnessed so much infirmity in his bench-mates, Miller had come to believe that impeachment should not be the only way to remove a Justice from the bench:

There are many matters which ought to be cause of removal that are neither treason, bribery, nor high crimes or misdemeanors. Physical infirmities for which a man is not to blame, but which may wholly unfit him for judicial duty, are of this class. Deafness, loss of sight, the decay of faculties by reason of age, insanity, prostration by disease from which there is no hope of recovery—these should all be reasons for removal, rather than that the administration of justice should be obstructed or indefinitely postponed.

In the absence of any such amendment addressing the issue of disability, the Justices had to make do with internal peer pressure. A prime example of this method occurred during the beginning of Miller's tenure, when Justice Robert Grier (1846–1870), who had always been malleable and indecisive, was pressured into retiring. The ailing Grier could not walk and needed to be carried to the bench. He could barely hold a pencil to write. Worse, his thinking was so muddled that he changed his mind during a single Conference on a crucial case reviewing the constitutionality of the Legal Tender Act. He thus provided the questionable fifth vote to invalidate what many considered a necessary exercise of congressional power to save the nation during the Civil War.

Philadelphia lawyer George Harding, an old friend, made the trip to Washington to investigate the Grier problem for himself:

> Called on Judge Grier saw Mrs. Beck [Sarah, Grier's daughter] & him for an hour. They are moving on to Capitol Hill—He feels his oats & doesnt talk of resigning. I sounded him but he wouldnt respond to my touch. I saw [Noah] Swayne—[Samuel] Nelson, & [David] Davis—They are greatly exercised at his not resigning—They declared they were going to crowd him about Dec 1 '69. He sleeps on the bench, drops his head down & looks very badly. Congress will also crowd him if he [does not] resign—. . . . Nelson, Davis & Swayne are loud in calling for you & they mutter at Grier saying how long—how long
>
> It is supposed that Mrs. Smith [Grier's other daughter] & Mrs. Beck support Grier in his wish to remain on the bench with a view to maintain their social status another winter in Washington—The Court are provoked at this—much of their time being spent in canvassing the subject.

Chief Justice Salmon P. Chase and the Senior Associate Justice, Samuel Nelson, paid a call on Grier a few weeks later. Sarah Grier Beck, the married daughter with whom the senile Justice lived when the Supreme Court was in session, informed Harding of their visit:

> The Chief & Judge Nelson waited on Pa this mor'n. to ask him to resign saying that the politicians are determined to oust him, & if he don't, they will repeal the law giving the retiring salaries. Pa told them if they wished him to resign he would do so, to take effect the 1st of Feb. What do you say to all this? Do you think he ought to do so? Excuse this rapid scribble—.

Apparently, Chase and Nelson were not the only ones concerned enough to pressure Grier. Justice Stephen J. Field (1863–1897), the Court's prodigious workhorse from the California frontier, also confronted him, a move that would come back to haunt him. Field's colleagues later would use the episode as their opener to pressure Field when his time came three decades later.

After twenty-eight years on the Court, Field suffered a knee injury and the chronic pain it precipitated caused him to emit unexpected outbursts of temper, often filled with profanity. By then he was no longer churning out solid opinions, but was either forgetting how he voted in Conference or simply doing nothing. The Justices sent the diplomatic John Marshall Harlan (1877–1911) to remind Field of the time when it had been necessary to encourage Grier to resign. But the plan backfired. Harlan later told the story of this encounter to Charles Evans Hughes (with whom he overlapped on the Court in 1910). Hughes recounts it here:

I heard Justice Harlan tell of the anxiety which the Court had felt because of the condition of Justice Field. It occurred to the other members of the Court that Justice Field had served on a committee which waited upon Justice Grier to suggest his retirement, and it was thought that recalling that to his memory might aid him to decide to retire. Justice Harlan was deputed to make the suggestion. He went over to Justice Field, who was sitting alone on a settee in the robing room apparently oblivious of his surroundings, and after arousing him gradually approached the question, asking if he did not recall how anxious the Court had become with respect to Justice Grier's condition and the feeling of the other justices that in his own interest and in that of the Court he should give up his work. Justice Harlan asked if Field did not remember what had been said to Justice Grier on that occasion. The old man listened, gradually became alert and finally, with his eyes blazing with the old fire of youth, he burst out: "Yes! And a dirtier day's work I never did in my life!" That was the end of the effort of the brethren of the Court to induce Justice Field's retirement; he did resign not long after.

With additional pressure from his nephew, David Brewer, who had joined him on the high bench in 1890, Field finally stepped down in 1897.

When peer pressure failed, the Court often resorted to a different tactic to encourage the retirement of Justices who were not yet eligible for a full pension. The Justices would lobby Congress to enact special one-time legislation providing a pension for a particular, ailing Justice—conditional, of course, on a prompt retirement. This worked for Ward Hunt (1872–1882), who, though "speechless with paralysis" for five years and limping from gout, had not resigned because he was totally reliant on his salary. Hunt's special pension provision set a precedent that did not go unnoticed.

In 1895 William H. Jackson, the brother of tuberculosis-ridden Justice Howell E. Jackson (1893–1895), asked the Chief Justice for similar treatment:

I have just returned from a visit to my brother, Justice Jackson, at Thomasville, Ga. and regret to say that I found his condition much changed and for the worse. . . . His local physician pronounces his present trouble dropsy [edema] and says he will probably have to be tapped both in the bowels and legs. He is further of the opinion that the disease will progress and that Justice Jackson will never be able to resume his official duties on the bench. Under these distressing circumstances and conditions it has occurred to me that Justice Jackson should be retired if it can be done. He feels it to be his duty to retire from the bench, but this ought not to be done, in my opinion, without giving him his salary. Since he has served the government faithfully on the Circuit & Supreme benches for nearly eight years, I think, and his health has been shattered we have a precedent in the case of Justice Hunt whose health gave way while he was on the Supreme bench and he was retired on full salary.

Justice Jackson has no income outside of his salary. His wife has valuable real estate near Nashville but it yields little or no income. It is a constant source of worry to him that he is unable to resume his duties on the bench. For him to retire without his salary annuity would hardly be just I think. I write to you on the subject of his retirement because of his admiration and friendship for yourself. Will you think the matter over and if you deem it proper confer with the President and Attorney General and give me your suggestions in the matter.

A bill was introduced to the Senate for Jackson's retirement on full salary, but he asked that it be dropped after a restorative trip to the West Coast enabled him to recover enough to resume his duties. Haggard and frail, Jackson made the arduous train trip to Washington to cast his vote dramatically in what would turn out to be his last case. Because his vote was expected to break the deadlock in the watershed case—which would decide the constitutionality of a national income tax—all eyes were on him. One journalist reported: "[Jackson] interests the crowd more than all the rest of the bench; that his life can last but a short time and that it will probably be shortened by the effort which he has made to attend the hearing." Jackson dissented from the majority decision, which invalidated Congress's power to establish the tax, and died three months later.

It often falls to the Chief Justice to finesse retirement situations. For example, Chief Justice William H. Taft had to maneuver delicately around Associate Justice Joseph McKenna (1898–1925) when his mental activity started to decline. As McKenna began to flip-flop in his votes and write shaky opinions, Taft grew concerned about his output: "In case after case he will . . . bring it into Conference, and it will meet objection because he has missed a point in one case, or as in one instance, he wrote an opinion deciding the case one way when there had been a unanimous vote the other, including his own."

Taft decided to assign McKenna only easy cases, but even then his opinions had to either be rewritten or reassigned. The lowest point came when McKenna circulated an opinion that Taft could not match to a readily identifiable case. Complained Taft: "McKenna's language is as fog. He does not know what he means himself. Certainly no one else does. I try to give him the easiest cases but nothing is too easy for him." Finally, in 1924, Taft invited the Justices to his home to discuss the situation. They concluded that no case could be decided on the basis of McKenna's muddled votes. The Court suffered several four-to-four deadlocks before Taft was finally able to persuade the recalcitrant McKenna to step down.

Potential departures from the Court are, of course, a subject of great interest to Presidents, who relish the prospect of filling as many vacancies as possible with candidates of their choosing. This can turn into a morbid sport. In 1970 President Richard Nixon asked to see the medical records of Thurgood Marshall (1967–1991), who had checked into Bethesda Naval Hospital with pneumonia. When the doctor asked Justice Marshall for permission to release the reports, he assented under one condition. Marshall first scrawled the words "Not Yet!" in large black script across the folder.

William H. Taft had the good fortune to be able to fill six vacancies during his single presidential term. Not long after he took office in 1909, Taft privately vented to an old friend his frustration with the Court's aging membership:

> The condition of the Supreme Court is pitiable and yet those old fools hold on with a tenacity that is most is discouraging. Really, the Chief Justice [Melville W. Fuller, 76] is almost senile; [John Marshall] Harlan [also 76] does no work; [David] Brewer [72] is so deaf that he cannot hear and has got beyond the point of the commonest accuracy in writing his opinions; Brewer and Harlan sleep almost through all the arguments. I don't know what can be done. It is most discouraging to the active men on the Bench.

But President Taft was exaggerating. The old-timers were performing well on this Court. Taft had long coveted Fuller's Chief Justice seat and his desire to occupy the center chair clouded his judgment of Fuller.

President Taft's hunger to be Chief was apparently both long-standing and well-known to the Justices. A Supreme Court staff member recalled witnessing this revealing scene back when Taft was serving as governor-general of the Philippines protectorate (six years before becoming President). It took place at a party given at Fuller's home to welcome a new Justice, William Rufus Day:

> While coffee was being served in the drawing room, a young officer called to say good-by to the Chief Justice and Mrs. Fuller. He had been suddenly ordered to the Philippines. . . . Mrs. Fuller . . . called from the floor above to the young officer, and said that, though she could not come downstairs, she would talk to him over the bannisters. After the exchange of farewells, and just as the young officer was going out the front door, Mrs. Fuller called to him . . . "And when you get to the Philippines you tell Willie Taft not to be in too much of a hurry to get into my husband's shoes."

Taft's wish was fulfilled in 1921—eight years after he left the presidency—when Warren G. Harding appointed him Chief Justice.

In the 1930s President Roosevelt grew so frustrated with the Court for opposing his New Deal legislation that he proposed a plan to add an additional Justice for each one over age seventy, up to a maximum of fifteen. His rationale for enlarging the Court was that the elderly Justices could not effectively keep up with the workload. But the very day the Senate Judiciary Committee was scheduled to vote on Roosevelt's hotly debated "Court-packing" legislation, Justice Willis Van Devanter, age seventy-eight, unexpectedly announced his retirement. Van Devanter (1911–1937)

had been a tactical leader of the conservative bloc striking down Roosevelt's economic initiatives, making the bill, already politically doomed,
seem even less necessary. A clerk to James C. McReynolds, Van Devanter's ally on the Supreme Court, recalled the dramatic turn of events:

> [McReynolds and Van Devanter] greeted each other very cordially [in
> McReynolds's apartment] and began engaging in some small talk. I then
> decided to leave and did so within a few minutes. My withdrawal may have
> seemed to be a gesture of politeness so as not to overhear their conversation,
> but the real reason was that I wanted to eat an early dinner and attend the
> circus that night. Besides, I considered Van Devanter's call a mere routine
> visit. In any event I did not realize that an historic meeting was taking place
> between two of the arch conservative Justices of the Supreme Court of the
> United States—their last meeting prior to Van Devanter's resignation.
>
> For months there had been rumors that one of the nine Justices would soon
> resign—either [Louis D.] Brandeis or [George] Sutherland or Van Devanter.
> However, I had always discounted such rumors as I felt that no Justice
> would leave the bench during the Court-packing struggle. It is true there had
> been no retirement from the Court in more than five years—not since Justice
> [Oliver Wendell] Holmes had resigned on January 12, 1932. This interval had
> been one of the longest periods in the history of the Court during which no
> change of membership had occurred. But I considered that a resignation dur-
> ing the heated debates on the President's proposed bill would resemble an
> ignominious retreat under fire. I therefore assured myself that there would
> be no resignation in the immediate future despite a recently enacted retire-
> ment law which had gone into effect on March 1, 1937.
>
> Early the next morning—Tuesday, May 18—Van Devanter telephoned to a
> newspaperman, whom he had known for years, and asked him to call at the
> Justice's apartment on his way to work. When the newspaperman arrived at
> 2101 Connecticut Avenue, N.W., Van Devanter gave him a copy of a letter
> of retirement which was not to be made public until after it had reached the
> White House. However, the original of the letter was at that moment on its
> way to the Executive Mansion in care of a messenger. . . .
>
> As soon as Van Devanter's letter was received at the White House, the
> copy given the newspaperman was made public. The capital was taken by
> complete surprise—especially as Van Devanter was apparently in the best of
> health. Only the day before he had delivered an opinion in Court and had
> spoken in a strong and clear voice for more than half an hour.

Justice Van Devanter's decision to retire was at least in part a result of
a bill Congress had passed a few weeks earlier expanding the incentives
for Justices to step down. The act formally introduced the concept of "resignation," as opposed to "retirement," which now meant a former Justice
could keep his senior status as a federal judge and serve on lower courts
(with permission from the Chief Justice). In retirement, Van Devanter

made good use of his talent and experience by filling in on appeals courts. In the 1960s Justices Stanley F. Reed and Tom C. Clark would also enjoy robust post-Supreme Court stints sitting as federal judges, just as Sandra Day O'Connor, David Souter, and John Paul Stevens do today.

Some Justices who resign while still in good form simply return to the practice of law. On a few rare occasions this has led them back to the Supreme Court and put them in the peculiar position of arguing cases before their former colleagues. Justice Benjamin R. Curtis set this precedent in 1858 when he decided to return to his law practice in his native Boston, where he had been earning more than double his Supreme Court salary. Only forty-seven when he retired, Curtis did not stay away along. He reappeared before the Supreme Court fifty-four times to argue cases on behalf of clients.

Although he was too tactful to say it openly, Curtis's other motive for resigning was one of principle. He had clashed with Chief Justice Roger B. Taney and his brethren over the slavery issue and felt slighted by Taney's lack of professional courtesy during the heated process of drafting the majority opinion (Taney) and dissent (Curtis) in the *Dred Scott* case. Curtis confided to his brother:

> I cannot again feel that confidence in the court, and that willingness to co-operate with them, which are essential to the satisfactory discharge of my duties as a member of that body; and I do not expect its condition to be improved. On the other hand, I suppose there is a pretty large number of conservative people in the Northern, and some in the Southern States, who would esteem my retirement a public loss, and who would think that I had disappointed reasonable expectations in ceasing to hold the office. . . . But I do not myself think it of great public importance that I should remain where I believe I can exercise little beneficial influence; and I think all might abstain from blaming me when they remember that I have devoted six of the best years of my life to the public service, at great pecuniary loss, which the interest of my family will not permit me longer to incur.

Justice John A. Campbell (1853–1861) also had a second act as a Supreme Court advocate. A native of Alabama, Campbell resigned during the turmoil of the Civil War after attempting to broker negotiations between the Confederacy and the Lincoln administration. As a states' righter who opposed secession, the South eyed him with suspicion for not having resigned sooner and did not appoint him to a significant Confederate post. Campbell came to regret his decision to leave the Court and he missed his colleagues. He settled into a successful law practice in New Orleans and was often rumored for reappointment to the Supreme Court, but nothing came of it. He did return frequently, though, arguing sixty-two times before the high bench. A Washington newspaper reporter described Campbell's final performance before the Court in 1884:

> He is a very old man. His form is thin and bent, his skin is in the parchment state, and his hair is as white as the driven snow; but a great mind looks out through his keen eye and a great soul controls his fragile body. He is a lawyer to the core—in some respects one of the wisest, broadest, deepest, and most learned in the United States. He has neither the presence, voice, nor tongue of the orator, but when he speaks in his thin, measured tones, never wasting a word, the Supreme Court of the United States listens as it listens to almost no other man.

A century later, in 1982, former Justice Abe Fortas (1965–1969) would return to argue a case in which he represented Puerto Rico. This was a dramatic comeback for Fortas, who had resigned under a dark cloud thirteen years earlier after it was disclosed that he had been paid consulting fees by a shady financier while sitting on the Court. Although Fortas had denied any wrongdoing and had returned the fees, his resignation preempted charges of judicial misconduct. Three of Fortas's former colleagues were still on the bench at the time of his argument, including Justice William J. Brennan, Jr. A reporter witnessed his welcome:

> [W]hen the nine Justices emerged from behind the red drapes to take their seats on the bench, Justice William J. Brennan, Jr., a normally undemonstrative man, looked down into the well of the Court and spotted a familiar figure at the counsel's table: Abe Fortas. Brennan's face burst into a broad, beaming smile—a fleeting public display of the behind-the-scenes warmth that no doubt accounts for Brennan's hold on the colleagues and the clerks who work most closely with him. Then Brennan quickly turned to Fortas's opponent, Philip Lacovara . . . and flashed another, more formal smile.

Fortas, who had excelled as an appellate advocate before being named to the Court, won his case in a unanimous decision. But he never knew it. The former Justice died suddenly two weeks later, before the decision was announced and his comeback was complete.

While almost all modern Justices have chosen to retire from active service, one particularly dramatic exception was Chief Justice Harlan Fiske Stone, who died wearing his judicial robe in 1946. All was well in the morning when Stone arrived at work, but in the afternoon when it was his turn to announce opinions from the bench, he faltered. Justice Harold H. Burton recorded the event dispassionately:

> The Chief Justice had repeated himself just a little in his oral dissent . . . , but looked all right. However, when it came his turn to give 3 opinions for the Court at 1:40, he was unable to speak or collect his papers. Justice Black

signaled for immediate adjournment. The Court rose at once. Justices Black and Reed helped the Chief to the robing room. He walked about not thinking or speaking clearly. He lay down there. The Marshal called [the doctor] from the Capitol. He reported good pulse and pressure but some blood circulation indigestion. . . . The rest of the Justices (except Justice Murphy) had lunch as usual and returned to the bench at 2:30. Justice Black presiding announced "in the temporary absence of the Chief Justice" the three cases which [Stone] had been authorized to announce. . . . We then proceeded with our regular business.

Stone died that evening of a massive cerebral hemorrhage, surrounded by his family. At Felix Frankfurter's urging, the Justices had quickly reconvened that afternoon to finalize the decisions handed down that day. They knew that Stone's votes could not be counted once he was dead and that the results needed to be announced formally from the bench to be considered official. Otherwise, the cases would have to be reargued.

As medical diagnoses have improved, Justices have been better able to judge for themselves when it is time to step down. Improvements in medical care and treatment have also enabled them to continue to function capably in their eighties. Hugo L. Black (1937–1971) began to question his abilities after his eyesight began failing and he suffered a mild stroke playing tennis in 1966. He kept asking family and friends for their advice on whether to retire. After much handwringing, he knew it was time to quit when, at age eighty-five, he was stricken with temporal arteritis and taken to Bethesda Naval Hospital.

By happenstance, Black's colleague, John Marshall Harlan (1965–1971), was being treated for spinal cancer in the next room. Although nearly blind and in terrible pain, Harlan had been keeping up with the workload from his hospital bed. One of his clerks recalled that they simply brought the Court—and some contraband—to him:

> For the next month [after Harlan checked into the hospital], we made frequent trips to the hospital, bringing him applications and other Court papers, going over them, and getting signatures. We also smuggled in Lark cigarettes, which he smoked constantly, and Rebel Yell bourbon, which he consumed sparingly after we transferred it to hospital cups with straws so the nurses couldn't tell.

Harlan patiently waited to resign until Black announced his retirement. Black's son, Hugo, Jr., recorded the poignant reason why:

> Meanwhile, I learned that Justice Harlan wanted to see me alone. When I got to his room, I shut the door behind me and said, "What is it, Mr. Justice?"
> "Did you lock the door, Hugo?"
> "No, sir. But I will." I did this, then said, "What's the matter, Mr. Justice?"

Pierce Butler's brethren attended his funeral mass in 1939. Pictured from left to right are: James C. McReynolds, Owen J. Roberts, Stanley F. Reed, Edward T. Sanford, Willis Van Devanter, William O. Douglas, Felix Frankfurter, Hugo L. Black, Harlan Fiske Stone, and Chief Justice Charles Evans Hughes. Butler died while serving on the Court; most modern Justices have retired. (Courtesy of the Library of Congress)

"Hugo," he said, "I need to know about your father's retirement. What is he going to do?" "Mr. Justice, I think he will retire very soon. Why do you ask right now?"

"I cannot do my job any longer; I believe I have cancer of the spine and I am going to have to retire." Tears ran down his cheeks as he continued, "But I do not want to do anything to detract from the attention your father's retirement will get. I don't have to tell you. He is one of the all-time greats of our Court. He has served with over one-third of the Justices who ever sat on the Court. Nobody's judgment ever exceeded his—his is just the best."

"Mr. Justice," I said, "you must do what you have to do. There will be time."

"Holding up until your father's retirement is recognized and commented on is the right thing to do," he said. Now he had brought tears to my eyes. "Mr. Justice," I said, "this is about as noble an act of friendship as there could be. I hate to say this, but I'm not even sure he would do the same thing for you."

"I think he would. But, really, it makes no difference, Hugo," he said. "I would wait anyhow out of respect for his greatness even if he were not my friend."

Before announcing his retirement, Black asked his son to help him with one last, highly unusual, request:

Practically the first thing Daddy wanted me to do once he was installed in the hospital was to go out and burn certain papers of his. According to him, publishing the notes of conversations between Justices inhibited the free exchange of ideas. "You remember how you told me that a tape recorder always chilled any real negotiation in a labor dispute, Son, with everybody spending all their time making a record?" he said. "What I'm talking about is the same kind of thing." He also felt that reports by one Justice of another's conduct in the heat of a difference might unfairly and inaccurately reflect history. As an example, he cited to me a biographer's accusation, based on Justice Harold Burton's papers, alleging that Daddy had hung back on the decision ending segregation of the races. "Good Lord, Son, you of all people know how false that is." When he requested me to burn the papers, I tried to put it off, since I did not think this should be done. "You'll have plenty of time when you retire to do it yourself. You know the ones you want to keep and the ones you want to destroy."

"I want you to do it. There isn't time for me." Then he changed the subject. "Son," he said, "I want you to send Spencer [Campbell, his messenger] over to the White House with my retirement letter right now. Then deliver it to each of the judges in the building, including the retired ones."

I had dreaded this. The doctors had told me and Elizabeth [Black, his wife] not to let him send the letter because they still felt he might recover his strength. But he insisted, "They don't know what they're talking about. I'm finished, Son. I want that thing sent before it happens."

I took a different tack. "Daddy, you don't want to send that thing before I get those papers out of there and burn them. I might not be able to get the same cooperation I can while you have the full power of your office as senior judge."

He thought for a minute. "You're right, Son. We'll hold up until you get them burned. But get right on it."

Hugo Black, Jr., stalled, but eventually complied when he saw that his father's condition would not improve.

With no hope of recovery, Elizabeth Black handled the mechanics of announcing her husband's retirement:

> With a sense of destiny I got up out of bed and retrieved from the file the two letters of retirement Hugo had signed, identical except one was dated and one was not. I took the undated one, ran it into the typewriter, and put in "September 17, 1971." I then addressed a letter to "The President, The White House, Washington, D.C." and put a notation on the bottom, "Delivered by hand by Mr. Spencer Campbell." With a numb feeling I gave it to Hugo, Jr., who was leaving to pick up Jo [his daughter Josephine] at the airport, and they would go thence to the Court. We also called and talked to the Chief,

Former colleagues paid their final respects to Justice Potter Stewart at his funeral in 1985. Pictured form left to right are: Warren Burger, William J. Brennan, Jr., Byron R. White, Harry A. Blackmun, Lewis F. Powell, Jr., William H. Rehnquist, John Paul Stevens, and Sandra Day O'Connor. (Courtesy of the Supreme Court of the United States, Office of the Curator)

who said he would send Spencer to the White House in his limousine. I went to Bethesda and had a call from friends saying they had just heard it announced by the White House that Hugo had retired. I turned on the television and heard a little about it through Hugo's bathroom door as I fed him, as he did not want a television in here. . . . That night Hugo, Jr., related his and Jo's experience at the office. They had met with the C.J. [Warren Burger], Frances [Lamb, Black's secretary], and the clerks. The C.J. assured all the office they would have a job. Frances Lamb was crying. Spencer made all the brethren a copy of Hugo's letter of retirement and also the "Memorandum to my Brethren" memo I had typed. Later in the evening Marion and [Justice] Byron White came by. Marion and I fell weeping into each other's arms.

Black died eight days later. Harlan had quietly retired six days after Black, no doubt satisfied with the outpouring of accolades his esteemed colleague received in the press. Although it can legally operate with as few as six members, the Supreme Court decided to delay hearing arguments in crucial cases until the two seats were filled.

Acknowledgments

The Supreme Court Historical Society is indebted to the many individuals who assisted in the preparation of this book. We wish to thank editorial advisors Timothy Bradley, Ross E. Davies, Lyle Denniston, James B. O'Hara, Todd E. Peppers, Melvin I. Urofsky, and Natalie Wexler, who lent their expertise and provided considerable guidance in editing the manuscript. The Society is also indebted to Catherine Fitts and Steve Petteway of the Curator's Office, who provided access to the Supreme Court's rich illustrations collection. A lot of thought went into how to make the book's index useful to the reader by Paul Cushman, Jr., whose contribution is very much appreciated. Morgan Stoddard, Jennifer Dowling, Sarah Morris and, particularly, Kate Wilko, are also to be commended for their tireless efforts at checking all the facts and citations in this reference work.

The Society gratefully acknowledges all the individuals and institutions who granted us copyright permission to reprint from letters, interviews, memoirs, and other firsthand accounts. These include Hugo L. Black, Jr. for excerpts from his biography of his father and for his stepmother's diary; Edwin Moloy, Curator of Modern Manuscripts and Archives, Historical and Special Collections, Harvard Law School Library; Robert Ferguson, executor of the Learned Hand Papers; Jeffrey Varn Rombauer, grandson of Edgar R. Rombauer, Sr.; Artemus Ward; John N. Jacob, Archivist of the Lewis F. Powell Jr. Papers; Robert M. Goldberg, son of Dorothy Goldberg; J. Harvie Wilkinson III; Carole E. Handler, daughter of Milton Handler; Todd E. Peppers; Randall Bezanson; Bruce Allen Murphy; and Ruth Bader Ginsburg.

Library, copyright © 2003 The President and Fellows of Harvard College.

Reprinted by permission of the publisher from *The Autobiographical Notes of Charles Evans Hughes*, edited by David Danelski and Joseph S. Tulchin, pp. 161, 163, 164–165, 171, 227, Cambridge, MA: Harvard University Press, copyright ©1973 The President and Fellows of Harvard College.

From *Some Memories of a Long Life, 1854–1911* by Malvina Harlan, copyright © 2002. Used by permission of Modern Library, a division of Random House, Inc.

From *The Court Years 1939–1975: The Autobiography of William O. Douglas*, by William O. Douglas, copyright © 1980 by the Estate of William O. Douglas. Used by permission of Random House, Inc.

From *Mr. Justice and Mrs. Black: The Memoirs of Hugo L. Black and Elizabeth Black*, by Hugo L. Black and Elizabeth Black, edited by Paul R. Baier, copyright © 1986 by Elizabeth Black, Hugo Black, Jr., Sterling Black, Josephine Black Pesaresi. Used by permission of Random House, Inc.

From *My Father: A Remembrance*, by Hugo L. Black and Josephine Pesaresi, Sterling Foster Black, copyright © 1975 by Hugo Black, Jr., Sterling Foster Black, Josephine Black Pesaresi. Used by permission of Random House, Inc.

From *Law and Justice in the Reagan Administration: The Memoirs of an Attorney General*, by William French Smith with the permission of the publisher, Hoover Institution Press. Copyright © 1991, by the Board of Trustees of the Leland Stanford Junior University.

The Society's Publications Committee, chaired by James B. O'Hara, approved this project and shepherded it to completion. Its General Counsel, Robert E. Juceam of Fried, Frank, Harris, Shriver & Jacobson, generously gave his time to draft and finalize the copublishing agreement between the Society and Rowman & Littlefield.

The Supreme Court Historical Society gratefully acknowledges its members for their ongoing financial support in its endeavors to educate the public about the Court's history. Similarly, all the firms, individuals, corporations, and foundations who have contributed to the Society deserve our appreciation as well.

Finally, the Society wishes to thank Jon Sisk, Darcy Evans, and Janice Braunstein at Rowman & Littlefield for their dedication to this project.

Justices of the Supreme Court
of the United States

Name	State Appointed From	Appointed by President	To Replace	Date Nominated+	Date Senate Confirmed	Judicial Oath Taken	Date Service Terminated	Years of Service
Chief Justices								
John Jay	N.Y.	Washington	New seat	9/24/1789	9/26/1789	10/19/1789	6/29/1795	6
John Rutledge	S.C.	Washington	John Jay	7/1/1795+	12/15/1795 Rej.	8/12/1795	12/15/1795	1
Oliver Ellsworth	Conn.	Washington	Rutledge, J.	3/3/1796	3/4/1796	3/8/1796	12/15/1800	4
John Marshall	Va.	Adams, J.	Ellsworth	1/20/1801	1/27/1801	2/4/1801	7/6/1835	34
Roger B. Taney	Md.	Jackson	Marshall, J.	12/28/1835	3/15/1836	3/28/1836	10/12/1864	28
Salmon P. Chase	Ohio	Lincoln	Taney	12/6/1864	12/6/1864	12/15/1864	5/7/1873	8
Morrison R. Waite	Ohio	Grant	Chase, S. P.	1/19/1874	1/21/1874	3/4/1874	3/23/1888	14
Melville W. Fuller	Ill.	Cleveland	Waite	4/30/1888	7/20/1888	10/8/1888	7/4/1910	22
Edward Douglass White	La.	Taft	Fuller	12/12/1910	12/12/1910	12/19/1910	5/19/1921	10
William Howard Taft	Conn.	Harding	White, E.	6/21/1921	6/30/1921	7/11/1921	2/3/1930	8
Charles Evans Hughes	N.Y.	Hoover	Taft	2/3/1930	3/13/1930	2/24/1930	5/30/1941	11
Harlan Fiske Stone	N.Y.	Roosevelt, F.	Hughes	6/12/1941	6/27/1941	7/3/1941	4/22/1946	5
Fred M. Vinson	Ky.	Truman	Stone	6/6/1946	6/20/1946	6/24/1946	9/8/1953	7
Earl Warren	Calif.	Eisenhower	Vinson	9/30/1953+	3/1/1954	10/5/1953	6/23/1969	15
Warren E. Burger	Va.	Nixon	Warren	5/21/1969	6/9/1969	6/23/1969	9/26/1986	17
William H. Rehnquist	Va.	Reagan	Burger	6/20/1986	9/17/1986	9/26/1986	10/3/2005	19
John G. Roberts, Jr.	Md.	Bush, G. W.	Rehnquist	10/6/2005	10/29/2005	10/29/2005		

Name	State Appointed From	Appointed by President	To Replace	Date Nominated+	Date Senate Confirmed	Judicial Oath Taken	Date Service Terminated	Years of Service
John Catron	Tenn.	Van Buren	New seat	3/3/1837	3/8/1837	5/1/1837	5/30/1865	28
John McKinley	Ala.	Van Buren	New seat	9/18/1837	9/25/1837	1/9/1838	7/19/1852	15
Peter V. Daniel	Va.	Van Buren	Barbour	2/27/1841	3/2/1841	1/10/1842	5/31/1860	19
Samuel Nelson	N.Y.	Tyler	Thompson	2/4/1845	2/14/1845	2/27/1845	11/28/1872	27
Levi Woodbury	N.H.	Polk	Story	12/23/1845+	1/3/1846	9/23/1845	9/4/1851	5
Robert C. Grier	Pa.	Polk	Baldwin	8/3/1846	8/4/1846	8/10/1846	1/31/1870	23
Benjamin R. Curtis	Mass.	Fillmore	Woodbury	12/11/1851	12/20/1851	10/10/1851	9/30/1857	5
John Campbell	Ala.	Pierce	McKinley	3/21/1853	3/25/1853	4/11/1853	4/30/1861	8
Nathan Clifford	Maine	Buchanan	Curtis	12/9/1857	1/12/1858	1/21/1858	7/25/1881	23
Noah H. Swayne	Ohio	Lincoln	McLean	1/21/1862	1/24/1862	1/27/1862	1/24/1881	19
Samuel F. Miller	Iowa	Lincoln	Daniel	7/16/1862	7/16/1862	7/21/1862	10/13/1890	28
David Davis	Ill.	Lincoln	Campbell	12/1/1862	12/8/1862	12/10/1862	3/4/1877	14
Stephen Field	Calif.	Lincoln	New seat	3/6/1863	3/10/1863	5/20/1863	12/1/1897	34
William Strong	Pa.	Grant	Grier	2/7/1870	2/18/1870	3/14/1870	12/14/1880	10
Joseph P. Bradley	N.J.	Grant	New seat	2/7/1870	3/21/1870	3/23/1870	1/22/1892	21
Ward Hunt	N.Y.	Grant	Nelson	12/3/1872	12/11/1872	1/9/1873	1/27/1882	9
John Marshall Harlan	Ky.	Hayes	Davis	10/16/1877	11/29/1877	12/10/1877	10/14/1911	34
William B. Woods	Ga.	Hayes	Strong	12/15/1880	12/21/1880	1/5/1881	5/14/1887	6
Stanley Matthews	Ohio	Garfield	Swayne	3/14/1881	5/12/1881	5/17/1881	3/22/1889	7
Horace Gray	Mass.	Arthur	Clifford	12/19/1881	12/20/1881	1/9/1882	9/15/1902	20

Samuel Blatchford	N.Y.	Arthur	Hunt	3/13/1882	3/27/1882	4/3/1882	7/7/1893	11
Lucius Q. C. Lamar	Miss.	Cleveland	Woods	12/6/1887	1/16/1888	1/18/1888	1/23/1893	5
David J. Brewer	Kan.	Harrison, B.	Matthews	12/4/1889	12/18/1889	1/6/1890	3/28/1910	20
Henry B. Brown	Mich.	Harrison, B.	Miller	12/23/1890	12/29/1890	1/5/1891	5/28/1906	15
George Shiras, Jr.	Pa.	Harrison, B.	Bradley	7/19/1892	7/26/1892	10/10/1892	2/23/1903	10
Howell E. Jackson	Tenn.	Harrison, B.	Lamar, L.	2/2/1893	2/18/1893	3/4/1893	8/8/1895	2
Edward White	La.	Cleveland	Blatchford	2/19/1894	2/19/1894	3/12/1894	12/18/1910*	17
Rufus Peckham	N.Y.	Cleveland	Jackson, H.	12/3/1895	12/8/1895	1/6/1896	10/24/1909	13
Joseph McKenna	Calif.	McKinley	Field	12/16/1897	1/21/1898	1/26/1898	1/5/1925	26
Oliver Wendell Holmes, Jr.	Mass.	Roosevelt, T.	Gray	12/2/1902	12/4/1902	12/8/1902	1/12/1932	29
William R. Day	Ohio	Roosevelt, T.	Shiras	1/29/1903	2/23/1903	3/2/1903	11/13/1922	19
William H. Moody	Mass.	Roosevelt, T.	Brown	12/3/1906	12/12/1906	12/17/1906	11/20/1910	3
Horace H. Lurton	Tenn.	Taft	Peckham	12/13/1909	12/20/1909	1/3/1910	7/12/1914	4
Charles Evans Hughes	N.Y.	Taft	Brewer	4/25/1910	5/2/1910	10/10/1910	6/10/1916	6
Willis Van Devanter	Wyo.	Taft	White, E.	12/12/1910	12/15/1910	1/3/1911	6/21/1937	26
Joseph R. Lamar	Ga.	Taft	Moody	12/12/1910	12/15/1910	1/3/1911	1/2/1916	5
Mahlon Pitney	N.J.	Taft	Harlan (I)	2/19/1912	3/13/1912	3/18/1912	12/31/1922	10
James C. McReynolds	Tenn.	Wilson	Lurton	8/19/1914	8/29/1914	10/12/1914	1/31/1941	26
Louis D. Brandeis	Mass.	Wilson	Lamar, J.	1/28/1916	6/1/1916	6/5/1916	2/13/1939	22
John H. Clarke	Ohio	Wilson	Hughes	7/14/1916	7/24/1916	10/9/1916	9/18/1922	6
George Sutherland	Utah	Harding	Clarke	9/5/1922	9/5/1922	10/2/1922	1/17/1938	15
Pierce Butler	Minn.	Harding	Day	11/23/1922	12/21/1922	1/2/1923	11/16/1939	17
Edward T. Sanford	Tenn.	Harding	Pitney	1/24/1923	1/29/1923	2/19/1923	3/8/1930	7

Name	State Appointed From	Appointed by President	To Replace	Date Nominated+	Date Senate Confirmed	Judicial Oath Taken	Date Service Terminated	Years of Service
Harlan Fiske Stone	N.Y.	Coolidge	McKenna	1/5/1925	2/5/1925	3/2/1925	7/2/1941*	16
Owen J. Roberts	Pa.	Hoover	Sanford	5/9/1930	5/20/1930	6/2/1930	7/31/1945	15
Benjamin N. Cardozo	N.Y.	Hoover	Holmes	2/15/1932	2/24/1932	3/14/1932	7/9/1938	6
Hugo L. Black	Ala.	Roosevelt, F.	Van Devanter	8/12/1937	8/17/1937	8/19/1937	9/17/1971	34
Stanley Reed	Ky.	Roosevelt, F.	Sutherland	1/15/1938	1/25/1938	1/31/1938	2/25/1957	19
Felix Frankfurter	Mass.	Roosevelt, F.	Cardozo	1/5/1939	1/17/1939	1/30/1939	8/28/1962	23
William O. Douglas	Conn.	Roosevelt, F.	Brandeis	3/20/1939	4/4/1939	4/17/1939	11/12/1975	36
Frank Murphy	Mich.	Roosevelt, F.	Butler	1/4/1940	1/16/1940	2/5/1940	7/19/1949	9
James F. Byrnes	S.C.	Roosevelt, F.	McReynolds	6/12/1941	6/12/1941	7/8/1941	10/3/1942	1
Robert H. Jackson	N.Y.	Roosevelt, F.	Stone	6/12/1941	7/7/1941	7/11/1941	10/9/1954	13
Wiley B. Rutledge	Iowa	Roosevelt, F.	Byrnes	1/11/1943	2/8/1943	2/15/1943	9/10/1949	6
Harold H. Burton	Ohio	Truman	Roberts	9/19/1945	9/19/1945	10/1/1945	10/13/1958	13
Tom C. Clark	Texas	Truman	Murphy	8/2/1949	8/18/1949	8/24/1949	6/12/1967	18
Sherman Minton	Ind.	Truman	Rutledge, W.	9/15/1949	10/4/1949	10/12/1949	10/15/1956	7
John Marshall Harlan	N.Y.	Eisenhower	Jackson, R.	1/10/1955	3/16/1955	3/28/1955	9/23/1971	16
William J. Brennan, Jr.	N.J.	Eisenhower	Minton	10/15/1956+	3/19/1957	10/16/1956	7/20/1990	34
Charles E. Whittaker	Mo.	Eisenhower	Reed	3/2/1957	3/19/1957	3/25/1957	3/31/1962	5
Potter Stewart	Ohio	Eisenhower	Burton	10/14/1958+	5/5/1959	10/14/1958	7/3/1981	22
Byron R. White	Colo.	Kennedy	Whittaker	3/30/1962	4/11/1962	4/16/1962	3/19/1993	30
Arthur J. Goldberg	Ill.	Kennedy	Frankfurter	8/29/1962	9/25/1962	10/1/1962	7/25/1965	3

Abe Fortas	Tenn.	Johnson, L.	Goldberg	7/28/1965	8/11/1965	10/4/1965	5/14/1969	4
Thurgood Marshall	N.Y.	Johnson, L.	Clark	6/13/1967	8/30/1967	10/2/1967	6/27/1991	24
Harry A. Blackmun	Minn.	Nixon	Fortas	4/14/1970	5/12/1970	6/9/1970	7/29/1994	24
Lewis F. Powell, Jr.	Va.	Nixon	Black	10/22/1971	12/6/1971	1/6/1972	6/26/1987	16
William H. Rehnquist	Ariz.	Nixon	Harlan (II)	10/21/1971	12/10/1971	1/7/1972	9/26/1986*	14
John Paul Stevens	Ill.	Ford	Douglas	11/28/1975	12/17/1975	12/19/1975	6/29/2010	35
Sandra Day O'Connor	Ariz.	Reagan	Stewart	8/19/1981	9/21/1981	9/26/1981	1/31/2006	25
Antonin Scalia	Va.	Reagan	Rehnquist	6/17/1986	9/17/1986	9/26/1986		
Anthony M. Kennedy	Calif.	Reagan	Powell	11/30/1987	2/3/1988	2/18/1988		
David H. Souter	N.H.	Bush, G. H. W.	Brennan	7/23/1990	10/2/1990	10/9/1990	6/29/2009	19
Clarence Thomas	Va.	Bush, G. H. W.	Marshall, T.	7/1/1991	10/15/1991	10/23/1991		
Ruth Bader Ginsburg	N.Y.	Clinton	White, B.	6/14/1993	8/3/1993	8/10/1993		
Stephen G. Breyer	Mass.	Clinton	Blackmun	5/13/1994	7/29/1994	8/3/1994		
Samuel Alito	N.J.	Bush, G. W.	O'Connor	11/10/2005	1/31/2006	1/31/2006		
Sonia Sotomayor	N.Y.	Obama	Souter	6/21/2009	8/6/2009	8/8/2009		
Elena Kagan	Mass.	Obama	Stevens	5/10/2010	8/5/2010	8/7/2010		

Source: Supreme Court Historical Society

Note: The length of service is calculated from the day of Senate confirmation and is rounded up. The length of service for Associate Justices who also served as Chief Justices is listed separately in the two sections. To calculate the total length of the member's tenure on the Court, combine the two sums.

+ = Recess Appointment

* = Promoted

Notes

INTRODUCTION

xi *Daniel Webster is speaking. . . . There is a tremendous squeeze. New York Herald,* February 10, 1844, quoted in Charles Warren, *The Supreme Court in United States History,* 2 vols. (Boston: Little Brown, 1926), 2:128–129.

xi *each particular whalebone in their wigs would stand on end. New York Herald,* February 6, 1844, quoted in Warren, *The Supreme Court* 2:128–129.

xii *The way the light system works.* Maureen Mahoney, interview by Mark Farkas, reprinted in Brian Lamb, Susan Swain, and Mark Farkas, eds., *The Supreme Court: A C-Span Book Featuring the Justices in Their Own Words* (New York: Public Affairs, 2010), 291.

xiii *in silence for hours, without being stopped or interrupted.* 1824 newspaper account quoted in G. Edward White, *The Marshall Court and Cultural Change 1815–1835,* Oliver Wendell Homes Devise 3–4 (New York: Macmillan, 1988), 182 n. 106.

xiii *cost him several months of absorbing labor.* Malvina Harlan, *Some Memories of a Long Life, 1854–1911* (New York: Modern Library, 2002), 112.

CHAPTER 1: SINK OR SWIM

1 *on Sunday before Day light.* Letter from Samuel Chase to Hannah Chase, February 4, 1800, Dreer Collection, Historical Society of Pennsylvania, reprinted in Maeva Marcus, ed., *The Documentary History of the Supreme Court of the United States, 1789–1800,* 8 vols. (New York: Columbia University Press, 1980–2009), vol. 1, pt. 2, 888–889.

1 *in preference to existing in an [element] become putrid. Baltimore American,* July 1, 1800, reprinted in Marcus, *Documentary History,* 3:439.

2 *For Heaven's sake.* Benjamin Harrison, *The Constitution and Administration of the United States of America* (London: David Nutt, 1897), 320.

2 *As I shall be absent from the next [Supreme] Court.* Letter from John Jay to George Washington, January 27, 1792, George Washington Papers, Library of Congress, reprinted in Marcus, *Documentary History*, vol. 1, pt. 2, 730.

5 *What with the non-acceptance of some.* The *Writings of George Washington*, ed. John C. Fitzpatrick, 39 vols. (Washington, DC: U.S. Government Printing Office, 1931–1944), 34:349.

5 *no Objection to take the place which [Jay] holds.* Letter from John Rutledge to George Washington, June 12, 1795, reprinted in Marcus, *Documentary History*, vol. 1, pt. 1, 94.

5 *daily sinking into debility of mind.* Letter from William Bradford, Jr. to Alexander Hamilton, August 4, 1795, reprinted in Marcus, *Documentary History*, vol. 1, pt. 2, 775.

5 *attachment to his bottle.* Letter from Edmund Randolph to George Washington, August 5, 1795, reprinted in Marcus, *Documentary History*, vol. 1, pt. 2, 776.

5 *he had long been a Judge & he knew no Law.* Letter from William Read to Jacob Read, December 29, 1975, quoted in Marcus, *Documentary History*, vol. 1, pt. 2, 820.

6 *[T]he chair [a kind of carriage] struck against a tree.* Letter from James Iredell to Hannah Iredell, April 26, 1792, reprinted in Marcus, *Documentary History*, 2:272.

6 *It has been this time very much crouded indeed.* Letter from James Iredell to Hannah Iredell, October 2, 1791, reprinted in Marcus, *Documentary History*, 2:212.

6 *I receive great civilities and distinction here.* Letter from James Iredell to Hannah Iredell, November 27, 1795, reprinted in Marcus, *Documentary History*, 3:82.

7 *I long for an Answer.* Letter from James Wilson to Hannah Gray, June 20, 1793, reprinted in Marcus, *Documentary History*, 2:408.

7 *The most extraordinary intelligence, which I have to convey.* Letter from John Quincy Adams to Thomas Boylston Adams, June 23, 1793, reprinted in Marcus, *Documentary History*, 2:408–410.

8 *Mr Iredell has by this, told you what will surprise you.* Letter from Hannah Wilson to Bird Wilson, July 28, 1798, Marcus, *Documentary History*, 3:281–282.

8 *I never should have forgiven myself if I had left him.* Letter from Hannah Wilson to Bird Wilson, September 1, 1798, reprinted in Marcus, *Documentary History*, 3:289.

9 *It was expected that the Senate would yesterday.* Letter from John Jay to Sarah Jay, April 19, 1794, reprinted in *The Life of John Jay with Selections from His Correspondence and Miscellaneous Papers*, ed. William Jay, 2 vols. (New York: J & J Harper, 1833), 1:311–312.

9 *The Supreme commenced their session on monday.* Letter from Jeremiah Smith to William Plumer, February 7, 1795, Plumer Papers, New Hampshire State Library, reprinted in Marcus, *Documentary History*, vol. 1, pt. 2, 752.

10 *the Stiffness of Connecticut.* Letter from John Adams to Abigail Adams, March 5, 1796, reprinted in Marcus, *Documentary History*, vol. 1, pt. 2, 842.

10   *[T]he Efforts repeatedly made to place the judicial Department.* Letter from John Jay to John Adams, January 2, 1801, reprinted in Marcus, *Documentary History*, vol. 1, pt. 1, 147.

10   *When I waited on the President with Mr. Jays letter.* Letter from John Marshall to Joseph Story (undated) 1827, reprinted in Marcus, *Documentary History*, vol. 1, pt. 2, 928.

CHAPTER 2: JOHN MARSHALL TAKES CHARGE

11   *[John] Marshall is of a tall, slender figure.* Letter from Joseph P. Story to Samuel P. P. Fay, February 25, 1808, reprinted in William W. Story, *Life and Letters of Joseph Story*, 2 vols. (Boston: Little & Brown, 1851), 1:166–167.

13   *gotten from some antiquated slop-shop.* George Van Santvoord, *Lives and Judicial Services of the Chief Justices of the Supreme Court of the United States* (New York: Charles Scribner, 1854), 363n, quoted in Albert Beveridge, *The Life of John Marshall*, 4 vols. (Boston: Houghton Mifflin, 1916–1919), 4:91.

13   *[T]he Chief Justice of the United States, the first lawyer.* Letter from George Ticknor to his father, February 1, 1815, reprinted in *Life, Letters, and Journals of George Ticknor*, 2 vols. (Boston: James R. Osgood & Co., 1876), 1:33.

13   *Meet him on a stagecoach.* From the eulogy delivered by Joseph Story to the Suffolk, Massachusetts bar, reprinted in Jean Edward Smith, *John Marshall: Definer of a Nation* (New York: Henry Holt & Co., 1996), 4.

15   *I watched for the coming of the old chief.* Margaret E. White, ed., *A Sketch of Chester Harding, Artist, Drawn by His Own Hand* (Boston: Houghton, Mifflin and Co., 1890), 196.

15   *When, however, the time came for him to open court.* Gustavus Schmidt, *Louisiana Law Journal* 1, no. 1 (1841): 85–86, quoted in Albert Beveridge, *Life of John Marshall*, 4:82.

15   *Marshall broke with English tradition.* The Justices of the Ellsworth Court wore black robes for a time as well.

16   *There are few families that make Washington their permanent residence.* Thomas Hamilton, *Of Men and Manners in America*, 2 vols. (New York: Augustus M. Kelly, 1968; Edinburgh: W. Blackwood, 1833), 2:37. Citations are to the Augustus M. Kelly edition.

16   *It is certainly true, that Judges here live with perfect harmony.* Letter from Joseph Story to Sarah Story, March 5, 1812, reprinted in Story, *Life and Letters of Joseph Story*, 1:217.

16   *I find myself considerably more at ease.* Letter from Joseph Story to S. P. P. Fay, February 24, 1812, reprinted in Story, *Life and Letters of Joseph Story*, 1:215–216.

17   *[W]e judges take no part in the society of the place.* Josiah Quincy, *Figures of the Past, From the Leaves of Old Journals* (Boston: Roberts Brothers, 1896), 189–190.

17   *Why, Mr. Reporter, the story is not only true.* Charles Henry Butler, *A Century at the Bar of the Supreme Court of the United States* (New York: G. P. Putnam's Sons, 1942), 90.

17 *I dined with them.* Letter from Charles Sumner to Simon Greenleaf, March 8, 1834, reprinted in Edward L. Pierce, ed., *Memoirs and Letters of Charles Sumner*, 2 vols. (Boston: Roberts Brothers, 1877), 1:137.

18 *Two of the judges are widowers.* Letter from Joseph Story to Sarah Story, March 12, 1812, reprinted in Story, *Life and Letters of Joseph Story*, 1:219.

18 *meanly furnished and very inconvenient.* Letter from Benjamin Latrobe to James Madison, September 8, 1809, reprinted in John C. Van Horne, Lee W. Formwalt, Derwin H. Stapleton, and Jeffrey A. Cohen, eds., *The Correspondence and Miscellaneous Papers of Benjamin Henry Latrobe*, 3 vols. (New Haven, CT: Yale University Press for the Maryland Historical Society, 1984–1988), 2:765.

18 *a most uncomfortable feeling. New York Daily Tribune*, March 26, 1859, quoted in Carl B. Swisher, *History of the Supreme Court, The Taney Period 1836–64*, Oliver Wendell Holmes Devise 5 (New York: Macmillan, 1974), 11.

18 *My boyish attention was fastened upon the seven judges.* Butler, *Century at the Bar of the Supreme Court*, 29–30.

20 *Long afterward when I went to Washington.* Butler, *Century at the Bar*, 30.

20 *It is by no means a large or handsome apartment.* Hamilton, *Of Men and Manners*, 127.

20 *The apartment is not in a style which comports with the dignity of that body. New York Statesman*, February 7, 24, 1824, quoted in Charles Warren, *The Supreme Court in United States History*, 2 vols. (Boston: Little, Brown, 1926), 1:460–461.

21 *The apartment is well finished.* Warren, *The Supreme Court*, 1:461. Presumably the reporter meant that some members of *Congress* "were sworn in" as members of the Supreme Court bar. The first woman to join the Supreme Court bar was Washington-based attorney Belva Lockwood, who succeeded in being permitted to practice before the Supreme Court in 1879 only after exhaustive lobbying.

21 *I did not fail to be at the courthouse the next morning.* Letter from H. M. Brackenridge to Walter Forward, September 29, 1817, reprinted in H. M. Brackenridge, *Recollections of Persons and Places in the West*, 2nd ed. (Philadelphia: J. B. Lippincott & Co., 1868), 283.

21 *The words and sentences seemed to flow.* Brackenridge, *Recollections*, 284.

22 *The effect of the female admiration and attention has been very obvious.* Letter from Mrs. Samuel Harrison Smith to Mrs. Kirkpatrick, March 13, 1814, quoted in Gaillard Hunt, ed., *The First Forty Years of Washington Society in the Family Letters of Margaret Bayard Smith* (New York: Frederick Ungar Publishing, 1906), 96.

22 *Although the Justices did sometimes ask questions of counsel.* See, for example, 3 U.S. 79, 84, 91, 94, 119, 124, 125 (1805) for examples of Chief Justice Marshall and the Associate Justices addressing counsel during oral argument. Thanks to Ross E. Davies for pointing out this evidence that the Justices did not always listen in silence as elsewhere reported.

22 *[Associate Justice Bushrod Washington was] a small, insignificant looking man deprived of the sight of one eye by excessive study.* Ben Perley Poore, *Reminiscences of Sixty Years in the National Metropolis* (New York: W. A. Houghton, 1886), quoted in Warren, *Supreme Court in United States History*, 2:470 n. 1.

23 *He pooh-poohed, as much to say it was not worthwhile to argue.* Peter Harvey, *Reminiscences and Anecdotes of Daniel Webster* (Boston: Little, Brown and Co., 1877), 121.

23 *Mr. Pinkney seemed to be waiting.* Harvey, *Reminiscences and Anecdotes*, 122–123.

24 *I can see the chief justice as he looked.* Harvey, *Reminiscences and Anecdotes*, 142.

24 *I was afraid I had said some foolish things in that debate.* Letter from John Marshall to Joseph Story, late 1844 or early 1845, recounted in a letter from Joseph Story to Alexander H. Stephens, quoted in Richard M. Johnson and William H. Browne, *Life of Alexander H. Stephens* (Philadelphia: J. B. Lippincott & Co., 1878). See G. Edward White, *The Marshall Court and Cultural Change 1815–1835*, Oliver Wendell Holmes Devise 3–4 (New York: Macmillan, 1988), 239.

25 *The Court sits from eleven o'clock in the morning.* 1824 newspaper account quoted in G. Edward White, *The Marshall Court*, 182 n. 106.

25 *Before this audience was the bench of reverend judges.* Charles Ingersoll, *Inchiquin: The Jesuit Letter* (New York: I. Riley, 1810), 55.

25 *from 98 cases in 1810 to 253 in 1850—forcing it to increase the amount of time allotted to oral arguments.* For information on the increasing workload and lengthening of the Supreme Court Term, see Gerhard Casper and Richard Posner, *The Workload of the Supreme Court* (Chicago: American Bar Foundation, 1976), 12–13.

26 *You heard him pronounce the opinion of the Court in a low, but modulated voice.* William W. Story, ed., *The Miscellaneous Writings of Joseph Story, Associate Justice of the Supreme Court of the United States and Dane Professor of Law at Harvard University* (Boston: Little, and J. Brown, 1852), 692.

26 *When I was on our State bench I was accustomed to delivering seriatim.* Letter from William Johnson to Thomas Jefferson, December 10, 1822, Jefferson Papers, Manuscript Division, Library of Congress.

26 *[H]e excelled in the statement of a case.* Joseph Story, LL.D., *A Discourse Upon the Life, Character, And Services of the Honorable John Marshall, LL.D., Chief Justice of the United States of America* (Boston: James Munroe and Co., 1835), 69.

27 *An opinion is huddled up in conclave.* Letter from Thomas Jefferson to Thomas Ritchie, December 25, 1820, Jefferson Papers, Manuscript Division, Library of Congress.

27 *I must comfort myself with the hope that the judges will see.* Letter from William Johnson to Thomas Jefferson, March 4, 1823, Jefferson Papers.

28 *[After my appointment] some case soon occurred in which I differed from my brethren.* Letter from William Johnson to Thomas Jefferson, December 10, 1822, Jefferson Papers.

28 *[While Mrs. Story] may be tempted by gracing our table.* Letter from John Marshall to Joseph Story, December 30, 1827, reprinted in John Stokes Adams, ed., *An Autobiographical Sketch by John Marshall* (Ann Arbor: The University of Michigan Press, 1937), 42–43.

29 *I think this is a matter of some importance.* Letter from John Marshall to Joseph Story, May 3, 1831, reprinted in Charles Hobson, ed., *The Papers of John Marshall*, 12 vols. (Chapel Hill, NC: University of North Carolina Press, 1974–2006), 12:63.

29 *At some moments this court presents a singular spectacle.* Harriet Martineau, *Retrospect of Western Travel*, 2 vols. (New York: Harper & Bros., 1838), 1:165.

29 *I miss the Chief Justice at every turn.* Letter from Joseph Story to Harriet Martineau, February 8, 1836, reprinted in Story, *Life and Letters of Joseph Story*, 2:226.

CHAPTER 3: JUSTICE BY SHAY, STAGECOACH, STEAMBOAT, TRAIN

31 *I have been elbowed by old women—jammed by young ones.* Letter from Levi Woodbury to his wife, Elizabeth Woodbury, undated, Levi Woodbury family papers, 1638–1914, Manuscript Division, Library of Congress.

32 *As you are about to commence your first Circuit.* Letter from George Washington to the Justices of the Supreme Court, April 3, 1790, reprinted in Maeva Marcus, ed., *The Documentary History of the Supreme Court of the United States, 1789–1800,* 8 vols. (New York: Columbia University Press, 1980–2009), 2:21.

33 *I have been advised to come from Savannah to Charles Town, by Water.* Letter from Samuel Chase to James Iredell, March 12, 1797, reprinted in Marcus, *Documentary History,* 3:154–155.

33 *I have been unwell, for the last Eight Week, five of which I have been confined to my Bed-Chamber.* Letter from Samuel Chase to William Paterson, March 17, 1799, reprinted in Marcus, *Documentary History,* 3:324–325.

34 *I . . . am happy in having an opportunity of obliging you.* Letter from William Paterson to William Cushing, August 9, 1794, reprinted in Marcus, *Documentary History,* 2:479.

34 *three Judges out of five (without consulting the sixth, [Justice John] Rutledge, who was on the spot.* Letter from James Iredell to Thomas Johnson, March 15, 1792, reprinted in Marcus, *Documentary History,* 2:246.

35 *an adequate Remedy can in my opinion.* Letter from John Jay to James Iredell, February 12, 1791, reprinted in Marcus, *Documentary History,* 2:135.

35 *a change in the system is contemplated.* Letter from George Washington to Robert H. Harrison, November 25, 1789, reprinted in Marcus, *Documentary History,* 2:10.

35 *it is expected some alterations in the judicial system will be brought forward.* Letter from George Washington to Thomas Johnson, August 7, 1791, reprinted in Marcus, *Documentary History,* vol. 1, pt. 1, 76.

35 *I have measured Things however and find the Office and the Man do not fit.* Letter from Thomas Johnson to George Washington, January 16, 1793, reprinted in Marcus, *Documentary History,* 2:344.

36 *We really, Sir, find the burdens laid upon us so excessive.* Letter from Justices of the Supreme Court to George Washington, August 9, 1972, reprinted in Marcus, *Documentary History,* 2:288.

36 *That the task of holding twenty seven circuit Courts a year, in the different States.* reprinted in Marcus, *Documentary History,* 2:289–90.

37 *In the most favourable view of the Subject it appeared, that the duties required.* Letter from Robert H. Harrison to George Washington, October 27, 1789, reprinted in Marcus, *Documentary History,* vol. 1, pt. 1, 36.

38 *They must, however, have the benefit of travel.* Tristram Burges (Rhode Island), *Congressional Debates,* 19th Cong., 1st sess., 1826, 1089–1090.

38 *We shall have these gentlemen as judges of the Supreme Court of appeals.* George Badger (North Carolina), *Congressional Globe,* 30th Cong., 1st sess., 1848, 596.

38 *completely cloistered within the City of Washington.* William Smith (South Carolina), *Annals of Congress,* 15th Cong., 2nd sess., 1819, 126.

39 *might also fall victim.* Abner Lacock (Pennsylvania), *Annals of Congress,* 15th Cong., 2nd sess., 1819, 134.

39 *Sir, I have not myself been sensible of any peculiarly corrupting influence in the air of Washington.* John M. Berrien (Georgia), *Congressional Debates,* 19th Cong., 1st sess., 1826, 534.

39 *I am here two thousand miles from home.* Letter from Peter V. Daniel to Martin Van Buren, April 8, 1843, quoted in John P. Frank, *Marble Palace: The Supreme Court in American Life* (New York: Knopf, 1958), 150.

40 *The discomfort of being about in immediate contact.* Letter from Peter V. Daniel to Elizabeth Randolph Daniel, April 8, 1851, University of Virginia Library, quoted in Frank, *Marble Palace,* 150.

40 *I have been painfully conscious of the delay of justice.* Letter from Salmon P. Chase to Samuel Miller, June 27, 1866, Papers of Salmon P. Chase, Manuscript Division, Library of Congress.

41 *My situation was somewhat like that of the parish committee.* Ebenezer Rockwood Hoar, quoted in Moorefield Storey and Edward W. Emerson, *Ebenezer Rockwood Hoar, A Memoir* (New York: Houghton Mifflin, 1911), 181.

41 *The District Judges at all points are in bad odour for common honesty.* Letter from John A. Campbell to Philip Phillips, June 4, 1870. Phillips Papers, Manuscript Division, Library of Congress.

41 *I find myself more affected by the hot weather.* Letter from Samuel F. Miller to William Pitt Ballinger, June 10, 1880, Samuel Freeman Miller Correspondence, Manuscript Division, Library of Congress.

42 *going up to be stamped all over.* Quoted in Charles Fairman, *Mr. Justice Miller and the Supreme Court 1862–1890* (Cambridge, MA: Harvard University Press, 1939), 416.

42 *When I came to the Court, I desired a Western Circuit.* Letter from Morrison R. Waite to Judge Thomas Drummond, April 20, 1878. Waite would have sat with him on the Seventh Circuit if he had switched circuits. Quoted in Bruce R. Trimble, *Chief Justice Waite: Defender of the Public Interest* (Princeton: Princeton University Press, 1938), 267.

43 *The Court tried to prepare far in advance as possible for these execution-night ordeals.* Edward Lazarus, *Closed Chambers: The First Eyewitness Account of the Epic Struggles Inside the Supreme Court* (New York: Times Books, 1998), 120.

44 *Unlike Chicago, however, where the judicial conference was open to about a thousand lawyers.* Dorothy Goldberg, *A Private View of a Public Life* (New York: Charterhouse, 1975), 158.

45 *Since I remain a federal judge and will likely sit on Courts of Appeals from time to time.* Retirement letter from Byron R. White to the Supreme Court Justices, June 28, 1993, reprinted in *United States Reports* 509 (October Term 1992): xii.

CHAPTER 4: WIVES, CHILDREN . . . HUSBANDS

47 *We had invited Carol and Abe Fortas for dinner in answer to an SOS.* Elizabeth Black, diary entry, March 1, 1965, reprinted in Hugo L. Black and Elizabeth

Black, *Mr. Justice and Mrs. Black: The Memoirs of Hugo L. Black and Elizabeth Black* (New York: Random House, 1986), 120–121.

48 *life had been ruined.* In a phone conversation between Lyndon B. Johnson and Mike Mansfield, July 30, 1965, President Johnson mentions that Agger used this phrase. Citation #8415, WH6507.09. LBJ Library, at http://whitehousetapes.net/exhibit/lbjs-nomination-abe-fortas-supreme-court-july-1965. Apparently, Fortas even asked the White House to delay his Senate nomination hearings to give him time to persuade his wife to support his nomination.

48 *almost as helpless as a Child.* Letter from Hannah Iredell to James Iredell, October 21, 1790, reprinted in Natalie Wexler, *A More Obedient Wife: A Novel of the Supreme Court* (Washington, DC: Kalorama Press, 2006), 53.

48 *I have made no visits.* Letter from Hannah Iredell to James Iredell, November 7, 1790, reprinted in Maeva Marcus, ed., *The Documentary History of the Supreme Court of the United States, 1789–1800*, 8 vols. (New York: Columbia University Press, 1980–2009), 2:105.

49 *I am perfectly well, but extremely mortified to find that the Senate have broken up.* Letter from James Iredell to Hannah Iredell, July 2, 1795, reprinted in Marcus, *Documentary History*, 3:66.

49 *traveling machines [with] no abiding place.* Quoted in *Old Scituate* (Boston: Chief Justice Cushing Chapter, Daughters of the American Revolution, 1921), 37.

49 *We have been roving.* Letter from Hannah Cushing to Abigail Adams, October 8, 1798, reprinted in Marcus, *Documentary History*, 3:296.

50 *We make out very well.* Letter from Sarah Jay to John Jay, May 15, 1790, reprinted in Henry P. Johnston, ed., *The Correspondence and Public Papers of John Jay*, 4 vols. (New York: Burt Franklin, reprinted, 1970), 3:399.

50 *Oh! my dear Mr. Jay should you too be unwell.* Letter from Sarah Jay to John Jay, November 13, 1791. Reprinted in *Selected Letters of John Jay and Sarah Livingston Jay: Correspondence by or to the First Chief Justice of the United States and His Wife*, eds. Landa M. Freeman, Louise V. North, and Janet M. Wedge (Jefferson, NC: McFarland Co., Inc., 2005), 201.

50 *Her judgment was so sound & safe that I have often.* John Marshall's Eulogy of Polly Marshall, December 25, 1832, by John Marshall, reprinted in John Edward Oster, ed., *The Political and Economic Doctrines of John Marshall* (New York: The Neale Publishing Co., 1914), 203.

50 *On going into the Chief Justice's room this morning.* Letter from Joseph Story to Sarah Story, March 4, 1832, reprinted in William W. Story, *Life and Letters of Joseph Story*, 2 vols. (Boston: Little & Brown, 1851), 2:86–87.

51 *Mrs. Miller, a matronly lady.* Randolph Keim, *Society in Washington: Its Noted Men, Accomplished Women, Established Customs and Notable Events* (Washington, DC: Harrisburg (Pa.) Publishing, 1887), 122–124.

51 *Mrs. Justice Miller . . . assisted by her grand-daughter . . . gives elegant dinners.* Mrs. E. N. Chapin, *American Court Gossip; or, Life at the National Capitol* (Marshalltown, Iowa: Chapin & Harwell, 1887), 249.

51 *I am afraid his wife will hurt him.* William Pitt Ballinger, diary entry, October 14, 1871, Briscoe Center for American History, University of Texas at Austin, Box 2Q425.

52   *His dissent (which many lawyers consider to have been one of his greatest opinions).* Malvina Harlan, *Some Memories of a Long Life, 1854–1911* (New York: Modern Library, 2002), 112–113. Malvina says her husband worked "several months" on the opinion, but it was argued in April and decided in May. She also remarks that he was the "youngest man on the Bench," when David J. Brewer, Henry B. Brown, and Edward Douglass White were younger. Thanks to Ross E. Davies for pointing out these inaccuracies.

53   *The memory of the historic part that Taney's inkstand had played in the Dred Scott decision.* Harlan, *Some Memories of a Long Life*, 113–114.

53   *wives cut an important figure.* Charles A. Kent, ed., *Memoir of Henry Billings Brown, Late Justice of the Supreme Court of the United States* (New York: Deerfield & Co., 1915), 96.

53   *It was customary in that era in Washington for visitors.* Milton Handler and Michael Ruby, "Justice Cardozo: One Ninth of the Supreme Court," *Yearbook of the Supreme Court Historical Society*, 1988, 54.

53   *The Stones in 1934–1935 carried through an appalling social calendar.* Warner W. Gardner, "Harlan Fiske Stone: The View From Below," *Supreme Court Historical Society Quarterly* 22, no. 2 (2001): 11.

54   *The Brandeises' "at home" was purposeful and austere.* Dean Acheson, *Morning and Noon: A Memoir* (Boston: Houghton Mifflin, 1965), 49–50.

54   *No judge can now live and pay his travelling expenses on his salary.* Letter from Samuel Chase to William Sprague, July 25, 1866, Chase Collection, Historical Society of Pennsylvania, quoted in Alice Hunt Sokoloff, *Kate Chase for the Defense* (New York: Dodd, Mead & Co., 1971), 191.

55   *When all these people leave their calling cards.* Dennis J. Hutchinson and David J. Garrow, eds., *The Forgotten Memoir of John Knox: A Year in the Life of a Supreme Court Clerk in FDR's Washington* (Chicago: University of Chicago Press, 2002), 105.

55   *I soon realized.* Hutchinson and Garrow, *Forgotten Memoir of John Knox*, 105.

55   *Those were the days of receptions—not cocktail parties, but afternoon teas.* Elizabeth Hughes Gossett, "Charles Evans Hughes: My Father the Chief Justice," *Yearbook of the Supreme Court Historical*, 1976, 11.

56   *Formal social life on the Court was quieter.* Dorothy Goldberg, *Private View of a Public Life* (New York: Charterhouse, 1975) 140, 143.

57   *There is [a] custom that we [Mrs. Powell and I] violated the first time.* Lewis F. Powell, Jr., "Impressions of a New Justice," *Report of the Virginia Bar Association*, 1972, 219.

57   *there is a courtliness.* Goldberg, *Private View of a Public Life*, 144.

57   *He took me by both my hands and sat me down on the sofa next to him.* Elizabeth Black, diary entry, September 9, 1957, reprinted in Black and Black, *Mr. Justice and Mrs. Black*, 85.

58   *Almost invariably, on an opinion he thinks to be very important.* Elizabeth Black, diary entry August 10, 1965, reprinted in Black and Black, *Mr. Justice and Mrs. Black*, 103–104.

59   *White took a proprietary interest.* Unidentified law clerk quoted in Dennis J. Hutchinson, *The Man Who Once Was Whizzer White: A Portrait of Byron R. White* (New York: Free Press, 1998), 438–439.

59   *Listen, Do.* Goldberg, *Private View of a Public Life*, 154.

59   *The code was brought home to me personally.* Goldberg, *Private View of a Public Life*, 154.

60   *I have been supportive of my wife since the beginning.* Gardiner Harris, "M.D. Ginsburg, 78, Dies; Lawyer and Tax Expert," *New York Times*, June 28, 2010.

61   *During my first months on the Court I received, week after week, as I still do.* Ruth Bader Ginsburg, "The Lighter Side of Life at the United States Supreme Court" (speech, New England Law School, March 13, 2009).

62   *Daddy is going.* Postscript on a letter from Oliver Ellsworth to Abigail Ellsworth, March 20, 1797, Marcus, *Documentary History*, 3:101.

62   *I remember well the rides in mother's electric automobile.* Elizabeth Hughes Gossett, "Charles Evans Hughes: My Father the Chief Justice," 8.

62   *All three of us girls happened to be in Washington.* Susan Blackmun recounted this episode at a dinner honoring her father. Quoted in Linda Greenhouse, *Becoming Justice Blackmun: Harry Blackmun's Supreme Court Journey* (New York: Times Books, 2005), 83.

63   *News of the impending Taft retirement reached the president.* Eyewitness Joseph P. Cotton told the story to his friend Felix Frankfurter who told it to his former student Frederick Bernays Wiener, who recounts it in "Justice Hughes' Appointment—The Cotton Story Reexamined," *Yearbook of the Supreme Court Historical Society*, 1981, 79–80. See also James M. Buchanan, "A Note on the 'Joe Cotton Story,'" which emphasizes the relevance of the visit to Hughes by Justices Willis Van Devanter and Pierce Butler prior to the President's phone call. *Yearbook of the Supreme Court Historical Society*, 1981, 92–93.

64   *I felt that . . . my dad's career, had been the great pride.* Transcript, Ramsey Clark Oral History Interview I, 10/30/68, Internet Copy, Lyndon Baines Johnson Library, 18.

64   *In the police community.* Phone conversation between Ramsey Clark and Lyndon B. Johnson, Tape No. K67.01, 1/25/67, 8:22 p.m. PNO:6, Lyndon Baines Johnson Library.

64   *[I]f my judgment is that you become attorney general.* Tape No. K67.01, 1/25/67, 8:22 p.m. PNO:6, Lyndon Baines Johnson Library.

65   *Tom Clark was a giver.* Ramsey Clark, "Tom Clark Eulogies," *Yearbook of the Supreme Court Historical Society*, 1978, 5–6.

65   *Then came my father's appointment to the Supreme Court.* Earl Warren, Jr., "My Father the Chief Justice," *Yearbook of the Supreme Court Historical Society,*1982, 9.

CHAPTER 5: YES, MR. PRESIDENT

67   *The job I have for you is just that.* William O. Douglas, diary entry, March 19, 1939, reprinted in Philip E. Urofsky, ed., "The Diary of Wm. O Douglas," *Journal of Supreme Court History*, 1995, 80.

68   *I have said that the appointment of a judge.* Letter from William Wirt to Martin Van Buren, May 5, 1823, quoted in John P. Kennedy, *Memoirs of the Life of Wil-*

liam Wirt, Attorney General of the United States (Philadelphia: Lea and Blanchard, 1850), 134–135.

68 *Who will be the next nominated no one knows.* Letter from Samuel F. Miller to William Pitt Ballinger, January 18, 1874, Samuel Freeman Miller Correspondence, Manuscript Division, Library of Congress.

69 *In the morning about seven o'clock.* Letter from Leonard Swett to William Herndon, August 28, 1887 (twenty-five years after the episode), quoted in Emanuel Hertz, *The Hidden Lincoln* (New York: The Viking Press, 1938), 339–340.

69 *He called up Fortas and invited him over to the White House.* Phone call from Lyndon B. Johnson to Abe Fortas on July 28, 1965, at http://whitehousetapes .net/exhibit/lbjs-nomination-abe-fortas-supreme-court-july-1965, citation #8406, WH6507.09, LBJ Library. While inviting Fortas over to attend the press conference, Johnson says, "I don't know what will happen or what questions I get but don't be surprised."

70 *Well, you know.* Reported by syndicated journalist Marianne Means, Hearst newspapers, July 29, 1965, confirmed in author interview with Means on January 7, 2011.

70 *To the best of my knowledge, and belief.* Abe Fortas Oral History, Oral History Collection, Lyndon Baines Johnson Library, 24–25.

70 *I just think it is the height of impropriety for a Supreme Court Justice.* Senate Committee on the Judiciary, *Hearings and Nomination of Abe Fortas of Tennessee to be the Chief Justice of the United States*, 90th Cong., 2nd sess., 1968, 1303.

70 *You will remember that you did me the kindness at one time to talk with me.* Letter from Wayne MacVeigh to Rutherford B. Hayes, August 21, 1877, reprinted in Malvina Harlan, *Some Memories of a Long Life, 1854–1911* (New York: Modern Library, 2001), 88–89.

71 *I found [Jackson] the most delightful of guests.* Charles A. Kent, ed., *Memoir of Henry Billings Brown, Late Justice of the Supreme Court of the United States* (New York: Deerfield & Co., 1915), 28.

71 *One day as we were returning from court.* Kent, *Memoir of Henry Billings Brown*, 28.

72 *[U]pon the occurrence of the next vacancy, by the death of Mr. Justice Lamar, I was instrumental.* Quoted in Kent, *Memoir of Henry Billings Brown*, 29.

72 *When President Hoover had under consideration the appointment of a successor.* Letter from Harlan Fiske Stone to George S. Hellman, November 30, 1939, George Sidney Hellman Collection, Manuscript and Archives Division, The New York Public Library, Astor, Lenox and Tilden Foundations, 1376.

72 *Your list is all right, but you handed it to me upside down.* William Borah recounted this interchange with Herbert Hoover to his biographer, Claudius O. Johnson, in *Borah of Idaho* (Seattle: University of Washington Press, 1936), 452.

73 *I'll do no such damned thing.* Letter from William Howard Taft to Charles Evans Hughes, April 22, 1910, quoted in Henry F. Pringle, *The Life and Times of William Howard Taft*, 2 vols. (Hamden, CT: Archon Books, 1964), 1:534.

73 *The salary is $12,500.* Pringle, *Life and Times of William Howard Taft*, 1:534.

73 *Don't misunderstand me.* Pringle, *Life and Times of William Howard Taft*, 1:534.

73   *There is nothing I would have loved more.* Letter from George W. Wickersham to Henry F. Pringle, January 23, 1935, quoted in Pringle, *Life and Times of William Howard Taft*, 1:535.

74   *Chase was a charming man with great faculties.* George H. Williams, "Reminiscences of the Supreme Court," *Yale Law Journal* 8 (1898): 297.

74   *The Presidency although high is only political.* Letter from Morrison R. Waite to his cousin John T. Waite, November, 1875, Morrison R. Waite Papers, Manuscript Division, Library of Congress.

75   *On Friday afternoon my husband called me from the office.* Marjorie Brennan, quoted in "The Ninth Justice: A Happy Irishman," *Time*, October 8, 1956, 25.

75   *As I approached the gates to go out, there was standing.* Donna Haupt, "Justice William J. Brennan, Jr." *Constitution*, Winter 1989, 53–54. See also, "A Fine Judge Ready for his Biggest Job," *Life*, October 29, 1956, 116, in which Brennan is quoted as saying "It seemed so fantastic I dismissed the idea [of being appointed to the Supreme Court] at once."

76   *Two others entered.* Harry A. Blackmun, "Some Personal Reminiscences and What They Meant for Me," *Journal of Supreme Court History* 29, no. 3 (2004): 328–329.

77   *I phoned Byron, and he was somewhat ambivalent.* Nicholas de B. Katzenbach, *Some of It Was Fun: Working with RFK and LBJ* (New York: W. W. Norton & Co., 2008), 58.

77   *[H]e was not very enthusiastic about it, really.* Recollection by Robert Kennedy of his phone call to Byron White on March 27, 1962, quoted in Dennis J. Hutchinson, *The Man Who Once Was Whizzer White: A Portrait of Byron R. White* (New York: Free Press, 1998), 317.

78   *[T]he confirmation of Justice O'Connor capped a four-month.* William French Smith, *Law and Justice in the Reagan Administration: The Memoirs of an Attorney General* (Stanford, CA: Hoover Institution Press, 1991), 63–69.

81   *I'm passing this long line of people and I remember.* John G. Roberts, interview by Jan Crawford Greenburg, Legal Correspondent for ABC News, *Nightline*, November 28, 2006.

81   *[The President] does not know who such friends of mine.* Letter from Pierce Butler to his son Pierce Butler, Jr., November 1–2, 1922, Pierce Butler Papers, United States Supreme Court.

82   *being named to the Supreme Court of the United States never crossed my mind.* Felix Frankfurter Reminisces, Recorded in Talks with Dr. Harlan B. Philips (New York: Reynal & Co., 1960), 278.

82   *On Tuesday, January 4 [1939] . . . while I was in my BVD's.* Felix Frankfurter Reminisces, 282–284.

83   *I am not having a very agreeable time just at present.* Letter from Ebenezer Rockwood Hoar to his wife, December 19, 1869, reprinted in Moorfield Storey and Edward W. Emerson, *Ebenezer Rockwood Hoar: A Memoir* (New York: Houghton Mifflin, 1911), 188–189.

83   *Then there was a committee hearing. Felix Frankfurter Reminisces,* 284–285.

85   *[O]nce a justice dons these robes, enters that inner sanctum.* Senator Joseph Biden, quoted in Mike Shanahan, "Senate OKs O'Connor nomination," Associated Press, September 22, 1981.

85   *Having laid aside their robes.* Randolph Keim, *Society in Washington: Its Noted Men, Accomplished Women, Established Customs and Notable Events* (Washington, DC: Harrisburg (Pa.) Publishing, 1887), 121.

86   *Exactly five minutes after we entered.* Charles Henry Butler, *A Century at the Bar of the Supreme Court of the United States* (New York: G. P. Putnam's Sons, 1942), 74.

86   *On Sunday evening after church.* Harlan, *Some Memories of a Long Life,* 99.

87   *Attended another poker party at the White House tonight.* William O. Douglas, diary entry March 11, 1940, reprinted in Philip E. Urofsky, ed., "The Diary of Wm. O Douglas," *Journal of Supreme Court History,* 1995, 93.

88   *Speaking of the punctuality of the Court in regard to adjournment.* Butler, *Century at the Bar,* 122–123.

88   *[P]acking the Supreme Court [with allies] simply can't be done.* Harry S Truman, lecture at Columbia University, April 28, 1959, quoted in Henry J. Abraham, *Justices and Presidents,* third ed. (New York: Oxford University Press, 1992), 70.

CHAPTER 6: LEARNING THE ROPES

89   *I was then conducted to the seat of the Chief Justice.* The Memoirs of Earl Warren (Garden City, NY: Doubleday, 1977), 279–280.

89   *It's quite a frightening experience to come here for the first time.* William J. Brennan, Jr., interview by Mimi Clark Gronlund, quoted in her book, *Supreme Court Justice Tom C. Clark: A Life of Service* (Austin: University of Texas Press, 2010), 178.

89   *the mule entered in the Kentucky Derby.* Donna Haupt, "Justice William J. Brennan, Jr.," *Constitution,* Winter 1989, 50–51.

90   *Notwithstanding [that] the emoluments of my present business.* Letter from Joseph Story to Nathaniel Williams, November 30, 1811, reprinted in William W. Story, *Life and Letters of Joseph Story,* 2 vols. (Boston: Little & Brown, 1851), 1:201.

91   *My appointment to the Supreme Court necessitated my removal.* Charles A. Kent, ed., *Memoir of Henry Billings Brown, Late Justice of the Supreme Court of the United States* (New York: Deerfield & Co., 1915), 29.

91   *When I came to Washington, I had never looked upon the face of judge Taney.* Samuel F. Miller's words, as recollected by Henry E. Davis, quoted in Henry E. Davis, Proceedings of the Bench and Bar of the Supreme Court of the United States in Memoriam Samuel F. Miller, held in U.S. Circuit Court in Omaha, (Washington: Publisher, 1891), 17, reprinted in Roger F. Jacobs, *Memorials of the Justices of the Supreme Court of the United States,* 6 vols. (Littleton, CO: Fred B. Rothman & Co., 1981–), 4:17.

91   *My brother Miller, I am an old and broken man.* Remarks by J. M. Woolworth, quoted in Jacobs, *Memorials of the Justices,* 60–61. Woolworth was Taney's close friend. Miller's biographer, Charles Fairman, says Woolworth's remarks "may be taken as a faithful recollection of what Miller had told him"; see Charles Fairman, *Mr. Justice Miller and the Supreme Court 1862–1890* (Cambridge, MA: Harvard University Press, 1939), 54.

92 *Saturday I went through my severest ordeal.* Letter from Morrison R. Waite to Amelia Waite, March 8, 1874, Morrison R. Waite Papers, Manuscript Division, Library of Congress.

92 *We live to learn, darlings.* Letter from Morrison R. Waite to Amelia Waite, March 13, 1874, Morrison R. Waite Papers.

92 *Every day in Court hard at work.* Letter from Morrison R. Waite to Amelia Waite, March 19, 1874, Morrison R. Waite Papers.

93 *A small white-walled room.* William P. Drew published his reminiscence of Fuller's swearing-in on October, 8, 1888, in *Purple and Gold, Official Magazine of the Chi Psi Fraternity,* 15, no. 4 (1898): 270–276, quoted in Willard King, *Melville Weston Fuller, Chief Justice of the United States 1888–1910* (New York: Macmillan Co., 1950), 123–124. Fuller took the Constitutional Oath before Samuel F. Miller, Senior Associate Justice, and the Judicial Oath in open court administered by the Clerk of the Court.

93 *A tremor as of reviving consciousness seems to pass.* King, *Melville Weston Fuller,* 124.

93 *During the first three months of my service on the bench.* David J. Danelski and Joseph S. Tulchin, eds., *The Autobiographical Notes of Charles Evans Hughes* (Cambridge, MA: Harvard University Press, 1973), 164.

94 *I found the work very difficult.* Danelski and Tulchin, *Autobiographical Notes of Charles Evans Hughes,* 164–165.

94 *It takes three or four years to find oneself.* Note made by Felix Frankfurter on July 3, 1923, of conversation with Louis D. Brandeis, reprinted in Melvin I. Urofsky, "The Brandeis-Frankfurter Conversations," *Supreme Court Review,* 1985: 299.

94 *A new Justice is not at ease.* Danelski and Tulchin, *Autobiographical Notes of Charles Evans Hughes,* 165.

95 *As Justice Harlan F. Stone said. The Court Years, 1939–1975: The Autobiography of William O. Douglas* (New York: Random House, 1980), 4.

95 *Justice White would often say that it takes about [five years].* Clarence Thomas, interview by Susan Swain, reprinted in Brian Lamb, Susan Swain, and Mark Farkas, eds., *The Supreme Court: A C-Span Book Featuring the Justices in Their Own Words* (New York: Public Affairs, 2010), 98–99.

95 *direct from a circus to a monastery.* Quoted in Mary Frances Berry, *Stability, Security, and Continuity: Mr. Justice Burton and Decision-Making in the Supreme Court 1945–1958* (Westport, CT: Greenwood Press, 1978), 27. Citing Hubert Holloway, "Notes & Quotes," undated and unpublished, Harold H. Burton Papers, Manuscript Division, Library of Congress, Box 27.

95 *One is "elevated" to the Court and consequently, in socially conscious Washington.* Abe Goldberg, speech to the American Bar Association, August 12, 1963, reprinted in Daniel Patrick Moynihan, ed., *The Defenses of Freedom* (New York: Harper and Row, 1966), 128–129.

96 *The greatest fear of Justices on the Supreme Court is of dying on the Court.* Abe Fortas interview by Bruce Allen Murphy, August 7, 1981, quoted in Bruce Allen Murphy, *Fortas: The Rise and Ruin of a Supreme Court Justice* (New York: William Morrow, 1988), 192.

96 *Yes—here I am—and more absorbed, interested.* Letter from Oliver Wendell Holmes to Frederick Pollock, December 28, 1902, The Mark De Wolfe Howe Papers, Harvard Law School Library, Box 4, Folder 14.

97 *In my few short days.* Letter from Harry A. Blackmun to Pat Mehaffy, June 19, 1970, Harry A. Blackmun Collection, Library of Congress, quoted in Linda Greenhouse, *Becoming Justice Blackmun: Harry Blackmun's Supreme Court Journey* (New York: Times Books, 2005), 54.

97 *I think psychologically it is a different world from the Court of Appeals.* Associate Justice Stephen G. Breyer, in discussion with the author, January 11, 2007.

97 *The day of my induction as Chief Justice. Memoirs of Earl Warren*, 275–276.

98 *I told them they were welcome to remain with me. Memoirs of Earl Warren*, 277.

99 *In a small room, my seven new colleagues.* Nat Hentoff, "Profiles: The Constitutionalist," *New Yorker*, March 12, 1990, 54.

99 *Hugo told me there was a possibility.* Elizabeth Black, diary entry, September 1, 1967, reprinted in Hugo L. Black and Elizabeth Black, *Mr. Justice and Mrs. Black: The Memoirs of Hugo L. and Elizabeth Black*, 175–6.

100 *On Tuesday, May 5, word came that the Judiciary Committee.* Harry Blackmun, "Some Personal Reminiscences and What They Meant For Me," *Journal of Supreme Court History* 29, no. 3, (2004): 334–335.

101 *I had taken my seat, and was examining things.* Mary Ann Harrell and Burnett Anderson, *Equal Justice Under Law, The Supreme Court in American Life*, 6th ed. (Washington, DC: The Supreme Court Historical Society with the cooperation of the National Geographic Society, 1994), 136.

101 *When I first went on the Court.* William H. Rehnquist, *The Supreme Court: How It Was, How It Is* (New York: William Morrow, 1987), 290.

102 *[B]y the time they got to me, I was either irrelevant.* Samuel Alito, interview by Brian Lamb, reprinted in Brian Lamb, Susan Swain, and Mark Farkas, eds., *The Supreme Court: A C-Span Book Featuring the Justices in Their Own Words* (New York: Public Affairs, 2010), 152.

102 *It was Justice White who gave me his chambers manual.* Todd C. Peppers, "The Modern Clerkship: Justice Ruth Bader Ginsburg and Her Law Clerks," in *Behind the Bench: Portraits of Law Clerks and Their Justices*, eds. Todd C. Peppers and Artemus Ward (Charlottesville: University of Virginia Press, forthcoming).

102 *The day that Sonia [Sotomayor] was sworn in.* Ibid.

102 *No one did more than Lewis Powell.* Sandra Day O'Connor, *The Majesty of the Law: Reflections of a Supreme Court Justice*, ed. Craig Joyce (New York: Random House, 2003), 150.

102 *Justice O'Connor's welcome when I became junior Justice.* Ruth Bader Ginsburg, "A Tribute to Justice Sandra Day O'Connor," *Harvard Law Review* 119, no. 5 (2006): 1239–1240.

103 *I eagerly awaited my first opinion assignment.* Ginsburg, "A Tribute to Justice Sandra Day O'Connor," 1240.

103 *Just do it.* Ginsburg, "A Tribute to Justice Sandra Day O'Connor," 1240.

103 *This is your first opinion for the Court.* Ginsburg, "A Tribute to Justice Sandra Day O'Connor," 1240.

103 *My first opinion was an opinion in which we were unanimous.* Samuel Alito, interview by Brian Lamb, reprinted in Brian Lamb, Susan Swain, and Mark

Farkas, eds., *The Supreme Court: A C-Span Book Featuring the Justices in Their Own Words* (New York: Public Affairs, 2010), 154–155.

103　*baptism by fire.* Lamb, Swain, and Farkas, *The Supreme Court*, 151.

104　*It took him a while to adjust to not being the junior justice.* Lamb, Swain, and Farkas, *The Supreme Court*, 154.

104　*As far as the composition of the Court.* Clarence Thomas, interview by Susan Swain, Lamb, Swain, and Farkas, *The Supreme Court*, 99.

104　*A new Justice comes into the Court and brings a personality.* Lyle Denniston, interview by Mark Farkas, Lamb, Swain, and Farkas, *The Supreme Court*, 257.

CHAPTER 7: INSIDE THE COURTROOM

105　*The deaths of some of our most talented jurists.* Robert Mills, "Report on the Extension of the Capitol," May 1, 1850, quoted in *Documentary History of the Construction and Development of the United States Capitol Building and Grounds*, 58th Cong., 2nd sess., 1904, H. Rep. 646, 433.

105　*[I was] grievously annoyed by the dampness.* Letter from John Catron to Clerk of the Court William Thomas Carroll, September 29, 1860, Clerks Files, quoted in Carl B. Swisher, *History of the Supreme Court: The Taney Period 1836–64*, Oliver Wendell Holmes Devise 5 (New York: Macmillan, 1974), 717.

105　*Midway in the rather dingy and ill-lighted.* E. V. Smalley, "The Supreme Court of the United States," *Century Illustrated Magazine*, December 1882, 163–164.

107　*The facilities afforded to the Court were then very slender.* David J. Danelski and Joseph S. Tulchin, eds., *The Autobiographical Notes of Charles Evans Hughes* (Cambridge, MA: Harvard University Press, 1973), 161.

108　*Each justice of the Supreme Court has a chair.* Smalley, "The Supreme Court of the United States," 164.

108　*But behind the massive bench, in dignified isolation.* Associated Press, "Supreme Court Takes Old Chairs in Moving," *New York Times*, October 3, 1935.

108　*The stage is a long dais.* Drew Pearson and Robert S. Allen, *The Nine Old Men* (Garden City, NY: Doubleday, Doran & Co., 1936), 10.

109　*At the head walks the Chief-Justice.* Smalley, "The Supreme Court of the United States," 164.

109　*the interior of a classical icebox.* Joseph Alsop and Turner Catledge, *The 168 Days* (Garden City, NY: Doubleday, Doran & Co., 1938), reporting on September 18, 1937.

109　*We had difficulty with the acoustics in the new Courtroom. The Court Years, 1939–1975: The Autobiography of William O. Douglas* (New York: Random House, 1980), 5.

109　*If your voice is low, it burdens the hearing.* Robert H. Jackson, "Advocacy Before the United States Supreme Court," *Cornell Law Quarterly* 37 (1951): 1.

109　*was strongly opposed and never moved into the offices.* Dean Acheson, *Morning and Noon: A Memoir* (Boston: Houghton Mifflin, 1965), 57.

110　*He thought the plans were too grand.* Frank Gilbert, interview, C-SPAN Supreme Court Experts, http://supremecourt.c-span.org/Video/Historians/SC_HIST_FrankG_02.aspx.

110 *The place is almost bombastically pretentious.* Letter from Harlan Fiske Stone to his sons, May 24, 1935, quoted in Alpheus Thomas Mason, *Harlan Fiske Stone: Pillar of the Law* (New York: Viking Press, 1956), 405–406.

111 *as useless and unnecessary.* Douglas, *Court Years,* 6.

111 *One of the amazing things about the courtroom.* David Souter, interview by Brian Lamb, reprinted in Brian Lamb, Susan Swain, and Mark Farkas, eds., *The Supreme Court: A C-Span Book Featuring the Justices in Their Own Words* (New York: Public Affairs, 2010), xv.

111 *Business begins promptly.* Smalley, "The Supreme Court of the United States," 164.

111 *Chief Justice Hughes nods to Justice [Benjamin] Cardozo.* Pearson and Allen, *Nine Old Men,* 10–11.

112 *After studying . . . Chief Justice [Charles Evans Hughes], I glanced at Justice McReynolds.* Dennis J. Hutchinson and David J. Garrow, eds., *The Forgotten Memoir of John Knox: A Year in the Life of a Supreme Court Clerk in FDR's Washington* (Chicago: University of Chicago Press, 2002), 96–97.

114 *kitchen-knifes, razors, and stings.* Danelski and Tulchin, *Autobiographical Notes of Charles Evans Hughes,* 227.

114 *[W]e don't shut up bores.* Letter from Oliver Wendell Holmes, Jr. to Frederick Pollock, March 17, 1898, reprinted in Mark DeWolfe Howe, ed., *The Holmes-Pollock Letters: The Correspondence of Mr. Justice Holmes and Frederick Pollock, 1874–1935,* 2 vols. (Cambridge, MA: Harvard University Press, 1942), 81–82.

114 *[B]efore the final game began, [Stewart] asked for scores.* Justice Potter Stewart's 1973 Term clerks—unnamed—told reporters Bob Woodward and Scott Armstrong this anecdote, quoted in their book, *The Brethren: Inside the Supreme Court* (New York: Simon & Schuster, 1979), 302.

114 *On one occasion Judge Grier complimented Mr. Phillips.* William A. Maury, Recollections (unpublished manuscript), 56, quoted in Charles Fairman, *Mr. Justice Miller and the Supreme Court 1862–1890* (Cambridge, MA: Harvard University Press, 1939), 105.

115 *They both loved candy.* W. H. Smith, "Supreme Court and Its Justices in Days Following the Civil War," *Washington Sunday Star,* April 22, 1923.

115 *Clifford was, in avoirdupois, the largest.* Smith, "Supreme Court and Its Justices."

115 *With an empty lobby he usually sat back.* Smith, "Supreme Court and Its Justices."

115 *I sat in the courtroom and heard the old man read.* Arthur E. Sutherland, quoted in David M. O'Brien, "Sutherland's Recollections of Justice Holmes," *Yearbook of the Supreme Court Historical Society,* 1988, 37.

116 *Opinions were announced on Mondays.* Douglas, *Court Years,* 39–40. Justice McReynolds's famous outburst, "The Constitution is gone!" occurred on February 18, 1935, when he announced his dissent (joined by Justices Van Devanter, Sutherland, and Butler) in response to Chief Justice Hughes's majority opinion upholding Congress's decision to take the country off the gold standard and outlaw public debts calling for payment in gold rather than paper currency. The official transcript has been excised because McReynolds's extemporized remarks were too vitriolic, and the Justice's exact words are disputed. One observer quoted McReynolds as saying: "The Constitution as many of us have

understood it, the Constitution that has meant so much to us, is gone . . . Horrible dishonesty! . . . Shame and humiliation are upon us." See Stephen Tyree Early, Jr., "James Clark McReynolds and the Judicial Process," (PhD dissertation, University of Virginia). Another eyewitness, Philip B. Perlman, Solicitor General of the United States, gave his own account in "Proceeding in the Supreme Court of the United States in Memory of Mr. Justice McReynolds (March 31, 1948)," *United States Reports* 334 (1948): ix–x.

116 *This is a remarkable proceeding.* John P. Frank, *Marble Palace: The Supreme Court in American Life* (New York: Knopf, 1958), 121.

117 *Is he going to read all of it?* Quoted in Bernard Schwartz, *Decision, How the Supreme Court Decides Cases* (New York: Oxford University Press, 1996), 18. The case was *Abington Township School District v. Schempp*, 374 U.S. 203 (1963).

117 *I personally do go up and want to hear the opinion.* Joan Biskupic, interview by Mark Farkas, reprinted in Brian Lamb, Susan Swain, and Mark Farkas, eds., *The Supreme Court: A C-Span Book Featuring the Justices in Their Own Words* (New York: Public Affairs, 2010), 206.

117 *Potter [Stewart] . . . is the Justice who told me.* John Paul Stevens, "Random Recollections," *San Diego Law Review* 42 (2005): 269–272.

117 *In recent years, dissenters only infrequently have given opinions.* Morton Mintz, "High Court Rules Judge Isn't Liable," *Washington Post*, March 29, 1978.

118 *Chief Justice [Earl] Warren announced the decision in a few brief words.* Anthony Lewis, email message to author, March 2008. See also, "Dissent by Frankfurter Provokes Warren to Rebuttal from Bench," *New York Times*, March 21, 1961.

118 *I took two friends into the Court to hear.* Elizabeth Black, diary entry, March 29, 1965, reprinted in Hugo L. Black and Elizabeth Black, *Mr. Justice and Mrs. Black: The Memoirs of Hugo L. Black and Elizabeth Black* (New York: Random House, 1986), 108. The cases she refers to are *United States v. Brown*, 381 U.S. 437 (1965) and *Griswold v. Connecticut*, 381 U.S. 479 (1965).

119 *The Supreme Court, regardless of what the ladies.* Barrett McGurn, *America's Court: The Supreme Court and the People* (Golden, CO: Fulcrum Publishing, 1997), 10.

119 *I wouldn't mind having the proceedings of the court.* Antonin Scalia, "A Constitutional Conversation," April 21, 2005, quoted at http://www.c-span.org/The-Courts/Cameras-in-The-Court/.

120 *The discussions that the Justices have with the attorneys.* Anthony Kennedy, "Appearance before the House Appropriations Subcommittee," March 8, 2007, quoted at http://www.c-span.org/The-Courts/Cameras-in-The-Court/.

120 *The aura of the place is always present.* Lyle Denniston, interview by Mark Farkas, reprinted in Brian Lamb, Susan Swain, and Mark Farkas, eds., *The Supreme Court: A C-Span Book Featuring the Justices in Their Own Words* (New York: Public Affairs, 2010), 263.

120 *When you go in for a big case.* Lamb, Swain, and Farkas, *The Supreme Court*, 264.

CHAPTER 8: SILVER TONGUES AND QUILL PENS

121 *After I took my place at the podium.* Lindsay C. Harrison, "9 Big Adventures: What if You . . ." *O, The Oprah Magazine*, June 2010, 146. The case was *Nken v.*

Holder 129 S. Ct. 1749 (2009). The plaintiff was Jean Marc Nken, a democratic activist from Cameroon, who was contesting denial of an asylum and deportation order on the ground that his life would be in danger if he returned to his country. Harrison won a temporary stay of Nken's deportation and continues to represent him.

122   *He was beyond any one whom I have known.* Letter from Samuel F. Miller to his brother-in-law, William Pitt Ballinger, February 27, 1881, Samuel Freeman Miller Correspondence, Manuscript Division, Library of Congress.

122   *Carpenter concluded.* Diary of William Pitt Ballinger, December 7, 1877, Briscoe Center for American History, University of Texas at Austin, Box 2Q425.

122   *Black, as a man, was simply abominable.* Samuel F. Miller's informal speech to the "law class at the University of Pennsylvania," October 1, 1888, as recorded by Samuel W. Pennypacker, *The Autobiography of a Pennsylvanian* (Philadelphia: The John C. Winston Co., 1918), 131. President James Buchanan nominated fellow Pennsylvanian Jeremiah S. Black (then his Secretary of State) to the Supreme Court in 1861, but Black's candidacy failed by one Senate vote. Black served briefly as the Court's Reporter of Decisions in 1861–1862.

123   *When [Jeremiah S. Black] was to speak.* W. H. Smith, "Supreme Court and Its Justices in Days Following the Civil War," *Washington Sunday Star*, April 22, 1923.

123   *There was a space back of the Bench.* Charles Henry Butler, *Century at the Bar of the Supreme Court of the United States* (New York: G. P. Putnam's Sons, 1942), 121–122. An unverified anecdote, cited to the *Denver Daily News*, February 1, 1903, is amusing: "according to one newspaper account, this luncheon system was abandoned after a lawyer, who had one day been talking steadily for an hour, stopped suddenly to hunt up a reference, whereupon from the mysterious apartment behind the screen resounded a clatter of dishes and a distinct: 'More coffee please, my man, and have it hot!'" Quoted in George Shiras, III and Winfield Shiras, *Justice George Shiras, Jr., of Pittsburgh, Associate Justice of the United States 1892–1903, A Chronicle of His Family Life and Times* (Pittsburg: University of Pittsburgh Press, 1953), 135–136.

124   *I arose and offered to present a motion.* Augustus H. Garland, *Experience in the Supreme Court of the United States with Some Reflections and Suggestions as to That Tribunal* (Washington, DC: John Byrnh & Co., 1898), 40–41.

125   *Very often I have seen lawyers.* Garland, *Experience in the Supreme Court*, 46–47.

125   *was stricken with apoplexy.* "Death Ended His Plea," *Washington Post*, January 27, 1899.

125   *In respect to time allowed for argument.* Butler, *Century at the Bar*, 86–87.

126   *In all cases before the Court, each side was allotted an hour.* Erwin N. Griswold, *Ould Fields, New Corne: The Personal Memoirs of a Twentieth Century Lawyer* (St. Paul, MN: West Pub. Co., 1992), 92 n. 25.

126   *I remember . . . there was the different rhythm of oral arguments.* Drew Days III, interview by Mark Farkas, reprinted in Brian Lamb, Susan Swain, and Mark Farkas, eds., *The Supreme Court: A C-Span Book Featuring the Justices in Their Own Words* (New York: Public Affairs, 2010), 223.

128   *to be able more quickly to separate.* Charles Evans Hughes, *The Supreme Court of the United States: Its Foundation, Methods, and Achievements, An Interpretation* (New York: Columbia University Press, 1928), 62.

128 *The judges of the Supreme Court are quite free in addressing questions.* Hughes, *The Supreme Court*, 62.

128 *I have just heard Mr. Brandeis.* Letter from William Hitz, Judge of the District of Columbia Supreme Court, to Felix Frankfurter, professor at Harvard Law School, December 17, 1914, quoted in Melvin I. Urofsky, "Louis D. Brandeis: Advocate Before and On the Bench," *Journal of Supreme Court History* 30, no. 1 (2005): 37. The case was *Stettler v. O'Hara*, 243 U.S. 629 (1917).

128 *No skill[ed advocate] can, or should try to, avoid questions here.* Dean Acheson, *Morning and Noon: A Memoir* (Boston: Houghton Mifflin, 1965), 98–99.

129 *"I thought you were arguing this case?"* Reported by Anthony Lewis, "The Justices' Supreme Job," *New York Times Magazine*, June 11, 1961.

129 *on the average I argued a case every two weeks.* Francis Biddle, *In Brief Authority* (Garden City, NY: Doubleday, 1962), 98.

129 *An extraordinary coincidence that was brought to the mind.* "Gen. Thomas Ewing Ill; Compelled to Suspend His Argument Before the Supreme Court," *Washington Post*, October 23, 1895. The case being argued was *Farmer's Loan & Trust Co. v. Chicago, Portage & Superior Ry. Co.*, 163 U.S. 31 (1896).

130 *Reed faltered this afternoon and sat down.* "Reed in Collapse; AAA Cases Halted," *New York Times*, December 11, 1935. The case was *United States v. Butler*, 297 U.S. 1 (1936).

130 *The critical document [in the case] was an affidavit. The Court Years, 1939–1975: The Autobiography of William O. Douglas* (New York: Random House, 1980), 181. The case being argued was *Hazel-Atlas Glass Co. v. Hartford-Empire Co.*, 332 U.S. 238 (1944).

130 *Thank you, but apologize to him.* Adam Liptak, "So, Guy Walks Up to the Bar, and Scalia Says," *New York Times*, December 31, 2005. The lawyer was Sri Srinivasan and the argument took place on November 28, 2005. The case was *Wachovia Bank v. Schmidt*, 546 U.S. 303 (2006).

130 *Justice Stephen G. Breyer said he did not see why providing a urine sample.* Joan Biskupic, "Supreme Court Looks Into the Locker Room; Urinalysis for School Sports Raises Questions of Privacy," *Washington Post*, March 29, 1995. The case was *Vernonia School District v. Acton*, 515 U.S. 646 (1995).

131 *My principle recollection of Justice [Hugo L.] Black.* Peter D. Ehrenhaft, "A Photographic View of the 1961 Term," *Supreme Court Historical Society Quarterly* 25, no. 2 (2004): 7.

131 *[Stone] was persistently bitter.* Warner W. Gardner, "Harlan Fiske Stone: The View From Below," *Supreme Court Historical Society Quarterly* 22, no. 2 (2001): 9.

131 *On your first appearance before the Court.* Jackson, "Advocacy Before the United States Supreme Court," *Cornell Law Quarterly* 37 (1951): 1.

132 *The first time I argued a case here.* From the filmstrip for visitors to the Supreme Court, quoted in Clare Cushman, ed., *Supreme Court Decisions and Women's Rights: Milestones to Equality* (Washington, DC: CQ Press, 2010), 240.

132 *I was very nervous.* John G. Roberts, interview by Susan Swain, reprinted in Brian Lamb, Susan Swain, and Mark Farkas, eds., *The Supreme Court: A C-Span Book Featuring the Justices in Their Own Words* (New York: Public Affairs, 2010), 20.

132 *it's a lot easier to ask questions.* Lamb, Swain, and Farkas, *The Supreme Court*, 20.

132   *The first is the lector.* William H. Rehnquist, *Supreme Court: How It Was, How It Is* (New York: William Morrow, 1987), 278.

133   *He has an excellent grasp.* Rehnquist, *Supreme Court*, 279–280.

133   *This lawyer has a complete grasp.* Rehnquist, *Supreme Court*, 280.

134   *One of the things the Justices do.* Drew Days III, interview by Mark Farkas, reprinted in Brian Lamb, Susan Swain, and Mark Farkas, eds., *The Supreme Court: A C-Span Book Featuring the Justices in Their Own Words* (New York: Public Affairs, 2010), 225.

135   *We come to [oral argument] cold as far as knowing.* John G. Roberts, interview by Susan Swain, reprinted in Lamb, Swain, and Farkas, *The Supreme Court*, 18–19.

135   *There are some questions that are real.* Drew Days III, interview by Mark Farkas, reprinted in Lamb, Swain, and Farkas, *The Supreme Court*, 225.

135   *[T]hrough the modern practice of questioning counsel.* Stephen M. Shapiro, "Oral Argument in the Supreme Court: The Felt Necessities of Time," *Yearbook of the Supreme Court Historical Society*, 1985, 29.

136   *In all my life as an advocate and observer.* Rodney A. Smolla argued the case, *Virginia v. Black*, 538 U.S. 343 (2003), for the ACLU. His recollection is quoted in Neal Devins and Davison M. Douglas, eds., *A Year at the Supreme Court* (Durham, NC: Duke University Press, 2004), 164.

136   *When I first came to the Court.* Clarence Thomas, interview by Susan Swain, reprinted in Lamb, Swain, and Farkas, *The Supreme Court*, 94.

136   *I learned when I got here.* Samuel Alito, interview by Brian Lamb, Lamb, Swain, and Farkas, *The Supreme Court*, 157.

136   *Often my whole notion of what a case is about.* William J. Brennan, *Harvard Law School Occasional Pamphlet Number Nine* (1967), 22–23.

137   *I think that in a significant minority of the cases.* Rehnquist, *Supreme Court*, 276.

137   *[I]t is probably quite rare.* Antonin Scalia, interview by Susan Swain, reprinted in Lamb, Swain, and Farkas, *The Supreme Court*, 61.

137   *think[s] differently about the case.* Stephen G. Breyer, interview by Brian Lamb, reprinted in Lamb, Swain, and Farkas, *The Supreme Court*, 132.

137   *[If] you have an associate.* Jackson, "Advocacy Before the United States Supreme Court," 1.

138   *The best advocates.* Samuel Alito, interview by Brian Lamb, reprinted in Lamb, Swain, and Farkas, *Supreme Court*, 158.

138   *You have to be extremely well prepared.* Maureen Mahoney, interview by Mark Farkas, in Lamb, Swain, and Farkas, *The Supreme Court*, 280.

138   *When the day arrives.* Jackson, "Advocacy Before the United States Supreme Court," 1.

139   *For some time after the decease of Justice [Horace] Gray.* Butler, *Century at the Bar*, 86.

140   *One young red-haired lawyer from Oklahoma.* Austin Cunningham, "The United States Supreme Court and Me," *Supreme Court Historical Society Quarterly* 18, no. 2 (1998): 9.

140   *[call] the attention of her gentlemen.* Quoted in Clare Cushman, "Women Advocates Before the Court," in Cushman, *Supreme Court Decisions and Women's Rights: Milestones to Equality*, 226.

140   *Along with my substantive preparation.* Paul Wilson, "A Time to Lose," *Journal of Supreme Court History* 24, no. 2 (1999): 173.

CHAPTER 9: NINE JUSTICES, ONE BENCH

143   *[W]hen you are going to serve on a court.* Earl Warren, "A Conversation with Earl Warren," WGBH-TV Educational Foundation, 1972.

143   *Before any opinion is formed by the Court.* Undated letter, John McLean Papers, Box 18, Manuscript Division, Library of Congress.

144   *The Chief Justice presided.* John A. Campbell, "In Memoriam: Benjamin Robbins Curtis," Memorial Address to the Supreme Court Bar, October 13, 1874, *United States Reports* 87 (1875): x.

144   *There is a long table.* Letter from David J. Brewer, July 15, 1890, Bradley Papers, New Jersey Historical Society.

145   *Often and often in coming out of the conference.* Augustus H. Garland, *Experience in the Supreme Court of the United States with Some Reflections and Suggestions as to That Tribunal* (Washington, DC: John Byrh & Co., 1898), 61.

145   *I have been fighting all day.* David J. Brewer, "[address to the] Thirty-third Annual Meeting of the Agents of the Northwestern Mutual Life Insurance Company," (1909 speech), quoted in Michael J. Brodhead, *David J. Brewer: The Life of a Supreme Court Justice, 1837–1910* (Carbondale, IL: Southern Illinois University Press, 1994), 82.

146   *I have the authority of Mr. Justice Holmes.* Quoted in Philip B. Kurland, ed., *Felix Frankfurter on the Supreme Court: Extrajudicial Essays on the Court and the Constitution* (Cambridge, MA: Belknap Press of Harvard University Press, 1970), 477–478.

146   *I think he was extraordinary.* Letter from Oliver Wendell Holmes, Jr. to Judge William L. Putnam, July 12, 1910, reprinted in "Judge Putnam's Recollections of Chief Justice Fuller," *Green Bag* 22 (1910): 529.

146   *Justice Harlan, who was oratorical while Justice Holmes was pithy.* Quoted in Kurland, *Felix Frankfurter on the Supreme Court*, 477.

146   *When members gather for a conference.* James F. Byrnes, *All in One Lifetime* (New York: Harper & Brothers Publishers, 1958), 137.

147   *I think that's a great custom.* Sandra Day O'Connor, interview by Susan Swain, reprinted in Brian Lamb, Susan Swain, and Mark Farkas, eds., *The Supreme Court: A C-Span Book Featuring the Justices in Their Own Words* (New York: Public Affairs, 2010), 188.

147   *[It's] a symbol of the work we do as a collegial body.* Ruth Bader Ginsburg, interview by Brian Lamb, reprinted in Lamb, Swain, and Farkas, *The Supreme Court*, 116–117.

147   *It's like being an attorney once again.* Anthony Kennedy, interview by Susan Swain, reprinted in Lamb, Swain, and Farkas, *The Supreme Court*, 73–74.

148   *The power to calm.* William H. Rehnquist, "Chief Justices I Never Knew," *Hastings Constitutional Law Quarterly* 3 (1976): 673.

148   *The C.J. certainly handles the conference in a masterful manner.* William O. Douglas, diary entry, April 22, 1939, reprinted in Philip E. Urofsky, ed. "The Diary of Wm. O Douglas," *Journal of Supreme Court History*, 1995, 82.

148   *[Hughes] accomplished in four hours.* The Court Years, 1939–1975: The Autobiography of William O. Douglas (New York: Random House, 1980), 219.

149   *Chief Justice Hughes radiated authority.* Quoted in Kurland, *Felix Frankfurter on the Supreme Court*, 491–492.

149   *[Associate Justice] Stone harbors a deep resentment at Hughes.* William O. Douglas diary entry January 12, 1940, reprinted in Urofsky, "The Diary of Wm. O Douglas," 87.

150   *It has been said that there wasn't free and easy talk.* Felix Frankfurter, "From Fuller to Stone: Chief Justices I Have Known," *Yearbook of the Supreme Court Historical Society*, 1980, 9.

150   *an increasing tendency on the part of members of this Court to behave like little school boys.* Quoted in Sidney Fine, *Frank Murphy: The Washington Years* (Ann Arbor: The University of Michigan Press, 1984), 3:244.

150   *To see people who are trying their best.* Clarence Thomas, interview by Susan Swain, reprinted in Lamb, Swain, and Farkas, *Supreme Court*, 94–95.

150   *[Van Devanter's] careful and elaborate statements.* David Danelski and Joseph S.Tulchin, eds., *Autobiographical Notes of Charles Evans Hughes* (Cambridge MA: Harvard University Press), 171.

151   *Not very much conferencing goes on.* Quoted in "Ruing Fixed Opinions," *New York Times*, February 22, 1988.

152   *And people are engaged.* Clarence Thomas, interview by Susan Swain, reprinted in Lamb, Swain, and Farkas, *Supreme Court*, 94.

152   *know how to write it in a way.* Antonin Scalia, interview by Susan Swain, reprinted in Lamb, Swain, and Farkas, *Supreme Court*, 63.

153   *I regret that my assignment of cases.* Letter from Morrison R. Waite to Nathan Clifford, December 25, 1878, reprinted in C. Peter Magrath, *Morrison R. Waite: The Triumph of Character* (New York: Macmillan, 1963), 261–262.

153   *As is well known, Byrnes was a southerner.* Bennett Boskey, "Opinion-Assigning by Chief Justices," *Supreme Court Historical Society Quarterly* 25, no. 1 (2004): 15. The case was *Taylor v. Georgia*, 315 U.S. 25 (1942).

153   *You can see the important function that rests with the Chief Justice.* Frankfurter, "From Fuller to Stone: Chief Justices I Have Known," 9.

154   *My colleagues upon the Supreme Bench were all men of distinction and ability.* Charles A. Kent, ed., *Memoir of Henry Billings Brown, Late Justice of the Supreme Court of the United States* (New York: Deerfield & Co., 1915), 30.

154   *If I'm in the majority.* John G. Roberts, interview by Susan Swain, reprinted in Lamb, Swain, and Farkas, *Supreme Court*, 7.

155   *Of course, sometimes what they think is a good opinion.* Antonin Scalia, interview by Susan Swain, reprinted in Lamb, Swain, and Farkas, *Supreme Court*, 64.

155   *You know the real persuasion around here.* Sandra Day O'Connor, interview by Bill Moyers, *In Search of the Constitution*, Public Affairs Television, 1987.

156   *was rare in those days for the Justices to comment.* Milton C. Handler, "Clerking for Justice Harlan Fiske Stone," *Journal of Supreme Court History*, 1995, 119.

156 *The proofs were folded four times.* Handler, "Clerking for Justice Harlan Fiske Stone," 119.

156 *Van Devanter . . . whose productivity ebbed as he grew.* Handler, "Clerking for Justice Harlan Fiske Stone," 119.

156 *If a justice is impressed with the opinion.* Byrnes, *All in One Lifetime*, 138.

157 *When an author concludes that he has an unanswerable document.* Tom C. Clark, "Inside the Court," in *The Supreme Court: Views From Inside*, ed. Alan Westin (New York: W. W. Norton & Co., 1961), 49–50.

157 *After an opinion is circulated.* Memorandum from Lewis F. Powell, Jr. to Eugene J. Comey, Tyler A. Baker, Charles C. Ames, and David A. Martin, September 1976, Powell Papers, Box 130b.

157 *Although the Judge was confident in his views.* Elizabeth Black, recollection from the 1956 Term, Hugo L. Black and Elizabeth Black, *Mr. Justice and Mrs. Black: The Memoirs of Hugo L. Black and Elizabeth Black* (New York: Random House, 1986), 83.

157 *I think this job is very competitive.* Quoted in John A. Jenkins, "Perchance to Dream," *New York Times Magazine*, February 20, 1983.

158 *When you get eight votes and the ninth one comes in.* John G. Roberts, interview by Susan Swain, reprinted in Lamb, Swain, and Farkas, *Supreme Court*, 27.

158 *I am surprised that exception should be taken.* Comment from Charles Evans Hughes to Felix Frankfurter on galley proof, reprinted in Elizabeth Hughes Gossett, "Charles Evans Hughes: My Father the Chief Justice," *Yearbook of the Supreme Court Historical Society*, 1976, 13.

158 *had a tiny pair of testicles.* Letter from Oliver Wendell Holmes, Jr., to Felix Frankfurter, October 24, 1920, Oliver Wendell Holmes, Jr. Papers, Harvard Law School Library, Box 27, Box 10. The case was *Western Union Telegraph Co. v. Speight*, 254 U.S. 17 (1920).

158 *When you write an opinion it will be well to cite.* William O. Douglas, diary entry, January 5, 1940, reprinted in Urofsky, "The Diary of Wm. O Douglas," 87.

158 *Negotiations often occur at two levels.* Memorandum from Lewis F. Powell, Jr., to Eugene J. Comey, Tyler A. Baker, Charles C. Ames, and David A. Martin, September 1976, Powell Papers, Box 130b.

159 *Five votes.* Quoted in Hentoff, "Profiles: The Constitutionalist," *New Yorker*, March 12, 1990, 60.

159 *He made us members of a huge family.* "Justice Souter's Eulogy," *Supreme Court Historical Society Quarterly* 18, no. 1 (1997): 5. Eulogy delivered by David Souter at Justice Brennan's funeral mass.

159 *I am not a playmaker.* Quoted in Hentoff, "Profiles: The Constitutionalist," 59.

160 *[A] rule which is absolute is what I call.* Steven G. Breyer, interview by Brian Lamb, reprinted in Lamb, Swain, and Farkas, *Supreme Court*, 148.

160 *A dissent in a court of last resort.* Charles Evans Hughes, *The Supreme Court of the United States: Its Foundation, Methods and Achievements, An Interpretation* (New York: Columbia University Press, 1928), 68.

160 *Dissents keep the boys on their toes.* "Proceedings in the Supreme Court in Memory of Mr. Justice Black," April 18, 1972, *United State Reports* 405 (1971): ix, lviii. Statement by Warren Burger.

160   *it would only aggravate the harm.* Quoted in Alexander M. Bickel, *The Unpublished Opinions of Mr. Justice Brandeis: The Supreme Court at Work* (Chicago: University of Chicago Press, 1967), 31. The case was *Western Telegraph Co. v. Foster*, 247 U.S. 105 (1918).

161   *I think this case . . . is wrongly decided.* Bickel, *The Unpublished Opinions of Mr. Justice Brandeis*, 31. The case was *Central of Georgia Ry. Co. v. Wright*, 248 U.S. 525 (1919).

161   *News stories sometime portray a picture of discord.* Lewis F. Powell, Jr., "Myths and Misconceptions About the Supreme Court," *ABA Journal* 61 (1975): 1347.

161   *You criticize the argument and not the person.* Antonin Scalia, interview by Susan Swain, reprinted in Lamb, Swain, and Farkas, *Supreme Court*, 65.

161   *"Ah," said Holmes with a sigh.* Quoted in Drew Pearson and Robert S. Allen, *The Nine Old Men* (Garden City, NY: Doubleday, Doran & Co., 1936), 107.

CHAPTER 10: (NOT SO) GOOD BEHAVIOR: DISCORD AND FEUDS

163   *I stepped out of a cloud.* Letter from Oliver Wendell Holmes, Jr. to Felix Frankfurter, March 28, 1922, Oliver Wendell Holmes, Jr. Papers, Harvard Law School Library, Box 27, Folder 13.

163   *Well, I like to get away.* Harry A. Blackmun, interview by Bill Moyers, *In Search of the Constitution: Mr. Justice Blackmun*, Public Affairs Television, Washington, DC, 1987.

163   *Nothing is more distressing.* Charles Evans Hughes, *The Supreme Court of the United States: Its Foundation, Methods and Achievements, An Interpretation* (New York: Columbia University Press, 1928), 68.

164   *The Chief Justice had now borne.* Undated report from Senator Uriah Tracy of Connecticut to Joseph Wood. Quoted in Henry Flanders, *The Lives and Times of Chief Justices of the United States* (Philadelphia: J. B. Lippincott & Co., 1858), 187–188. Chase and Ellsworth were presiding together on a circuit court in Philadelphia.

164   *[McReynolds is] selfish to the last degree.* Letter from William H. Taft to Helen Taft Manning, June 11, 1923, quoted in Alpheus Thomas Mason, *William Howard Taft: Chief Justice* (New York: Simon & Schuster, 1965), 215–216.

165   *[That] was the dullest argument I ever heard.* Quoted in Marquis W. Childs, "A Minority of One; A Dissenter Finds Himself Leader of a Court That Won't Stay Packed," *Saturday Evening Post*, September 20, 1941, 15.

165   *An imperious voice called me out of town.* Letter from James C. McReynolds to William H. Taft, November 23, 1929, quoted in Mason, *William Howard Taft: Chief Justice*, 216.

165   *a savage, with all the irrational impulses.* Brandeis-Frankfurter Conversation, Felix Frankfurter Papers, Manuscript Division, Library of Congress.

165   *The difficulty is with me and me alone.* Letter from James C. McReynolds to William H. Taft, circa March, 1924, quoted in Mason, *William Howard Taft: Chief Justice*, 217.

165 *afflict the Court with another Jew.* Quoted in Drew Pearson and Robert S. Allen, *The Nine Old Men* (Garden City, NY: Doubleday, Doran & Co., 1936), 225.

166 *Mr. Justice James Clark McReynolds of Tennessee.* Dean Acheson, *Morning and Noon: A Memoir* (Boston: Houghton Mifflin, 1965), 70–71.

166 *Justice McReynolds, a cantankerous bachelor.* Harriet Ford Griswold, "Justices of the Supreme Court of the United States I Have Known," *Supreme Court Historical Society Quarterly* 8, no. 4 (1987): 7–8.

167 *Hostility between the two blocs was inevitable and open.* Joseph L. Rauh, Jr., "A Personalized View of the Court-Packing Episode," *Journal of Supreme Court History*, 1990: 93–94.

167 *As it is told in the cocktail parties and congressional corridors.* Lewis Wood, "Vinson Expected to Bring Supreme Court Harmony," *New York Times*, June 9, 1946.

168 *was inexhaustible in his energy.* Arthur M. Schlesinger, Jr., *The Crisis of the Old Order, 1919–1933* (Boston: Houghton Mifflin, 2003), 419.

169 *It has been a most difficult one to decide.* William O. Douglas diary entry June 1, 1940, reprinted in Philip E. Urofsky, "The Diary of Wm. O Douglas," *Journal of Supreme Court History*, 1995, 94. Note that Brandeis was no longer on the Court when Douglas conferred with him.

169 *uniformly gracious.* Bayless Manning Interview, May 14, 1981, Stanley Forman Reed Oral History Project, Oral History Collection, University of Kentucky, Lexington, Kentucky.

169 *Reed is largely vegetable—he has managed.* Letter from Felix Frankfurter to Learned Hand, November 7, 1954, The Learned Hand Papers, Harvard Law School Library, Box 105C, Folder 20.

169 *Felix would come all hotted up.* Bayless Manning Interview, May 14, 1981, Stanley Forman Reed Oral History Project.

170 *Except in cases where he knows.* Felix Frankfurter diary entry, January 30, 1943, reprinted in Joseph P. Lash, ed., *From the Diaries of Felix Frankfurter* (New York: W. W. Norton & Co., 1975), 175.

170 *[Frankfurter] was . . . a prosyletizer. The Court Years, 1939–1975: The Autobiography of William O. Douglas* (New York: Random House, 1980), 22.

170 *When some incompetent soul was wasting our time.* Douglas, *The Court Years*, 178.

170 *[A]fter Felix spoke in order of seniority.* Quoted in Bernard Schwartz, *Super Chief: Earl Warren and His Supreme Court, A Judicial Biography* (New York: New York University Press, 1983), 53.

172 *When [Frankfurter] took more time than Bill.* William J. Brennan, Jr., "Remembrances of William O. Douglas on the 50th Anniversary of his Appointment to the Supreme Court," *Journal of Supreme Court History*, 1990, 105.

172 *When a priest enters a monastery, he must leave.* Felix Frankfurter diary entry, January 11, 1943, reprinted in Lash, *From the Diaries of Felix Frankfurter*, 155.

173 *Hugo is a self-righteous, self-deluded part fanatic.* Letter from Felix Frankfurter to Learned Hand, November 7, 1954, The Learned Hand Papers, Harvard Law School Library, Box 105C, Folder 20.

173 *we tear up law with complete indifference.* Felix Frankfurter diary entry April 20, 1943, reprinted in Lash, *From the Diaries of Felix Frankfurter*, 227.

173 *With all his brilliance, charm and stratagems.* Hugo Black, Jr., *My Father: A Remembrance* (New York: Random House, 1975), 227–228.

174 *Murphy was a special target of Frankfurter.* Douglas, *Court Years*, 25.

174 *We have [conferences] all the time these days.* Letter from William O. Douglas to Fred Rodell, October 25, 1943, Fred Rodell Papers, Haverford College Library, Haverford, Pennsylvania, Special Collections, Special Manuscript Collection, coll. no. 827.

174 *I have had much difficulty herding my collection.* Letter from Harlan Fiske Stone to Sterling Carr, June 13, 1943, Harlan Fiske Stone Papers, Manuscript Division, Library of Congress.

174 *[T]hey are sowing the wind.* Letter from Learned Hand to Felix Frankfurter, February 6, 1944, Frankfurter Papers, Manuscript Division, Library of Congress.

175 *He is confident and easy-going and sure and shallow.* Felix Frankfurter, diary entry, October 19, 1946, reprinted in Lash, *From the Diaries of Felix Frankfurter*, 274.

175 *Vinson conducts the Conference with ease.* October 27, 1946, diary entry, Lash, *Diaries of Felix Frankfurter*, 283.

175 *would discuss in his presence the view.* Quoted in Richard Kluger, *Simple Justice: The History of Brown v. Board of Education and Black America's Struggle for Equality* (New York: Knopf, 2004), 587–588.

175 *If war is declared on me, I propose to wage it with the weapons of the open warrior.* Robert H. Jackson to Chairmen, House and Senate Judiciary Committees, memorandum, June 7, 1946, page 5, with a copy to Harry S Truman, Robert H. Jackson Papers, Manuscript Division, Library of Congress, Box 26.

176 *We are all shocked by Jackson's statement.* Letter from Charles C. Burlingham to Geoffrey Russell, June 18, 1946, quoted in George Martin, *CCB: The Life and Century of Charles C. Burlingham: New York's First Citizen 1858–1959* (New York: Hill and Wang, 2005), 513.

176 *An unusual aspect of the Justice's civility.* Statement of Norman Dorsen, in Norman Dorsen and Amelia Ames Newcomb, eds., "John Marshall Harlan II, Associate Justice of the Supreme Court, 1955–1971: Remembrances by His Clerks," *Journal of Supreme Court History* 27, no. 2 (2002): 147.

176 *I think he came to realize very early.* Bernard Schwartz, *Decision: How the Supreme Court Decides Cases* (New York: Oxford University Press, 1996), 36–37.

177 *Bill [Douglas] is the most cynical.* Letter from Felix Frankfurter to Learned Hand, November 7, 1954, The Learned Hand Papers, Harvard Law School Library, Box 105C, Folder 20.

177 *In conference, Frankfurter became violent.* Richard S. Arnold diary entry, May 5, 1961, quoted in Polly J. Price, "*Mapp v. Ohio* Revisited: A Law Clerk's Diary," *Journal of Supreme Court History* 35, no. 1 (2010): 63.

177 *The continuous violent outbursts against me.* William O. Douglas, Memorandum to Conference, November 21, 1960. William O. Douglas Papers, Manuscript Division, Library of Congress.

177 *clashed often at the ideological level.* Melvin I. Urofsky, ed., *The Douglas Letters: Selections from the Private Papers of Justice William O. Douglas* (Bethesda, MD: Adler & Adler, 1987), 97–98.

177 *Frankfurter had a basic weakness.* Douglas, *Court Years*, 23.

178 *Bill is like an old firehouse dog.* Quoted in Bob Woodward and Scott Armstrong, *The Brethren: Inside the Supreme Court* (New York: Simon & Schuster, 1979), 399. James F. Simon confirmed this quotation with an anonymous Court source in his book, *Independent Journey: The Life of William O. Douglas* (New York: Harper & Row, 1980), 453.

CHAPTER 11: A PEEK INSIDE CHAMBERS

179 *On the Monday when the opinion was due.* Dean Acheson, *Morning and Noon: A Memoir* (Boston: Houghton Mifflin, 1965), 79–80.

179 *This job of being a law clerk.* Letter from William O. Douglas to Chester C. Maxey, a political scientist at Whitman College, December 27, 1944, William O. Douglas Papers, Library of Congress. Quoted in David Danelski, "Lucile Lomen," *Journal of Supreme Court History* 23, no. 1 (1999): 44.

180 *Though I had some doubt.* Samuel Williston, *Life and Law* (Boston: Little, Brown, 1941), 87.

180 *My employer's method.* Williston, *Life and Law*, 92.

181 *My work consisted in part.* Edgar R. Rombauer, Sr., *Rombauer Memoirs: To Our Dear Children* (privately printed, 2000), 39.

181 *Most of the Justices had secretaries.* David J. Danelski and Joseph S. Tulchin, eds., *The Autobiographical Notes of Charles Evans Hughes* (Cambridge, MA: Harvard University Press, 1973), 163.

181 *Stone interviewed me.* Milton C. Handler, "Clerking for Justice Harlan Fiske Stone," *Journal of Supreme Court History*, 1995, 113.

182 *During my second year out of law school.* Arthur E. Sutherland, quoted in David M. O'Brien, "Sutherland's Recollections of Justice Holmes," *Yearbook of the Supreme Court Historical Society*, 1988, 19.

182 *On Saturday, the day of the conference.* Handler, "Clerking for Justice Harlan Fiske Stone," 115.

183 *Stone would tackle.* Handler, "Clerking for Justice Harlan Fiske Stone," 115.

183 *When Stone had completed the draft.* Handler, "Clerking for Justice Harlan Fiske Stone," 116.

183 *He made one feel a co-worker.* Walter Gellhorn, January 21, 1974, Stone Papers, Box 48, Manuscript Division, Library of Congress.

183 *From the assignment slip.* Acheson, *Morning and Noon*, 80–81.

184 *Following this latest conference.* Dennis J. Hutchinson and David J. Garrow, eds., *The Forgotten Memoir of John Knox: A Year in the Life of a Supreme Court Clerk in FDR's Washington* (Chicago: University of Chicago Press, 2002), 192–193.

185 *[H]e quietly reached across.* Hutchinson and Garrow, *Forgotten Memoir of John Knox*, 136.

185 *In the early 1940's at least.* John P. Frank, *Marble Palace: The Supreme Court in American Life* (New York: Knopf, 1958), 116–117.

186 *The tasks of the clerks.* Frank, *Marble Palace*, 117.

186 *There isn't one chance in a thousand.* Comment made by Brandeis to John Knox, quoted in Hutchinson and Garrow, *Forgotten Memoir of John Knox*, 56.

187 *selecting mates in a foxhole.* Quoted in Adam Liptak, "Choice of Clerks High-lights Polarization on Supreme Court," *New York Times*, September 7, 2010.

187 *Naturally I want law clerks.* William H. Rehnquist, *The Supreme Court: How It Was, How It Is* (New York: William Morrow, 1987), 262–263.

187 *From across a broad, nearly bare desk.* Edward Lazarus, *Closed Chambers: The First Eyewitness Account of the Epic Struggles Inside the Supreme Court* (New York: Times Books, 1998), 23.

188 *I ask the new clerks to begin work.* Rehnquist, *Supreme Court*, 263.

188 *Aside from chance encounters.* Lazarus, *Closed Chambers*, 36.

188 *It's good for me.* Quoted in Artemus Ward and David L. Weiden, *Sorcerers' Apprentices; 100 Years of Law Clerks at the United States Supreme Court* (New York: New York University Press, 2006), 49.

188 *[Clerks] bring a continual infusion.* Robert Von Mehren interview, Stanley Forman Reed Oral History Project, University of Kentucky, quoted in Ward and Weiden, *Sorcerers' Apprentices*, 48–49.

189 *The floor of the entire room.* Hutchinson and Garrow, *Forgotten Memoir of John Knox*, 14.

189 *The purpose of the cert memo.* Letter from William O. Douglas to William H. Alsup, Richard L. Jacobson, and Kenneth R. Reed, April 22, 1971, reprinted in Melvin I. Urofsky, ed., *The Douglas Letters: Selections From the Private Papers of William O. Douglas* (Bethesda, MD: Adler & Adler, 1987), 53.

190 *With regard to each of these requests to be heard.* Peter D. Ehrenhaft, "A Photographic Review of the 1961 Term," *Supreme Court Historical Society Quarterly* 25, no. 2 (2001): 6.

190 *I like to go over these petitions personally.* Memorandum from William O. Douglas to Warren E. Burger, July 13, 1972, Blackmun Papers, Manuscript Division, Library of Congress, Box 1442.

190 *Reed was not as interested in full-blown.* Julian Burke Interview, Stanley Forman Reed Oral History Project, quoted in Ward and Weiden, *Sorcerers' Apprentices*, 109–110.

191 *On the cert petitions we had to learn what his views were.* Lewis F. Powell, Jr. to John J. Buckley, John C. Jeffries, and Jack B. Owens, August 20, 1973, Powell Papers, Box 130b, quoted in Ward and Weiden, *Sorcerers' Apprentices*, 129–130.

191 *[T]he cert pool was controversial.* Randall P. Bezanson, "Good Old Number Three: Harry Blackmun and His Clerks," in *Behind the Bench: Portraits of Law Clerks and Their Justices*, ed. Todd C. Peppers and Artemus Ward (Charlottesville: University of Virginia Press, forthcoming).

191 *In our day, HAB.* Bill Murphy, 1979 clerk, quoted in Peppers and Ward, *Behind the Bench*.

191 *I thought I could handle the cases more efficiently.* John Paul Stevens, interview by Brian Lamb, reprinted in Brian Lamb, Susan Swain, Mark Farkas, eds., *The Supreme Court: A C-Span Book Featuring the Justices in Their Own Words* (New York: Public Affairs, 2010), 46.

192 *In Justice Blackmun's Chambers.* Bill Murphy, 1979 clerk, quoted in Bezanson, "Good Old Number Three: Harry Blackmun and His Clerks," in Peppers and Ward, *Behind the Bench*.

192   To Justice Brandeis [bench memos were] a profanation of advocacy. Acheson, Morning and Noon, 97.

193   Several of my colleagues get what are called bench memos. Rehnquist, Supreme Court, 272.

193   to be a road map. Quoted in Peppers, "The Modern Clerkship: Justice Ruth Bader Ginsburg and Her Law Clerks," in Peppers and Ward, Behind the Bench.

193   Douglas clerks had to do this. Charles E. Ares, "Remembrances of William O. Douglas OT 1952," in Remembrances of William O. Douglas by His Friends and Associates, In Celebration of the Fiftieth Anniversary of His Appointment to the Supreme Court of the United States, ed. William Cowen and Catherine Constantinou (Washington, DC, 1989), 10.

193   One of the highlights of our work occurred. Bezanson, "Good Old Number Three: Harry Blackmun and His Clerks," in Peppers and Ward, Behind the Bench.

194   The function of the clerks in relation to the writing. Frank, Marble Palace, 116–118.

194   On a couple of occasions each term. Quoted in Ward and Weiden, Sorcerers' Apprentices, 203.

195   And some opinions he would ask us to do a draft. Edwin M. Zimmerman interview, March 19, 1981, Stanley Forman Reed Oral History Project, quoted in Ward and Weiden, Sorcerers' Apprentices, 154. Zimmerman clerked in the 1950 Term.

195   What the hell do you mean—not clear! Quoted in Silas Bent, Justice Oliver Wendell Holmes: A Biography (New York: Vanguard Press, 1932), 306.

195   Hugo has certain steps to warm up for writing. Elizabeth Black, diary entry, March 1, 1965, reprinted in Hugo L. Black and Elizabeth Black, Mr. Justice and Mrs. Black: The Memoirs of Hugo L. Black and Elizabeth Black (New York: Random House, 1986), 103.

195   The draft is then turned over to the clerks. Daniel J. Meador, "Justice Black and His Law Clerks," Alabama Law Review 15 (1962): 57, 59–60.

196   We made our own legal arguments to the Justice. Richard W. Benka, 1972 Term clerk, "Remembrances of William O. Douglas on the 50th Anniversary of His Appointment to the Supreme Court," Journal of Supreme Court History, 1990, 106.

196   One of the problems which we encountered last term was that I became the "bottleneck." Lewis F. Powell, Jr., to Larry Hammond, William C. Kelly, Jr., Thomas W. Reavley, and J. Harvie Wilkinson III, April 2, 1973, Powell Papers, Box 561.

196   He would tell you to go start an opinion. Quoted in Ward and Weiden, Sorcerers' Apprentices, 206.

197   Justice Blackmun's opinions were very much his own. Bezanson, "Good Old Number Three: Harry Blackmun and His Clerks," in Peppers and Ward, Behind the Bench.

197   The law clerk is given, as best I can, a summary. Rehnquist, The Supreme Court, 300.

197   I read over everything. Peppers, "The Modern Clerkship: Justice Ruth Bader Ginsburg and Her Law Clerks," in Peppers and Ward, Behind the Bench.

198   Clerks rarely appreciate until much later. Harold Koh, 1981 clerk, "Unveiling Justice Blackmun," Brooklyn Law Review 72 (2006), 18.

198   Here you shall see a good deal. Paul Freund, "The Supreme Court: A Tale of Two Terms," Ohio State Law Journal 26 (1965): 225.

198 *You will learn things, hear things.* Daniel A. Rezneck, 1960 clerk, interviewed by Polly J. Price, December 12, 2005, quoted in Polly J. Price, *"Mapp v. Ohio* Revisited: A Law Clerk's Diary," *Journal of Supreme Court History* 35, no. 1 (2010): 54.

199 *Eight out of nine opinions were written.* Quoted in Ward and Weiden, *Sorcerers' Apprentices*, 155.

199 *The vote in the case presently stands.* Memorandum from Benjamin S. Sharp to Harry A. Blackmun, January 17, 1974, Blackmun Papers, Box 175. The case was *Renegotiation Board v. Bannercraft Co.*, 415 U.S. 1 (1974).

199 *When you need five votes and you only have four.* Quoted in Ward and Weiden, *Sorcerers' Apprentices*, 168.

199 *talking out of school.* Quoted in Ward and Weiden, *Sorcerers' Apprentices*, 81.

199 *Of course you can listen.* Louis Jaffe, *Harvard Law School Bulletin*, April 1957, 11.

199 *While sharing views on pending cases.* Lewis F. Powell, Jr. to David A. Charney, Robert M. Couch, Joseph E. Neuhaus, Cammie R. Robinson, October 11, 1983, Powell Papers, 130b. Quoted in Ward and Weiden, *Sorcerers' Apprentices*, 161.

200 *There were points of relief.* J. Harvie Wilkinson, *Serving Justice: A Supreme Court Clerk's View* (New York: Charterhouse, 1974), 37.

200 *But the greatest of all clerking sidelines.* Wilkinson, *Serving Justice*, 39–40.

200 *With Justice Blackmun.* Lazarus, *Closed Chambers*, 38.

201 *David [J. Vann] and I lived.* Charles A. Reich, "A Passion for Justice," *Touro Law Review* 26, no. 2 (2010): 394.

201 *It is common knowledge.* Richard L. Jacobsen, quoted in "William O. Douglas Remembered: A Collective Memory by WOD's Law Clerks," *Journal of Supreme Court History* 32, no. 3 (2007): 328–329.

201 *Ten thousand dollars.* Fay Aull Deusterman interview, March 3, 1991, quoted in Bruce Allen Murphy, "52 Weeks of Boot Camp," in Peppers and Ward, *Behind the Bench*.

201 *You get an inappropriate idea.* Quoted in Tony Mauro, "Corps of Clerks Lacking in Diversity," *USA Today*, June 5, 1998.

201 *I have occasionally reflected on the experience.* Letter from William H. Rehnquist to Robert H. Jackson, undated, Rehnquist papers, Library of Congress.

202 *It is one of the most enjoyable parts of the job.* Antonin Scalia, interview by Susan Swain, reprinted in Lamb, Swain, and Farkas, *Supreme Court*, 56.

CHAPTER 12: "WELCOME TO THE CHAIN GANG"

203 *Sometimes the Chief.* Merlo John Pusey, *Charles Evans Hughes* (New York: Macmillan, 1951), 1:282–283.

203 *a lonely, troubling experience.* William J. Brennan, Jr., "Construing the Constitution," *U. C. Davis Law Review* 19 (1985–86): 3.

203 *The notion that we are awesome men is wrong.* Donna Haupt, "Justice William J. Brennan, Jr.," *Constitution*, Winter 1989, 57.

203 *entering upon a life of slavery.* Quoted in Tom Clark, "The Supreme Court Conference," address before the Section of Judicial Administration, American Bar Association, Dallas, Texas, August 27, 1956, *Federal Rules Decisions* 19 (1957): 303–304.

203 *Welcome to the chain gang.* William O. Douglas, diary entry, April 17, 1939, reprinted in Philip E. Urofsky, ed., "The Diary of Wm. O Douglas," *Journal of Supreme Court History,* 1995, 81.

203 *First and foremost, complete absorption in the work.* Letter from Felix Frankfurter to an English friend, Master Oliver Gates, October 29, 1953, Felix Frankfurter Papers, Manuscript Division, Library of Congress.

204 *When I first got here.* Clarence Thomas, interview by Susan Swain, reprinted in Brian Lamb, Susan Swain, and Mark Farkas, eds., *The Supreme Court: A C-Span Book Featuring the Justices in Their Own Words* (New York: Public Affairs, 2010), 88–89.

204 *Reading and summarizing.* J. Harvie Wilkinson, *Serving Justice: A Supreme Court Clerk's View* (New York: Charterhouse, 1974), 21.

205 *The electronics industry.* William O. Douglas, "The Supreme Court and Its Case Load," *Cornell Law Review* 45 (Spring 1960): 414.

205 *I am worked almost to death and have hardly time to breathe.* Letter from Morrison R. Waite to his brother, Richard Waite, February 2, 1877, quoted in Bruce R. Trimble, *Chief Justice Waite: Defender of the Public Interest* (Princeton: Princeton University Press, 1938), 271.

205 *On the front of this building.* William Suter, interview by Connie Doebele, reprinted in Lamb, Swain, and Farkas, *Supreme Court,* 325.

206 *We receive about nine thousand requests a year.* Clarence Thomas, interview by Susan Swain, reprinted in Lamb, Swain, and Farkas, *Supreme Court,* 89.

207 *You develop a pretty good eye.* John G. Roberts, interview by Susan Swain, reprinted in Lamb, Swain, and Farkas, *Supreme Court,* 15.

207 *I read the rich man's* and *the poor man's.* Quoted in Richard L. Williams, "Justices Run 'Nine Little Law Firms' at Supreme Court," *Smithsonian,* February 1977, 91.

207 *I try not to delegate.* William J. Brennan, Jr., "The National Court of Appeals: Another Dissent," *University of Chicago Law Review* 40 (1973): 477.

207 *Reading all of it you wouldn't have time to sleep.* Quoted in Barrett McGurn, *America's Court: The Supreme Court and the People* (Golden, CO: Fulcrum Publishing, 1997), 125. Burger was speaking to members of the foreign press on June 17, 1978.

208 *The inhuman practice.* Dean Acheson, *Morning and Noon: A Memoir* (Boston: Houghton Mifflin, 1965), 80.

208 *The hour of the meeting.* Augustus H. Garland, *Experience in the Supreme Court of the United States with Some Reflections and Suggestions as to that Tribunal* (Washington, DC: John Byrnh & Co., 1898), 62.

209 *Chief Justice Taft could inhale.* Austin Cunningham, "The United States Supreme Court and Me," *The Supreme Court Historical Society Quarterly* 18, no. 3 (1997): 9.

209 *I suppose you know more than those who drafted.* Frank Murphy Papers, No. 13, 1944, roll 131. The case was *State of Georgia v. Pennsylvania Railroad,* 324 U.S. 439 (1945).

209 *The largest conference list.* Robert H. Jackson, "The Supreme Court as a Unit in Government," in Alan Westin, ed., *The Supreme Court: Views From Inside* (W. W. Norton & Co., 1961), 25.

210 *The Court decided over 1800 questions.* Clark, "Inside the Court," in Westin, *Supreme Court: Views From Inside,* 46.

210 *The pressure of time may induce an attitude.* Jackson, "The Supreme Court as a Unit in Government," in Westin, *Supreme Court: Views From Inside,* 25–26.

210 *Hughes had a custom.* Transcription of conversation between William O. Douglas and Professor Walter F. Murphy, Cassette no. 14, April 5, 1963, Princeton University Library, 1981, quoted in Artemus Ward and David L. Weiden, *Sorcerers' Apprentices; 100 Years of Law Clerks at the United States Supreme Court* (New York: New York University Press, 2006), 42.

211 *The rule basically is that everyone writes one majority [opinion].* Justice Stephen G. Breyer, in discussion with the author, January 11, 2007.

211 *There is nothing so conducive to brevity.* Quoted in Williams, "Justices Run 'Nine Little Law Firms' at Supreme Court," 89.

211 *The art of writing legal decisions.* Letter from Oliver Wendell Holmes, Jr. to Felix Frankfurter, December 19, 1915, reprinted in Robert M. Mennel and Christine L. Compston, eds., *Holmes and Frankfurter: Their Correspondence, 1912–1934* (Hanover, NH: University Press of New England, 1996), 40.

211 *Only a few naturally write lean prose.* John P. Frank, *Marble Palace: The Supreme Court in American Life* (New York: Knopf, 1958), 132.

211 *When [Douglas] was in the office and in the room, he worked.* David Ginsberg interview, August 28, 1987, quoted in Murphy, "52 Weeks of Boot Camp," in *Behind the Bench: Portraits of Law Clerks and Their Justices,* eds. Todd C. Peppers and Artemus Ward (Charlottesville: University of Virginia Press, forthcoming).

213 *The Justice's writing was so good.* James M. Marsh, "Supreme Court Justice Without a College Degree," *Supreme Court Historical Society Quarterly* 21, no. 4 (2000): 19.

213 *Justices Rutledge and Black were of like mind.* Frank, *Marble Palace,* 132–133.

213 *By the time the lawyer and litigant get to the Supreme Court.* Victor Brudney, 1942 Term law clerk to Wiley Rutledge, interview by John M. Ferren, quoted in Ferren, *Salt of the Earth: Conscience of the Court, The Story of Justice Wiley Rutledge* (Chapel Hill: University of North Carolina Press, 2004), 230.

214 *frail body and weak heart.* Joseph Rauh, Cardozo's last law clerk, 1936 Term, quoted in Joseph Rauh, Melvin Seigel, Ambrose Doskow, and Alan Stroock, "A Personal View of Justice Benjamin Cardozo: Recollections of Four Cardozo Law Clerks," *Cardozo Law Review* 1 (1979): 5. The full quotation is "he gave the law, from love, or more likely from a feeling of duty to his fellow man, the last measure of effort that his frail body and weak heart could summon to his judicial tasks."

214 *Dad would come in every night.* Haupt, "Justice William J. Brennan, Jr.," 54–55.

214 *This place can become like a pressure cooker.* Quoted in Warren Burger, "In Memoriam: Hugo L. Black," *Supreme Court Reporter,* 92 (1973): 78.

215 *I had thought of the Court.* Powell, "What the Justices Are Saying," *ABA Journal* 62 (November 1976): 1454.

215 *One characteristic of this place.* Quoted in Williams, "Justices Run 'Nine Little Law Firms' at Supreme Court," 91.

215 *The suggestion . . . that we don't talk to each other.* Stephen G. Breyer, interview by Brian Lamb, reprinted in Lamb, Swain, and Farkas, *Supreme Court,* 144.

215 *He doesn't live his life reacting.* David Souter, "Tribute to John Paul Stevens," *Journal of Supreme Court History* 35, no.3 (November 2010): 195–197.

215 *It was my duty to report to Justice Harlan's house.* Edgar S. Rombauer, Sr., *Rombauer Memoirs, To Our Dear Children* (privately printed, 2000), 41.

216 *Giving up smoking.* David J. Danelski and Joseph S. Tulchin, eds., *The Autobiographical Notes of Charles Evans Hughes* (Cambridge, MA: Harvard University Press, 1973), 176–177.

216 *When I came to the Court there were many traditional habits.* The Court Years, *1939–1975: The Autobiography of William O. Douglas* (New York: Random House, 1980), 5.

216 *I think physical fitness.* Quoted in Pam Hait, "Sandra Day O'Connor, Warm, Witty, and Wise," *Ladies Home Journal,* April 1982, 40.

217 *One of the nice things about the job.* Antonin Scalia, interview by Susan Swain, reprinted in Lamb, Swain, and Farkas, *Supreme Court,* 57.

217 *When I came to Washington to meet the Justice.* Nathan Lewin remembrance in Norman Dorsen and Amelia Ames Newcomb, "John Marshall Harlan, II, Associate Justice of the Supreme Court, 1955–1971, Remembrances by His Law Clerks," *Journal of Supreme Court History* 27, no. 2 (2002): 154.

218 *As a matter of fact most of the [headnotes].* Charles Henry Butler, *A Century at the Bar of the Supreme Court of the United States* (New York: G. P. Putnam's Sons, 1942), 80.

218 *There was an immediate argument against the idea.* Barrett McGurn, *America's Court: The Supreme Court and the People* (Golden, CO: Fulcrum Publishing, 1997), 37.

219 *I have an office suite of only three rooms.* Lewis F. Powell, Jr., "An Overburdened Supreme Court," address to the Fourth Circuit Judicial Conference, June 30, 1972.

219 *My brothers gently rejected.* Powell, "What the Justices Are Saying," 1454.

219 *All of the memos and certs.* Randall P. Bezanson,"Good Old Number Three: Harry Blackmun and His Clerks," in *Behind the Bench: Portraits of Law Clerks and Their Justices,* ed. Todd C. Peppers and Artemus Ward (Charlottesville: University of Virginia Press, forthcoming).

220 *The necessaries and comforts of life.* Quoted in Charles Warren, *The Supreme Court in United States History,* 2 vols. (Boston: Little, Brown, 1926), 1:416.

220 *The expenses of living have so largely increased.* Letter from Benjamin R. Curtis to Millard Fillmore, September 1, 1857, reprinted in Benjamin Robbins Curtis, ed., *A Memoir of Benjamin R. Curtis L.L.D. With Some of His Professional and Miscellaneous Writings,* 2 vols. (Boston: Little, Brown, 1879), 1:250.

221 *It is very important.* Letter from Salmon P. Chase to Samuel F. Miller, June 15, 1866, urging him to write to Congress, Salmon P. Chase Papers, Collection 0121, The Historical Society of Pennsylvania, reprinted in John Niven, *The Salmon P. Chase Papers,* 5 vols. (Kent, OH: Kent State University Press, 1993–1998), 5:113.

221 *The truth is Dr., I might have been rich, but am poor.* Letter from Morrison R. Waite to Dr. A. F. Bissell, October 21, 1877, quoted in Trimble, *Chief Justice Waite,* 279.

222 *In consequence of the illness of the Chief Justice.* Letter from Samuel F. Miller to his brother-in-law William Pitt Ballinger, January 18, 1885, Samuel Freeman Miller Correspondence, Manuscript Division, Library of Congress.

223 *Few are aware.* Quoted in Alpheus Thomas Mason, "Extra-Judicial Work of the Judges: The Views of Chief Justice Stone," *Harvard Law Review* 67, no. 2 (December 1953): 214–215.

223 *The administrative work.* Sherman Minton to Harry S Truman, Minton Papers, Harry S Truman Presidential Library, Box 9.

223 *The debate was long and heated.* Douglas, *The Court Years,* 230.

223 *Warren brought the proposal to Conference.* Douglas, *The Court Years,* 230.

224 *Asked about his bruisingly long workweeks.* McGurn, *America's Court,* 82.

224 *[T]he summertime is a break.* Antonin Scalia, interview by Susan Swain, reprinted in Lamb, Swain, and Farkas, *Supreme Court,* 58.

225 *The Justice worked long and hard.* Acheson, *Morning and Noon,* 78.

225 *Not at the price you have to pay for it.* Letter from William H. Taft to M. Strauss, June 5, 1927, Taft Papers, Manuscript Division, Library of Congress, quoted in Alexander M. Bickel and Benno C. Schmidt, Jr., *History of the Supreme Court of the United States: The Judiciary and Responsible Government, 1910–1921,* Oliver Wendell Holmes Devise 9 (New York: Macmillan, 1984), 84.

225 *All at the table knew that the annual workload.* McGurn, *America's Court,* 122.

225 *My only concern is that we might abuse this privilege.* Lewis F. Powell, Jr. to Warren Burger, memoranda, December 15, 1981, Lewis F. Powell, Jr. Archives, Washington and Lee University.

226 *The court's docket tends to increase.* Quoted in Robert Barnes, "Roberts Supports Court's Shrinking Docket," *Washington Post,* February 2, 2007.

226 *It's a real mystery to me.* Jessica Marmor, "Alito on the Shrinking Supreme Court Docket," *Wall Street Journal Law Blog,* February 7, 2007, http://blogs.wsj .com/law/2007/02/07/alito-on-the-shrinking-supreme-court-docket/.

226 *I think we could do more than seventy-five.* Antonin Scalia, interview by Susan Swain, reprinted in Lamb, Swain, and Farkas, *Supreme Court,* 55.

227 *The most important thing we do.* Quoted in Alexander Bickel, *The Least Dangerous Branch: The Supreme Court at the Bar of Politics,* 2nd ed. (New Haven, CT: Yale University Press, 1986), 71.

CHAPTER 13: TIMING IT RIGHT

229 *I won't be down tomorrow. Washington Post,* March 6, 1935.

229 *The time has come.* "Retirement of Mr. Justice Holmes," *United States Reports* 284 (1932): vii.

229 *It's a whole lot better to go out.* Press Conference of Lewis F. Powell, Jr. following the announcement of his retirement, June 26, 1987.

230 *I should die happier.* Letter from John H. Clarke to Louis D. Brandeis, September 13, 1922, quoted in Alpheus Thomas Mason, *Brandeis: A Free Man's Life* (New York: Viking Press, 1946), 536.

230 *Although I finally concurred.* Dorothy Goldberg, *A Private View of a Public Life* (New York: Charterhouse, 1975), 198–199.

231 *[T]he death of Mr. Justice Barbour.* Letter from Joseph Story to Sarah Story, February 28, 1841, reprinted in William W. Story, *Life and Letters of Joseph Story,* 2 vols. (Boston: Little & Brown, 1851), 348–349.

231 *the oldest looking man on the bench.* Oliver Hampton, *Early Indiana Trials and Sketches: Reminiscences* (Cincinnati, OH: Moore, Wilstach, Keys & Co., 1858), 138.

231 *Judge [Duvall] is eighty–two.* Edward L. Pierce, ed., *Memoirs and Letters of Charles Sumner,* 2 vols. (Boston: Roberts Brothers, 1877), 1:137.

232 *I much fear I shall lose my sight.* Letter from Henry Billings Brown to Charles Artemus Kent, December 7, 1903, *Memoir of Henry Billings Brown, Late Justice of the Supreme Court of the United States,* ed. Charles A. Kent (New York: Deerfield & Co., 1915), 93.

232 *While it involves a good deal.* Henry Billings Brown, "Dinner given May 31, 1906, by the Bar of the Supreme Court of the United States to Mr. Justice Henry Billings Brown Upon His Retirement from the Bench of the Court" (Washington, DC: W.F. Roberts Co., 1906) 18. Harold H. Burton Papers, Manuscript Division, Library of Congress.

232 *I venture the assertion without fear or contradiction.* Letter from Richard Peters, Jr., to Joseph Hopkinson, March 18, 1838, Hopkinson Papers, Historical Society of Pennsylvania.

233 *In Sup[rem]e Court today.* Diary entry by Edward Bates, April 11, 1864, reprinted in Howard K. Beale, ed., *The Diary of Edward Bates 1859–1866* (New York: Da Capo Press, 1971), 358.

233 *A proposition has been introduced into the Senate by Mr. Harlan.* Diary entry by Edward Bates, December 20, 1863, in Beale, *Diary of Edward Bates,* 322.

234 *There is no man on the bench.* Letter from Samuel F. Miller to his brother-in-law, William Pitt Ballinger, March 18, 1877, Samuel Freeman Miller Correspondence, Manuscript Division, Library of Congress.

234 *Judge Clifford reached Washington.* Letter from Samuel F. Miller to his brother-in-law, William Pitt Ballinger, November 28, 1880, Samuel Freeman Miller Correspondence.

235 *If I had been made Chief Justice.* Letter from Samuel F. Miller to his brother-in-law, William Pitt Ballinger, December 5, 1875, Samuel Freeman Miller Correspondence.

235 *The "shorter handed" the Court is.* Letter from John W. Wallace to William A. Maury, November 9, 1880, quoted in Charles Fairman, *Mr. Justice Miller and the Supreme Court 1862–1890* (Cambridge, MA: Harvard University Press, 1939), 382.

236 *Having reached the age of Seventy–three years.* Theron G. Strong, *Landmarks of a Lawyer's Lifetime* (New York: Dodd Mead and Company, 1914), 28.

237 *I have no doubt you will resign.* Letter from Noah Swayne to Joseph P. Bradley, March 16, 1882, Bradley Papers, New Jersey Historical Society, Box 3, Folder 10.

237 *very tired of the labour and indifferent to the honors.* Letter from Samuel Miller to his brother-in-law, William Pitt Ballinger, November 21, 1881, Samuel Freeman Miller Correspondence.

237 *I do not believe a healthy man.* Letter from Samuel Miller to his brother-in-law, William Pitt Ballinger, October 13, 1885, Samuel Freeman Miller Correspondence.

237 *There are many matters which ought to be cause of removal.* Address by Samuel Miller to New York State Bar Association, 1878, quoted in Fairman, *Mr. Justice Miller*, 379.

238 *Called on Judge Grier saw Mrs. Beck.* Letter from George Harding to Joseph Bradley, November 17, 1869, Bradley Papers, New Jersey Historical Society, Box 3, Folder 10.

238 *The Chief & Judge Nelson waited on Pa.* Letter from Sarah Grier Beck to George Harding, December 9, 1869, Sumner Papers, Harvard Law School Library, quoted in Charles Fairman, *Reconstruction and Reunion, 1864–1888*, Oliver Wendell Holmes Devise 6, pt. 1 (New York: Macmillan, 1971), 730.

239 *I heard Justice Harlan tell of the anxiety.* Charles Evans Hughes, *The Supreme Court of the United States: Its Foundation, Methods, and Achievements, an Interpretation* (New York: Columbia University Press, 1928), 76.

239 *I have just returned from a visit to my brother.* Letter from William H. Jackson to Melville W. Fuller, January 28, 1895, quoted in Willard King, *Melville Weston Fuller, Chief Justice of the United States 1888–1910* (New York: MacMillan Co., 1950), 208–209.

240 *[Jackson] interests the crowd more than all the rest.* Arthur Brisbane, *New York World*, May 7, 1895. Jackson's vote ended up not being the tie-breaker in the rehearing of the case, *Pollock v. Farmers' Loan & Trust Company*, 157 U.S. 429 (1895), affirmed on rehearing, 158 U.S. 601 (1895). In a five to four vote the Court found the income tax unconstitutional; Jackson, however, voted with the minority, indicating that one of the other Justices had switched his vote from the time the Court first heard the case argued.

240 *In case after case he will.* Letter from William H. Taft to Horace D. Taft, November 2, 1923, Papers of William Howard Taft, Manuscript Division, Library of Congress.

240 *McKenna's language is as fog.* Letter from William H. Taft to Helen H. Taft, May 8, 1924, Papers of William Howard Taft.

241 *The condition of the Supreme Court is pitiable.* Letter from William H. Taft to Horace Lurton, May 22, 1909, Papers of William Howard Taft.

241 *While coffee was being served.* Charles Henry Butler, *Century at the Bar of the Supreme Court of the United States* (New York: G. P. Putnam's Sons, 1942), 165.

242 *[McReynolds and van Devanter] greeted each other.* Dennis J. Hutchinson and David J. Garrow, eds., *The Forgotten Memoir of John Knox: A Year in the Life of a Supreme Court Clerk in FDR's Washington* (Chicago: University of Chicago Press, 2002), 230–231.

243 *I cannot again feel that confidence in the court.* Letter from Benjamin R. Curtis to George Ticknor, July 3, 1857, reprinted in Benjamin Robbins Curtis, ed., *A Memoir of Benjamin Robbins Curtis L.L.D. With Some of His Professional and Miscellaneous Writings*, 2 vols. (Boston: Little, Brown, 1879), 1:247.

244 *He is a very old man.* Reporter for the Philadelphia Record, 1884, quoted in Henry G. Connor, *John Archibald Campbell, Associate Justice of the United States Supreme Court 1853–1861* (Boston: Houghton Mifflin, 1920), 260–261.

244 *[W]hen the nine Justices emerged from behind the red drapes.* Jim Mann, "The Court Hears One of Its Own," *American Lawyer*, June 1982, 46.

244   *The Chief Justice had repeated himself.* Harold H. Burton, diary entry, April 22, 1946, Harold H. Burton Papers, Manuscript Division, Library of Congress.

245   *For the next month.* Statement of James R. Bieke, 1971 clerk, in Norman Dorsen and Amelia Ames Newcomb, eds., "John Marshall Harlan II, Associate Justice of the Supreme Court, 1955–1971: Remembrances by His Clerks," *Journal of Supreme Court History* 27, no. 2 (2002): 174.

245   *Meanwhile, I learned that Justice Harlan wanted to see me.* Hugo Black, Jr., *My Father: A Remembrance* (New York: Random House, 1975), 260–261.

247   *Practically the first thing Daddy wanted me to do.* Black, *My Father*, 261.

248   *With a sense of destiny.* Elizabeth Black, diary entry, September 17, 1971, reprinted in Hugo L. Black and Elizabeth Black, *Mr. Justice and Mrs. Black: The Memoirs of Hugo L. Black and Elizabeth Black* (New York: Random House, 1986), 278.

Index

Note: Italicized page numbers indicate the subject is in the illustration on that page. Supreme Court Justices' names are boldfaced.